Evelyn a woman's life in
20th Century troubled times.

Seven Maids with Seven Mops

Evelyn Chadwick

authorHOUSE®

AuthorHouse™ UK Ltd.
500 Avebury Boulevard
Central Milton Keynes, MK9 2BE
www.authorhouse.co.uk
Phone: 08001974150

First published by AuthorHouse 12/17/2009

ISBN: 978-1-4490-4809-9 (sc)

This book is printed on acid-free paper.

Contents

Part 1

Part 2

Part 3

✦ For Gabilu ✦

My thanks to Elspeth Jack and Anne Hyatt for their patient corrections and suggestions, also to Stephen and Liesl Hearst, Peter Huhne and above all to Alan, for his calming and perceptive influence during the many years of soul and memory searching.

Seven maids with seven mops

...seven generations of women, mothers to first daughters in one family with birthdates from 1847 to 2002, holding hands across the centuries, like cut-out paper-dolls... are re-created from letters, photographs, or handed-down tales. Only from time to time a little 'inspiration' is allowed to take wing.

The first two are born in a peaceful mountain town in Europe. Others move across continents, learn new languages.... know and suffer terrible wars, discover unimaginable cruelties in this threatened world, *our* world. Some have to learn sobering truths. Four of the seven women have been on the 'wrong' side, should you be observing from the British viewpoint. Having been 'on the wrong side' can be...no, is still, uncomfortable.

As these lives inter-twine, some events recur immutably; even so, there are endless 'shifting sands' and changing patterns to learn in the school of life.

Whatever comes can usually be cleaned up, turned into 'acceptable' on the scale of things. Some less acceptable events become history, and in the end give color to all that un-predictable stuff, washed up on the 'sands of life'.

The Walrus and the Carpenter, were walking close at hand.

They wept like anything to see, such quantities of sand;

If seven maids with seven mops, swept it for half a year,

Do you suppose, the Walrus said, that they could get it clear?

I doubt it, said the Carpenter, and shed a bitter tear.

'Alice in Wonderland'

Lewis Carroll

Mathias Klander, b.1763, d. 1839
Maria Magdalena Jost, b.?, d. 1855
Josephine's grandparents

Slovenia, 2004. Setting the scene:

Two hours in the air, half an hours' drive by taxi, and here it is at last: that small town snuggled against green hillsides. Years ago my grandmother said I should come here, see it, *her* birthplace, *her* home, until she was eighteen years old. In later years she did return, but only once, by then the place had become part of Yugoslavia and 'unbearably changed', she claimed, aggrieved, many old memories shattered.

Clutching a folder of family history, I emerge mole-like into the blinding sunlight, find myself ambling up a narrow road, probably the main road of Neumarktl, as my grandmother knew it. Now the place is called 'Trizic'. Both words mean 'new market', one is German, the tricky one, Slovene.

What a setting! I stop, marvel at houses, stylish, very Austrian but so neglected, hundreds of years old. One of the bigger ones could surely have been the family hotel owned by my great- *and* great-great grandparents; all this was Austrian then, governed by the Habsburgs from early 1300.

"If *only* they were still here, all these ancestors"..., I'm on edge, frustrated by the passing of time and the fragility of ties..."how can I possibly get inside their personalities, quirks and dreams; so many memories, already slipping away, fading photographs.....?

The place appears to have only three roads, at the top of the hill, where the buildings stop, a narrow stream sparkles opposite a modest 'Town' Museum. I step inside, manage a self-conscious 'dober dan' (good morning), while my driver explains I am a guest from London related to...and then follows a string of family names: Klander, Hofbauer, Malli, Pollak, Wuk, Kotnik, all 'ghosts' from my grandfather's papers. The curator falls about, gesticulating, then a torrent of words which, alas, are Slovene. "Magdalena Klander" he laughs, "she married at the age of thirteen and had twenty-five children"... even in Slovenia this appears a tale worth telling. One imagines Neumarktl was a dull place with little to do other than go to bed in those distant days! He shuffles off to find the *official* history: there they are, all the family names: Klanders have lived here since 1600. Well, I already know that! I buy the book, awed, flattered, ever more frustrated: it's in Slovenian. Who knows what I'll discover!

There is, allegedly, a painting in Trizic, of a Great Fire, which consumed the entire village. A careless worker in the <u>Klander</u> foundry left un-extinguished flames smoldering in the night, these were fanned by a strong mountain wind...the result, a huge disaster, almost 100 people perished. Wanting to find the picture, I tried two churches, finally came across a stained-glass window depicting the disaster in a little restaurant, quite by chance....

Why do I feel a touch of guilt on behalf of *my* careless ancestors, two hundred years ago?

Ridiculous!

A painting of St. Florian, with the depiction of the Great Fire below him can be seen in a church in Trižič to this day.

Here they are, the 'seven maids' and their birthdates:

Josephine   1847

Cölestine   1882

Erika   1907

Ingeborg-Evelyn   1935

Gabrielle   1959

Polly   1983

and little Leela   2003.

Part 1

Josephine's story

(....truly in a nut-shell....)

Josephine Klander, born in February 1847,
christened on that very day in her home, house
no.134, in Neumarktl, was the seventh and last
child in a prosperous Austrian German-speaking
family, who had, since 1600, married women with
Slovene names.

After primary school and a few years with nuns in
a nearby convent Josephine stayed at home and
helped to run the family hotel. At last, in 1881 she
found a man she liked enough to marry; she was
by then a thirty-four year-old spinster, on the shelf,
really old! Husband Karl Hofbauer, some years
younger, a successful man in 'wood', had inherited
the business from his father. What did he see in
Josephine? A solid, practical no-nonsense person,
a devout daughter of the church, who 'got on' with
things, a bit plain perhaps? "How pleasing, married
at last", she must have thought.

Their first child, born almost within the correct
number of months, was christened Cölestine,
in 1882. Three years on the family moved into
a newly built mansion in St. Anna, a tiny village
nearby, with some industry, the "Illyrian Quicksilver
Company".....and timber works, saw-mills, a
brewery........

3

Karl Hofbauer's highly respected family had come, two generations ago, from a small village near Vienna.

Josephine helped her husband in the ever-growing business; she enjoyed working in the office. Her little girl was sent to board with aunts in Neumarktl, as soon as she was sensible enough to attend school. Josephine's need to be free to help the family business was, for some reason, overwhelming.

In 1894 Josephine's mother dies. This old lady had for some time been living with her daughter, helping to take care of the growing family...by now *three* girls. Josephine's twelve-year old, Cölestine, learns about death, black clothes, coffins and funerals.

Many relatives have come to St Anna, to pay their respects... "another venerable Klander gone," they mutter darkly, the house gloomily full of relations from everywhere; visiting cousins are told to behave, admonished to sit quietly or to walk in the garden. "No shouting, no running today, children," whispers Josephine, at regular intervals, to all five of them.

Cölestine, in black, looks pale, feels ill: she sees her grandmother in an open coffin in the drawing room; flickering wax candles throw light on the face of the corpse, the eyelids seem to move. The startled child makes a sign of the cross, then stares hard at the yellow, not-so-wrinkled face; a little voice in her head reassures: "her soul must be in heaven now, she looks much happier than when she was alive.... I know she was only my grandmother, but

I loved her just as much as I love my Mama...the saddest day is the day one's mother dies...please, St. Florian*, take especially good care of her"...* Patron saint of Austria

• • •

The aged nun leans forward across the table, trying to appear friendly and encouraging: "I'm so sorry your grandmother has died. You must be missing her. And Josephine, your dear Mama,...whom we loved dearly when she was here, please tell me about her and your *old* school in Neumarktl and about your little sisters, perhaps they too would like to be here, in the convent school?"

"Wish she'd stop asking so many questions" thinks Cölestine, "and why does she have such a bristly chin?" Politely, she confides she is quite glad to have some peace from her sisters, but in a 'grown-up' sort of way, so she does not appear to be lacking in charity.

"My school was tiny, only two rooms and a playground" she continues, "the boys and girls spoke German and Slovene, but our lessons were in German. Sometimes we sang songs in Slovene..."

The nun nods..."and here you will speak Italian as well, dear child! You will know many languages. We hope you like it here and will make friends soon; there is also a new girl from Triest! ... But let me take you to your dormitory ......The new boarder

5

stands up, follows demurely, suddenly overwhelmed with the wish to be home again...(that black misery-inducing homesickness), "perhaps," she thinks, "it's as well I'm here, I must be brave....there are far too many cousins at home now; my Mama will be too busy to miss me."

Two years later, back home in Neumarktl: Another death, this time an uncle; his widow needs comforting, with all her children, for an undetermined length of time. Poor Josephine: fortunately the family villa is huge, as usual overflowing with children and someone is expected to look after them. Cölestine, now fourteen, has left boarding-school and is put in charge. She has turned into a young woman of surprising practical good sense. 'Young woman' is too strong...a very 'mature teenager.' A tutor is engaged to coach all seven children.

Under one roof there are: Josephine, her husband, one widowed aunt, seven children, Josephine's bearded brother Sepp and his wife, a shadowy figure from Triest, apparently fabulously rich, ('Sepp', derived from Joseph, very common in these parts). Josephine's husband, the busy veneer merchant, travels far and wide through Austria, Croatia, Serbia and Hungary to choose and purchase fine timber. All these persons live in a big house, at the foot of a stunning mountain range. Sepp, a professional zither virtuoso, loves to entertain the assembled family with fantastic performances. Everybody clamors to learn to play; the first showing any talent is his sister-in-law, Josephine. There exists a photo of her with her teacher and three daughters out in the summery garden, both adults poised to play zithers on the table.

Cölestine looks truly bored. Her father is frequently away on business and Mama and Uncle Sepp are always so happy, doing everything together. They go to work at the factory (well, somebody has to supervise the Slovenian workers), then Cölestine and Josephine have their zither lessons and later Sepp goes to talk to his own wife or does new experiments with his inventions. He has a dream:... to invent a 'Perpetuum Mobile'!

• • •

Josephine, uncomfortable in a high-necked dress, leans across the table to inspect her brother-in-laws' hand on the zither: "what fingers are you using, Sepp, what *are* you doing? Show me again!" They sit outside, relaxing with music, enjoying the sunset, the cool mountain air. Every one loves staring at the spectacular color change of the rocks, this warm pink glow, and no-one knows why it happens. What can it be? "Sepp, *you* are the scientist, explain why the rocks go pink!"

"I can teach you to play the zither, but alas, I have no idea about the color..... I must admit: teaching music is not so much fun as it used to be, now I'd much rather read books about physics and photography. And I love lithographic stones. My dear wife has paid for all my new interests, but complains her funds are dwindling!" "Aha, mein Lieber, we've heard about your extravagances! Don't you even enjoy teaching *us*?" He smiles, enigmatically......

"We've been talking about you, you know, Karl and I, *you surely* know how much we'd like you to work with us again in the saw-mill, the office so needs another man and you could earn enough to buy anything you need for your intriguing scientific studies.....

Sepp *had* been offered a job at the factory, made *some* attempts, but simply could not settle into such routines...

Brother Karl, a businessman with vision, tried to interest Sepp in a post in Vienna: the family firm had just opened a branch outlet of the wood veneer industry. This potential goldmine for the entire family Sepp couldn't come to grips with either and returned to Neumarktl, to *try* 'working' in the office, once again ...but really to renew his obsession with the Perpetuum Mobile.

<u>According to the Laws of Thermo-dynamics a 'Perpetuum Mobile' is an impossibility.</u> Like eternal life, like raising the dead....but then, musicians are accustomed to overcoming 'impossibilities'. Perhaps they can <u>will </u>them to give way, remove the barriers....?

Josephine is no fool, she has a subtle strategy: some old papers, found among her Mama's possessions, which (*she* hopes) may open poor Sepp's mind to the dedication *some* men have, just *trying* to make a living. While the children romp about in the garden she surprises Sepp with the following document, penned laboriously by her mother, many years ago.

Adjusting her tiny spectacles, she sniffs the musty old pages, arches her eyebrows, then begins to read to her brother-in-law:

The 'Great Fire' 1811. This terrible event in Neumarktl , started accidentally in the foundry of the Klander family. The fire was fanned by a strong wind and the flames passed down the entire village and destroyed most of the houses. 100 workshops were burnt down. At least 70 people were killed.

I am married to Andreas Klander, but I do not feel guilty. My parents did not know about this fire. They might not have arranged this marriage for me, had they known. Or perhaps they knew, but thought it was a good thing since Napoleon gave Neumarktl 80.000 Fr. to rebuild itself.

My father-in-law Mathias swears it was not his fault, but I'm not so sure. He did penance anyway, by providing free iron shutters for every new house that was built.

Napoleon *stayed in our family hotel, when it was called "Pri Klandru", for three whole days in 1809, during his advance through Europe"..*

Loosening her tightly encased stoutness Josephine continues:

"Andreas Klander, born 1807, son of the slightly hunchbacked Mathias and Magdalena;

(Josephine looks up: "their portrait hangs in the living room!")

He married me in 1837, he was just a boy really..... medium height, clean-shaven and could not pronounce 'V' because he has polyps on his lips. His own family and even his children say he is 'serious, strict, a despot, a tyrant.' Although not lacking in entrepreneurial spirit his many ventures failed one after the other".......Here they are:

<u>Andreas' misfortunes</u>: He was postmaster of Neumarktl and needed an assistant. His brother Alois, employed as helper, helped himself to some money...so Andreas had to pay the costs and was relieved of his post.

In <u>Transport</u>....he took a waggon-load of sugar over the Loibl Pass, was caught by a snowstorm and had to over-winter, inadequately covered...lost the entire load. 7000 florins in the red!

<u>Roadworks to Pristava</u>...mudslide, continuous rain. Discontinued.

Vienna, 1848: Revolution. Andreas was the owner of a <u>saw-mill </u>and also of a <u>grain-mill </u>in St. Anna. Several wagon-loads of freshly sawn veneers en route to Vienna were requisitioned by revolutionaries to build barricades in street-fighting. There was no recompence, the saw-mill had to be sold.

"Enough, surely! There can't be more?" Sepp is getting restless...

....*Gasthaus zur Post.* Or "*Pri Klandru.*) This was later re-named "Hotel zum Grafen Radetzky" because the famous field Marshall stayed for a few weeks. I will have to sell this place. It is so in debt that there will be hardly any profit. I don't quite know what to do with Napoleon's bed, somebody in the family should keep it. He was a very nice man and friendly with Andreas' mother Magdalena. Evil tongues had much to say about her little boy Johann Nepomuk who was born about the correct number of months after Napoleon's departure."

"Du lieber Gott", Sepp pretends to be shocked, "why did you never tell me before, dear Sister-in-law, are you too loyal to spread this appalling story about? These papers do make sense: one day *your* children will read all about *their* grandfather from a reliable source... this *is* important ...you must keep these papers safe, and of course I know that your sawmill was bought by *my* father, *and that I should really be involved with it...*"

"For sure," nods Josephine, "you know how we need you! Believe me, even I had no idea my father was such a loser......perhaps this was the reason my parents quarreled so much? Now villagers 'talk' because I work in the office, I should be a man. I don't care: Karl and I make a good team, *we* never quarrel and I enjoy feeling useful ...besides, it stops me eating all the time......."

Sepp looks forlorn; he feels trapped...even mildly guilty: "What I really can't bear is spending so much time with all those Slovenes", he confesses," they are

so rough, dirty, stupid and noisy....*I don't trust them...*"
He gives her a long look....Josephine, aghast, stares
back at her brother-in-law, *tries* to ignore this remark,
but it rankles. If her own husband, his brother, is
pleased with the Slovenian workers, thinks them
loyal and strong, and if *she* is glad to know each one
of them...why must Sepp be so trying, so contrary? Is
it his 'artistic temperament?' Or perhaps *his* family,
only second generation in Neumarktl, are simply
not used to Slovenian ways and their language? The
Klanders have been marrying wives with Slovene
names for centuries!

"There are always people like that," she thinks to
herself, "he's never even *tried* to learn Slovene...a
shame really and so unhelpful. One day I will tell
him what I *really* think. It just won't do!"

Mothers' and daughters' lives are by nature
interlinked for the years up to a daughter's
puberty. It would be unnatural to try to
prise them apart. Josephine and Cölestine are
already sharing their history, so we may as
well observe them through the younger eyes
of the teenager, the one with the adult mind:

Cölestine's Story

"When I was old enough to go to school my Mama and my Papa who had to go to work every day, deemed the half hour walk from St. Anna to Neumarktl too exhausting for my small person and so I was sent to live with my father's sisters. They lived near the school.

After two years I was moved to the house of three cousins of my mother's, none had husbands and they ran a grocery store. The youngest of them was an uncontrolled person who would throw cups and plates against the wall when things did not suit. I was afraid. After a short while my parents gave me to Miss Pirz, an elderly daughter of our doctor, who was extremely old. Only on Sundays I went home to my family. When my grandmother died I went to the convent." (from a letter, written some years later).

By 1896, after her time at the convent, she feels quite grown-up.

Cölestine now inhabits her own little room at home. She has crept away after the morning's lessons with the tutor to rest, her back aches and she often wonders why her right shoulder looks a bit higher than her left,.... peering into the spotty old mirror... could she be a little hunch-backed? Instead of brooding on this unhappy fact she decides to write a letter to her favourite nun, a sister Angelica:

"I do so miss you all and think of you specially each day. Now we have a new tutor. He insists I read from a fat History book and then he asks me questions about it. For *tomorrow I must memorise a poem by Goethe and I also hope to have some music lessons from my Uncle who used to teach music in Triest, but now he is living with us; I love him very much; he plays to us all on his zither and teaches us Italian. Mama has lessons too. My cousins are all here. The girls both paint and make a great mess with all their colours and brushes. When I scolded them, saying their paintings were too big ...and so was the mess...they decided to paint a very small picture as a joke...no more than five centimeters square. I love it: it is 'my' mountain, the one I see from our garden and the rickety old fence. I will ask the woodcarver to make a special frame for it. No-one has ever given me a painting before and I like it because I can take it with me wherever I go....*

During the passing months Cölestine really learns to take charge of family matters. Tutors come and go. In the summer there is a notable visit from two further cousins:

Dearest Sister Angelica, we have had a busy time with visitors from Triest...two gentlemen. I did not know them before: yet both are cousins! I'm ashamed to tell you I cannot stand the younger one, only a 'second' cousin he is called Manfred Ragg, very haughty and always mocking me, just because he thinks he is very clever having graduated from University. He says he is a scientist. He has endless arguments with others as well, for example with my favorite Uncle Sepp, the zither teacher, who is inventing a strange machine which has many glass pipes filled with mercury from the mine nearby.

I so dislike it when grown-ups argue. It is so frightening.

Arguments between Dr. Manfred Ragg and Uncle Sepp get nowhere. Josephine, as always, stands between, protects and pacifies the irritable men-folk in her family. Cölestine is horrified.

As soon as the visitors leave Neumarktl the others return to their routines while the unhappy 'scientist' continues his experiments. One night the entire household is woken by cries of delight: "It's up and running", he repeats over and over as he runs from one room to the next," for all eternity...for ever, just like I *knew* it would!"

All those awake enough to do so pad along to admire the miracle machine.

On the following morning the Perpetuum Mobile comes to a halt.Uncle Sepp had been warned by his own relative and by a professor at the University in Graz, to abandon this dream, but he simply could not, would not, give up.

On that fateful day he wanders off before breakfast, into the early morning fog in the forest nearby, with his wife and his gun, (in case of brown bears)..."you go ahead, dear, the path is a bit narrow..."

and shoots,.....first, his wife, then himself...

September 1897. Again there is a coffin in the drawing room, *two* coffins, everyone in black, stunned. Josephine, in shock, has guilty feelings about the long lecture she gave Sepp: had she upset him? Karl, the strong silent 'head' of the family stands by her side, Aunt Ludowika has all her children around her, while Cölestine comforts her younger sisters. "How could he do this terrible thing" whispers Josephine, "he was so talented, he *knew* how much we loved him"....Karl Hofbauer, shading his eyes, reminds her that there will be a Christian funeral after all. Fortunately the village priest was Sepp's teacher when the boy was young and had noticed the child's' sensitive and somewhat unstable nature. The priest clears his throat before he declares: "Joseph Hofbauer was *not* an evil murderer; he is with God now." The monstrous sin of murder has been softened by the Church.

Cölestine can hardly speak, her wild and frightened thoughts can't be tamed...:"we all loved him ...he was always here and such fun and he loved Mama so much... *two mortal sins*...surely he isn't a murderer.... why do they call him a wastrel.....perhaps he simply could not bear to disappoint us all? Oh, poor Uncle Sepp, why did you do it?" Gradually friends and guests from the village filter into the house. The priest says prayers, consoles the sorrowing family as best he can, under such circumstances.

Cölestine flees to her room, kneels on her grandmother's prayer-stool. She wonders if Uncle Sepp had been a little in love with her mother, because she was always so nice to him, teaching him to be a business man just like her own handsome husband. "It's quite easy to fall in love with one's teacher", she reflects. But still, how could he do it, surely not...please St. Florian, look after him in heaven...we all loved him so and he was a nice person really..."

After the mourners have gone Josephine collapses in the chair by the window, gazes at the Klander crucifix, made a hundred years ago in the Klander foundry. All she feels is numbness, and then, increasingly, rage. How shameful it all is! How wasteful!

Needless to say, there was much talk in both St. Anna and Neumarktl. Almost everyone was connected to the family in some way, and the Hofbauers had much power and influence over the well-being of their workers and employees.

Josephine was proud of her husband's success at work but very perplexed by his young brother, who, with all his talent for music and science had shown skill for neither business nor for living.

• • •

In earlier days there had been gossip about the boy Sepp who seemed un-biddable at school and tended to drift off, to be found again in the woods, or just playing by the river.

When his talent for music came to light the family wondered from whom he had inherited his gifts. Someone had given him a zither and he seemed to know everything about the instrument before he even got near a teacher. Within a few months he was packed off to have lessons in Triest. To his family's surprise this Hofbauer was one who became well-known, who actually made a living from music. "A virtuoso," they thought admiringly, wishing him well.

Could it all have come to be because of the unusual circumstances of his baptism? During a freezing winters' afternoon the new-born baby was carried in a padded cushion on a sleigh ride to Neumarktl. Midwife and godparents had fortified themselves with mulled wine for the return to St Anna but when they reached home there was *no* new-born in the cushion. They returned and eventually found him head-first in the snow...already turning blue.

When Josephine heard about this, decades later, she did wonder if there had been some indefinable damage to the small boy.

Some curious re-arrangement perhaps, in Sepp's tender little skull?

Cölestine had few friends in Neumarktl. But there were enough people in the house to keep her occupied all day long: her younger sister's lovely voice was trained by a teacher who came to the house while the youngest needed much help with reading and writing.

Cölestine had suffered a lot more from the 'shame' of her Uncle's tragic and inexplicable actions and for some time she could hardly bring herself to leave the house.

"People might see me and ask questions" she thought. "How could I explain to them what a nice man he was? I so wish we could go away from here."

All tutors were dismissed while Josephine, in deep depression, tried to return to normal life. Dealing with office work, and settling the children after the tragedy were tasks she felt she could barely handle. Her sister, with *her* brood, had returned to Graz which made the house seem even emptier. It was then decided to send the younger sisters to a convent school in Graz. Cölestine, not much older than fourteen, would stay at home, perhaps she was to keep her mother company when the head of the family was away on his lengthy business trips. The teenager tried to help her Mama in every way. She went along to the office and the saw-mill, where they had to speak Slovene. She began to feel like a grown-up herself.

All Uncle Sepp's belongings were given to the church, for the poor, apart from his zither, which now belonged to Cölestine. His wife's clothes were also given away, but for one very lovely pale blue silk gown. Josephine felt that Cölestine could perhaps be cheered up with a new grown-up garment suitable for some as yet unspecified happy event, difficult to imagine. The dressmaker from Neumarktl was called to take measurements. She knew how to conceal the slightly uneven back of the young girl, so no-one would even notice .

While folding and wrapping the beautiful gown, Cenzi shed a tear for poor Aunt Marie. "I'll always remember her now", she thought.

In later years, when she was already a mother of grown-up children of her own she wrote an account of a **mysterious event** she and others experienced at this difficult time:

"It goes without saying that the suicide of Uncle Sepp affected our lives very deeply. Once the tutors were dismissed my little sisters were packed off to a convent school in Graz.

When Christmas drew near we simply couldn't bear the thought of staying in the house still so full of dark memories. It was decided that we would all spend Christmas with Mama's sister Ludowika in Graz. My father hoped that Mama would come out of her deep depression if she spent some time away from Neumarktl and that she might begin to forget the pain of the terrible mishap.

Papa travelled back home to Neumarktl on St. Stephen's Day and promised to return on St. Sylvesters' Day. We received a letter from him in the morning: there had been a breakdown of the machinery in the factory and he could not return to us until it was all running again, until any defect had been put right. He also said he might arrive on a late train, but if he had not arrived by 10pm we should not expect him.

On the last day of this terrible year we waited from one train to the next for my fathers' appearance. That evening we all sat in the drawing room, there were eight of us and we passed the time playing parlour games. We heard the clock strike ten times. My Mama said, sadly: "I don't suppose he'll come now..."

At that moment we heard Papa's characteristic footsteps passing through the entrance hall, through a second room and we saw the doorknob turn. We leaped up and shouted 'Papa' or 'Uncle', hurrying towards the door. But there was no-one at all! All the other doors were securely shut and we experienced a terrible feeling of emptiness. We discussed it at length and could not understand it.

Exactly fourteen days later my Papa died from Typhoid fever. But first he'd sent a request that Mama should come, that he was very ill, and that he had not wanted to spoil our fun over New Year.

Thus ended my childhood. From then on I shared all my mother's cares, and believe me, she had more than her share. I was fifteen years old." The deaths of Josephine's mother, then Uncle Sepp and his wife and now her husband, all in such a short time was simply too much to bear and soon she became so ill that the family doctor feared she would only live for another fortnight. It was said to be some illness of the spleen. "Praise be to God," writes Cölestine, "the doctor was in error, because my dear Mama eventually reached the age of ninety-seven. But at the time all this was very trying, when I was still so young with two younger sisters and no male relatives apart from my eighty-four year old guardian.

After a spell of about two years my Mama recovered. She even spent time in Laibach, (Ljubljana) for a health-cure. By then she had actually decided to sell all the business and property, no matter what the price. My brave widowed Mama, assisted by me, continued to run the business for about three years. Then the venture was sold to the cotton-spinning merchants Gassner and Glanzman. They brought huge benefits to Neumarktl because they decided to use the waterpower of the river to run their factory and also to create electric power for the entire area. The deal was completed in the summer. On the 10th October 1900 we left St. Anna and Neumarktl and moved to Graz. After the long loneliness of life in the valley we enjoyed town-life to the full...theatre, concerts and ball after ball in the winter months. I did still sometimes think about my cousin Fred (Manfred Ragg). Clearly, none of us longed to return to St. Anna. Graz had a great deal to offer and as time passed we, the Hofbauer girls, were much in demand. ... I was thought to be a most desirable dancing partner.

Josephine, now well-off, spends money on her daughters. Artistic photographers in town immortalize the three young sisters in wonderful gowns, looking desirably marriageable.

The 'retired' business-woman becomes the focus of her children, and enjoys watching their lives take shape. She creates a new home and sees to it they meet young persons of both sexes, to secure their own futures. ...

Cölestine claims, in her own account, to be a popular dance-partner in the ballrooms of Graz. There are also homely occasions, and a photograph exists, showing an unpromising array of young gentlemen, nearly all mustachio-ed and sadly, rather stupid-looking. This may be explained by earlier photography, because in those days people had to hold still counting up to 20 (at least!), to ensure sufficient exposure.

It has to be said, however, the girls don't look nearly as stupid.

'Formalised mating games' then, carefully but discreetly supervised by mothers and aunts, anxious to place their daughters into lives of their own.... and surely always a hotbed of intrigue and hopes.

"In the back of my mind there was always the ghost of cousin Fredy", notes Cölestine in a letter. Despite the attentions from other suitors she holds herself in check, more like an amused by-stander. And yet, when they finally meet again, along with some other relatives, the young and fairly dashing Dr. Manfred Ragg seems to take little notice of her, and, if anything, repulses her, while being utterly charming to everyone else.

How does one interpret such behavior? Why...true love, of course!

"A visit to Vienna where we met once again, proved that all had changed and before we knew we had become engaged, secretly of course, and for a long time, as Fredy didn't have anywhere to accommodate a bride", writes Cölestine in another letter. One summer later the two have a terrible outburst because Cölestine has danced all too eagerly at some ball, which has caused her secret betrothed much displeasure. For two whole years they lose interest in each other. Time is passing. Cölestine's 'little' sisters play a quiet role, in the background:

Valerie, two years younger than Cölestine, was thought to be a 'wild' child who preferred to play rough games mostly with boys. She liked to befriend the dirtiest children about. Like her sister she was sent to a convent school, where her very promising voice was trained to a high level of proficiency. The voice was suitable for the opera and she soon had engagements in larger towns such as Klagenfurt, Teschen and Innsbruck. One wonders how such instant careers came about 100 years ago? She allegedly had good reviews but somehow lacked the correct temperament to be able to establish herself in the jealous world of performers. She disliked life in the theatre, so all that glamour was short-lived and she returned home to her mother, to take care of Josephine for the rest of her life. Neither reproduction nor romance there, none whatsoever! After her mother's death, about forty years later, she became an alcoholic and was found alone, on the floor, surrounded by empty bottles. She had been dead for many days.

The youngest child Margarethe, very beautiful, not too bright, is remembered mainly for her unhappy love-affair with a Jewish gentleman, who could not bring himself to leave his wife. Margarethe travelled with both of them in Syria, Egypt and Palestine and ended up eventually, broken-hearted in Vienna where she learned to run an office for a lottery organization and after many years she was totally in charge of it. As she aged, still ethereally lovely, she gradually lost her mind and she too died alone, in Vienna.

A mere nineteen pages and you have an outline of the earlier years of Josephine and Cölestine, sensible women, practical and devoted to their family, in their differing roles as mother and daughter, both of them interested in running a business, which must surely have been a brave thing to do in those days. One can't help feeling sorry for 'Cenzi', Cölestine's new nickname. She had no choice: she became an adult at the age of twelve.

Josephine had not been afraid to send her children away to board with relatives, nuns or other responsible persons. Here was a woman who needed a career. Although it made her very ill, she enjoyed controlling the lucrative veneer business, and feeling responsible for the Slovene workers and their families. Both mother and eldest daughter spoke German with a heavy Slovene accent for the rest of their lives. Josephine had become very wealthy, for a while.

However, soon after this time, Europe was to experience 'The Great War' and a recession of epic proportions: a great 'leveler', for over ten years.

Cölestine's miniscule framed oil-painting of her beloved mountains near Neumarktl travelled with her wherever she went.

We jump ahead too fast: First Cölestine must leave the nest.......

Cölestine's New Life.

In 1905 Fredy, or, more importantly, Dr. Manfred Ragg, the chemical engineer, is offered a job in London.

This triggers a conciliatory mood and without too much fuss he and 'Cenzi' become engaged officially. Any remaining doubts evaporate. Finance too is a factor. In the good old days gentlemen had to come up with complex proof of their abilities to keep the cherished daughters from 'good' families.

Here there is no father to ask awkward questions about such things, so Fredy probably gets round his prospective mother-in-law Josephine with charm and wit. Cenzi, a good sport and more than ready for the big adventure of a new life in England, tries to learn to cook, and attempts some English grammar! Even Josephine joins in the new challenge, when the twice weekly English teacher appears, with her 'hau du juh du' and 'pliezd tuh miet juh!

In April 1906 Fredy arrives to gather up his bride. Josephine breaks down while embracing her first-born, fearing for the young couples' future in such a distant and foreign place as England. She sobs, Fredy shuffles about in embarrassment. Travelling with them was Cenzi's step-mother-in-law, Hermine, a large, fearsome-looking lady, and, having heard about English food they also imported a lady cook! Their first home is in Woodford Green, North London, a splendid three-story Edwardian villa called 'Upwey'. One can't imagine why they would want such a big place. Perhaps they knew that Cenzi was already pregnant? The first-born to be is already more than just a twinkle in her father's eye.

Cölestine must have learned a creditable amount of English in those early years. She was, allegedly, quite homesick.

Judging from photos there was a steady stream of visiting relatives, to fill life with chatter and antics in the garden, such as a bizarre custom of putting on ridiculous garments and clowning about, looking quite silly. Was this something one did in the 'old days'? The young Raggs are sharp and funny, but definitely not ridiculous. There is one of Fredy sitting on the top rung of a tall ladder, wearing a hat and carrying an open parasol, supported right and left by his still slender young wife and his corpulent stepmother. Seated on the rungs is a young woman in a white apron, hands demurely resting on her lap. Is she the cook? Just from that photograph one deduces the instigator of this nonsense is Fredy, the scientist.

It is hard to be a young person suddenly uprooted into a new country and having to cope with developing a different persona. Cölestine was engrossed with her husband, mother-in-law and being pregnant. She had been tough and adaptable from her earliest days when she was farmed out to stay with aunts and other persons in Neumarktl, and sent off to boarding school for a bit of serious grooming from the nuns, to say nothing of the events from the age of 14 and onwards. There must have been other help in such a big house, but learning to communicate with the British all about was surely a cause for concern. Yes, she was certainly strong enough to cope. Without modern props such as 'counselling'. In those days it was swim...... or sink. She swam.

Her dearest Mama, Josephine, who by then looked formidably old, came just once; did she also try a few words of English? And Cenzi's sisters came to stay. She was never alone! It would be fair to speculate that Cölestine was leading a pleasant life, doing things surrounded by helpers and family. She spoke some English, for sure, but she never had to cook!

On the 10th of January 1907 Cölestine's first daughter arrives: 'Erika, Hermine, Josephine' was well-named: Ericaceae are the hardiest and least demanding of plants.

Fredy sloped off each morning to work in a bleak laboratory belonging to the firm of Suter, Hartmann, Rahtjen in a place called Silvertown, an area near the docks, in London. Now fading photographs give little clue as to his activities. There is a horse with its nose in a nosebag, standing near mountains of barrels, in the distance a very depressing building with a 30ft chimney. His tasks were something to do with the invention of a rustproof paint for use on ships and trains. Small wonder he needed to let off steam when he was at home with his family and guests...

Little Erika had an English nanny, Nurse Mary Parker: we have a photo of her pushing an elaborate metal push-chair containing her charge into what looks like a dense thicket. No doubt Erika's later talents conversing in English stem from this early age. One needs to learn languages as young as possible otherwise you never 'get' the accent.... well, Erika Ragg learned English in the cradle.

Four years later a second daughter was born, and then yet another. By then Erika had begun her schooling in Woodford Green. The three little girls surely reminded Cölestine of her own childhood in Neumarktl, although Erika was fortunate enough to return to her own home each day during her schooldays.

Cölestine will have pored over Erika's first Term Report from 'The Convent', Woodford Green, Essex. It shows that her child was in Infants Division and that her general Progress was 'Very Good.'

There was 99/100 for conduct and the same for politeness, however only 90 for punctuality and, even worse, only 85 for order!The adult Erika, later to be known as 'Eka' was already fully encapsulated by the Rev. Mother de Sales in 1912 at the tender age of five and a half. Can it be true that all our traits are there by that age? There are six reports, from Sept.1912 to Sept 1914. The last report is blank but for a date, Sept.9th. 1914, a signature by the Rev. Mother, and scrawled across the page; 'not examined'.

This is testimony of the first real dramatic event in tiny Erika's life and, by extension, in the lives of her sisters and their resilient mother: the First World War had begun. Family Ragg are labeled 'aliens' in a country which had been their home for nearly eight years.

All three Ragg daughters succumb to whooping cough during the summer months, and 'Papi', who seems to have absconded to Austria to get a quick break from the misery at home, finds himself trapped and separated from his family when war breaks out in August. Telegrams fly between 'Mami' and 'Papi,' while the small girls are tended by their long-suffering nurse and grandmother. Whooping-cough tends to go on for weeks and weeks. There is no stopping for either the war or the infection.

Papi/ Fredy/ Dr Manfred Ragg was in a real pickle: no extra money in the bank for five tickets to return home to Austria, even worse: he had been summoned by the military and assigned to run the kitchen of a military hospital. In later years this was seen to be very funny indeed because Papi had never set foot in any kitchen in his entire life. Any sick and wounded he had to keep nourished were in more serious danger than they realized! But his family in Woodford was also in difficulties: no money, three small sick children and suddenly labeled an 'enemy'!

Now cool, practical Cölestine comes into her own: she simply passes the hat round in her husband's firm and asks for the necessary funds to return to Austria. It is a matter of some urgency because the family has been informed they would be interned in a camp with other aliens currently being rounded up in England.

"Mami, please can I come with you, I promise I will not cough, not even once?" Little Erika is beside herself with misery. "I haven't been to school for ever and ever and I want to see my friends to say goodbye to everyone... please, please, let me come too..."

"Ekalein, please be sensible. Just imagine how cross Sister Mary St. Paul will be if she sees you in the building, I'm only going to pick up your report." Tears stream down Erika's pale cheeks.

"Now listen, this is a good plan: I'll help you to write GOOD BYE and much love from Erika Ragg and I'll give it to your teacher to show to everyone...." "and will you come back very quickly and tell me what they said..?" Little Erika has given in...but not without resentment. "I hope the snakes bite you on Snakes Lane !..."

But she adores her Mami..... it is only a joke they say every time they walk into the village to do the shopping.

How well-organised they must have been. Was there a telephone in the house? Who knows how they dealt with their belongings and with the children.

By the time they arrived in Den Haag, by boat, the second daughter, Dagmar, came down with pneumonia so they had to stay in Holland until she'd recovered. The poor wee thing was only three and baby 'Ene' (Irene), one year old. Cölestine will have had a testing time, again. No doubt Erika played a responsible role in all this, she was seven after all! And how much of this acquired 'Englishness' will stick, one wonders? Both Cölestine and Erika had a good dose of it, especially Erika. Time will tell.

Less than one year later Erika has a splendid report from her new school in Hollabrunn, Austria, dated

28.5.1915. She is given the mark of 1 for every single subject, which is the highest you can have in the Austrian system. She had been assigned to the 2nd year class, so her English education had obviously been seriously good. Well done, little Eka! Perhaps she didn't miss England at all.

Mind you, Hollabrunn may not have been up to the standards of the English education system. It is a very tiny town, in wine lands north of Vienna and only about 15 miles from the Czech border. No doubt a scenic place it is above all the new home of 'Grossi', (Grossmutter= grandmother) the famous widowed business-woman of the Klander clan, who used to play the zither, spoke Slovene and is now a gaunt old lady, thin as a matchstick, wearing tiny glasses on the end of her nose. Cölestine is so very happy to be with her mother and to be able to speak her own mother-tongue: Austrian German with a thick 'Schlag-Ober' of Slovenian! What a relief. When she remembers her daily struggles in Woodford Green.........

Grossi lives in a small house with a tiny walled garden full of potted plants and has little to worry about.... other than having to water the plants and buy her daily provisions. Suddenly her house is full and for the foreseeable future there are three grandchildren to take care of. Her son-in -law is an officer about to be sent to the Italian front, but the family is safe and content for the time being. There is sufficient food; the War is far away, somewhere in France, somewhere in the Ukraine......

And Cölestine? What is going on in her head? "My poor little Mama...how patient she is with this invasion! She seems to have lost weight in the eight years we were away in England...and such terrible eyesight! I must get her to wear some more cheerful clothes though, always this dreary black... how can she stand living here, Hollabrunn is almost as boring as Neumarktl, and she knows almost no-one? One thing is sure, this little house really can't hold us all...I simply must find some place to rent, if Fredy's pay allows it. Erika's school fees are higher than those in Woodford, but we're saving money because we have no Nurse Parker here. Oh dear, how I miss her, she was such a 'nice' English girl. And Ekalein will forget all her English! For the moment she just has to learn more about this country. It's 'home,' of course. ...we'll all feel better when we have a house of our own....and soon my sisters are coming for a weekend! They just don't seem to find themselves the 'right' men... I can't think why they are so hard to please...Here comes Erika now, back from school for today. ...."

Months, years go by. The Great War seemed unreal in Hollabrunn. Apart from not having a husband and father about, and having little money, 'home' for Cölestine was normal, despite cramped conditions with her ageing mother, who gladly devoted herself to small grand-daughters, just as her own mother had done, in Neumarktl, when she was getting old and feeling useless. But they did begin to savor poverty: clothes were handed down and turned, shoes carefully repaired, passed on,...they had to become inventive.

The once so busy Josephine, now a busy Grossi, often marveled at her own past courage, when she, a fine lady in the late 1800's had supervised some undoubtedly rough Slovenian woodcutters each day. How she missed them! What an unusual thing that must have been. And when her husband passed away, she had run the business single-handed and become so ill from all that stress. The family doctor had predicted her death...within a few months! But here she was. Useful again!

Her only dream, buying a home in Bad Ischl, the Kaiser's family summer residence, had come to nothing with the outbreak of the war. Now she was the wizened old lady, faced with three little girls, but their mother had no intention of going out to work. Just two women in the house then, small as it was, cooking, cleaning and coping. There was a sound, strong, sensible bond between them.

The war, begun in September 1914, dragged on... If only Papi, the scientist, would reappear from wherever he might be! First at the Italian front, later deemed more suitable to work as an industrial chemist for the War effort, he was posted to an island, Arbe, off the Dalmatian coast, with full responsibility for the running of a Bauxite mine. This meant he had annual leave. His modest salary kept the entire family going.

Josephine, Cölestine, the children, prayed the War will be over 'soon'. Food shortages were beginning to 'bite', people learned to 'make do', becoming under-nourished. In 1917 Papi is able to visit, and leaves behind the prospect of yet another addition to the family:....a son is born in October 1918, just when the Austrian Monarchy collapses. Having been granted leave to be with his family at this time he was spared from unthinkable disasters: newly appointed as Commander of the island... the Croats had put a price on his head.

Sometime, in November drizzle,...an Armistice.... the war was over! Now there was a tiny new Manfred, soon known as 'Pucki'...Was Cölestine content? She must have been extremely worried: four children, a husband without a job, no home of their own.... what prospects were there?

Papi Ragg, after months of searching, followed up an advertisement in a specialist newspaper offering employment in a paint factory in Norway. The family would live in a small whaling town near Oslo, and his brief was to continue his research from the pre-war days, and oh, how glad they all were! Another upheaval for the children, but a blessing, although mixed, for Cölestine: still not much money, rented accommodation, (only two rooms) and then all that cooking, scrubbing, shopping and learning to cope... in Norwegian! Was it fun to run her household under such primitive conditions? They were so poor. As always, she just had to get on with things.........

One can only try to imagine how Gross-mama Josephine felt, all alone again, in her tiny house in Hollabrun. The family watched with interest from distant Norway: Grossi had new friends, the notary and the house doctor. They came regularly to her house to play cards. It was very 'gemütlich', for many, many years.

In Norway there was yet another new school and a new language for Erika. Such big changes surely leave their mark? However, Erika, Dagi, Ene and a tiny Pucki, mostly up to their ears in ice and snow (if the photographs are to be believed) had the happiest of times, despite domestic constraints. Norwegians were friendly and kind, the country was interesting and Papi's salary, at last, very acceptable.

And then there was the jack-pot: Dr Manfred Ragg invented a rust-proof paint called Arcanol, used worldwide to this day. The family became wealthy. Just like that! He was offered a job in Hamburg, during the big recession after WW1, yet the Raggs had no financial problems at all. Soon they bought themselves a house of some elegance in a suburb called Reinbeck. They named their villa 'Jotun' in gratitude to Norway: Jotun is the name of a mythical Norse giant, and plainly a bringer of good fortune.

As the Arcanol business grew Papi grew richer and richer while Germany became an uneasy place to live. They began to toy with ideas of returning to Austria, back to Carinthia, close enough to 'where we both come from'. "We don't really belong here!

I shall buy you a castle, liebes Mamilein, to make up for all the bad years. We will end our lives in style!" Mami thought he was joking, of course. A fairy tale! Did Cölestine/ Mami, see it like that?

She was practical and sensible, not given to romantic notions. Her first duty was to bring up all her children and send them out into the world, the second was to look after her man. Everything was orderly, relaxed, patient and kindly.

They employed a cook and a maid, just like the good old days in Neumarktl and in Woodford Green.........

The Raggs were fun to be with. They were great hosts, they were cultured (Papi owned a pianola on which he played Mozart and Beethoven symphonies), they read books. Both had a sarcastic, caustic streak, but with it there was humor, sharp humor.

Because of the business they entertained 'personages'. They were 'stylish'! In the 1920's, for example, they often had dealings with a young man from West Africa, someone to do with shipping. They saw him every time he came to Hamburg on leave, he more or less adopted them, they made him feel part of the family. His own family lived in Pomerania...their lives devoted to shipping, one maternal grandfather an admiral, earlier ancestors had been farmers.

Erika, by then a shy fourteen-year old, mentions this young man in her diary. One feels she was quite put out by her parents being so nice to him. "Der olle Ihlenfeldt" she calls him (that old Ihlenfeldt), and even worse: "der olle Kaffer" when she had been sent out by her mother to buy some champagne and tulips before his next invitation. "Let's hope he's soon sent back to his black people," she records.

Note this man's name. He re-appears three years later!

Excerpts from Erika's diary between 1923 and 1926 allow insights into a very young lady's psyche: having shown her classmates some photographs of a family gathering including 'Reinhold Ihlenfeldt and co", she reports: "gales of laughter from everyone. Ellen (her friend) was quite beside herself. How is it possible all the girls think he is so smashing? I'm quite well informed about him now..." This was June, 1923. Erika is 16 years old.

On the 9th she writes: "Tomorrow the boys are coming. How I hate these creatures!" 10thJune: "Sunday passes.... homework, housework and boys. Oh how I hate that Ihlenfeldt. Such arrogance and disregard! Even the others noticed it. I did not say a word to 'Mr. I'. If only he didn't come. Mami forces me to be downstairs with them."

Only 18 months on she writes: "...and now Ihlenfeldt: I was terribly anxious when he came. Well, we all rushed to the door at the same time, so details were lost. He has become, oh miracles, quiet and modest and a bit fatter and less beautiful. I had the best intentions to be nice and talkative, but it seems to be an impossibility with this person. Thank God I only blushed once, when he said "you're just as quiet as you used to be"....but I'd had too much champagne and, with a headache, showed myself from my worst side: I said nothing at all. He is staying in Hamburg, but I hope they soon send him back to his black Mammy. I don't know why he makes such a strange impression on me. I secretly compared him to William, and I have to admit that my poor little friend seems to lag behind somewhat". (Willy Hacker, her current boyfriend.)

Raggs senior have settled into comfortable armchairs in Papi's study, with a glass of cognac ...Papi lights the stub of an unfinished cigar... it is late, the last of the guests left. Mami, exhausted, needs to put her feet up,"it's been hard work tonight" she sighs, "I really don't feel much like clearing up the table and glasses now, let's just leave it all until I have some help tomorrow". ...... Papi's eyes are shut: "Entertaining after work is really just like 'more work' these days "he thinks to himself, but doesn't like to upset his wife who has just put on such a splendid show, for his benefit. ... "and have you ever seen such an exquisite bouquet as the one young Ihlenfeldt brought today, it is quite outstanding. I suppose he must be doing rather well for himself... isn't it strange how much he seems to enjoy being with us here in Reinbeck,...why, no sooner his ship docks in Hamburg he wants to come out to see us...nice really. He's almost like a son now. Too bad he is a Lutheran, do you suppose he fancies Erika? I must say, she does seem to have a soft spot for him!" Papi's nose glows from an evenings' wine and brandy; he considers the fine young Reinhold who has so attached himself to his house and home: "we must keep an open mind about all our daughters.... we'll need to find men with prospects... I dare say, Reinhold does make a very good impression, how long has he been coming here now...nearly five years is it?"...Papi stares up at the ceiling and at his large china eagle on the bookshelf..."we'll just have to see...keep our 'eagle' eyes open...but I'm sleepy now, my dear, let's go upstairs and get a good night's rest.

To imagine any ones' life in Germany a bed of roses in those troubled times, between the two World Wars, would be ridiculously unrealistic. There was inflation, deprivation, hardship and political trouble in spades. It was during these threatening years that Josephine Hofbauer, alias 'Grossi' became old, and, in the years of inflation, quite hard-up....and that Cölestine, the by now quadri-lingual mother of four, had matured and was even thinking of 'retirement', back home, somewhere in the south of Europe.

"Where is home", she must have wondered:... "Neumarktl, Woodford, Hollabrunn... Sandefjord,..... Hamburg ? And Erika, now an appealing young woman in her final years of ferociously serious German high school, is toying with the idea of becoming a student of archaeology. After years of being the oldest child, which, needless to say, can be a wearying task to say the least, the escape from school, even from home, seems a tantalizing prospect. Would she admit, even to herself, that all she really wants is to be wooed and carried off by such a man as Reinhold Ihlenfeldt, and never have to do a stroke of work of any kind? They had been writing to each other for quite some time, discussing heavy topics such as religion and philosophy and Reinhold regularly sends photographs of his adventures on the Gold Coast to Papi Ragg and all the family...not just one or two, but many. Everyone involved is quietly heading for some eternal bond, no-one ever says it out loud, but later events show that dreams, however secret, can come true...... Or, one must will them to come true.

There is a photo of Erika dancing on the lawn of their very grand garden, looking coy, but nevertheless in the arms of some young man, perhaps a school friend. There was indeed some romance with such a person, but intended or not, the entire Ragg family had captured the heart of this affectionate young Ihlenfeldt who appeared each time he was sent back from Africa on business. In his diaries there are remarks about the delightful Ragg children and how pretty the girls were, especially young Erika, who had turned that corner from teenager with long pigtails to shy enchantress. She even began an earnest correspondence with him ...that poor lonely fellow slaving away in Africa. Well, not only earnest, but regular and very, very serious topics chosen to impress each other. There was debate about the undesirability of 'mixed-faith' marriages (Reinhold's brother had just had a bad experience) and about Faith and God. Two years of gentle hints how important it seemed to keep in touch, quoting fragments of poetry and clever philosophical thoughts. Erika had an axe to grind about the need for a young woman to be 'independent' of her parents' support, wanting to learn something that would allow her to stand alone, to keep herself. Reinhold firmly argued against this need, upholding the idea of a pure, unsullied woman who lives only for the man she will marry. Reinhold must have done a lot of reading in those two years to keep up this intellectual level! Could it be that the best way to get to know another person is by correspondence? In 1928, shortly after Reinhold Ihlenfeldt comes to Hamburg for a month to recover from his now seven year stint in the tropics.... they get engaged.

He knocks on the door to Papi's study, trembling from head to foot, to ask for Erika's hand in marriage. Papi has known all along that this was 'a good thing' but nevertheless feels obliged to explain that he is in no position to offer a large dowry as he has yet another three children to bring up, but aware of Reinhold's respectable place in the world of shipping he knows his daughter will be well cared for. When Reini emerges from the study the entire clan is gathered outside the door to witness the official 'engagement kiss'.

Erika's Story

Here it is then: the dreaded 'mixed marriage', that is, between a Catholic from Austria and a Lutheran from Pomerania. This frequently discussed topic in the family had led to the view it could/should never be allowed...the strain on everyone too great. "Quite unthinkable..." because everyone from Neumarktl and everyone from Marburg, meaning all of Mami and Papi's ancestors, going back for nearly 300 years, had been Catholic!

A beautiful, innocent virgin is claiming the right to disappear from her Catholic family into darkest Africa...with a Protestant! It is to the credit of the family that, despite everything, there is minimum fuss, other than the usual vows to the Holy Mother Church to bring up any children in the 'only true faith'.

Erika's three semesters of archaeology at Hamburg University are abandoned— to be replaced by 'holy matrimony.' Forsaking Germany...to its then current universal 'impoverishment', a country on the verge of a mostly unforeseen change, Erika Hermine Josephine becomes Erika Ihlenfeldt, on the 13th March 1929.

What a fine couple they are! Mami, normally so balanced and stable and full of jokes clings to her intrepid husband weeping, full of foreboding because her firstborn is going to blackest Africa, to live in the jungle, amongst foreigners. Well, to a British Colony.....

The honeymoon takes Eka and Reini via Vienna to Hollabrunn, where the young bride introduces her brand-new husband to the beloved Josephine, her 'Grossi'. On to Venice and Genoa and the Italian and French Riviera; they did things in style those two, and there is an entire photograph album to prove it.

With hindsight Erika never had such a good spoilt time again in all her life; it really was an all-time high. One supposes she was much too young and inexperienced to really take it in.

Most of us only realize the *good times* when they are long over!

Stand back, observe the three generations at this moment:

<u>Josephine</u> (Grossi), 82, lives alone in her now quite empty home. Sometimes she has the company of one or the other of her unmarried daughters. Most of her considerable fortune has vanished due to the terrible years of inflation after the first World War- but she lives comfortably enough. She enjoys her little garden, likes to play cards with her gentlemen friends, misses the 'old days'. For the past ten years Neumarktl is called Trizic and is in Yugoslavia. How strange!

Her eldest, <u>Cölestine</u>, now called 'Mami' by everyone, is 45 years old and has four children, so this is entirely appropriate; <u>Erika,</u> her eldest, met *her* husband-to-be aged only fourteen, just as Cölestine had. Now she lives in Africa; perhaps there will be a grandchild. As Erika's siblings pass through their schooldays, Mami and Papi begin to envisage retirement and the possibility, *no*, need, to return to their roots. They sense uneasy developments in the daily events surrounding them, they read between the lines. The Nazis leave Papi alone: fortunately he is protected by an Italian passport, since he was born in Triest. "Not immediately, but very soon: ...perhaps once the children have left school... we should get out of here," is, no doubt, what they think. Son and heir Pucki, begins to have a curiously striking resemblance to Mathias Klander, in Neumarktl, whose portrait, painted in the early 1800's, hangs in Papi's study.

There were many other far-seeing individuals for whom Germany was becoming a questionable proposition at this time. Herr Doktor Manfred Ragg and Frau Cölestine Ragg began by taking a few holidays in Austria, calling on relatives in Klagenfurt and Vienna and Hollabrunn, carefully weighing up the possibility of returning to this part of the world. They were missing neither England, nor Norway.

And <u>Erika</u>, Cölestine's eldest? Well, she's 22 and in love and by this time has a change in life style that borders on the fantastical. She travels by ocean liner, first class, to the Gold Coast, lounging about on deck-chairs with her glamorous tall husband, who knows everyone and adores her. She speaks English with a very slight German twang! Nothing like as terrible as Reinhold's.......

The happy couple settles into a tropical home (with an old slave cellar) in the native town right on the seafront of down-town Accra. From the raised veranda they gaze across the sea to the ships being unloaded in the distance. There was no harbor; in those days whatever arrived by boat had to be transferred into narrow long-boats rowed by athletic black men glistening in the spray. Reinhold's life consisted of one dramatic event after the other: the bay of Accra became littered with goods that had dropped into the ocean, never to be retrieved.

Soon Erika realizes there is nothing else to do but 'take an interest', look pretty, and entertain numbers of multinational guests.

The cook tolerates her presence, nods politely at all her requests, and produces great meals in spite of her attempts to meddle.

She's blissfully happy. During this time they become known as 'Eka' and 'Reini'.....

Accra, a fast developing town with an indigenous population of 60.000 and about 900 whites from various countries, had electricity, telephone, water supplies, roads were paved, cinemas and bars added to the lively social scene. After work, at

5pm, everything ground to a halt so people could rush off to tennis, golf, riding, swimming,...it was all available. Then followed the 'sundowner'- and evenings were mostly enjoyed with some sort of party. There was no racial discrimination, everyone mingled naturally, based of course on interests, education and social stratification.

For Germans living in the country the most difficult aspect was British social distancing, still in place in 1927, nearly 10 years after WW1. By the time Erika came to Africa these hard feelings were dying down; the young couple was soon seen in the 'best circles' of Accra, at the garden parties of the Governor, as on smaller occasions at Government house and at the Accra Club. The fact that Erika spoke passable English with only the slightest trace of an accent made life a lot more pleasing.

The Club was housed in an 'old' building dated 1895 offering a library and billiard room, a bridge-room and of course a bar and restaurant. Members could sit out on the veranda and were entertained, on Sunday evenings, by the Accra Police band. After the constraints of life in Hamburg with all the family, Erika, in fashionable new clothes and with a handsome, popular husband, must have been more or less in heaven!

He found time to drive her inland to visit African villages and lush landscapes and took her on business trips to adjacent African countries; hot, new, strange, entrancingly romantic and exotic adventures. Her embarrassingly large number of servants, who cleaned and cooked and served and laundered and shopped and planted and carried and drove ... all in immaculate uniforms, milled around her, the centre of their attentions. She soon picked up the required 'pidgin English,' a linguistic experience all on its own.

Reini's passion is photography, he develops his own pictures. He's an artist making an attempt to keep a record of all they see (for almost 10 years) and creates albums. They send pictures to both sets of parents. But then Reini had been doing this all along, for as long as he'd known the Raggs...for the past seven years! Meaning to impress them, of course. This is a very good thing. It means we can not only imagine Erika's new life but we can see a great deal too. Erika believes she is the luckiest woman alive. In later years she would look back on those ten years in Accra as the best years of her life. She was a little homesick of course, just as Mami had been during her years in England, and just as Grossi must have felt, forlorn, widowed, friendless, in Graz and Hollabrunn.

As these three women moved through their allotted lives they all had their share of adjusting to do, learning to fit in, learning to change, communicate with strangers, and understand. It's called 'broadening the mind'.

There was much of that.

Dearest Mami ,dearest Papi,
Accra, Jan.3rd,1930.

Imagine this: after breakfast Reini took me down into the court yard and there it was: a new car, just for me. It is a Chevrolet Roadster (no roof!) He just said, "happy birthday", even though it isn't my birthday until next week...can you imagine how I feel! He has been showing me how to drive in his car for some weeks now, and tonight we are going out for a careful drive along the beach road, where there is not a great deal I could bump into. He is worried I might feel bored sitting about all day long but he is wrong: I have several books from the Club library, plan my wardrobe for our busy social life (the ladies here like to look glamorous) and of course I have to tell cook what to do! Reini trusts him because the cook has worked for him for many years. Cook doesn't really like me to make any suggestions because I obviously don't know what is available here.

Reini always has his hair cut by the chauffeur. Should I let him cut mine? I'm a little worried about this. We are looking for a picture of the 'Bubi' hair-cut, for him to copy! Can you cut out something from a newspaper and send it? Now that I have my own car I must have a sensible and practical hair-do, don't you agree? There are so many new friends here, we go to the Club often and drink gin and tonic..

How are my 'ugly 'sisters and my 'horrible' brother. When does he start at his new boarding school with the monks in Lavanttal? I do miss you all and wish you could all come and see how happy we are. Reini is adorable and we have two little kittens, both stripy and very funny. Before I forget: sometimes African traders come to the house, selling strange carvings and metal sculptures. Shall I buy something bizarre for House Jotun? I can just see an object like that on the veranda in Reinbeck. Please let me know. All love, Erika.

Liebe Erika, we think of you so much, all of us! Your 'ugly sisters 'are at school and green with envy when you write about your new life. A car, just for you! Is it really necessary? We always managed without one. Anyway, I don't think I could drive because of my bad eye.

Do be careful you sleep properly tucked -in under those mosquito nets, I can just imagine how sweet your blood must taste to hungry mosquitoes, to say nothing of those cockroaches...Yes, Pucki has been accepted as a boarder, and I'm sure it will do him good when he starts there in September.

I don't know what to say about the African things. They sound interesting. Please remember to take your Quinine every day. And drive with care! Be embraced by your loving Mami and Papi.

Erika sometimes forgets to take her preventative medicines and has several very bad bouts in hospital with Malaria and Black-water fever ... Being the wife of a shipping agent has one very great advantage: free boat journeys home. After Erika's illnesses she invariably returns to Hamburg to recuperate.

By 1933 radical political changes have taken place in Germany. These trends were felt even in the depths of Africa, and the repercussions and results were not remotely understood by expatriates working abroad. Reinhold had never shown any interest in politics, it appears both he and Erika lived very much on the edge of these happenings, even though they were closely linked with their 'Heimat' through work, literature, music and family feelings.

An unexpected event occurred in the early months of 1934 when Mami and Papi in Hamburg received a telegram from their daughter and son-in-law in Accra with the news that Reini had been appointed German Consul for the Gold Coast and Togo-land. He posts cuttings to them from the Gold Coast Gazette.

THE GOLDCOAST GAZETTE, 7th April, 1934.
It is hereby notified for general information that the King's Execquatur, empowering Herr Reinhold Ihlenfeldt to act as Honorary German Consul at Accra received His Majesty's signature on the 12th February, 1934.

Needless to say their social life escalated with this appointment. Not that they weren't sufficiently in demand already! By now the Ihlenfeldts both spoke very passable English, they were young and good-looking, and the British community as well as their diplomats were friendly. They were able to get a taste of an enviable social life, from visits to the race course, to garden parties and elegant soirees and even dinners for visiting royalty from other nations.

• • •

Infant mortality amongst Europeans was very high. Over and over again the decision was: no family-building— not until they were posted to a better climate, or until they returned to Europe. This was endlessly discussed, corresponded about, weighed up........mulled over.

After four years together Erika and Reini felt they had the solution: they would have a baby and leave it in Hamburg with Mami and a trained nurse; with any luck there would soon be a posting to a better climate and then they could enjoy being a proper family. They had been warned against this plan by wiser and older persons such as the family doctor and by their parish priest ...but the urge to procreate was so very strong!

What a splendid idea, what a generous offer from Mami and Papi.! To have another baby in the house, even with a trained nurse, would be a challenge: Mami was already fifty. One can still be a 'mother' aged fifty......the house in Reinbeck was very large and so, when all was said and done, there was little in the way of this grand design. On evening walks, in the cool ocean breeze, the would-be parents in Accra strolled to the lighthouse and back, discussing, more than once, the name for the as yet un-conceived offspring. If it were a boy he could be 'Wolfgang' and if a girl, Reinhold had a weakness for 'Ingeborg' or for 'Eva'. Erika didn't really have strong feelings. A close friend of theirs, Evelyn Dade wished to be godmother and so a combination of Ingeborg- Evelyn came into orbit.

The 'Evelyn' bit was, of course, the first little step to being the tiniest bit British....along with being conceived in a British Crown Colony!

So, an infant, conceived in Accra was transported in utero to Hamburg three months before the birth. Judging from Erika's dimensions it was surely a very large Wolfgang?

ETA was the end of December, 1934: everybody stood by, Reini in steamy hot Accra, Eka in freezing snowy Hamburg, the nurse, Sister Erna, in her starched uniform and the saintly Mami, ready to supervise yet another infant, in her care.....her own remaining children, Dagmar, had already left home, Irene was finishing school, while Pucki appeared for holidays from his boarding school in Austria . It shouldn't be too bad!

Erika expanded in a bloated sort of way and lolled about. Christmas came and then New Year. She went for careful walks in the snow. Still nothing.

The doctor suggested there had been some mistake in the calculations made in Accra. Well, not even Erika's birthday celebrations on the 10th of January made the slightest birth tremor appear. The resident in poor Eka's stomach was very, very lazy and comfortable.

At last, on the 23rd of January, an 8-pound Venus made her belated appearance, only a month late but, according to the Vereins-Hospital staff, a remarkable specimen, by any standards. Many photographs were taken, of both the shattered mother and the surprised newly-born.

Examining her offspring Erika's unflattering assessment was:

"a Pomeranian peasant-child with slitty blue eyes..."

Not only does the new-born have a large brown birthmark on the top of her left arm, but also: it is shaped like the map of Africa. Next to Erika's bed are photographs of a benign, smiling Reinhold, amongst the vases of flowers sent by friends and relations.

Now Erika had a daunting new task : to be a 'mother'. In those days new mothers rested in bed for at least a week.

By February the youngest resident of Haus Jotun was well established with an entourage of doting uncles, aunts, grandparents and a noticeably slimmed-down mother. There is a picture-book cradle with much floaty white muslin, a cot, a white pram, and early potty-training,(yes, really, it was thought the thing to do: holding a potty under a baby would achieve a result!) all photographed to allow the absent father to take part at a distance.

Unbelievably, at 7 weeks, the mother-substitute Sister Erna goes into action with baby gymnastics! There are photos of a writhing infant suspended by her ankles... can it be that all German babies are treated like that in the first months of their lives? Or was this simply a trained nurse, showing off?

By March Erika hardly appears in the photos; she's obviously weaning herself from mother-dom and leaving her offspring in more experienced hands. Or possibly preparing herself for the martyr-dom of abandoning her baby? But first there is christen-dom with all the family gathering and the celebration deemed necessary for such an event when Ingeborg-Evelyn is received into the bosom of the Catholic Holy Mother Church.

Erika returns to Accra, probably with mixed feelings.

As time passes at least ten photographs of Ingeborg's developing activities are taken monthly and posted to her distant parents, who cling to each other with great love and affection, while enduring the bittersweet pangs of guilt of both having - and not having a baby. The blue eyes are now golden, hazel. Never mind.

By December the parents return to Hamburg and Reini meets his child for the first time.

This momentous event takes place in the nursery, with only Erika (and the Nurse, in case of an emergency) in discreet attendance; the rest of the family stands in the corridor peering through a gap of the door...they all want to witness this first meeting, to see how father and daughter behave. Reini admits later that his heart rate was up and that he was very moved, but also terrified of doing anything that might arouse the displeasure of the 'princess.' One attempt of lifting her into his arms ends with screams and tears while small arms reach out imploringly to Nurse Erna.

Erika and Reini had not expected miracles, but the well-known 'call of the blood' was not in evidence for the moment.

It took a while. The next clever ruse was for Erika to dress in a starched uniform just like the nurse and to attempt feeding and bathing ceremonies. After four weeks of patient effort Ingeborg-Evelyn began to accept her mother. Dad was rejected time after time. This non-acceptance lasted until a week before the planned parental return to Africa, when her highness fell for his cigarette lighter, which she wanted to blow out. Blowing out candles on the first Christmas tree had been her greatest thrill. Ingeborg-Evelyn would continue blowing out imaginary candles in the corner where the tree had stood, for many months. Father and daughter began, warily, to be friends of a kind. For one whole week, anyway.

Photography continued: the difficult first encounter between father and daughter (blank disbelief on a one-year old face quite sad to see) and the magical German Christmas tree with real candles, sparkly lametta, and gingerbread rings.

Then Eka and Reini rented a car and took off to enjoy a two month trip around Europe. First there was a call of duty (as consul) to attend a party given by von Ribbentrop in Berlin, at that time acting ambassador to Britain. After that the young couple seemed to need to get about in Germany because they had seen so little of it in their student days, and they were now obliged to talk more knowledgeably about their own country, a place they only knew while still at school. Did they have any idea what was going on in Germany, one wonders?

Spending all ones home-leave with a one year-old, who would then get too used to you and therefore make the next new parting too painful all round, was something the young parents had discussed at great length. They had a distressing row in Linz, as described in one of Reini's numerous diaries, almost as if it was the first misunderstanding since they were married. Going on long car-journeys can bring out the worst in people, as can visiting relatives.

In 1936 the 'Africans' returned to Accra.

Mami had already coped with three changes in nurses by then, which can't have helped in the fostering of Ingeborg-Evelyn. Pleasingly, there was an inspired intervention by young Pucki, home for his holidays from boarding school. His favourite cartoon clown in a newspaper, a character called 'Knups', led him to observe that the chubby baby had an uncanny resemblance and was henceforth known as Knups, a useful short blend of plumpness and affection, above all, it was amusing. This caught on at once! A good shrink may remonstrate that giving a male name to a young female might have deleterious effects on her development, warp her mission in life, change her hormones, appearance and so forth. For now 'Knups' was a well-proportioned, adorable package of cute smiles, golden eyes and shiny blonde ringlets. A model baby. We shall see.......

Erika knew that life was about to change dramatically: they had news of a posting from Accra to Cape Town, probably in 1938. At last, a chance to become a proper family!

Mami and Papi too were now free to plan their long-hoped for escape to Austria, where Papi had, in a mad moment, acquired a 13th century castle with four towers (no draw-bridge). He might have liked a drawbridge: to get away from Hamburg in 1938 seemed just the thing, an escape to a quiet backwater near the border of Yugoslavia. In any case the Nazi's ignored him, with his Italian passport.

Besides, he was sixty-five years old and wanted nothing else but to play Mozart and Beethoven symphonies on his pianola and to enlarge his stamp-collection. No more science, no more business, no more babies and nurses, just peace and quiet. Wishes of a sixty-five year old must be respected.

They could not move in straight away, the place needed wiring, painting, central-heating. While all this was going on they would rent a villa nearby. There was plenty of time to plan, and dream about life in their castle and some trips across the mountains to Yugoslavia , where Mami's (and Papi's) roots were.

1939 was to be a year of momentous change for Mami, Erika and the 'nearly four year old '. ....

Nothing much new for Grossi, however, still alive, nearing ninety, and peering through little spectacles on the end of her pointy nose. She was known to beat her elderly gentlemen friends into submission by winning at most of their regular card-games. One pleasing fact was that her eldest, Cölestine, would soon pack up life in northern parts and take residence in Schloss Mageregg just outside Klagenfurt. This was at least a three-hour train journey away from Hollabrunn, nevertheless Grossi felt reassured by the relative proximity...........

1939, Klagenfurt, Austria. Moving into an ancient 'Schloss' focuses the mind. Not only did Papi need an assistant to help with the running of it, but also to keep a horse (for the carriage), to see to repairs and plant things in the fields and scythe the meadow. He knew nothing about such matters....and to be honest, stuck mostly to his stamp-collection. Now there was also Yugoslavia, just across the mountains!

Mami rolled up her sleeves bravely and 'got on', which was what she always did. This time it was curtains and unpacking and feathering the nest, if one can call such a huge place a nest ! It was a pleasing thought, having all the family here, enjoying the countryside and being together, from time to time....that was what really kept Mami going. And to be only a few miles from Neumarktl, her old home. Papi soon settled down in his study, along with the wise china eagle one sees on all his photos, and began to study the past.

His castle, called Mageregg, was only one treacherous mountain pass (the Loibl Pass) away from Yugoslavia (now called Slovenia) and he was soon accessing old church registers, village priests, distant relatives, finding both alarming and delightful tales about earliest ancestors, the Klanders and others.

And Cölestine-Cenzi-Mami?? After all those early uncertainties, here she was, in her new incarnation: the 'queen' of her castle. How often did she go down into her own chapel at the base of the front right-hand tower to thank God for her good fortune?

She had all she'd ever hoped for: a fairly grumpy but loving and successful husband, four children - eventually dotted all over the globe, financial stability, a huge kitchen in which to bake unbelievable strudel with dough so thin you could read the newspaper through it, and good health. If there was anything missing she never let on.Her mother, Josephine, now in her nineties, still lives in Hollabrunn, cared for by spinster daughters...Compared to these sisters Cölestine is thought to be living a picture-book life, fulfilled and successful beyond all dreams.

We now expect to see her seated in her castle, wearing elegant gowns and being waited on by servants.

Not so: she has hard work from dawn to dusk: the place is vast and the distances from room to room take it out of her! The kitchen can be reached only after a stately descent past knights in coats of armour (well, just the coats of armour) to an ancient grey stony kitchen, quite dark and below the ground, when one tries to look out of the window. Mercifully, there is a pulley in a tunnel on which plates and glasses and food can be transported up and down between the lower ground floor and the dining room. People still have to march up and down themselves. If they need a rest they can step into the chapel just before the stairs begin. Once at the top you find handsome rooms with high tiled stoves for heating and wooden parquet floors covered with Persian rugs. Hidden by one of the windows in the tower is Papi's pianola. While he sits listening to the sounds of symphonies on his piano rolls he can gaze out across fields and parklands all the way to the Karawanken, those towering mountains separating Austria from Yugoslavia . "Here is where we belong" he no doubt thinks to himself, "this is good and we are lucky, despite the hard work and the expense." The family is agog! To visit the Schloss is quite an adventure. It dates back to the fourteenth (or was it thirteenth?) century, had been built by Italians. Everyone feels somewhat 'different', perhaps a bit grander and more privileged, or romantic, wandering about inside and outside in such lovely surroundings and, when passing by the ancient Roman urn, imagines all the others who had seen it ....and had once lived and died in such a place..

But clouds are beginning to form on the horizon, ominous rumblings, for all to hear and fear. Where-ever they are, the Josephines, Cölestines, Erikas and Ingeborgs, something is about to happen to them all that none could escape – let alone understand.

Shortly before Mami's 'apotheosis' in her wondrous castle, in September 1938, Erika bundles up her child, travels by train to Vienna and Hollabrunn, to meet with and say goodbye to Grossi before the sea-journey to CapeTown. Knups is ecstatic about sleeping in a 'room on wheels'...seems unperturbed by leaving her first home and indeed her Mami in Hamburg. She is introduced to Mami's mother! This is an impressive array of mothers to take in.

How pleasing to imagine four generations in such proximity: Grossi, Mami, Erika and Knups, for one brief moment, touching, chatting, smiling together. There is no recorded account of this great moment, not even a photograph. It would almost be worth trying 'regression' to re-live such an event.

Then,....a quick flight to Genoa to board the ocean liner called 'Tanganyika.' Knups befriends the entire crew and passengers on the flight from Vienna: her mother has fainted (altitude sickness?) and the small traveler blithely entertains, and is cared for, by everyone. Erika reported to Reini that "Knups seemed to prefer male passengers and flirted with most of them." Not bad going for a three and a half year old.

Meanwhile, in the castle:

"How about a special dinner party to celebrate our return to Carinthia, my dearest...I mean, we need to build up a circle of acquaintances here,".....Papi rambles on at bedtime, after another long evening re-assessing his stamp collection ....

Mami, darning something, agrees: "Of course, Papilein, that would be splendid....but you forget: it may take a while before we get to know anyone. I mean, um, there's the priest, he's kind and intelligent and well perhaps we can call on some of our Klagenfurt relatives, they've hardly noticed our settling here. I know they're distant cousins. Let's think about it! And you know, we certainly need a maid again, one who lives in, otherwise I really can't manage ...a Slovenian one would be nice...If only Eka and Reini weren't so far away. Dagi and Ene telephoned from Vienna and are planning a visit soon, won't that be wonderful."

Papi decides to say nothing for now -pondering the news he'd gleaned from the wireless: Hitler and Chamberlain had come to some "agreement" in the matter of the Sudeten problem....a relief, but not a real solution. For the moment a war has been averted. He imagines how nice it would be to have some friends, new or old, to talk about the troublesome politics...even better, to forget all about it......"

For a short time-span Grossi, Mami and Erika, as well as the rest of Europe, hold their breath as it dawns on them all that another war is imminent ......and then the danger passes. Most of Europe breathes a huge sigh of relief. Everything continues as before.

The Ihlenfeldts, journeying via the Mediterranean through the Suez Canal, (where Reini proudly remembers his Admiral Grandfather accompanying German royalty whenever it was in 18 hundred and something) and then right around Africa, make numerous interesting stops. Reini's new job in Cape Town requires being acquainted with harbor facilities and staff along the entire East Coast of Africa. There are calls to be made in Port Said, Port Sudan, Aden, Mombasa, Daressalam, Porto Amelia, and finally Beira and Lourenco Marques, East London and Durban. The entire journey takes over six weeks and temperatures are unbearable. In those days there were fans.... but no air-conditioning.

A model *new* father, Reini takes matters into his own hands and carries his daughter to the ship's hairdresser to have her shoulder-length locks cut off...... without consulting Erika, the *new* mother! A serious row takes place, although Knups feels much cooler! The child isn't used to such heat and is becoming rather difficult to handle.

Fortunately the Tanganyika has a well-organized nursery and there is also a young lady missionary, who loves looking after little children. This is a bonus for everyone concerned. Erika (and Reinhold) are still finding their way as parents and Knups plays her part in testing their so-called skills! She even announces to other passengers that her *real* parents are in Hamburg; this causes surprised questions to be asked and discomfort to all concerned.

To top it all Erika is endlessly 'unwell'. In Beira, an Indian medic diagnoses mercury poisoning caused by the combination of calomel and orange juice. Whatever it is, Erika is very sick and her offspring has some quick growing up to do.

The three year old becomes stubborn, resentful and intractable. The seemingly endless journey has become a trial for all.

Six weeks later the new 'home' becomes a reality: Table Mountain, that unforgettable sight!   It is the 9th of October, 1938. The best way to arrive in **CAPE TOWN** is by ocean liner.

Spread along the horizon is Table Mountain, flanked on the left by Devil's Peak, on the right, Lions Head... once you've seen this sight you never forget it. The closer you get, the more personal it becomes, a great majestic enveloping power. A bit like a God. You gaze at it and want it to hold you, protect you, devour you.

Erika and Reini settle in speedily. They've spent most of their savings on their first 'own' house, which nestles on the ribs of the Lion...just before he magically turns into Signal Hill. A boring little bungalow built at the top of a steeply sloping garden with at least 30 steps to climb before you reach a tiny veranda, from which there are magical day and night views of the bay and of course, the harbour. Sitting on the veranda one can hear distant calls of the muezzin in the Muslim quarters, a few streets down. Subconsciously, they must have been trying to reproduce their rather more substantial residence in Accra. They call their new home 'Accra'.

During those early months of acclimatizing and meeting new friends and colleagues there are murmurings and daily threats of political turmoil in the news. Erika remains in close touch by post with all her relatives and soon gets the hang of 'coping' with only one maid. There is a part-time gardener, and Wilmot, who drives the office car.

Mother and daughter are getting quite fond of each other, perhaps because the infant knows how to pretend to be more stupid than she really is. She knows this will gain her increased affection. When the new regime doesn't suit she says: "I'm going back to Reinbeck", or just simply: "Mami never said that".

One day Erika discovers the child packing a suitcase with some clothes and toys. When questioned, she tells her mother she is ready to... 'go back home'.

There is much wrangling about food and serious punishment when there is any rebellion. Eating meat is a huge obstacle: that loathed lump of chewed matter carried from one cheek to the other and then secretly spat out, always, without fail, discovered by

Erika; or downright disobedience when locked in the nursery for something or other, such as jumping out of the window....Reini gives his child her first hiding.

During this time the nightmares about 'wild' animals began, real night terrors which ended in tears, sweating and screams, alarming parents, even neighbors. Somebody must have said something to the child, long ago, in Europe perhaps, and because there really were snakes and creepy-crawly beasts everywhere, even quite large monkeys one afternoon, munching away in a tree, the poor city-child from northern Europe had developed some un-staunch-able fear. Reini's theory: his daughter was simply spoilt and wanted attention; then he decided a dog and later, a cat, were needed, to help her get over these nightly fears.

Erika types *long letters* to her mother asking for advice. When Mami receives news of her first grandchild's obstreperous behavior she expresses genuine surprise. Then follows much sound advice on child-rearing sent across the globe to help the inexperienced mother understand how best to cope with a nearly four-year old troubled mind. It can only have been homesickness ...turned into some sort of rebellion. In her letters Mami often mentions how terrible her own longing for Knups is, how much she misses the child, holding her and hearing her talk.

Ten months after arrival in Cape Town there comes the day the whole world and particularly Erika, Grossi and Mami, hear news: World War II has begun.

Hollabrunn, Austria 1939. Grossi and her two middle-aged spinster daughters are clearing away supper dishes.

They settle down on their uncomfortable Biedermeier furniture listening to the radio, before it is time for bed. An interruption in the usual Opera evening from Vienna.... a solemn voice declares *that Germany and Britain are now at war* .

"How appalling" Grossi gasps, "the Germans are fighting again. What on earth do they want Poland for? Perhaps Austria will not have to be involved?" "But we've had that Anschluss, Mama, *we are Germany now!*".....the sisters look at each other helplessly. "Shall we telephone Magaregg? Fredy will know more about our role in all this...perhaps there is nothing to worry about." We're quite safe here, Mama, in Hollabrunn. No-one even knows where Hollabrunn is, so small and unimportant....Just so long we don't lose any more money, that would be terrible...let's call them right away..."

Papi manages to reassure his frightened female relatives. They have a long discussion about 'poor little Ekalein' in South Africa: "South Africans belong to the British Commonwealth...don't they all speak English there? Oh my God, shouldn't Reini and Eka come back home"? *Indeed, everyone is very worried. Telegrams fly across the globe. But it is all too late. History repeats itself: the Ihlenfeldts are 'enemies' in South Africa: just like the Raggs, in England, in 1914.*

• • •

The British secret service had been active long before the outbreak of this war, compiling lists of Germans who were functionaries of the NSDAP (Nazis) or those who were prominent in business or industry such as Siemens, Krupp, AEG, Bosch, Opel, Mercedes etc, or shipping. There had been press releases during the 2nd half of September: relatives of enemy representatives would not be interned, but it was not long before "black Marias" appeared to transport male prisoners to camps in South Africa.

Erika put on a brave face.

Her man was one of the first to go, even though he had never joined the NSDAP. He was called at 10am to be ready by 5 pm, for transport to Johannesburg escorted by two plainclothes policemen.

Both policemen were simple Afrikaaners, mildly embarrassed by what they had to do, and as there was time before departure they took Reinhold Ihlenfeldt to the station bar and had several drinks while assuring him that the war would soon be over and "Mr. Hitler is bound to win, so that 'Meneer Illeveld' would soon be back home"…"in time for

Christmas", they suggested, trying to prove they were kindly and humane. They probably were!

In Johannesburg there was a limousine waiting at the station, to take them to 'LEEUWKOP", one of three internment camps. "Perhaps the war is already over," they suggested this time. A fine thought.

Reini did wonder then whether this civilized treatment was in some way due to the fact that he had once been a 'consul', even if not in South Africa. On arrival he was advised by the camp commandant he could complain officially to the Chief Control Officer, Sir Theodore Truter, as only Germans thought to be 'dangerous' were interned.

The next five months proved to be a severe test for Erika . While her man left no stone unturned to be released from the camp by writing careful letters to Sir Theodore Truter and other dignitaries explaining he was *the most harmless non-political man* in the world, not even a member of the Nazi party, he was not amongst those who managed to be set free.

There was a mountain of censored daily letters between Erika, Reinhold, and some carefully controlled censored mail (via the Red Cross) to relations in Europe. The camp was in the Transvaal, a 1000 mile train journey away; the distraught couple were separated ~and helplessly so. How long was this war going to last? No-one had the slightest idea.

Worst of all, there was no income! With the breadwinner locked up and every penny spent on the house Erika found some help and distraction by taking in lodgers. Mother and daughter slept in the nursery while two bachelors and a lady were bedded and fed in the rest of the house. It was the only way forward Erika could devise. One imagines it even began to be quite entertaining... a lot of chatter and drinking and entertaining each other. It became a busy and lively and yet worrying, often melancholy time.

The pampered Gold Coast 'madam' has a rude awakening. In daily letters Erika and her man make frequent references to a growing estrangement and coolness after ten years of married life, which had been developing between them and how they now regretted any unkindness and wished they could be together again.

Absence was making hearts grow desperately fond.....
Erika admits she longs for Europe and feels they'd made a mistake coming back to Africa.

Her imprisoned man tries to keep a cool head and clear perspective. The continued gossip was always that the war would be over in a month or two...just 'hang in' there and be hopeful...!   Poor Erika.

Five months later Sir Truter is finally convinced of Reini's notorious harmlessness: the prisoner is released and given orders to dissolve his home in CapeTown within a fortnight and to move to one of four smaller towns inland, away from the coast:

Bloemfontein, Paarl, Ceres or Elgin. The latter was only 65 km from CapeTown; the place was full of retired British colonial and military officers, and these would surely keep an eye on 'the jerry'.

At last, a happy reunion with some fast action: letting the Cape Town house, fully furnished, stowing away personal things, renting a cottage in Elgin and finding a job with an apple farmer in Elgin...all this was just about feasible in fourteen days.

Once monthly the 'new' apple farmer has to report to the police-station in Caledon....the rest seemed like the land of milk and honey.....

May 1940: German troops over-ran Belgium and Holland and the war took a turning for the worse. South African prisoners on parole were instantly gathered up and re-interned. This time it was no longer possible to protest. Reini landed in Baviaanspoort just a few miles from Pretoria, along with 1600 other German men.

After several months living out of suitcases with friends in Cape Town Erika 'bites the bullet', boards a train to Pretoria, the nearest town to the camp. She reports in the first of hundreds of letters to Reini that their child had observed the slag-heaps from the mines outside Johannesburg and declared "this must be the place where they make mountains". In Pretoria she moves into a hotel/boarding house along with six other German women, who also want to be in a position to visit their men.

This will be allowed once a month, for ½ an hour, separated by two high fences of barbed wire with an armed soldier on guard duty. Children are not permitted.

Pretoria, October, 1940

A 'house-boy' carries two suitcases and a small cardboard box full of toys across Church Street, a busy road. The annexe to Belvedere Hotel can be reached no other way. Several German ladies have already taken up lodgings in the main building. Another three, from the annex, including Erika, must cross the road before breakfast, lunch and supper.

Erika's room, one of seven, opens up onto a large courtyard with a polished red stone floor. A narrow covered walkway, held up by pillars keeps the residents dry as they emerge from their doors to find two bathrooms at the far end. Even further, across a roughly paved alleyway is the only toilet for at least ten residents. Next to this 'outhouse' are several other brick structures, single rooms, for the black servants of the Belvedere. All buildings are covered with corrugated iron. A strip of garden in the front with two high palm trees and Canna lilies just about everywhere makes the annex appear reasonably friendly, typically South African.

Black servants come from the provinces and are all male, known as 'house boys', whatever their age. The 'boy' puts Erika's cases down and looks at her expectantly. She finds a 'tickey' and gives it to him. (ticky= approx. 3 pence)

He nods mutely, then slopes off as she looks around at her daughter, silent by her side. Erika lugs two cases on the beds...then opens a door to see what appears to be a larder, with shelves, on the opposite side an open door revealing a small room with a window and a bed. Against one wall a metal sloping surface and a large metal basin with a tap....finally the penny drops: "this is a kitchen! No-one told me it's so cheap because that's what it is, with tiled walls floor to ceiling. They've just stuck in two beds, a wardrobe and a table and a dressing table with two lace doilies.

Knups throws herself on one of the beds, sucking her thumb: "Look up here, Mutti, this is a funny house....the windows are on the roof!" Erika has to agree, quickly points out that lying in bed could be very much more interesting if one can see the moon and the stars and the birds flying by. "You're sucking your thumb again................!"

"Poor child, what a come-down" she thinks, beginning to unpack. A place of honor for a photograph of Reini... cases and toys can go into the 'larder'. "Why not go out and see if there are other children; but don't go on the road, promise ?......"

Half an hour later things are stowed away. This is home, for the foresee-able future, and "please God, not for too long.....it will do of course, but only just... given poor Reini has to share a shabby little hut in his camp with two other complete strangers -this is more or less on a par with..." a commotion in the courtyard, three ladies appear, speaking German:

"Willkommen, Frau Ihlenfeldt, we saw you and your little girl arrive so we've come to help you settle in...in this...unusual room...well, it's nice and big and light! And with those windows up there" ....
All heads turn up and gaze at the ceiling......

"I'm Pev Brinkman and this is Ilse, we are bringing you a thermos of tea and biscuits and some flowers... wait, I'll get a vase ..." Pev disappears and returns in no time at all: "We, my son Peter and I, have a room in the corridor, so I can help you get used to all this. Is the little room over there for your daughter? "Perhaps," says Erika warily, "I haven't really worked it out." She notes Pev has a wasted, lame arm, which she cradles in her good arm. She seems really friendly, things are looking up.

"We'll all be doing a lot of letter-writing", Pev remarks wryly noting Erika's typewriter ready for action on the table," why not come with me now and I'll show you where *my* room is and then we'll all go over to supper together this evening... the management will bring some cups and spoons and glasses for you. You must come and meet the others...no, let *me* get you cups and we can have tea first". By suppertime Erika and Knups have met Pev's son Peter in his hand-knitted suit, all of four years old and definitely ready for bed, judging from his behavior in the dining room.

"What a pest", sighs Knups, "if *you* are friends with the lady with the floppy arm then I will have to play with her boy! I'm nearly six and he's still a baby!" Erika's thoughts are on a similar track: "well, only for a few weeks, one hopes".....

The going-to-sleep ritual is to sing a verse of Brahms' Lullaby to each other, then the lights are put out and Erika goes to the side room to read for a while. After this unusual day she creeps back into the 'Kitchen'....into the bed next to her child. Being together is comforting. When she looks up she really can see the stars......

Within days the side-room has a different occupant... an Inge Mueller from Tanganyika (now Tanzania). The boarding house, now completely full, had turned her away, but when Erika heard she immediately offered up the side room, thus *reducing the rent* for her own abode. Erika knows how to scrimp and save, remembering life during the First World War. *She is just the most parsimonious person in the universe* with a true talent for martyrdom. Even having another lady walk through her bedroom at various stages of the day and night, although not entirely pleasing, makes Erika feel she is not alone: she is doing a good deed, but above all, saving money.

The first thing the other woman put up on her wall was a watercolor of Mount Kilimanjaro, to stop her from feeling miserable and missing home. There were hints of Zebras and Giraffes on the plains below. It made a great change from gazing at white tiles.

All Erika has is a framed photograph of her man. Priorities are the typewriter and her camera, (both belong to Reini of course.) With these she creates a daily routine of being a mother and keeping her man posted about their lives.

A big bonus: the child was coming up for school and, in the hours of her absence, there would be plenty of 'new' friends about, and no cooking or other domestic duties. Erika's only luxury is a small Opel; it greatly increased her popularity. She was always giving lifts to people and so useful for getting to know Pretoria, a town with aspirations. Just down the road was one of Pretoria's most famous landmarks, the Union Buildings, home of the government and stretching out before it a vast handsome terraced garden, always open to the public; a marvelous place to explore and romp about, especially for the young inhabitants of the Belvedere Hotel.

12th November,1942. "Bad news, our daughter has whooping cough. Rest at night is much curtailed and I'm just waiting for my numerous neighbors to complain. I can't leave her for a single moment because she starts to cry immediately. Last Sunday I pulled out her first tooth. At first she said nothing, but when she saw the blood she began to cry horribly, - surprised perhaps by her own courage."

16 November. "My entire life is governed by this. The child looks terrible, her face swollen, I'm glad you don't have to experience it. On top of this she has lost a second tooth, which doesn't exactly improve her looks. She coughs and wheezes and chokes, especially at night. I have not been up more than five times a night, lucky me! During the day I let her sit outside... that seems to help. Apart from rushing across the road to eat I'm always with her."

19th November. "Knups' illness has worsened. It usually starts at 9 pm, she vomits all over the bed, screams, hits everything in sight and this goes on every hour or two during the night. During the day it's not so bad."

21 November. "I've also got it now....Knups does seem a lot better, thank goodness, we're halfway through." By mid December it was over. Erika concedes, after much complaining about her daughter's difficult nature that, "in all fairness she is more reasonable than most of the other children."

As always, Christmas was celebrated in the traditional German way, with every mother decorating her own tree in her room, then inviting everyone to come and watch the usual scenario of a German carol, followed by the opening of gifts.

Erika's pitiful conifer stands scraggily in the sink, the draining board hidden with a white tablecloth. She has made a crib with hay, moss, some toy sheep and a cut-out Holy Family. Parcels and presents are on the floor. The main present is a shiny leather satchel for school, also a flowery umbrella and a doll's pram...when candles are lit Tante Inge plays 'Stille Nacht' on her mouth organ. At 8pm Erika and Reini close their eyes and transmit their thoughts to each other, as promised.

31st December. Erika takes her child to be checked by the doctor, who pronounces her fit to go to school.

14th January 1941. "A big day your daughter went to school for the first time. Indescribable excitement: for a week before she'd enquire each day how many more days until...?Die dumme Kuh! (the silly cow) If only she knew how much she'll learn to hate it! I have taken many photos for you so you can enjoy this event with us. I made a big 'Schul-tüte' (a German custom: a large colorful cone ending in a point filled with sweets and little gifts) and most of the *new* children were carrying one. Your daughter is one of about twenty tiny people in grade 1 and we, the mothers, were allowed to stay at the back for the first hour. The teacher, an older lady, looks like a toad but is gentle and confidence inspiring.....

When we, the mothers, were told to leave I noticed Knups' lips trembling and I have to admit that I too had to fight back the tears. The car felt empty, the room feels empty. I've been very depressed. These poor little worms have to sit there from 8am till 12.3o..."...

Erika's life is centered around her child's welfare and on keeping in touch with her husband. She discusses with him whether they can afford ballet lessons and later swimming lessons for their six year old who is beginning to show signs of poor nutrition such as endless lethargy and constipation.

Feb.4th 1941. "Three of the women lodgers had to help me hold the child down for an enema. She became like a wild animal and screamed and kicked, it was indescribable. I don't suppose she'll ever forgive me. I can't cope with this sort of behavior. She is full of sudden fevers and un-explained pains."

It was the old story about 'crying wolf'. Erika had begun to ignore her child's endless complaints and self-pitying whininess. But then she discovered an infected tooth, which had to be pulled out.....

Letters flew between Reini and Eka. When they were not speculating about the war they were endlessly analysing their offspring. The verdict was not great: slow to learn, does not listen, remembers nothing, lazy, rude, shy, clumsy, ferociously stubborn, morose, and permanently constipated. Erika felt she recognized some of those traits from her own side of the family and that she would have to apply some conscientious character-training.

The first (inspired) thing she does is to buy a light bulb for the outside lavatory. The problem was partly that awful darkness, far too distracting for a six-year old. Daily prunes did the rest, so much more pleasing than enemas. From this time onwards there wasn't a month when Erika didn't have to call the doctor. Her child had endless fevers, infections and childhood illnesses. During one of these illnesses the bored child studies Erika's hands: "Mutti, why have you got such ugly hands...and why has your face got so many lines? All Erika can afford is a large pot of Nivea Crème. Poor Erika. She is in her mid-thirties and feels cheated. Her day-to day existence is dreary and predictable.

Would she have liked another child...well...on balance, no.! She is aware of the lack of a real home, that her child is growing up surrounded by strangers and without a father, that a child *should* really have siblings as she herself had experienced, and that Knups was behaving like a spoilt brat, receiving far too much attention from one person,... her own mother.

There was little to fill Erika's life apart from the daily routines. She writes proudly to tell about a green dress she had sewn for 'Knubslein'.... made from an old garment of Pev's. Another daily occupation is repairing the ladders in her stockings. This is done by holding a minute hook on a wooden handle with which she pulls up the laddered bit stretched over a wooden mushroom-shaped tool.... with much peering and frowning.

Some of the German ladies took jobs of one sort or another. Erika began to regret she'd had no specific training, recalling her long letters to Reini when he was already working in Accra while she was still at school in Hamburg. At that time she had been talked *out* of studying or learning some skills, and all that by the very man who was now helplessly imprisoned and unable to provide any money.

In all likelihood Erika was clinically depressed. The only way forward was to *teach* something. German perhaps? But who wanted to learn German in those days? It wasn't too long before she had a few pupils, a life-line of sorts, and how nice it must have been to collect a few pence per lesson! The one big expense was the permanent ill health of her child: there was something unresolved in both body and soul of Knups, who was dragged from one specialist to another. Theories were put forward: the altitude, dietary faults,... faults in the absorption of nutrients, to nerve ends 'starved' of nutrients.....to water retention. Supplements and tablets were prescribed and exercise or perhaps ... *less* exercise, whatever came to light was soon superseded by another theory. The child remained morose, fearful, un-co-operative, tired, unfriendly, tearful and worst of all, a thumb-sucker. Erika was not enjoying motherhood.

At least she was not alone. The German wives were able to socialize, support, entertain, one another by having picnics and tea parties. They talked about their men, and one expects they had views on the war. There is a yawning gap here, such matters were censored in correspondence and probably not aired in front of children. According to occasional 'bioscope' newsreels, the War looked very frightening indeed.

Erika had achieved *one* notable thing: her child had settled into the German school and was learning to read and write in three languages, albeit with spectacularly bad results. When one thinks about it, a six-year old brain bombarded in such a way can only produce a modest and messy end-product: letters penned by the tri-lingual offspring are touchingly, embarrassingly bad. Erika would have welcomed a better school but there was no money for such luxuries. A convent school nearby offered free *religious* instruction to small heathens such as Knups. Erika would have loved to hand her daughter over to nuns but the schooling was just too expensive; besides the child became hysterical when faced by wrinkled nuns, even to be taught the catechism, so this venture was soon abandoned. There was no silver lining.

By 1942 everyone has settled down to boarding-house life and the grown-ups have become increasingly resilient:

The German women guided their brats through sicknesses and health, through swimming lessons, picnics, birthdays, Xmases, school holidays and all the long daily events of mothers and children, without any input from fathers, grandparents or any relatives at all. Everything was recorded in letters and photographed for posterity. A notable event was the smashing of Knups' two new front teeth after an unsuccessful leap down the stairs.....she was then delivered bleeding and screaming by a big boy (who happened to be passing) to the horrified Erika!

From that day onwards, thanks to much clever filing by a dentist, a new Mona Lisa was created, with a mysterious tooth-hiding smile. 1942: ballet lessons for Erika's lumpen offspring, 1943: exams, Eisteddfods..... curious illnesses.....

Dearest, you can't imagine how depressed I feel. Will this bloody war ever end? I know you'll be completely un-impressed when I confess I wasted some money on a fortune teller in town. Some of the other ladies told me how fantastic she was, how many things she said that seemed to fit. So I went along and within ten minutes she told me all about our daughter and also that you and I will soon be together again, unexpectedly soon! I hope she's right. I had told her that you were 'away', so as not to give her too many clues. As for Knups....she will become 'an artist of some kind', according to the woman. She was a bit stumped when I pressed her. 'Maybe music, maybe painting'....was her best shot. There's been no post from you for six days, is everything alright?

1944. Suddenly: some wind of the 'authorities' planning an exchange of prisoners of war! The Belvedere wives had all but given up thinking about the war. It just went on and on ~ so being offered the possibility of returning to Europe seemed improbable and an unwise too, surely? The cinema newsreels in Pretoria were no inducement to return to Germany!

Even so, when the offer came, halfway through 1944, to be transported by ocean-liner, fully protected by both British and German navy, first to Portugal and then by train through Spain and France to the 'homeland', many of the long-separated couples decided to risk it and go home. Had they been listening to inflated German propaganda on the radio? How else could they possibly have considered leaving the safety of South Africa?

The internees had endured camp life for four whole years; most had elderly parents in Germany, some suffering frightening hardships.

After four years in the 'kitchen' the adjoining larder contained a fair number of books, cradles, crayons, comics and even a dolls-house, made by Reini in the camp...all the property of nine-year old Ingeborg-Evelyn. None of this was permitted as luggage on the return journey; parsimonious Erika stood her child on the street corner outside the boarding house, along with her possessions. "Ask everyone to buy your toys", she said......................

Proceeds went towards a wristwatch....as well as sweets. "There will be absolutely none to be found in Germany, because of the War," Erika warned. Then followed an exciting 30 hour train journey from Pretoria to Port Elisabeth, where a vast Swedish ocean liner, the Drottningholm, lay in the docks awaiting boarding of about 990 passengers, all German. The gleaming white vessel was clearly marked with the Red Cross sign and also had a green line encircling the body of the ship. This was the international signal to denote 'passage without hindrance.'

But first there were the customs officials: no-one was allowed off the train until luggage and persons had been carefully searched. Each traveler was allowed one piece of luggage and £25 in cash. (The British and South African exchange prisoners, who would be embarking in Europe to return home, had similar restrictions.) There were controls and documents and formalities. The blinds of each carriage were pulled down and the officials did a careful search for hidden diamonds, weapons, illegal things, military information, whatever they might have been. It took hours and hours.

Any sweets destined to travel to war-torn Europe were confiscated by S.A. Customs. Might they have contained smuggled diamonds? Knups was devastated. Erika had some difficulty in getting through to her distraught daughter, who had never been that close to armed and uniformed officials before, and was behaving appallingly.

Well, in retrospect this was a small hurdle: out there was this huge ship and somewhere was a man called "Vati", which sounds terrible in English but pleasing in German, and never mind the sweeties, in a minute "we will see Vati again and we will be on that big ship"...

Women were allowed to board first and Eka, who discovered they had a 4-bed inside cabin on E-deck, ie. the lowest deck on the ship, started to get the luggage down to move in.

She was greeted by a missionary's wife who enquired how big Erika's family was. "Only three," the wife exclaimed, "we are five! Would you mind if one of our children shared your cabin?"

Erika smiled wanly but nevertheless did an instant 'star-turn' as an ex-shipping agents' wife: a steward in charge of assigning passengers was found and she begged him to see if there hadn't been some mistake.

"But no, madam, you are down for a cabin with two children, Ingeborg and Evelyn". She smiled at the friendly Swede, her most winning smile of course and pleaded with him to try once more.

"I know from years of experience in the shipping world that there are always some free cabins at the last minute, please have another look"... Indeed, a cabin for three was found: the luck of the Ihlenfeldts,....they were assigned a luxury cabin, with a small seating area and a curtained-off double bed for the parents.

Married men were permitted to board as dusk fell. Their women stood near the gangway, screaming, weeping, rejoicing, singing, waiting to embrace the men folk, whom they had not been allowed to touch, even with their fingertips, for four years. Later that evening the child was bribed, in view of dramatic refusal of and protest to the 'going-to-bed' idea, with chocolate and many loving promises, to get some sleep,— while the re-united Eka and Reini explored the topography of the boat and even found a bar, which was already doing big business with the men celebrating their freedom. Four alcohol-free years had passed! The reserves of the Drottningholm were reduced to such an extent that the passengers only had beer and some wine left to drink after the first fortnight of the journey had passed.

The trip to Lisbon was to take four weeks, allowing for only very modest speeds. The idea was to keep a distance from any coast, travelling more or less up the middle of the Atlantic due north. Every two hours the captain reported his position to the German and the British admiralty who had given orders to all warships in the area to leave the Drottningholm in peace.

During this crossing the invasion of the Anglo-American troops in northern France had begun. The French partisans or resistance fighters became very active, exploding bridges and closing down railway lines, in short, the counter transport of British prisoners from France was delayed and so the South Africans, once arrived in Lisbon, were lodged in 5-star hotels, organised by the German embassy. 900 Germans took over Lisbon, Cascais, Estoril and Domingos. These places used to be the homes of exiled royalty! Luggage was tagged with DIPLOMAT labels and each family was given handsome amounts of cash by the German government. Everyone felt they'd turned into wealthy tourists!

And even then, in 1944, at the height of the war, there were British, French and American guests at other tables in the hotels, and everyone behaved politely and correctly, if in a somewhat restrained manner. Living in this way, with daily excursions and shopping for things which were going to be useful 'at home,' (once one got there), was completely delightful. This idyll lasted almost one month.

Great Return to the 'Fatherland'!

Close to departure time a doctor had to be called: Erika was 'unwell'. She had to remain horizontal. So the Ihlenfeldts had a sleeper-coach, to share with her. This was good because the journey, which was to take one day lasted a whole week. Good in one way, bad in another: Erika would have had a second child more or less mid-May 1945 had 'it' not decided there and then that being a new-born child in Germany at this time was just not on...needless to say, this whole matter was never discussed in front of Knups.

The much loathed 'boches' edged their way through France, via Biarritz (another very royal hotel) and escaped, by the skin of their teeth, several partisan attacks and explosions. As they crept along, hiding in tunnels, changing over onto coaches, but in the end a safe arrival in Heilbronn, Germany, the little family was finally quartered in barracks for two days to undergo an indoctrination of heroic dimensions: they were issued passports, food coupons, clothes coupons, train tickets, pocket money......

Family Ihlenfeldt stepped out, all on their own, for a walk in a park in Heilbronn and soon saw what a bombed city looks like. In a restaurant they ordered roast venison for three, and learned, (too late) that they had consumed their entire months' meat ration. At night, when they were woken by air-raid sirens, they slipped into their elegant silk dressing gowns, Erika's with swans-down collar and sleeves and appeared in the shelter looking like extras from a film-set. The expressions on the soldiers' faces with their steel helmets and gasmasks were hard to describe: Reini and Eka were a triumphal success...

In 1944 the rail system in Germany was a somewhat haphazard affair. We learnt that to get from one place to another was a question of sitting on the required platform and waiting..........

Erika, was as excited as a small child before Christmas.... even though she had been sitting on a platform in Salzburg for hours, gazing at the ruins of the once glamorous Hotel de l'Europe, (where they had stayed in better times)... even though there was no way she could contact her parents in their castle: the telephone connection had been requisitioned by the army stationed nearby.

Eventually a pathetically slow, stopping train deposited them in Klagenfurt at 3 o'clock in the morning. The station, partly destroyed by bombs, harbored a Red Cross office which took them in. The Ihlenfeldts slept... huddled together on a bench and a birthing chair! After a very uncomfortable night the Red Cross contacted the military station nearby who sent a messenger on foot to the castle. And now: here they are: Papi and Mami outside the station in an open carriage, horse-drawn of course. What a moment!

Soon there were questions : "What on earth are you doing here...why didn't you wait for the war to end before you returned...are you completely crazy coming back now...did you really have to....?"

The older generation examined their exhausted daughter, their grandchild, the bedraggled state of the weary travelers and decided what was needed now were not questions, but a hot bath and sleep.

Magaregg, the castle in warm Autumn sunshine,... a most welcome sight! The 'refugees' made it their home, loving every precious moment, relaxed and safe for four happy weeks. The only sign of a war were the military barracks close by, which Ingeborg-Evelyn-Knups got to know rather well: the care-taker's daughter, exactly the same age, invited the 'South African' to come along to a school run especially for children of soldiers stationed in the area, in this way half of each day was spent catching up on basic skills, reading and writing German and presumably some arithmetic.

Could Erika persuade her parents that returning had been wise?

"It's almost as hot as Pretoria, sitting out here in the sun". Erika moves her chair into the shade, Papi pulls his hat further over his bulbous red nose; the 'Jause' (coffee-break) on the lawn by the fantastically ancient Roman urn, is a family tradition.

"Where is the child?" Mami pours the coffee, offers Erika freshly baked Streusel cake... "I tried yesterday to explain to her about my sisters and Neumarktl, but I'm not sure she was really listening, she was so surprised to see the mountains turning pink.... actually, she was in danger of falling out of the window in the tower, ...not even Papi seems to know why the Karawanken blush at sunset..."

Mami did try so very hard not to crowd in on Knups, who appeared to have no real memory of her earliest years in Hamburg. This was hard to understand. But then, they had been separated from the child when she was only three and a half.....for six whole years.

"She does seem a very innocent ten-year old! Has she accepted her father yet, after the camp, do you think it's all going to be 'normal' now, Ekalein? What a miserable four years you've had. We thought about you every day, you know; but we still believe you should not have returned."

Erika, in a strange state, disoriented and weakened by the miscarriage is relieved to get her child off to school, relieved that her own parents are 'parenting' her, and relieved Reini is by her side. But, and there always is a 'but'...he wants to move on to his own parents, up in that small town on the Baltic, where he knows he is really needed, assumes his own father, now eighty years old, is no longer able to run the business without help. Reini certainly does not want to be going off alone. The pressure is on his wife to agree to travel with him once more; a case of divided loyalties, choices must be made.

Erika's man had made a vow to be a non-combatant and carried papers to prove he'd been locked up in a camp for four years. He had come 'home' to be of help to his old parents.

Erika, however, was confused; she'd seen little of her in-laws and   admitted not feeling too comfortable in their home during two or three short visits in the 1930's. Their small-town attitude and unworldly ways were not to her liking. Reini understood and really couldn't hold this against her, if anything, he agreed. But he was a dutiful, loving son, there was a job to be done, they had to go. Reini and Eka were either completely fearless or totally uninformed about the war. Can it be possible that Germans, even Austrians, had no inkling what lay ahead in the next six or seven months?

Erika was an exceptionally intelligent adult. She was also stubborn, ambitious and snobbish. Above all she tended to be very, very negative. Reini was often 'up against it' when it came to important decisions which had to be resolved jointly. Her surprising decision to go with him was probably based on two facts: the memory of those four years alone in Pretoria and the fear that something might happen to him, another separation, or worse.

Neither of them seemed to know what they'd let themselves in for.

After an adventurous train journey, passing the ruins of Berlin; (look Knupslein, can you see all those broken houses....don't forget this sight, this is Berlin, a very important town) father, mother and child moved in with the next set of grandparents and Reini went straight to work with his father in the office downstairs.

The double-story house was directly in the harbor, separated from the ships by a wide cobbled road and ancient trees as well as some railway tracks along the docks. Erika had seen it all before, during happier times on visits from Africa: from the balcony on the second floor there was a spectacular view of much of the harbor of Swinemünde.

Next to the house, on the right, was a large low concrete air-raid shelter for the entire dock-area, somewhat sunken into the ground. This was certainly something new!

Erika rolled up her sleeves and 'mucked in'.

The old, dark, now neglected home was on the second floor: downstairs were the offices of the shipping agency. Up from the large entrance on the harbor road was a wide staircase of bare dusty wood, on the second floor you pulled a chord to ring a brass bell inside. A darkly curtained drawing room, cobwebby and antiquated, displayed: in one corner a five foot tall, dusty ornate porcelain vase, decorated elaborately with raised china flowers and leaves, gracing the other end was a spittoon and an upright piano with fancy brass candleholders attached, a stool to match with velvet tassels festooning the cushioned part. It was awkward to move about: a cumbersome dining table took up most of the centre; this normally would have 'lived' in the dining room, but it was impossible to keep so many rooms heated in the winter. There were no servants.

The rusty bathroom tub with clawed feet, the wooden toilet a long way from the house, was at the back of the garden. Musty disturbing smells pervaded all rooms, indefinably worrying, everything so dark. Decrepit Ida and Alexander Ihlenfeldt, both in their eighties, must have been struggling for a long time! ...

Through the floor boards one heard the telephone and voices from the office staff, down below.

For the first time Erika is face to face with real problems in Germany: nothing in the shops, daily and nightly visits to the air-raid shelter, artificial fog, (smoke-screens) in the harbor area, (to fool the bombers), and a bitterly cold winter. The family 'manages' a Christmas Eve, with tree and carols (and a dolls-house made by Reini, for his child) there has even been a fair, in the small town, where one can buy a few handmade wooden toys and crafts and arty things. It does feel Christmassy in a way Erika used to dream of during the hot summer Decembers of Pretoria...............

Now there is snow and ice, an outside loo ....intolerable....

Because of the constant air alarms and smoke-screens to protect the harbor area, Knups is kept at home, the school being quite a distance from the house. Erika manages to sign up her offspring for a weekly piano lesson with an elderly lady, about ten minutes away. Once the route has been absorbed by the eager pianist-to-be she is sent off on her own. Erika is surprised how the child makes rapid progress, sits at that piano completely absorbed, for hours. She devises school-work, to stop her daughter, who seems baby-ish and immature, from falling even further behind in the three R's.

On the way home from piano lessons the alarms begin to wail, the smoke screen wells up and Knups, who has to traverse a park to get home chooses a wrong turning... "all the bushes look the same"... and, hopelessly lost, running this way and that, does not know what to do, experiences panic for the first time. Erika stands in front of the house looking in every possible direction and cursing herself, for not taking the trouble to accompany the child. Fortunately there is no air-raid and Knubs arrives home some 15 minutes later to be smothered with hugging and a few tears.

Erika begins to learn you can not be too careful.

One morning in January 1945 Reini receives a call from the local SS Headquarters ordering to present himself at 9.30 am. on the following day.

"May I ask what this is about", enquires Reini.

"You will find out when we see you tomorrow."

Reinhold would have been only marginally less surprised if a bomb had exploded next to him. What possible interest could the Gestapo have in a man who has come back to a near-destroyed Germany from the safety of South Africa to assist his old parents?

When called by the Gestapo you must expect anything and everything. He is worried. Is it because he had not signed up with the Territorial Army? He had papers issued by the highest authority   in Berlin that he was free from any military duties as an exchanged prisoner of war. Reinhold instructs his secretary to telephone the Chancellery in Berlin if she has not heard from him by 5pm, after his interview. She was to tell them he had been taken by the Gestapo, explaining all the circumstances and to ask for immediate intervention.

At Gestapo headquarters he is told to sit on a wooden bench in a corridor for an hour. Were these unnerving sixty minutes designed to intimidate candidates before such an interview?

"Mr Lewien will see you now..."Reinhold is not sure he's heard correctly: Levin, Levy, Lewien... there are many possibilities. He is offered a chair and wonders about that too. There are the usual questions; name, address, age, occupation religion etc.

"Why are you not registered with the Territorial Army?"

So that was it! Reini explains the whole story about the oath he'd made in South Africa, as an exchange prisoner.

"An oath made in front of a British citizen does not count as an oath in Germany," is offered as response.

"I have documentation signed by the highest authorities," ventures Reini.........There follows a very long silence.

"Alright, let's leave it at that. But would you mind telling me why your daughter never says "Heil

Hitler" when she fetches the milk from the milk cart in the morning?"

There were lengthy explanations about growing up in South Africa, where no-one says Heil Hitler and that the nine-year old has not yet got used to living in Germany.

"Well, see to it you re-train her! I had actually planned to keep you here, but you'd better go and pay more attention to matters of this kind!" So much for Gestapo methods.

From then on Erika goes to fetch the milk herself and Knups' adventures in Swinemünde become even more curtailed. Erika did let her go tobogganing, in the park area by the air-raid shelter. This was within shouting distance of the house and office and needless to say, a fascinating treat for a child brought up in Africa. In January and February it snowed heavily, later the frost was severe.

Hundreds of refugees were coming off the ships every day, poor people carrying shabby cases and sacks, they were homeless, with nowhere to go. Desperate persons came into the doorway of the house and begged if they could stay the night, even if it was just on the floor of the entrance hall. It was pitiful. In return they offered a measure of flour from their miserable supplies salvaged in the flight from the Russians. Erika crouched on the floor and scooped some flour from the sack. She became hysterical because her wedding ring had fallen off her finger into the sack and could not be found. She had lost a lot of weight, as had everyone.

Things were getting scarce. The only thing Erika's mother-in-law seemed to have a lot of.... were bottled gooseberries, rows and rows of them. The grown-ups spoke endlessly about getting on a ship and leaving Swinemünde. Yet to persuade the older generation that safety was a problem seemed almost impossible.

"The Russians won't do anything to us" they said, "we can't leave all our things..."

Peenemünde, on the island Usedom, was only a few miles away. This was where the V2 rockets were developed and made. It did therefore seem surprising that Swinemünde harbour had never been bombed. The Russians were making advances on sea and land along the Baltic and, by the 12th of March could already be heard clearly in the distance. It was perhaps at their request that the allied forces deployed 700 American bombers to drop 1435 bombs onto the harbour and town.....

The alarm started at lunchtime. Reini escorted his mother down to the shelter (a Splitter Schutz-bunker), an above-ground,thick-walled concrete construct, and Erika was to follow with her father-in-law. Suddenly the old man became unreasonable. He sat down on his rocking chair, in the centre of the living room and refused to budge. "I want to die in my own home. Go away, leave me alone!"

Erika, too frightened to hang about hurried her child down the stairs and outside. Within ten yards was the bunker. Its door was shut. Erika knocked and banged on the iron door but there was no response. She took off her shoe and hammered the heel hard on the door. It opened, just a little. Someone admitted them, reluctantly, and slammed the door shut again.

Not long and the inferno began. With each mighty explosion the building rocked and swayed. People moaned, wept and screamed. Erika notes that her child decides to pray. The nuns in Pretoria had achieved something after all! "That's where we should have stayed," crosses her mind, with each frightening explosion......

One hour later, after the 'all-clear,' the door is unbolted by the air-raid warden, traumatized Germans step outside, clinging to each other in a blinded, careful way. Erika can hardly breathe. Where-ever she looks there is fire. Stepping out into uncertainty, bits of people scattered and piled about, no-one can walk in a straight line, one must climb over bodies. She sees the house still standing, hidden in a haze of dust. There had been seven ships in dock, full of refugees from the East. Where are they ....?

The stubborn eighty-year old sits in his rocking chair, grinning inanely, unharmed, apart from a covering of plaster,.... the inside of the house just about habitable although some window frames have been blasted out , hardly any glass left in the windows......

The place is filthy, freezing, but it stands and can be sorted.

Erika's time has come: She is in charge!

The days after the raid are unspeakable. Over 20.000 inhabitants, refugees and soldiers are declared dead and half of the town is completely flattened, roads blocked, the park a mess of toppled trees, scattered with dead bodies. Many days pass until all the corpses are put to rest in a mass grave on the Golmberg, about 5kms outside Swinemünde.

The remaining town too, was dead: no water, gas or electricity supply, and no prospect of repairs. Reini had to carry buckets of water from a mediaeval pump several blocks away and sanitation, well, that was mediaeval too. There was lots of wood to burn and the old wood burning stove in the kitchen was just the thing, under the circumstances. Official recommendation to 'vacate' the town had been posted everywhere. It was time to go. The old Ihlenfeldts were in complete denial of the reality around them. They had witnessed the streams of refugees passing their home for months now, seen the stiff corpses unloaded in nets like so much dead cattle, seen children dragging the dead on toboggans to the mass graves.....

"You must go", they said, "we want to stay, in our house...we won't be harmed......"

Eventually an old friend, a former Africa-captain, bumped into Reini on the street, and managed to persuade the old folk to accept a cabin on a freighter going to Lübeck. He was able to contact friends in Lübeck who arranged a room in an Old Age Home. They arrived safely, 'luxury' refugees' but their spirits broken.......

Some days later Ihlenfeldts-junior were safely stowed in a small cabin (vacated by the ship's cook,) of a freighter going to Kiel. Erika left the fire in the kitchen stove burning when she handed over the house key to yet another captain known by Reini. This good man would act as caretaker.For the first time in months Erika felt happy and relatively safe. God knows there was little enough reason to feel safe, but there was nothing more she could contribute to every-ones' well-being. She obviously had no idea what the ships' cargo was...

The Baltic was heavily mined and ships were torpedoed each day. It was wise to move only very slowly and only at certain times. One might have been blown sky-high at any moment, and even worse: the cargo the boat carried was...torpedoes!

The 24 hour journey lasted nine days......In Kiel the ship dropped passengers off at the furthest end of the harbour, right opposite the railway station. Later, in the afternoon they arrived in a small town called Eutin, where they were met by old friends, the Heyers, from the CapeTown days. They brought a small wooden waggon for transporting the luggage; Knups was allowed to help pull it over the cobbled streets, and what a racket it was! No wonder it was called a 'Bullerwagen'! By a lake stood a beautiful old half-timbered house: an attic room, three beds with big puffy featherbed covers, a table carrying a large bowl and water jug for washing was three floors up where Reini's head hit the eaves and door frames every time he moved! No matter: all the Ihlenfeldts had made it to the other side of the Yalta 'Elbe-Trave' line, out of reach of the Russian invasion!

The name Eutin derives from 'Uit' and 'In', because the little settlement was surrounded by a town wall and two gates: 'Out 'and 'In'. In medieval times it was populated by people who spoke Danish, Dutch and German and to this day there is a local dialect called 'Platt-Deutsch' (low German') which has its charms...but is actually totally incomprehensible, a little like Danish.

Eutin is a charming, romantic place, with a castle, a market place, nearly every house has trellised roses growing up the walls and at the bottom of a slight hill lies the lake, surrounded by forests and ever more lake, in fact it is part of the 'Switzerland' of Schleswig Holstein. After the dour Swinemünde Erika feels reassured, full of hope. They make contact with the old folk, now settled in their Old Age home in Lübeck, about an hour's drive away. Soon a better attic is found at Bahnhof-strasse 10, offered by a distant family member of the Heyer clan: this is to become home for a very long time. The wall paper, unforgettably yellow, with ornate curly roses and leaves, one queen-size bed for the parents and, horrors... a prickly straw filled mattress for the child... by the door, a coal stove and on the other side a bowl and jug for washing. There are two windows. When you open them you come pretty close to being able to leap across into a post office window. Erika is grateful, for everything.

Meals and social life take place downstairs with the kindly hostess and her daughter, a large girl with staring eyes. Ursula is a year older than Ingeborg-Evelyn-Knups, but can't go to school because she is mentally retarded. Ingeborg doesn't mind: Ursula does everything without protest! Ursula's mother, Inge Heyer, is coping as best she can without a husband, who is still at the front.

In some ways she is pleased to have refugees, and soon finds many things for them to do.It's all 'go' with the 'refugees'; first a school has to be found (easy, 10 minutes away!) then a job is needed for Reini, (not so easy, where were the ships?) and what about Erika? As it turned out, this was the easiest of all: Inge Heyer ran a crafts shop, right there in the house, opening out onto the pavement, with a window displaying pottery, brass and wooden objects... although it wasn't exactly brisk there were always customers, hoping to buy a birthday present or two. Erika offered to help and was soon running the shop and loving it, while Mrs Heyer, who took care of herself and her refugees, and of course her strange daughter, did the rest.

Remarkable how she put a hot meal on the table when there was absolutely nothing in the shops. She had recipes up her sleeve Erika could only marvel at: the unforgettable 'Grosser Hans', more than likely a Danish dish: if you could lay your hands on some flour, fat or lard and bottled pears you could shape a huge dumpling, steam it and serve it up with the heated fruit in it's own thickened sauce, indescribably delicious! Then there was elderberry soup, also served hot, with dumplings. Erika had never heard of such delights, and indeed, when there is simply nothing else everything becomes a treat. Scratching about in a coop were a few chickens, who conscientiously laid very precious eggs from time to time.

One evening word got round: a military train was stuck in the station, just four minutes along the road...After sunset, in the dark, Reinhold and two friends decided to 'inspect' the train for provisions and did indeed come home with sugar, butter, coffee and flour, stowed away in their jackets.

"Stealing for your family does not count," said Erika, and besides, the soldiers always had more than anyone else. There didn't seem to be a war in Eutin.

Some weeks later, when the British advanced and occupied Eutin, and the war had actually been declared 'over'(May 1945), Erika's man was at last able to find something more sensible (and less dangerous) to do. He realized the Brits would need an interpreter. He penned a letter to the Commander of the military government, offering his services. They 'snapped him up'.

After initial enquiries about Reini's past politics and general skills (he had never joined the party) he was asked to appear for work on the following day, along with several other Germans who had language skills. They were all allowed into the military canteen to have a substantial lunch! Erika envied him.

Critical events at this time were: finding rooms, halls, anywhere at all, for the constant stream of refugees from the East, finding food and clothes for everyone. Reini had to requisition homes from the good citizens of Eutin, for military personnel or for refugees. The population of the little town was gradually swelling to a 100% increase. Medical supplies were unavailable. The workload was indescribable.

After two weeks of stress Reinhold Ihlenfeldt was instructed by the Commander he was to take on the role of 'Bürgermeister' ie. Mayor of Eutin. At first he could hardly believe his ears and his reasons for refusing this honorable task were numerous.

There were meetings with other possible candidates and with British officers, but in the end, when even gentle bribery wasn't making him relent ("you will be well paid, you will be respected, you only need commonsense and there will always be experts on hand when you feel you don't have specialized knowledge, the military government would requisition a suitable home for you..."), Reinhold still could not see himself in this role.

The persuasive Brits nagged on. They finally swayed him by reminding him he'd "come back to his homeland to help his country," and now was the time he was truly needed. That got to him...he finally said 'yes'.

"I will do this work on one condition," countered Reinhold," if you come across someone better qualified to do this job you will release me from my duties at once!"

"Splendid", said Colonel Gray, shaking the new mayor by the hand.

On the 17th May 1945, printed notices were to be seen in all the shop-windows announcing the name of the new mayor, Herr Reinhold Ihlenfeldt and that all his instructions were to be obeyed. Signed :

THE BRITISH MILITARY GOVERNMENT

W H. Gray   Lt. Colonel R.M

Erika was stunned. Here she was, in her tiny attic, with the mayor of Eutin! The man who had recently robbed a German military train in the dark night! And who had turned down the offer of better accommodation! (She would have welcomed a better place than the attic.) Still, she was so proud of him.

With other ladies she immediately took on the role of distributing the famous American CARE parcels to refugees and other needy folk. For her child (the mayor's daughter!) there were no civic duties until a year later, when she had to present a bouquet of flowers to some dignitary at a conference for European Unity. Wearing a borrowed white dress and white ribbons at the ends of her pigtails, her photo appeared in the local rag.

Erika's 'job' got her out into the midst of people far less fortunate than she was—those who slept on hay in sheds and barns, wrapped in rough grey army blankets, who needed medical attention, and had little to eat and nothing to do but wait until 'something' might happen, whatever that could be? A new home perhaps? In those first years after the war there was simply nothing to do but wait and see. Refugees continued to flow in and out of towns all over Germany and the British, American and French occupiers had their in-trays full of chaos and misery.

Erika watched and learned how to cope with even less than she had ever imagined possible. Everyone had to improvise, especially the mayor's wife, setting a good example. ...She also learned how one chats up a farmer for a few baskets of sugar-beet, how to get them home and how to turn them into a sticky brown substance, to smear on bread or to use as sweetener.

Tante Inge had an old-fashioned copper bowl, large enough to scrub down the two girls (which she enjoyed doing with mind boggling thoroughness from time to time, there was no bathroom). This cauldron was kept in a very basic laundry room down in the cellar.

One did wonder about its multiple use when a log and coal fire would be lit under the pot, then filled with chopped beet to simmer, bubble and spit in a friendly way, emitting an unforgettable odour. Huge numbers of glass jars filled with the stuff were lined up on the shelves in the cellar, along with other bottled fruits and berries. Hanging on bent metal coat hangers were sad stretched furs of rabbits, like small discarded coats, their owners having given their all to keep us supplied with protein. In the corner, on the floor lay a heap of potatoes, and the inevitable shriveled apples. The cellar was endlessly fascinating.

Erika had no idea that her daughter thought it somewhat piquant to be scrubbed together with Ursula in the same cauldron as the sugar beets!

Some months after arrival a larger, more pleasing room with kitchenette on the second floor was made available to us. Erika turned this space into a mayoral bed-sit while the attic became the domain of her almost teenage daughter. By now a real housewife Erika owned saucepans of her own (one unforgettably, made from an army helmet). And, things being as primitive as they were, there was a basin in the kitchenette which had to do for ablutions as well. There was only one WC for all persons in the house and no bathroom. Erika soon discovered the Public Baths, a quaint affair only five minutes away, where, after a long wait, one had to pay for ten minutes in a small cubicle containing an old-fashioned bathtub with clawed feet. Did the poor mayor ever have enough time, in those post-war years to have a bath?

As seasons, years passed, friends and colleagues invited each other to dinner and to the yacht club and each others' homes. Like in Cape Town and Accra Eka and Reini were much appreciated.

The old Ihlenfeldts, who never really recovered from the shock of their flight from the Russians, and having to make do in an Old Age home, died peacefully, in quick succession of each other, and were buried in Lübeck. In many ways this was a relief to all. Their son had neither means nor time to ease their plight.

After two years Erika longed to see her own parents again. The slow process of the German recovery after total destruction of railways and roads made travel generally chaotic. She did make it for a few weeks eventually, but endured great hardship, at one stage even traveling in a cattle truck. She was much given to exaggeration, but no-one was ever able to disprove this.

Her husband's greatest happiness was sailing on the Eutiner See. He never owned a sailboat of his own but knew enough persons who were honoured to lend him theirs and the annual regattas and events kept him fit and content. Capsizing once or twice was all part of the fun. Neither of his two women were all that keen,... however, with some bribery, Reini's 12 year-old spent many afternoons baling out a slightly less than watertight boat and learned to keep her head down when the sail changed sides in the wind. A valuable lesson in life's vicissitudes, perhaps?

Life-long friendship developed between the Ihlenfeldts and Col. Reginald Jones, the man in charge of Eutin and the surrounding area in Schleswig Holstein as representative of the British military government. The Joneses lived in Pulverbeck, a grand requisitioned house on the edge of the lake. He and his wife Betty were only too delighted to find some Germans like Erika and Reini who spoke English and were willing to give them insights into the current situation. Such personal friendships were considered irregular at the time, but mutual sympathy carried them all through any unspoken criticism. (Criticism from both German and British circles.)

Ingeborg had by then made creditable progress as a pianist and relished the presence of a concert grand in the Jones' house, where she could practise for as long as the grownups were chatting away. The

Ihlenfeldts never owned a piano, not counting the one left behind in Swinemünde.

There is a modest (instantly suppressed) sadness in Erika. She sees that Reini has made a conquest at the many parties they attend and how his eyes give him away during conversations with and about the lady in question. Always sitting together, always touching each other.... "How could this be, after all we've been through together," Erika sighs, when she herself has never entertained such feelings about anyone else. "Such a betrayal, such" ....no, she can't even admit it to herself.

"Never show anyone you care that much" was her motto, and "don't give anyone the satisfaction knowing you are so dependent," was another. All she does is to turn in on herself in a negative way. Still young, she feels that terrible question endlessly haunting her: "what am I doing here, and what good is it, what use am I?"

Erika, an old-fashioned woman, believes she exists for her man, her daughter, and for her ageing parents. Somehow this no longer adds up. It never occurs to her that she could perhaps do or learn something new. There is no incentive. She feels trapped and depressed. She doesn't know what to do. She is only 42!

Luckily her man, 48 years old, had persuaded himself that Europe was no longer the place for him: the only way forward was to return to Africa. They did after all still own that funny little bungalow called

'Accra' on the edge of Lion's head, in Cape Town. He'd resigned from being Mayor in 1947, was doing some fairly mundane civil service job for the military government and was 'going nowhere,' achieving nothing. It was 1949. Time for a change!

Erika was appalled. When it came to the crunch she didn't want to go back to Africa after all........

Once her man really got his teeth into something he would not let go until everything was carefully organized; every detail weighed up, corrected, planned, from every angle possible. This sounds tedious, but that's how he was, a stickler.

In retrospect his efficiency seems a miracle. There were no international telephone calls, e-mails had not been invented. There was 'snail mail' and also lovely old-fashioned telegrams, of course. The Post Office was right next door!

Within weeks he'd booked a cargo boat from Oslo, organized friends in South Africa to pay for it, accepted invitations from various persons to come and stay in South Africa, particularly some dear friends, with a guest farm and starting a business 'in jam'.

"Please, come soon, dear Ihles...the berries are ripening; we need you to help make Youngberry Jam while you find your feet in Africa... Can you bring a large copper cauldron from Germany?"

Of course, Reini will fix it!

A cauldron is specially constructed in Hamburg and shipped to the farm in South Africa. Other old friends who have survived the terrible air raids on Hamburg are also planning to return to S.A....with hopes to set up a 'factory for brassieres.' These are the lovely Brinkmans, Pev, with her lame arm, her husband and their son Peter, the bane of Ingeborg's life in those Pretoria days, when all fathers were in the camp.

So, Reini, dashing about, sometimes with, often without his family, organizes the great trek back to Africa, while Erika and child get on with normal life.

Just at this time poor Erika has the unpleasant task of explaining menstruation to her teenager. When it happened there was that inevitable mother/daughter moment, when things had to be talked about. Erika was not much given to talk about 'things'.

But, as an enlightened and final treat Erika allows her daughter to spend an idyllic day bicycling with the young admirer to a place called the Bungsberg, where they swear undying love.

There will be some 'fast-forwarding' now. It is summer 1949 and the Ihlenfeldts have reached Oslo by slow trains, via Denmark and Sweden. Reini's two women are sleepy and moody, but he is bubbling over: A fresh start and a boat-trip, albeit on a freighter!

Well, not everybody can be happy all the time: Erika, once settled in her cabin, is embarrassingly withdrawn and appears only for meals, her own quiet way of showing displeasure. "To be honest," she admits later, "living in Europe has been a terrifying adventure, but I've understood at last that it is where I belong." Too late. A good wife sticks with her man, through thick and thin. She can always come back and visit.

Different problems loom in Africa. The most pressing one is finding a job for the head of the family.

After some time on a dreamily beautiful farm near Plettenberg Bay, with the most kind and generous friends anyone could hope for, Reini, ever positive, ever optimistic, sets out again to knock on the doors of former contacts in CapeTown. Ten years have gone by since his last job had been so suddenly whisked away by WW2; he is now nearing fifty. Even then that was a bonus only to those who were hoping to take early retirement!

For Reini it seemed hopeless. No one had anything for him. After several months of to-ing and fro-ing and much practical work on the farm, he began to feel he'd made another mistake. Bottling Youngberry jam was not exactly his idea of a career. Erika said: "I told you so".....He had left no stone unturned.

Erika however, had grown to like living on the farm and would have been perfectly happy to stay there for ever!

In the end something worth considering did come up: a managerial post in South West Africa, Walvis Bay, a small settlement in the Namib Desert with a fairly important harbor. At that time (1950) it was South Africa's only harbor on the West coast. In 1878 this natural deepwater harbor and the Namib Desert had been annexed by the British. When the Germans acquired Southwest Africa from native chiefs in 1884 the British enclave was excluded and put under the administration of the Cape Province in South Africa.

The Norwegian whale-industry had stationed itself in Walvis Bay: it processed both whale meat and fish-oil. This installation burnt down in 1950. Reini, who inspected the remains of the buildings, found numerous cans of Arcanol rustproof paint, the brainchild of Erika's father, which had made Papi Ragg a wealthy man thirty years earlier. What a heart-warming, extraordinary coincidence!

By the 1950's Walvis Bay was a miserable dump with 8000 inhabitants, a few sandy roads , eight fish meal factories, a few houses and shops, many on stilts (because the place was prone to flooding), and the Railway Institute, the hub of what little social life there was. Most inhabitants were native laborers in the harbor and factories, along with their families.

Constant sandstorms, the finest sand imaginable forced itself into doors and windows, however well sealed. When there was no wind the stench from the fish meal factories pervaded the entire area. There was no sanitation, no paved road. Electricity was available from 8pm-10pm via a generator from the Cold Storage Co. So, if what you wanted was a cold beer, the way forward was to hang a bottle outside in the wind, inside a wet sock. After 10pm it was back to petroleum lamps or candles. No-one had a fridge, and Erika's culinary disasters could all be blamed on her petroleum oven.

Strangely, Erika found great happiness in Walvis Bay.

She was queen of her 5-room, grey breeze-block house, her own home for the first time since 1940 when the war had begun. Even though there was an outside bucket loo, and only about 3 sq. yards of sand called a garden, fenced off from the worst of the blowing sand (the only thing growing was a Tamarisk tree, about 3ft tall and an amazingly hardy Oleander plant)....a challenge if ever there was one!

Sturrock & Woker, the firm Reini was working for, employed 20 Europeans and 120 Namibians.

Very shortly after his arrival a branch of the international Seamans' Mission opened in Walvis Bay and Reinhold Ihlenfeldt, as director of the firm, was able to assign two smallish rooms to this enterprise. An English reverend, along with a few boxes of books were the beginnings of this scheme. Erika, voted in as member of the "harbor lights Guild" (ladies who offered tea to visiting sailors), sold knick-knacks from a kiosk to any takers. There were dances and other entertainments.

Before too long Ihlenfeldt was headhunted and offered the post of mayor of Walvis Bay. He declined most firmly! It has to be said they soon had a pleasing circle of friends and there were always ocean liners with captains on board, who invited and entertained the hardy 'locals'. By then the municipality had progressed to a modest power station, which functioned for several hours each day. Life was transformed! By the time the Ihlenfeldts left Walvis Bay eight years later there was in existence a newly built Seamans' Mission, complete with chapel, library, a hall for dances and events and a residence for the pastor and his assistant. In such a very small and primitive settlement it was impossible not to get involved with the great demands for 'progress'. Reini, a Lutheran in word but a total heathen in deed, assisted with the building of a Lutheran church and Erika, with the help of a friend, laid the foundations for a public library, spending much time classifying and setting up a workable system. Some years later the municipality of Walvis Bay took on the task of providing professional personnel.

Erika, now in her forties, had only two wishes: to ensure her child had a good education, preferably in a Catholic school, and to own a fridge! All this had come to be: Evelyn (the German bits were dropped) was now boarding at the Holy Cross Convent in George, where there were still many about who hated anyone or anything German. Two years on she was transferred closer to 'home' to Windhoek Holy Cross Convent, only 14 hours by train from Walvis Bay! Mind you, trains were slow in those days. And when Erika turned 46 her daughter was ready to go to University in CapeTown. For those three years the fond parents in Namibia seemed to be as happy and content as 'sand-boys'.

Well, mostly......In 1955 there was a bombshell, the cosy existence of the Ihlenfeldts shattered: their daughter had become pregnant, with her long-time lover Pierre, a Lebanese, and they were about to be married.   In those days there was no alternative. Ingeborg Evelyn almost killed her mother with this blow to the family pride, honor, you name it. Erika's only child got married quietly in CapeTown. She writes a letter to her parents in Austria:

Es schmerzt mich, Euch eine unerfreuliche Nachricht mitzuteilen. Vor wenigen Wochen kam ein Brief von unserer Tochter, dass sie aerztliche Bestaetigung haette, sie erwarte ein Kind. Der Vater ist angeblich dieser Pierre Attala, von dem wir Euch ja schon berichtet hatten. Eure Hoffnung, (unsere auch) dass sich das Verhaeltnis mir der Zeit verwachsen wuerde, ist hiermit zerstoert, sie sind bereits kirchlich getraut. Knups studiert dennoch weiter und hofft ihre Schlusspruefung zu bestehen. Ab Mitte Dezember wird sie nun mit ihrem Kamel-treiber in Nord Rhodesien leben.

Wir sind am Boden zerstoert mit diesen Ereignissen.

(Dear Mageregg-people! It pains me to give you bad news. Some weeks ago we received a letter from our daughter that she has been confirmed to be pregnant. The father is allegedly this Pierre Attala, about whom we had already informed you. Your hope (and ours too) that the relationship would die away in time is therefore destroyed; they have already got married in church. Despite all Knups continues to study and do her finals. From the middle of December she will live in Northern Rhodesia with her camel-driver. We are gutted by these events.)

Erika and Reini eventually pulled themselves together. They came to CapeTown to buy their child a 'trousseau', to meet Pierre's stepmother Josephine, and generally to make peace. The little 'German' family of yore had suffered a serious shock and had been tested.

Despite all difficulties it would be absolutely true to say that Erika put down deep roots in those sand-dunes. Surprisingly, in 1959, when the time had come to return to CapeTown it was an unbelievable wrench. In all its quaint ghastliness Walvis Bay left her with unforgettable, bonding memories. They boarded a boat along with their belongings and with their black cat Peter. In German, "der schwarze

Peter" is a symbol of good luck. Nevertheless, a melancholy day but also an important one: Reini was close to retirement and it was high time to get back to the wonders of civilisation for those years that were still to come.

We've reached the half-way point in our tale of seven generations. Here is the snag: Because the next incumbent lives inside my head, and because it_is me, ...there is the temptation to delve in and show how the events of my life still quiver on, half alive, sometimes vehemently alive... which may cause some repetition of Erika's life, *but with the additional emotions of how I felt, how I saw her.*

I'd hate it if you were bored ... do feel free to skip about 40 pages! It's a case of 'Know thyself' or, in Latin, 'Nosce ipsum'....written on a Holy Card by my maths -nun when I left school...

It is excellent advice....

Ingeborg-Evelyn's Story

What a poor start: I don't like any of my names. I can't relate to them at all. Who am I supposed to be? Somehow all the others have real names, names that fit and work. But *Ingeborg* and *Evelyn*, well, they don't feel like me, inside. Mind you, it has been useful at times, to become just plain Inge, and I have been an Inge and still am one, to several people who are dear to me.

In my English incarnation 'Evelyn' has been invaluable. But just the sound of it makes me feel hot and prickly...that elongated 'eee' and the 'vil' to follow. What *was wrong* with my parents' tonal sense? So all that, for starters, is uncomfortable.

Then there is that birth in H a m burg. Another stupid name. Now that I think about it. No, I'm just trying to be lighthearted.

I was treated like a princess, cosseted by at least three if not four ladies, dressed, fed, weighed, bathed and potty trained, to say nothing of the baby gymnastics. I could hardly tell them apart although one was dressed all in white and wore a white cap. She did most of the work, briskly, I expect. Others came and went. No doubt the best was 'Mami', she was always there. After a month the woman who had given birth to me vanished, and a year later the nurse in white did too. A new nurse in white took over the chores. A *year* later I was visited by a stranger who, I was told, was my mother. I didn't care for her. After three weeks of her dressing up in a white uniform I allowed her to feed me, touch me. My father also tried to befriend me: I gave them both a hard time. People kept coming and disappearing. Only 'Mami' was always there. And as I became bigger there was an occasional encounter with Papi, who made a lot of pleasing noise on his pianola or allowed me to type on his typewriter. No doubt he was a formative influence. After all, that is just what I am doing now!

I was a very fortunate small person, for as long as I can remember I was 'das Knupslein' or 'der Knups'. Now there is a very subtle distinction between the two: <u>der</u> Knups is masculine, the effect is one of a stubby, stubborn, stumpy, willful and somehow comical person. <u>Das</u> Knupslein, being both diminutive and neuter brings out shades of something cute in need of protection. People should take care when they choose names for their children.

My parents lived and worked in Africa, shadowy figures who came and went, once, sometimes twice a year. I don't suppose they registered in my two or three-year old mind. I was endlessly photographed for them, so that they could at least see what was happening to me. To be honest, I remember little from that time, apart from one cold, white day when I was allowed to stick a carrot nose into a snowman's face fashioned by my 16 year old uncle Pucki. It was his idea I'd been re-christened 'Knups' after a cartoon character in a Hamburg newspaper.

• • •

Early years in any child's life are very important as the personality forms itself. Don't Jesuits say the first five years of a child constitute the entire nucleus of the eventual person?

All I can say now, looking back over this time, the notion that I would be in good hands, groomed to make a new start, aged nearly four, with Erika and Reini, was a very bold move. I force myself not to romanticise this. But there are some things that do come to my mind, things that must have left a mark. (Like sins leaving 'black marks on the soul', as the nuns would have it, in later convent education). Erika and Reini had no experience as parents. I expect they were really quite nervous, trying very hard. We were to sail around the east coast of Africa to Cape Town. My father, had to fly to Basle on business, my mother took a train to Hollabrunn to show me to her grandmother, the famous Grossi, my great-grand mother, by then in her 90's. From an early letter I have learned that I didn't weep but could think of little else than sleeping in 'a little room on wheels'. And on the following day there was to be a trip on a plane! Whatever that was??? A long room with wings of a bird?

I have been told these things, they are not memories. Strangely I do remember, vividly, my first flight, from Vienna to Basle. In those early days of travel by plane, my mother was in a state of terror: she had never flown before. There we were, boarding a tinny, tiny plane, without a man to 'take care' of everything. I assume it was tiny: I have seen pictures of planes from 1938, and let's face it, they were puny things. Small wonder she passed out in a dead faint as the propellers took us up and away. 'Altitude sickness,' was the explanation.

I had a great time, walking up and down the aisle and befriending everybody. I sat on the laps of countless lovely 'daddies' while my mother got herself together again. Strangely, this is my very first real memory...loving all that attention and being liked by strangers. In Basle we were met by the concerned Reini, who then took care of wife and child in the time-honored way. Another little box on wheels and we were ready to board the 'Tanganjika', a respectably large ocean liner.

What does a nearly four-year old need? Regular meals, warmth, clean clothes, a nice bed? 'Tante Nika' provided all these and more: there was a nursery with trained staff and toys. Children were fed separately and food was excellent. A six-week journey in unbelievably hot climates does not bring out the best in anybody: Tempers flared all round. There are photos of the family sweating it out on a rickshaw in Port Said, wearing tropical helmets and looking reasonably cheerful, my mother languidly detached.

On board I caused a flurry of excitement by telling others that my real parents lived in Hamburg. It all fitted, since Erika was very quick to have her child taken off her hands, not just by the nursery but also by a young missionary lady, who seemed to like other people's children. Of course I didn't understand. But somehow, as far back as I can remember, I recall the feeling that I knew better and perfectly well what the grown-ups were up to. I certainly sensed my parents' efforts at parenting were not quite of the standard I was accustomed to. They were nice, I liked them, but they didn't get it right... Erika, mostly exhausted, the heat was getting to us all.

I spent much time in the deck pool, floating about, in a rubber ring with a net underneath. My father liked water. My mother had a lumpy figure and did not care to reveal it too often. I suppose I was homesick for my Mami and Papi in Hamburg.

But exciting things happen too: everyday there is a violinist who entertains passengers at noon, tea-time and in the evening. His speciality is to encode the letters of a passenger's name in his daily program, quite a feat.

For example:

Midday Concert:	
Immortellen, Walzer	Gungi
Naschkätzchen, Intermezzo	Siede
Gedämpftes Licht, Tango	Meisel
Ein liebes Mädel, Tango	Reuter
Afternoon	
Ich tanze mit dir, Walzer	Schroeder
Hochzeitstag/Trolthaugen	Grieg
Liebesgruss, Lied	Elgar
Elfengeflüster, Intermezzo	Rhode
Nachts ging das Telefon	Kollo
Evening	
Fruehlingstimmen, Walzer	Strauss
Eine kleine Nachtmusik	Mozart
Liebestraum, Lied	Bochmann
Dreimädelhaus	Schubert
Tango Bolero	Llossa

Read down the first letter of each musical item and you will find:.. INGE IHLENFELDT. What an honor! Did this violinist leave a mark on my soul? Did I become a violinist? Strangely...... well, read on.

I cannot claim to remember all this. I neither knew nor heard anyone else in all the years to follow, right up until my twelfth year, who played a violin. I was not taken to concerts and had not been to any schools which taught music other than singing.

SS. Tanganjika, Sunday the 11th September, 1938. "...but please can I come too, Mutti, I want to put on my nice dress like you did and have cake in the big room with the grown-ups....all the time I have to play in the sandpit with the other children and then it's bedtime and I want to be pretty like you...I promise I won't talk ..."

Erika gazes at her daughter and shakes her head: "but you're covered in sand, look at you. You'll have to have a bath first and will you really be quiet? Completely quiet?"

"Yes, I promise" says Knups. Eka gets her child ready, very proud in a new dress with dots and a white collar. A large place has been cleared in the bar, a pianist and violinist will perform ladies and gentlemen, sitting at tables, sipping their tea. Knups cranes her neck to find the waitress with the cake-trolley who appears in no time at all ....to satisfy her youngest customer on this rather warm afternoon.

"Which cake would you like?" The most colorful one is chosen... "For once my child behaves in an exemplary way," Erika notes.

The musicians walk on, to friendly applause. Erika has a quick look to locate the nearest exit. As the violinist tunes Knups takes a swig of juice, puts her glass down, examining the man getting ready,..... The concert begins. The child has stopped eating and listens with eager concentration. "Why does the violin sing when you stroke it with a stick... it sounds so sad?" she whispers after they'd come to the end of the first piece.It was a well-known song in ¾ time, smooth and romantic and Eka said the words to Knups, very softly when the musicians stopped. Knups looked at her gravely. "Can I play that song one day?" "Shhhhhhh, you promised, shhhhh!

My parents were great keepers of letters, telegrams and photos. To be confronted with so much material is like being treated by an expensive shrink. Could my inexperienced parents, aged 38 and 31 respectively have been treating me too strictly, too critically? I was expected to behave like an adult, on the 'children should be seen and not heard' principle. Am I kidding myself when I seem to remember not being able to take them seriously?

Vivid fragments of memory from the early times in Cape Town: I am almost four years old: Auntie Eve, a tall thin lady, has an easel and tubes of sticky paint, and she makes me sit still while she paints and paints and paints...a picture of me! She is gentle, funny and I love her. Her son Boris is ten.

Something radiates from her, such an encouraging thing, such acceptance, I can still feel it now. I really loved her.

Less pleasing: nightmares. Once we had moved to our bungalow I recall frightening wild beasts which made me wake up and scream. My parents came running. It happened again and again. My father thought I was being 'naughty.' He was wrong because I couldn't make them not happen..... And then that circular glass-topped coffee-table in the 'lounge' which my mother liked to polish: it produced a thin whiney squeak...one of my favorite things, I never tired of it! My mother liked to hear me sing: she would stand me in a circle of friends expecting me to entertain them. I did, allegedly, with great aplomb. I can see now where all this is leading: performing on a violin, perhaps?

My father comes home from work one day with a puppy in his pocket! "Take it out!" he orders. It's small, wriggles, legs, tails everywhere, and needs a drink, we think. Then a wee, then a chew of my teddy, another wee......

Soon Erika is writing extremely critical letters to her mother about the difficulties with her 'exasperating' offspring. Disobedient, stubborn, willful, lying, always wanting to be entertained, refusing to eat normal food (only macaroni was acceptable) rude to the colored maid Lucy and even worse to the Zulu gardener....in short, a pest. A bit like the puppy, I suppose.

Letters from Mami, (sent at the time when she was packing up to leave Hamburg and move into her castle in Austria,) were full of good advice saying she really didn't understand 'Knupslein' was difficult, she had been like a lamb in Hamburg, and if a child was lying it was usually through fear of punishment.

Well, my father certainly believed in punishment... "if you do this, then we'll do that" approach. "If you don't eat that meat now you will sit here until you do" ....and so on. One afternoon, locked in my room for some misdemeanor, I decided to jump out of the window. It was just my bad luck my father was in the garden and caught me doing it. He pulled down my knickers and slapped my bare bottom.

This deeply humiliating event left an indelible mark on my four-year old psyche, the indignity of it, the cheek and how- dare- he!- feeling is there to this day! I mean, a clout around the ear is one thing, but the other was just too much. From then on I suppose something inside me closed down, perhaps for eighty years ... until he died.

By then he thought I was wonderful and adored me. And I had accepted him, in a fashion. But, in 1938 it was just as well he was interned in the camp, not long after my 'chastisement!' When he'd gone I consoled my mother with "never mind, we can buy a new daddy",..which went into the family chronicle. As it turned out, I did see very little of him over the years. Perhaps this was a good thing.

It allowed me to form closer bonds with my mother, as there was no-one else to get in the way. We never discussed this, even forgot about it. But there was always a foreigness between us: I thought of him mostly as someone who got in the way. Much later, as the decades passed I remained politely distant... always. He lectured me, he demanded replies to his endless letters. I did an absolute minimum and there were always barriers. I feel bad about this now and wish he'd drop in for a chat. But he's dead.

He loved writing to his many friends and to record his life in minute detail. When I was older, I saw him as a pedant and despised his files full of letters, dating back to his earliest days. But if he hadn't done this scribbling, and kept so many pictures, well, where would this account go now?

By 1940 my mother and I had left CapeTown for Pretoria. Recollections from this time are, in my case, selective and only vaguely coming into focus, in a disturbing way. Is it normal or not to remember the fabric of ones mothers' dress, a delicate silk georgette garment, grey with large orange dots, very 1930's?

Or the shine of the red polished courtyard outside our strange new abode? There are vivid snippets-- such as the day I returned with my little friend Peter, from one of our "gold and silver" expeditions, slow, eyes- to- the ground searches for treasures,' mostly in the slums just beyond our courtyard, where the black servants had their dark, mysterious rooms. We carried about an old jam jar in which we collected anything shiny, especially small coins or pretty stones and on this particular day, longish white balloons, which we found strewn about. My mother, followed by Peters' mother, and other ladies, seemed much exercised by our gathering up these 'balloonies" as we called them. We were told they were dirty and that we should never go there again. Six and four years old, we were wide-eyed and bewildered...

A more pleasing area for letting off steam were the gardens of the Union Buildings, just three minutes away. Once we'd been coached in the skills of crossing the road, a small and very un-busy side road, we had a vast kingdom of lawn and rows of still young trees to play in, on, and under. We tore about, shouted as loud as we pleased, I had my own favorite tree, which I climbed and felt happy. Each child had its own undisputed 'fav' tree. I don't remember any mothers hanging about. Perhaps they'd come with us at the beginning, or I'm remembering later years, when I was six, or seven, or eight? We felt wild, sweatily grubby, wondrously free. There's nothing quite like sitting above ground on a branch, probably no more than about six feet off the ground, a seriously good feeling.

We communicated in a Babel of tongues, English, German and Afrikaans, a splendid and exuberant cocktail with a flavor of nowhere else on earth. At first I had only selected friends, like little Peter who spoke German, English was what we heard all day long, with Afrikaans limping along in third place.

I was the only child regularly in bed with some illness. Apart from all the normal childhood complaints such as mumps, measles, whooping cough there were bouts of lethargy, when I remember lying on my bed, sucking my thumb. This maddened my mother. At night she covered my thumb with iodine tincture and bandaged it up tightly to make it inaccessible. Only those who sucked their thumbs as long as I did (up to twelve years old) will know what a primeval urge it is, this unstoppable need to do it again and again. With it came a relaxation of reality and living, a dissolving into another dimension, which is impossible to describe in words. I would chew and gnaw at the bandages, suffer the taste of the iodine, anything, to get at that thumb. What does it mean? Looking back at this behavior I can only remind myself that we are little animals when we are young, and there are some things little animals need to do. Like snuggle up to a grownup. My mother did not like physical contact with me and pushed me away, usually with a joke. "Fass mich nicht an!" she'd say, looking embarrassed. She and my father seemed affectionate enough. This I noted in later years; in Pretoria she had only me. Her determination to shape me into a better scholar, better dancer, better eater, more amenable person, did nothing but make me more and more stubborn. And yet, at school, I was nearly always top of the class, teacher's little helper and generally a GOOD THING!

I was dragged to specialists, to find out why I was so bloated, so tired, so constipated, so bad-tempered, so melancholy. If she bought a bowl of fruit I'd gobble everything up, and this she didn't like either. "We can't afford it," she'd say. The boarding house food was scorned, only fish and chips and fruit were 'in'. Doctors tried their luck with all sorts of remedies but not one said "she needs a home, a father, or even, she is missing her home in Hamburg," to say nothing of her grandparents. Holistic healing had not arrived. Soon I was signed up for ballet and swimming lessons: I hated both at first, I was very cowardly, but my mother had the steely determination I lacked!

Another vivid memory is returning to our white-tiled room, sobbing, not really being able to explain what was wrong. I had been in the room of an elderly couple who liked to listen to music. I had sat with them and started to blub. I actually remember this, a feeling not all that different from the need to suck my thumb. Something inexplicable and hopeless, the sound of a slow orchestral piece, I have no idea what it was. But with hindsight, the misery was very probably triggered by a memory of my grandfather playing on his pianola, some arrangement of a Beethoven symphony. Did my mother put her arms around me? I don't know...perhaps.

Talking of steely determination: a sight I shall never forget is that of my mother massaging her legs with an ebony ribbed rolling pin; she believed this torture would improve circulation and give her more shapely legs. She suffered from water-retention, her upper arms were also not very pleasing. This strange tool of torture she called a 'vaytootsmere', which derives from 'weh tut es mir'...meaning 'it- hurts-me', in German.

She was also a great believer in independence: from age seven onwards I was dispatched to school on Pretoria's public transport, on my own. She'd always pick me up in her Opel, but even the ballet classes were soon reached by bus. I made a huge fuss at first, to no avail, she was bigger and stronger. It was good really: I needed that toughening up for later years. It was customary to slap children about the ears. This is called an 'Ohrfeige'. I had plenty of those! Not at school, only 'at home'.At school it was rulers, struck on the palms of your hands. That happened twice in those four years. German school consisted of two large rooms divided by a sliding wall, and a playground. The classes had about twenty children in each room who were taught in three languages; German, Afrikaans and English. How this was divided up I can't recall, but I know my mother was puzzled by my curious tasks and slow progress. Although German-speaking at home I preferred to read English books but spelling was appalling in all languages. I hated sums but was thought to sing nicely. At first reports were average, later I became teacher's pet with top marks, despite frequent absence due to illness. My mother kept me on track: homework sessions in the afternoon. I saw no fun in that and pretended to be really stupid, just to annoy her. Another ruse was pretending to be baby-ish, to make her love me more. I desperately needed hugs, praise and affection, even protection, but she was adamantly hardened against that sort of thing. I wonder why?

There was constant manipulation, one way or the other. I needed her, she needed me, but we were not very 'good at it'! She was so critical!

In my head is a patchwork of snippets of those four years in Pretoria, vivid, palpable and real. Just imagine the moment of disbelief, when I rose from our potty...(yes, we used one, as neither of us could face the long walk to the outside toilet adjacent to the native quarters, especially at night)..and found a bright red pool of blood. What was this?

My mother, in shock, couldn't believe her eyes, called the doctor immediately. He guessed at a burst vein, or bilharzias, or a bladder infection. Laboratory tests confirmed an infection caused by a lung infection I'd recovered from recently. News went round Belvedere Hotel that I was on my deathbed, having some bizarre female complaint at the tender age of eight. I felt fine, but was not allowed to get up. It meant staying in bed for nine days, before the infection cleared. No problem: I was an experienced 'being-in-bed' person, having had one throat, chest, ear, tooth infection after the other for three years running. These were The Treats: my mothers' jewellery box: I put on every brooch, necklace, ring there was and gazed at myself in a hand mirror. Or: provided with a tray and matchboxes, glue, paper and scissors I constructed chairs and wardrobes for my dolls house. Then the typewriter, my favorite pass-time: I typed a letter to my father, not at all bad, it is right beside me now, in German, with questionable spelling, but certainly literate.

"How does she know how to type?" he queries and my mother's reply was: "modern children simply know how to do this". The equivalent of present-day babies fiddling around with computers?

A hard knock was giving up my first solo performance at the Eisteddfodd in the Town Hall, the illness had made me weak and wobbly so the ballet teacher cancelled my slot.

For special events I was taken to a boiler room just opposite the infamous 'balloonie' area. (This had become forbidden territory). My mother sat on a stool and turned (sometimes burnt!) my longish hair into ringlets with tongs heated in the wood stove for providing bathwater. It must have been quite hard to judge just when to take the tongs out of the coals as there was always that memorable smell of singed hair! How I loved the attention and the transformation! I felt special. The first time I was squeezed into a frothy pale green tutu and saw myself in the mirror, with curls and pointed toes in satin ballet shoes, well, it was the start of an astonished realization I was 'cute'. In a puddingy sort of way!

Other awakenings during those tender years: a short holiday with a school friend on a hot, dusty Transvaal farm, still under construction; the only entertainment was swimming in a circular corrugated iron dam, stuck right in the middle of nowhere, probably rainwater, perhaps for crops or animals: there was a tiny ladder to get in...the water murky and warm with wriggly things, frogs, beetles? Three or four of us, the boys rather braver, were putting their heads under water. Taunted by them and finally persuaded to dive under, I come face to face with a boy who then kissed me under water. No-one could see! Well, the others laughed and teased us. Afterwards he told me he loved me. We were both eight, and this was my first kiss, never forgotten.

What about the chickens on the run after they'd had their heads chopped off? What a nightmare! I began to miss my mother and the Belvedere Annexe. Eventually returned, burnt brown and looking more grown-up than my mother remembered, I fell into her arms and sobbed how happy I was to be home. How gratifying.

By 1944 the war in Europe was becoming intolerably dangerous. One would have thought that South Africans would take it out on their large contingent of German wives and children, but if there was any trouble I certainly had no inkling of it. There were so many children in the boarding house that the innovative manageress of the Belvedere suggested an evening show with folk-dancing and singing and a play, acted only by children: each child was to take part in some capacity. The play was a thriller, a murder I seem to remember, with an Afrikaans text, and to this day I can say my line which was:

"heer is die pragtige pêrels", (here are the wondrous pearls) although I haven't a clue who or what I was! Did Erika keep this memory alive? In later years, whenever either of us handled pearls, we'd get the giggles and say, with great delight: "pragtige pêrels" using impressive Dutch back-of-the throat gutturals. After the 'cultural' input there were games, with forfeits: I had to kiss a boy fifty times, he was the favorite amongst the gaggle of kids, twelve years old, with a mighty stammer. I reported to my mother that the kisses had been 'lovely and soft'. She on the other hand informed my father that I would turn into a really bad lot one day!

And what about the unforgettable 'little blue flowers'? Pretoria is famous for these now. The Jacaranda trees were originally South American, now there was hardly a street in Pretoria which did not turn into an enchanting shade of blue in the Spring. The flowers looked even prettier after they'd dropped on the ground. Both canopy and carpet radiantly blue; to this day blue flowers mean more to me than any others.

And now the crowning memory: a combination of little blue flowers with the Afrikaaner ice-cream man on his horse-drawn cart. He was so friendly, let me jump on to sit with him as we ambled around the block, selling his wares. The road next to the annexe was on such a steep incline, I feared for the poor horse in front; did the man have brakes on his cart? Surprising, really, that my mother allowed this...I wonder if she even knew? "You are the nicest little girl in his area", he said, would I like to have a job selling ice-cream......... This was not to be.

My last memory of Pretoria is standing on the street corner with my toys on the pavement and price tags on each item. Everything was going cheap. Passers-by were kind and curious: why this was happening?

"I am going back to Germany" I said," because my father is coming out of the camp"...They said nothing. They must have thought it was a death sentence.

What on earth were my parents *thinking* about?

Blurred memories of the train journey to Port Elisabeth: the dramatic confiscation of my sack full of sweets (bought from the street sales) and the big moment when my father came up the runway. Why is this not more clearly etched, could a nine-year old brain shut down due to overload? My first recollection is of my father ordering *ten* eggs for breakfast, all boiled. He had not had eggs in the camp for four years. I sat and watched him devour them one after the other. I was embarrassed, he was a stranger. I do remember my resentment: I was no longer the focus of my mother's attention. He was always there and had views about me that did not coincide with my mother's. I knew I was *supposed* to like him. Instead I made friends with a different grown-up gentleman. He was an artist who sat on deck painting, every day. We got on really well and I liked sitting near him with my own pencils and crayons, drawing while he occasionally looked over and encouraged me. He told my parents I had talent. I liked him a lot.

After four whole weeks of cruising up the west coast of Africa we got to Lisbon. Earlier there had been two 'refueling' stops, and 'fresh provision' stops, but we had not been allowed off the ship.

Once installed in the Grand Hotel in Estoril, home of the abdicated kings of Europe, I'd got used to the idea of a 'father' being around. We had a huge room; my parents could close off their sleeping area with red velvet curtains and I slept on a sofa opposite. I can still see the view down to the sea. Day after day my father jollied us along to see many places, Cascais, Lisbon town centre, the beaches. There is a vivid memory of an old castle on a hill with strangely shaped chimneys (Cintra?) and of a shoemaker from whom my father bought some leather sandals for me, made of shiny brown leather half-saucers over the toes. We walked and walked and ate much ice-cream. The hotel smelt of olive oil, everywhere we went was that special smell of Portuguese olive oil.

One night I was awakened by noises. I looked across to my parents' bed. They had no clothes on and were playing some rude game. I watched for a while. What they were doing reminded me of the day I had been punished for playing 'doctors' with my friend Gisela, when we were caught looking at each others' bodies and punished...a horrible and embarrassing afternoon in Pretoria, a few years before. I gazed at them for a while, fell asleep eventually. I hated their game and decided I would never speak to them again. I really did *not speak to either of them for a whole week*. I felt cross, disgusted, dismayed. Whenever possible I went out of their way and did my own thing, as far away from them as possible. I couldn't smile. I merely nodded or shook my head when appropriate. "What's the matter?" they enquired, over and over. I just stared. After a week of this my father threatened to take me to a doctor if I didn't speak. So I let them have it...the whole sorry tale about their 'rude' games at night.

I have no insight into their feelings about all this. I expect they found a way to make me feel better about it. I talked again.........

"My God, I had no idea we hadn't drawn the curtains around the bed, we must have forgotten.....how could we be so careless"...

Erika was more upset than she liked to admit. How does one explain to a nine year old what parents do after dark, when they are in love, after such a long separation, when they'd had a few drinks. After lame reassurances they bribed their aggrieved daughter with money, sent her off to the swimming pool to find some friends and buy ice-cream. "We'll come down later and join you, and then we'll go out together to see a castle..."

An involved face-saving stratagem was put into place by Eka and Reini, largely a case of 'attention lavished and money spent on' the confused young person. In those six weeks in Lisbon the primal scene was soon overlaid with other impressions. Overlaid, but not erased. Such things are etched for ever. Would I really have behaved like that if I'd 'known' my father better? He seemed like such an intruder, always talking to my mother, and paying the wrong sort of attention, I felt, to me. And she was different too, now that she had him back. Why did she like him so much?

I'm not sure I didn't prefer our kitchen in the Belvedere Hotel.

Boarding the train to France I knew this delightful 'holiday' had ended. For some reason we had a compartment with beds, while others had second class accommodation without beds. My mother had been taken ill in Lisbon shortly before the onward journey, it was very mysterious, she had to lie down all the time, and could not carry anything. In later years I was told she had miscarried....

First stop was Biarritz just across the boarder between Spain and France. The hotel, even grander than Hotel Estoril was right on the beach: one huge room for parents, mine, ballroom-sized adjacent to theirs contained a king-size bed with velvet curtains on a platform and a pillow shaped like a long sausage. Too scared to go to sleep alone I begged my parents to stay until I dropped off. Another one of those 'etched' memories. What a far cry from the cosy intimacies of our tiled kitchen in Pretoria. So... this is how kings and queens sleep!

Food was scarce in France, dinner and breakfast meager, to say the most. Here was the first taste of hardship. Watery soup with dry bread? My father tells how we walked to the station on the following morning, sitting on a park bench next to an elderly French 'granny'...who asked: "what is that long train standing on the siding?"......"We scratched together our pitiful remains of school French and gave her the required answer. The little grand-mère gazed at us with sad eyes, stood up and walked off without a word". (from a letter written by my Dad.) The German occupiers were hated, naturally. My parents had much to learn.

During the onward journey our train was attacked several times. Even the grown-ups had to learn to stretch out on the floor when the shooting started. I was not afraid. Lying flat on the floor was uncomfortable, boring and just look how filthy it was, seen from three inches away for an interminable time. We were not allowed to budge in case a partisan (resistance fighter) would get frisky with a gun. Everything was threatening really, my father, the train, the war, the lousy food, to say nothing of the swastika flags we were given to wave out of the windows, unbelievably, and stopping for hours in dark tunnels to be safe from the partisans... ....“Sh....no more whispering...” they might shoot into our carriage” said my father, huddled up on the floor,”make yourself flat as a snake and don't move or anything,”.... “but I must go to the toilet...” “Don't you dare move now, we could all get killed...”

The authorities got us all back to Germany safely. On arrival in Heilbronn the grown-ups were taught how to use ration books and to go into air-raid shelters.

“I am nearly ten now, just a few more months, but even I can see my parents are getting things wrong! We ate food in a restaurant and used up all our ‘meat rations’. We also had to learn how to jump out of bed quickly and not bother to get dressed before the bombs started falling, but to run to the shelter, a horrible grey place with hardly any light, under the ground. Later, when the soldiers said ‘good-bye’ they gave us the Hitler salute and then we went to the station and sat about waiting for many hours. The idea was to go to the castle in Austria, which is about four or five hours by train.”

“Do the grandparents know we were coming? All I remember is sitting on a platform, falling asleep with my arms crossed to cradle my head, on a suitcase. It's so easy to sleep when one is really tired! When we arrived it was the middle of the night: we couldn't reasonably wake up my grandparents. There was a place for sick people at the station and they let my mother and me lie down on a bed. My father had to sit on a chair with a hole in it, all night. I felt sorry for him.

In the morning the nurse who let us sleep also let us use her telephone. Then, at last, Mami and Papi came with a carriage and a horse. It was a sunny day and we all fitted in the carriage, with our luggage and the horse was strong enough to pull all of us through Klagenfurt out into the countryside where Magaregg is. I liked the ride much more than those horrible trains; people were just starting to get up and some waved to us. I was happy to see Mami and Papi but I didn't remember them at all."

August. September, 1944. "Another girl lives here, in a little house near the stream, not in the castle. Her name is Karla and she is my friend. We play all sorts of games...like going up in the attic where there are dusty trunks full of old clothes. We put them on and pretend to be someone else. Out of the windows we can see far away mountains and fields. On hot days we paddle in the stream. There was a snake slipping along the pebbles and now I'm not so keen to go back..... Karla says they don't do anything. She goes to school not far from here; you pass the gates and walk along a dusty road with very high trees on each side. At the end are more gates and small houses where soldiers live with their wives and children. There is a school ...I'm supposed to go every day. I have to do everything in German now. I really like Karla.

On Sunday mornings a priest comes to say Mass in the chapel in the round tower. It is big enough for Mami and Papi, for us too and the maid. Karla comes with her mother. Mass here is much more fun than in the cathedral in Pretoria, where it was so hot and there were so many people, I know I am not supposed to say this, but going to Mass is quite boring. I'm glad the priest can talk to God in Latin, but I really don't know what he's saying. After Mass Mami invites the priest to have coffee with us; he's just an ordinary man without his special holy clothes on. He talks to Papi, who plays music on his pianola on Sundays. You don't need to use your hands for this. He prefers it to going to church. My father also does not go to church. He says his parents belong to a different church, so he believes in God in a different way; I suppose that's alright? Sometimes I feel sorry for my Dad. I must hug him more and tell him things. He wants us to go away from here and go by train to visit *his* parents who live by the seaside. His father is very old and needs help in the office, he is waiting for my father to be there *now*.

November 1944. "On a train again....we should be there in two hours. My father says there are no partisans here to attack us. "What about the bombs?" I asked, but he said the bombs were for towns, not trains. "We've just seen a horrible thing: a broken, grey town, all the buildings fallen to bits. The train went along the outside of the town. My father said: "look, remember this for ever!

This town is called Berlin. It has been bombed. This is what happens in wars. It used to be a very important place and now it is nothing." When we get to the seaside it will be cold. My father says we will not go to the beach for a long time, only in June. I am missing Karla and she has promised to write and send me her photograph... I wish I was still in the castle with Mami. She cried when we left."

Swinemünde. December. "My other grandparents have a dark house with a piano. I have my own room! It is next to my parents' room. We have to go up a small wooden stair case because downstairs is the office where my father helps *his* father do all the work with ships. From the balcony one can see many ships, first there is a cobbled road, then a railway track and after that the ships. It's fun to sit on the balcony because it has glass windows so one is warm and dry. We've been here for a few weeks now. Soon it will be Christmas with ice and snow. My grandmother says there is a market for Christmas toys and presents and maybe even cakes. When I looked at her piano she said *she knows a lady who will teach me to play on it!*

I got into big trouble last week. When I was standing next to that vase by the window, which is bigger than I am, I told my Dad: "one day, when your parents are dead, I would like to have that vase". He gave me an 'Ohrfeige' and said I was not to talk like that. I wasn't sure why he hit me so hard. I suppose he doesn't want his parents to die. He's very bossy these days. The other day I put some butter on my bread and asked if I could have the jam and he said: "From now on the rule is: because of the war one can have either butter, or jam, but not both at the same time." My mother *and* my grandparents agreed with him. Soon it will be Christmas.

It was jolly cold at the Christmas market. We had hot red lemonade and spicy cake. I was allowed to buy, for my room, some wooden painted dwarves, cut out of wood and I bought a holy thing, to hang by the door, it is made of baked red earth and looks like Mary over a little bowl for holy water. I don't have any holy water, but I tried ordinary water which slowly came out. I like it though. It's no good for making the sign of the cross, but I'll hang it over my bed along with the dwarves. I wonder where one gets holy water from. They had some by the chapel door in Magaregg. The market people sold candles and trees; being out in the dark was really nice!

My new task: because I'm not going to school I have to go each morning to get the milk from the man with the cart. Grandmother gives me a tin can with a handle and a lid. I pay him. Here one has to say Mark and Pfennig; everywhere money is different. My mother makes me sit down every morning to write and do sums in German.

When I was writing with my left hand the other day my father said it was a bad sign. I'm not sure what he means, but I can write and draw with both hands. If one hand fell off I would have a spare one, how can it be bad? Sometimes I don't like my father. I will soon forget how to say things in English and Afrikaans. Anyway, no-one would understand what I say.

My piano teacher is very old, and kind. I practise for a long time. I like doing it. I can already play a tune and my mother says I am quick. For a change! Now that she has walked me a few times she tells me I'm old enough to find my own way. I'm happy to go out on my own. Soon I will be ten. I have no friends. There are bad things sometimes. We see many poor people who have come off the ships with their luggage. They are called refugees. They have no homes, they look tired and worried. Every day more arrive. My father says they are running away from the Russians, who fight and kill everybody. I hope the Russians don't come *here*...It has snowed again. Everywhere looks white and beautiful. I can have my Dad's toboggan from the attic. He has not seen it since he was little.

When my grandmother was young she could sing very well, and play the piano and she could also draw pictures. Next to the piano hangs a small drawing she did of blossoms on a branch. She says they are apple blossoms and in a few months she will show me her apple tree with those same flowers, in the garden. We must go through the garden every day, when we go to the wooden box lavatory. There is a big hook on the wall with torn newspaper. At the top is a shelf with green berries which my grandmother keeps. There is also a proper lavatory in the bathroom, but it is so old it can only be used for pee-ing and we have to pour water in it, because it's broken. Lots of things are broken in my grandparents' house and some things are weird, like that large pot of sand next to my grandfather's chair. It is called a 'spittoon' and one should spit in it. I'm not sure why. The second weird thing is a small long basin with a wooden cover on tall legs by the foot of my grandparents' bed. It looks a bit like a donkey on which you can sit; my mother said it was for washing your bottom.

Because it is so cold the dining table has been moved into the piano-spittoon-living room. Usually it lives in a big room across the passage to the veranda. But in the room where we all do everything like sitting and playing, doing lessons and smoking and eating, is a huge tiled 'oven' which my father fills with wood and coals and it makes the room very hot. All the other rooms are very cold. I have one warm cardigan and a very small coat because I'm growing a lot. I get wet feet in the snow but there are no boots in the shoe-shop. My mother is cold too and she is getting thin because she has to work harder than before. The other day she was crying: a poor woman rang the bell and asked if she could sleep in the entrance and my grandmother said it was alright and gave her a blanket, so then the woman said thank you and let my mother take some flour out of her sack. When my mother put her hand into the flour her wedding ring fell off and she couldn't find it, she was on her knees, putting both hands in and feeling for her ring and then *she* started to cry.

I didn't know what to do, so I stroked her back....
she *did* find it in the end. I think my mother is very
tired. I have never seen her cry before".

The grown-ups are arguing about leaving this house,
going away *before it is too late*. When I come they
stop arguing and talk about other things. They
look upset.

January 1945. "More and more strangers come to
our door every day. They get off the boats and ask
us where to go, or, can they stay inside until the
trains come, or something. We have nothing to
give them, but they usually stay downstairs in the
hallway, huddled together. They go to our lavatory
in the garden There are no bottled gooseberries
left. Outside is ice and snow, just like my father
said, but it's not *that* good without boots and warm
clothes. I play with the toboggan sometimes, there
is a little hill in the park next to the air-raid shelter,
but yesterday a man asked me to let him use my
toboggan for pulling heavy things from the ships.
He has not brought it back. Some bigger boys come
to play there too. I don't know them. We have to go
into the shelter sometimes and it is very dark and
boring.

They do a scary thing here, whenever they think
airplanes are coming ...they switch on some metal
bowls to blow out a white fog over the whole town.
Every street has them and soon you can't see where
you are, the ships are invisible, the roofs are invisible
and it is best to be at home. Then the bombers fly

over a cloud and don't know what to do and go back home.

Tomorrow is my 10th birthday. I have no friends here, so no party. Maybe I will have a cake and a present."

February 1945. "Every day my father tells his parents that we should leave this place because the Russians are coming nearer and nearer......they think I'm not listening, but I am. My grandmother says, no, no, you three go and leave us here, we can't leave our home and all our things. Then my father tells them, quietly,...so I can't hear...what bad things the Russians do to all women, even old ones. My grandparents are sure the Russians would never do anything bad to them. It is amazing how they all say the same things over and over again. After that my parents go to their own room and say to each other: "What can we do to persuade them...how can *we* go, and leave them, helpless?" I feel sorry for the grown-ups because it is all such a mess." I am afraid.

12 March 1945. "Today I was nearly killed, but the bombs missed. Nearly all the windows are smashed, we were in the shelter when it happened, except my grandfather, who wouldn't go.

"I'm tired of going there all the time" he said. "I want to stay here. I don't care any more if the bombs kill me."

So my mother and I ran down...but the shelter was shut. My mother banged on the iron door, no-one could hear us. She took off one shoe and banged the door with the heel, then the door opened a little and a man said what do you *want*,... OK.OK... and let us in. My mother found my father and my grandmother and we sat together with lots of other people. We heard loud bangs and distant bangs and when they were very loud the shelter rocked and shook, like a big ship. Some women were crying and holding each other. The lights went out. I decided to pray, in case God could stop the bombs falling on us. I had my rosary in my pocket and held it hard, but no-one else was 'doing it', so I didn't either. The most frightening thing was when the floor rocked. A few times my father said: "that was close"...and my grandmother, who held his arm very tight looked like a small grey mouse shriveled up. She thought her house must be broken by now with my grandfather in it. My mother looked straight ahead and said nothing. The noise stopped. We stumbled out into a fog of dust and smoke, it was hard to breathe and hard to see so I held my fathers' hand. We clambered and stumbled over stones, broken trees and torn-off bloody legs and bodies. My father said "they are dead". We were so close to our house and it was not burning, many things were burning, but not *our* things. Inside we found grandfather... he had white dust all over him and was still in his chair. He looked silly but quite pleased with himself."

Now there was a lot of trouble! My father had to nail the broken windows shut in some way. It was becoming dark. My grandmother found candles. There was no electricity, it was bitterly cold. No water was coming out of the taps. Also, we had no food. When the new day came my father took a bucket to find an olden-days pump near by and he did that again later in the day. My mother and I tried to go along the road to see if anyone had food for sale, most shops were bombed or closed or had nothing on their shelves. Later people started leaving Swinemünde because the place was full of dead bodies and sunken ships. Luckily my father, who had gone to fetch water in our bucket, bumped into an old friend, a captain of a ship which had not been bombed. This captain said he could get us all away, first my grand-parents, then us, on two separate ships.

So that is what happened. It was nice to leave Swinemünde. I am ten years old and I did not meet a single child to play with in the five months I spent there! It was like being in prison.

<u>Interlude 2009.</u> The writer, myself, now grown-up, in fact quite elderly: what is described on the previous page is the closest brush with death my family had. *We were the lucky ones*, what was going on around us, a hell of subhuman events, of cruelty, incomprehension and fear, as though every living creature was to be crushed, ground into fragments, pulped, dissolved. Human beings, remorselessly brushed off the face of the earth, burned, drowned,

gone for good, plans dreamed up in safe clean offices, by stunted, blunted bullies: who had the power to command others to do the dirty work. No country's war can be described as good. Not even Britain or America can claim a Good War, yet, undeniably, they *had* to destroy the evil of those Nazis, that noxious avalanche advancing from minds of mad men calling themselves leaders, stunted by devils; scientists, laboratories, factories, all mindlessly producing, catering for, making possible an Armageddon of indescribable cruelty.

Events in Germany, the persecution of Jews and other disadvantaged minorities, the cruel killing, the hounding of dissenters, remains to this day the sort of thing that gives survivors and the following generations nightmares for life. The slate can never be wiped clean, the cruel events linger, like demons, hidden....lurking. Is this *one* form of punishment? *It is not easy, being a German.* It is especially not easy in Great Britain, or should I call it England? *They* cherish their victory, and so they should.

But they forget to look inside the cracks of history, to see the huge numbers of ordinary, powerless, frightened Germans bullied into a system and how many may never have truly understood the consequences nor meaning, of Nazism, of saying 'Heil Hitler', or any other childish role-playing that was expected of each and every ordinary citizen. I see it clearly now, the demonic Vorsprung of those Nazi maniacs.....but I truly had no notion whatsoever of what was going on then, over sixty years ago. Not one single time did I see my parents raising their arms in this Nazi salutation, but then we were there only for the last terrible months. In the end only misguided milkmen and simple-minded bureaucrats had the energy for displays of loyalty to the Reich.

And it was perilous not to conform, even at the bitter end.

<u>April 1945. Flight from the Russians.</u> Now new things happened: we had good food like butter and cheese and cake on our ship, but I was ill and spent most of the journey curled up on a bunk.

Our new town was a fairytale town. Every house had roses growing up the walls. It was called 'die Rosen Stadt' with cobbled roads, like the ones in Swinemünde but no ships, only a lake with rowing boats! Nothing was broken or bombed at all. I didn't think there even *was* a war in Eutin...it felt like a holiday place. Our friends gave us food and helped us settle down while we told them all about the bombs. My father called it a "terror raid".

At first we lived in a very old house right high up, under the roof. My father had to bend all the time. A week or two later we moved to a newer house, also belonging to this same family. They were called the Heyers, one of three sets of Heyers in Eutin. These new Heyers gave us a room with a higher ceiling, right at the top of *their* house. My father could stand up straight.

There was a bed for two people with shiny brass railings, I slept on a prickly straw mattress on the floor; with a puffy blue and white checked featherbed. Two windows opened up to the Post office, where friendly ladies sat waving and laughing, we could have touched hands if we really stretched! Our room was tiny, the toilet downstairs on the next floor we shared with the whole house. No-one had a bathroom. The owners of this house lived on the ground floor. Their daughter Ursula had big staring eyes. She was eleven. Her father was still in the war, no-one knew where, nor when he would come home. They said things in a different way from my parents. I liked the way they spoke and I *loved* the way Frau Heyer cooked! We were allowed to use their kitchen, but soon we all became a big family, with Tante Inge (I was allowed to call her that) doing all the cooking which we ate together at a long wooden table with a low lamp hanging over it. Tante Inge knew how to cook unusual things, always delicious. She used fruit and vegetables; lucky Ursula to have such a mother! Ursula stayed at home. She had something wrong with her brain, she couldn't read or write. She could play though. For almost a year I missed proper school, but now I had to go again. After school we picked dandelion leaves for the rabbits outside. We made a dark den in the roof of the outhouse; it was full of spiders and cobwebs, but we swept it and got old boxes and cloths and cushions. It was our own little home.

<u>May 1945</u>. There were no air raids in Eutin. Once I saw dirty, ragged people walking down the middle of

our road, at least five in each row. Were they going to the station, just around the corner, about thirty or forty of them? They carried nothing and looked sort of burnt. My mum told me they had come on trucks from Hamburg where there had been a terror-raid like in Swinemünde. They were refugees. Somebody must have had a plan where they could go? Sometimes there were dirty ragged soldiers walking on our street. They also had nowhere to go. The town was filling up with refugees from everywhere. Then British soldiers were coming. The Germans were afraid. Tante Inge said we should spend the night in her wooden summerhouse next to a nearby lake. It was quite a long walk. Nobody had cars so we loaded up a little wagon to pull, with bedding and bread and apples and stuff and walked for about three hours, after dark, to this place. It was very exciting. If the British came to Eutin and the FGG (fierce German grandfathers) put up any resistance, there might be danger in staying at home...best to hide until it was all over! Ursula and I crept up a little ladder and made ourselves a bed under the eaves of the summerhouse. The grownups slept on chairs downstairs. No-one heard even a single shot. It was a silent night. In the morning, Tante Inge stuck her head out to see if anything was going on. The lake lay still, even the birds seemed completely quiet .

We soon discovered the British had entered Eutin from the *other* side and were already running the town. After a day or two when there was nothing left to eat we walked back to town, feeling sheepish but also a little wary. It was not long before I saw my first British soldier. There were plenty of them in jeeps but this one was strolling along. I did the V for victory sign and said: "I can speak English" and he laughed and said "how come?" so I told him I was from Pretoria. Then he gave me some CHOCOLATE! And guess what: it worked every time!

Tante Inge decided we needed new dresses for Pentecost, a special holiday in Germany. We would go for a long walk through the woods and right round a lake to a restaurant where one could eat jellied eels at Pentecost. I didn't know or care what jellied eels were, but I loved the dresses the dressmaker made for us: pale blue with large pleats front and back and white lace collars. Ursula and I looked like sisters. Tante Inge enjoyed seeing her daughter playing so happily, I don't believe Ursula had ever had any friends.

My new school was only 10 minutes walk from home. I loved going there and all the things we had to do. The war was finished now and although the fighting had stopped there still was no food. Small girls were not vain then...my mother found me some boots for the coming winter from the CARE parcels she helped to distribute. One boot was brown and the other was black but they were warm and dry. The hand-knitted knee length socks made from thick sheep's wool scratched and prickled, but they helped the boots to stay on. I also owned a winter coat, made out of an army blanket. The words

'DEUTSCHE ARMEE' were printed in large letters, fortunately only on the inside. For Christmas the big surprise was a muff made from rabbits' fur. The fur came from the rabbits Ursula and I had been carefully feeding in previous summer months. One must learn, to 'harden one's heart', said Mutti.

The British were super: they came to our school and we had to take off our clothes so they could decide who was too thin. I was one of the lucky ones! From that day onwards thin girls were allowed soup with fatty blobs swimming on top, as well as a cream cracker. I brought mine home, so my mother could have some too.

Eutin was fun. There was a convent where a nun taught me to play the recorder and piano. She was quite hunched, with a twisted crippled foot....as we had no piano my mother sent me to practise across the road: our grocer owned an upright in his tiny storage room. There, amongst sacks of flour and weevils, I sat each day, practising on a honkey-tonk, but I didn't know the difference; I was happy. Sometimes happiness *is* like that: *not* knowing!

Soon I had friends, who invited me to come and play at their houses, or even to sleep there sometimes. This put an end to the thumb-sucking habit. My best friend Jutta would laugh for sure, if she noticed. It stopped, for ever, there and then, a triumph! We went to recorder lessons together. She thought me clever because I played the piano. Her mum was a professional singer who showed off like mad, wearing ex-tra-or-di-nary clothes! She'd come to our house, stand outside the windows, sing a sonorous bit of opera full blast, to make us hear she'd arrived. The whole street knew! My own parents were so dull by comparison. Mind you, they made friends with Colonel Jones, and his family, who were the British 'rulers' of Eutin. Now these people lived in an old-fashioned smart house, with a huge grand piano and they had a car and amazing food. Going there was *really* something. They gave me a book of Arthur Mee's 'Everlasting Things'."

"My parents were always out. This was because my father was an important person, a Bürgermeister, which means everybody knows you. I was the 'Bürgermeisters daughter'! When they went out at night they just said: "go to bed when you've done your homework and you can borrow our radio." It was a very little radio. I remember them listening to it, when the war ended and my mother cried. They had more and more friends. One New Years Eve they felt sorry for me and said: "Here is an alarm clock. We will set it to wake you up at midnight and we will give you a glass of port-wine and our radio, so you can listen to the music at midnight and drink a toast to the New Year." That's how my parents were.... They *had* to go out, because my father was so important. One morning after they'd been out to dine with friends, my father woke up, and managed, but *only just* to get out of bed and open a window. He had smelt gas. My mother was still *fast* asleep. It seems I had left the gas on just enough to almost kill them both. After heating my supper and eating it alone, I'd gone to my attic room and gone to bed." This is *one* way to learn to be more careful.

"I had long thick pigtails in those days. It's strange, but I don't remember washing my hair very much, maybe one doesn't need to when one is only eleven or twelve. My birthdays were fun too: I was allowed to invite a few girls from my class to come to my attic where we giggled and laughed and ate cake with lemonade.

The lemonade is much better now... during and straight after the war German lemonade tasted vile. I can't imagine what it was made of. Anyway, it was pink. I learned about old customs like walking two-by two in procession, while carrying a paper lantern with a lit candle and singing:

"*Laterne, Laterne, die Sonne Mond und Sterne, Brenne aus mein Licht, brenne aus mein Licht,   Nur meine kleine Laterne nicht....*"

This was to mark November the first, a gloomy day for so many reasons and yet the happiest for young children in Schleswig Holstein. In the icy winters I built up fond memories, wearing my new winter coat with fur hem and a fur muff, going to midnight Mass in sparkly snow, and yes, I *did* remember the rabbit, but it felt so lovely wearing this, especially at night!   Unforgettable too was Spring, with snowdrops and carpets of primroses and later that scented lilac along the way to school; how lucky I was!

Tante Inge liked to sunbathe in her deckchair in the backyard; she'd go really brown, already in May. Chatting to her, baking in the sun, I had my first brush with psychic matters: "When will my husband come home from the war" she asked and I replied, (chancing it, I knew): "in exactly four months from today".... Surprisingly this is what *really* happened. I acquired a reputation for soothsaying.

I never succeeded again. Mind you...curing warts in the Schleswig Holstein way might just fall into this category: *If you wish to cure a wart, first wait until full moon, then sit outside under the moon, but it has to be midnight, then, allow a slimy snail to creep over the offensive growth.* Mine fell off three days later, not just one, but a whole nest of them on my left knee. Really!

In summertime everyone's attention was turned towards our beautiful lake, the Eutiner See, where there were long wooded walks around the shores, sailing boats and regattas and, passing over a little wooden bridge, an area given over entirely to swimmers. Each summer a patient, a very brown man in swimming trunks, held onto a fishing rod *at the end of which was a child*, learning to swim. It was probably an especially strong construct, with a harness to be strapped around the prospective swimmer. I wished I'd been taught that way!

It has to be said that swimming in natural lakes takes some getting used to: there are ducks and 'bits' and slimy things, unlike the Pretoria swimming pool.

Lakes have a strange odour, which changes with the seasons, and when certain algae take over... even I refused to go in! Those four years In Eutin were the richest and happiest ever: real parents, real friends, real seasons, excellent teachers, adventures of a kind that I had not had before.

One 'adventure', never revealed to my parents, was the day a 'Tommy' said I could have some chocolate if I came with him to his barracks, not very far from my school. I was happy to be engaged in a conversation with this nice young man, who had enough chocolate to *give away*! The barracks were empty and he took me to his bed where we sat down. Chatting he went to his cupboard to get the chocolate. Then he put his arm round me and stroked my upper leg. His hand went under my skirt......

Grabbing my chocolate I pulled away and ran out shouting: "you are very rude"....and ran and ran, until I was sure he was not following....

Admittedly there were few chocolates, no treats and new clothes, only that intangible thing called 'culture'. This sounds so pompous.

I was learning to savor and appreciate the things that stay with you for life: smells, tastes, poetry and songs, classical music, art, theatre, even a brief bit of ballet, school excursions, friends who were weavers, potters, painters... a total life experience. As soon as the war ended creative activities sprang back to life. Most adults we knew were making things, useful things, such as thickly woven sheep's wool rugs, or warm prickly knee length socks, these admittedly, I came to loathe. We knew potters and furriers and tailors and the most indescribable medieval shoemaker who worked in a dark 'cave-like' cellar by the market. Another regular was a man who beat brass into ashtrays and wall hooks and ornamental candlesticks. In those dark years after the war, when there was *nothing* to be found in the shops, these wonderful creative persons were the salt of the earth.

Right in the midst of *general renewal and rebirth* I also *began* to understand about dying: my grandparents in their dismal Old Age home died one after the other. Poor Ida and Alexander had become two ancient, grumpy persons, with an unpleasant odor and nothing but complaints. Their flight from the Russians, leaving behind their lives, home and possessions, had broken their spirits. There was nothing we could do for them.

My father was relieved when their suffering was over. They died about one year apart, in 1947 and 1948 and were both buried in Lübeck. The organist played Handel's Largo, both times. To this day I can't hear this without thinking of dismal wintry funerals....mixed with guilt that I'd felt no love for them at the time when they most needed it.

• • •

My 'best' friend Gabriele lived on a farm. She invited me to spend time there; an amazing experience, because of the good food, the horses which were 'mating', the family's own small lake where we swam in the nude,...the golden glow around all this early sensuous awakening of the innocent kind!

We played recorder duets, folksongs, little pieces by Bach, Telemann. Once I'd left Eutin we lost touch. I liked her name so much that it was passed on to my first daughter. But my very, very 'best' friend was Jutta. I wish I could remember why. It is complex: we were classmates; she had this loony singer-mother. We also played recorder duets. We roller-skated, with some gusto; I fell and broke my right arm in three places. This was established only one day later, when I had been dragged along to visit the grandparents in Lübeck, all the time moaning about my arm. My parents thought I was trying to get out of going! The following day an X-ray revealed three fractures; my poor arm was in plaster for months. How quickly one learns to do everything with the left arm. My teachers were impressed by both handwriting and drawings. In all these events Jutta was always around. We gave each other confidence, advice, and exchanged secrets. Teenage private ones!

I had become a teenager who was called "Fräulein" for the very first time: I no longer had to do a 'Knicks' when shaking hands with grownups, (a 'Knicks' being a small curtsey) but also, I had a crush on a boy called Uwe. By then I was a pianist of roughly Grade Vlll level, and, at the very end of our four years in Eutin, a beginner violinist. A late start, better late than never! I'd been roped into a group of young musicians who were being trained to play Haydn's Toy Symphony. What an honor! Uwe was the concertmaster and I sat at the back, assigned to the *vital* task of playing the 'cuckoo'. This meant I had to count carefully and come in with my lamentable 'cuckoo' at just the right split second. If ever there was a task I was not able to fulfill, this was it! I soon learned to fake the counting and came in, *often* in the right spot, by ear. Story of my life. But this is when it all started: my love for the violin was born. I pleaded and my parents actually managed to track one down. It was 'mine' on an indefinite loan from the kind Heyer family who owned one, stored in their attic. A lovely thing it was too, with gut strings and a carved scroll in the shape of a lion. I was entranced.

Nearly all young violinists in Eutin had lessons with a gaunt old lady called Lila Kroening-Devantier. (She was actually the first female violinist to be employed *professionally* as rank and file player in a German symphony orchestra.) To get to her I had to walk up Bahnhof-strasse, turn right past the station and the windmill... and at the end of the road was her ancient house with low-beamed ceilings, a sanctum of magic mystery: the sound of violins. I was not taught in her large dark music room with mysterious objects and pictures, but in a tiny, sunny spare room. On the wall a beige cloth wall-hanging with embroidered and appliquéd Egyptian figures of the antique variety, entered my subconscious then and has just resurfaced, as I write. I worshipped this teacher...and everything about her.

Within four months she invited me to perform at one of her prestigious pupils' concerts: I played, with piano accompaniment, an arrangement of a song by Mozart called 'Komm lieber Mai'. One of the three Frau Heyers present told me afterwards that the violin sounded wonderful and that she was proud of me. As it was really *her* violin I was gratified. My parents could not come for some reason. After the concert I was accompanied home, with a longish detour, by Uwe. On this walk we promised each other to correspond when I had arrived in Africa and that we would *never* forget each other.

It took half a century before we saw each other again.

I was just 14 years old; four of the happiest, and also the most dangerous years of my life in Germany were over. We left with many tears, said goodbye to vast numbers of friends and got on a train to Oslo, to catch a cheap freighter sailing for CapeTown.

I was numbed, leaving behind my first boyfriend, my friends and my violin-teacher. Life was no longer worth living.

My mother was sulking too. We couldn't share my fathers' vision of our future in Africa.

July 10th, 1949. The Bay Beach Hotel, Seapoint, CapeTown.

Dear Uwe, my parents are spooked by the coincidence that they have the same room number as in 1938. It's nice here, very windy, as we are just by the sea...I see it from my window. Every day my father goes to town to find a job with various former colleagues, but so far he has no luck. I look in the newspaper each morning to see if I can find one, for him, but it seems I'm not old enough to get this right. Most friends from before the war have gone elsewhere, even their favorites, the Kraemers, who now live on a farm many miles from here. We are going to buy a car and drive there. I miss everyone in Eutin and all I can do now is practise my violin, but quietly, as we are in the hotel.

It is hard for my parents. Perhaps it will be fun to go to that farm. I can't remember the Kraemers, he is called Pop, she is called Eve. Please write to me at the farm next time. I wonder if I'll ever go to school again!

Love, Inge.

As far as my father's job was concerned the weeks in CapeTown appeared to be fruitless. The way forward was to stop spending money on the hotel, to borrow a car and drive off into the unknown.

There could be no 'unknown' spot nicer than the 'Heidehof', a farm very near Plettenberg Bay, about 5 hours' drive from CapeTown. Our friends from pre-war days had bought the land in 1940, built their own house, in the style of a old Cape

Dutch farmstead, along with a few outhouses and had established wheat fields, youngberries, bees, helped of course by black workers and learning new skills as they went. A brave move. Their kind offer, taking us, poor refugees,in... was one of the nicest things that happened to me: to live out in the 'bush', surrounded by breathtaking scenery, plants, birds, all the business of the daily chores, the space and sounds and smells... unforgettable, priceless. Eve Kraemer, a painter by profession and farmers wife by necessity, became my adored grown-up role model. She was so gentle, so funny, positive and kind; I was informed that ten years ago we had loved each other just as much. This was in the CapeTown era, when my father was locked up as prisoner of war and the Kraemers had be-friended us. Now 'Auntie Eve' took it upon herself to mother us all and feed us delicious food and, no doubt, stopped my parents from despairing. They were given jobs to do ...woodwork for my Dad, cementing stone steps, building a rondavel, soon we learned how to open beehives, wearing helmets with nets and gloves, we harvested youngberries and grenadillas, and cooked jam, to be bottled and sold. It was satisfying, fulfilling, bonding and exhausting......
After all that work we'd sit on the wide covered veranda of the thatched homestead and allow our eyes to scan an expanse of shrubs and trees dipping down into a valley framed in the distance by the mysterious Tsisikamma Mountains.

Just 15 minutes' drive down a winding road lies 'Nature's Valley', the most beautiful, then little known, beach in South Africa, where one picnics and swims. In no time we became *new* people, *new* South Africans, forever spoilt and unfit to live anywhere else! We were in paradise, underscored with a permanent chorus of crickets, birds and ominous rustlings in the grasses. My father drove along the 'garden route' several times, staying with old friends in Cape Town, still hunting for a suitable post in the world of ships, but he was already close to 50, no-one wanted him. The Ihlenfeldts were on the point of becoming 'farmers", just like the Kraemers! This pleased Erika...but Reini had doubts. I never believed, not even for a moment, that we'd end up as farmers. My parents were far too unpractical. I had no faith in their skills whatsoever.

After months of idyllic farm-life I was kitted out for the Holy Cross Covent in George, about two hours drive away. The farm food had built me up somewhat, I also had no idea how a beret should be placed on my head, without making me look like a complete idiot. Two stupid pigtails, long black stockings and a suspender belt along with four pairs of voluminous navy bloomers, tie and a pleated uniform, completed the picture. Who *was* this unbelievable hideous lumpen creature?

Mother Superior, in great wisdom, decreed I should sleep in the junior dormitory, as my English was somewhat poor, and attend school with juniors, until acclimatized. I recall my first night in the dormitory, surrounded by 'tinies'. I wasn't going to show how I hated being with them, but when those lights went out I burst into hysterical tears. Somebody reported this. I was questioned.

On the following day I was established with girls in my own age group, within days all was well. Well? *Quite* well........

One of the hardest things is to be woken at six by a nun ringing a bell: you are expected to leap out of bed and kneel down to pray. Unforgettable: semi-conscious sliding out of bed onto your knees... putting your head on the bed to imitate prayer and yet sleeping another twenty odd seconds. One or two early risers could be heard murmuring prayers but I don't think I ever managed! Twenty or more beds then had to be made by us unfortunates and were measured by a nun armed with a ruler; she closed one eye to judge the alignment. *Everything had to be perfect.*

There were *lurking* difficulties...not to do with language or bed-making .....but with the simple fact that I was German. The War had not been forgotten in 'Wasp' South African schools...where most nuns came from England or Ireland. One or two really had it in for me. Someone, not a nun of course, stole my tuck box, a miraculous gift of assorted goodies, sent to me by a friend of my parents in CapeTown. I felt crushed on all fronts, battling with all the holy stuff such as Mass first thing before breakfast,... daily prayers of the Angelus, when the bells rang... all this was so alien and yet, as a Catholic, one had to conform. I felt trapped. Later in the term there was 'retreat' for the Catholics, which meant *no* talking, *no* school work, for three whole days! I was speechless, (which was the whole idea, of course.) Then I pointed out there was all that catching up to do and I could not afford to spend three days reading improving tracts about saints and so on .... This was not appreciated. "She's behaving like a 'bloody German", is no doubt what they thought.

On Saturdays there were 'etiquette' lessons. We were instructed what *not* to say at dinner parties (*never* talk about religion or politics) what *not* to wear (nothing too short or shiny) and which books to avoid. There were all manner of humiliations on a daily basis, nuns inspecting your nails, your closet, your bathtub, your bed-making and woe to anybody who wasn't towing the line. Every Saturday there was dry-cleaning ones uniform with a little damp rag, and shine ones shoes, a discipline similar to that in the army, only more ferocious, with feral nuns, giving black looks with their unfailingly sharp eyes...and black marks. All-powerful and constantly breathing down ones neck: the enemy!

I kept my head down for a while, becoming more outspoken as time went by. My only comfort was the splendid music hall, where I spent as much time as possible, practising both violin and piano. This was my salvation. The nuns began to soften when it appeared I had won several gold-medals at the local Eisteddfod, bringing glory to the school.

None of these troubles were relayed to my parents. Our letters, written under weekly supervision, were censored. I had the advantage of writing in German of course, and I doubt if any of the nuns could cope with that. Still, one never knows.....I even managed a correspondence with Uwe in Germany; changing his name to Ewu seemed to fool the nuns. In this way we stayed in touch, even under these most trying conditions! Innocent letters told him about my first experience of Gilbert and Sullivan's "Mikado", studying the role of Katisha, the ugly sub-heroine. I had memorized all my arias and soon found myself on the stage, feeling rather silly.

To my relief my operatic career was short-lived...,I was complimented into the orchestra pit instead, my voice, allegedly, too soft to carry more than about three yards. It has to be said that playing the violin in the pit did me a lot of good. I had only been at it for about a year after all!

While all this fitting in, adapting and adjusting was going on my parents had set themselves up in the Namib Desert. My father left no stone unturned, and of course, he found a right worm under one of them: a job in South West Africa, in a god-forsaken harbor called Walvis Bay. He was to be in charge of a firm called Sturrock & Woker, which ran an agency with offices right in the harbor. The job came with a grey breezeblock house, and loo, out in the sand-dunes. Yes! Walvis Bay *really* is in a desert, with almost daily sandstorms, no electricity, no sanitation and one main road. A Railway Institute, mainly used by desperate and drunken sailors provides entertainment.

In 1950 the Ihlenfeldts took up residence in their first real home since 1939,... and there they stayed for eight years! To visit South West Africa from school was unthinkable...a three-day / four-night train journey both ways! So eventually I was moved to another Holy Cross Convent, this time in Windhoek, only about 12 hours away from Walvis Bay, same sort of nuns, running a rather less 'frightening' establishment, or perhaps I'd just got used to boarding schools by then. The girls were a mixture of German, English and Afrikaans speakers, the nuns as before, mostly Irish or from England. I didn't miss George, so cold and wet.... and so very strict.

Windhoek Convent, hot and dusty, with a swimming pool and daily siestas during the hottest part of the day, offered a great deal less holiness than the George Convent, where our fanatical Mother Superior had ruled with such an old-fashioned iron rod.

Things were more relaxed. I felt in control of my own destiny. Only two more years and I would go to university somewhere, perhaps even back to Europe, to an aunt in Vienna?

How nice to be sixteen, to begin noticing ones body, ones hair and clothes, to make friends in a more meaningful way! School seemed a doddle, I had chosen the easy way out and there was in any case nothing seriously difficult to contend with: the nuns taught neither physics nor chemistry, so I left out maths, my worst subject, and coasted along on English, German, Afrikaans, history, geography, botany and music. Leaving out maths was a big mistake. I realized, six months before my final exams that this very subject is needed to study science at University. However, at first my new school was great and I made huge advances in every way, even to being nominated prefect for several terms.

During my final year I was allowed out of school to have private violin lessons with a local professional, now sorely in need of a more methodical approach. My teacher, a German aristocrat who, unforgettably, had a small gold crown painted on his car doors, not only had high standards, but was also very kind. Whenever I played badly I blamed it on the lousy food at the convent; he always took the hint by inviting me into his kitchen and offering me salami and liver sausage bread-rolls. Now that's the way forward!

Several events stood out during that time:

We were starved in more ways than one: girls of 16 and 17 feel the need to befriend the opposite sex. I was beginning to gaze at the priest and the altar boys, or anything in trousers in a somewhat hypnotic way. It was surprising the nuns allowed me out to spend time with the aristocrat violin teacher. But we both behaved immaculately. This was the time when 'attachments' could become both troublesome *and* pleasurable. My class teacher, Sister Dympna, who could speak German, was a large ungainly nun, palpably unhappy in her own skin. She would walk up and down in our senior dormitory saying her rosary when we went to sleep, restless as a caged lion. She had a crush on me; I found cream cakes in my desk and she made me a brown taffeta party dress, God knows why. I suppose she enjoyed taking my measurements. It was all very proper. And nice for me, to be thought so wonderful,....even by a poor, dumpy, disturbed nun.

During holidays teenage hormones were on the rise. Our group of boys and girls who met up on bicycles, somehow managed to enjoy life, despite the god-forsakenness of Walvis Bay. There were long afternoons in a beach hut, reached after much heavy pedaling through sand-dunes (this was horrible if not impossible) where we sat about, picnicking and flirting. We met in each others homes and listened to strange songs like "I'm a lonely little petunia in an onion patch,"Charlie Kunz creations and pop songs of the forties such as 'Always' and 'Yes, my darling daughter.' The infamous Railway Institute showed appalling films; we saw each one through. There was little else to do.

My *special* boyfriend, Patrick Hamilton, was also keen on Elaine Bramwell, who had a rather handsome brother called Leslie, whom I fancied as well. We all fancied each other! And, oh yes, the local baker's son, Karl-Heinz Maischatz, how could one ever forget such a name, he fancied me for my musical skills, a kindred soul, a decent pianist. His father baked marvelous pastry. This bespectacled boy was not part of our bicycle group...., a much too studious and earnest fellow, who, I heard later, died very young.

Then there was a German boy, who fell madly in love ...he had a memorable way to remind me of his feelings: a job in the new Power Station allowed him to send me nightly greetings by switching off Walvis Bay's power supply in three short bursts at 10pm. He also had the deplorable habit of visiting my mother, when I was back at school. He'd sit and sit, wanting to talk about me. At first she felt sorry for him, later it was decided to be brutal, send him on his way.

So, a pattern emerged,...innocent gadding about, no drinks, no drugs, only simple clean fun. We were 'good' children, and very well controlled by the strict morals of the time. I'd as good as forgotten Uwe in Germany, although we did still write occasional letters. There were new attachments, nothing too serious, and for us all an imminent reversal of the state of dependence on parents to the state of 'going out into the world'. Of all these young persons I was the only one to go to university. I was still a very immature and babyish person. My obsessive violin playing, after only four years was not quite of a high enough standard to take up further studies. "Don't even think about a career in music", was my parents' advice. "It's not 'done' for a woman to play in orchestras. " "Besides", said my mother," you'll never find a husband with this terrible scar on your neck...do you *have* to practise all the time?" (Parents! They have such antiquated, annoying ideas!)

"Why not become a scientist, like your grandfather," they suggested, meaning well ......about six months before my 'matric.' I pointed out one needed maths for that.

I was easily 'led' then, and without much ado settled down to catch up on a subject I hated and had successfully avoided for over a year.

A marvelous Irish nun, Sister Mary Anthony, took it upon herself to sort out what little math's I had, and added the missing bits in record time. It was she who discovered I needed glasses, as I sat frowning at the blackboard. (I passed, but only with a C, when all other subjects had been A's or B's.) This was my life's story so far...always catching up, learning at great speed things that others had done long before me. Learning English and Afrikaans aged five, then sorting out German once settled in Eutin, discovering violin aged fourteen, (really a dead loss if you're serious about it,) endlessly changing schools, countries, friends, ...*nothing but hurdles and more hurdles...... ....*

There was another (secret) plan my parents had: to send me to Vienna, to study violin with some illustrious guru, but I only heard about that much later.

Well, I'd managed the maths. The next hurdle: a degree in science.If only I had stood up for myself.

I was uselessly, feebly submissive.   A push-over, a door-mat. "....and you can have violin lessons too," they said. What a hope.

Without a single physics or chemistry class in my life I would soon be attending first year lectures! The only preparation for this was a little book I had exchanged for a voucher I'd won in an essay competition in South West Africa. There it is, on my bookshelf to this day: "Die Welt in der Retorte," a modern Chemistry for everyone, with 180 drawings and 16 charts! It did not help that it was in German, but reading it proudly, carefully, I believed I'd have a fighting chance as a serious student. Ironic: the prize-winning essay had been on the subject of my greatest love...the violin. It was no big deal winning the first prize in South West Africa in 1952: in such a huge country there were very few schools!   Touchingly, inside the cover it gives my address: E. Ihlenfeldt, P.O. Box 18, Walvis Bay. Why is this so moving, 55 years on? There is also a holy card, the kind that nuns give their pupils on special occasions.   It says: Unum est necessarium!   In sua voluntate, nostra pax.

Josephine and children's zither lesson 1890s

Coelestine c1900

Coelestine and Erica, London c1910

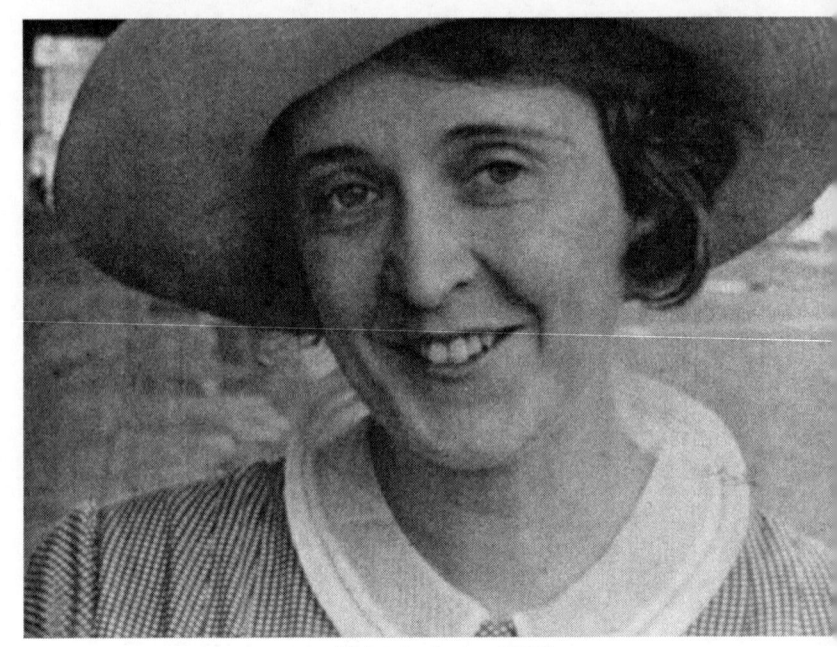

Erica in Accra 1936

Erica and 'Knups' in Pretoria 1943

'Mami's castle' Mageregg c1960

Evelyn and Gabi in Ndola 1964

Part 2

Growing Up.

1953. I've burnt my school books. I am 18 years old and 'reside' in Fuller Hall, the official residence for 200 girls, on campus in Cape Town. (should I say 'young women'?) My mother was in tears when we said goodbye. I can't bear it when she cries. I know she loves me. I love her too.

Everything is thrilling, I feel so excited! We all have our very own room, part of H Flat, there are nine of us and we're mostly from distant parts of southern Africa...Nyasaland, South West, Transvaal, Eastern Cape, Southern Rhodesia and Natal. What a collection of travelers! It will take me 3 days and four nights to get back home by train. Now that I live away from parents and school I am classified an ex-enemy alien, which means I have to visit a police-station every three months to show what I am up to. What if I forget? It's too bad I'm still on my father's passport...why can't I have one of my own? Why do I have to be a German?

Perhaps 'freedom' is overrated, I'm not sure yet. By my modest standards (little money, the War, convents etc) I'm on a roll and simply can't believe my luck. 'Freshettes' like myself pin a green bow to their clothes. But only for 3 months. This is one of the rules our delightful lady warden, Mrs. Emmett, tells us to obey. We are also expected to sign out whenever we leave the residence, stating time and destination, have to be in by midnight; only one night a week though, having told the warden with whom and where we are going. Modified 'freedom' then, modified rapture, for a while.

Should one dare infringe there is a house committee, who are very strict indeed; one would probably be 'gated'. Still, compared to the convent this isn't at all bad: it's sheer heaven.

I am Cinderella compared to the lovelies in H Flat: everyone has more and better clothes. Some of them even use make-up!

And they have loads of pocket money. Here I am, still in a navy-blue convent skirt with one of my Mum's hand knitted pullovers. She makes all my clothes and they are terrible. Do I mind? Yes. But my parents pay for my fees and residence, so I try not to. And for my music lessons.

There are more pressing things to worry about: getting to lectures in the morning, practicals most afternoons. Being signed up for Physics, Chemistry, Botany and Zoology leaves little time for much else. I have white lab coats, regularly laundered by the colored maids; I slice up smelly dogfish or peer into a microscope, all this is much better when one wears a lab gown that goes with the job. It's all rather fun. For dinner we don academic gowns, mine is venerable, has seen many previous owners. The effect of such garments is all-powerful.

Reality soon sets in: the worst is Physics. I recall sitting far back in one of those sloped lecture theatres trying to understand what a startlingly shriveled old man is talking about, and simply not finding the way into a single sentence he utters. There are no tutorials. No-one knows of my agony and disbelief. I have never been faced with something I couldn't at least grasp just a little bit. I try and try and take notes and looked at them. It is hopeless. I am too proud to tell anyone. No-one else in H flat is doing physics. "So much for my convent education", I think,.... "what shall I do?"

Anyway,.... there are more interesting events. Like Rag week, and the fun of staying up all night with the men from Smuts Hall across the road. For once there are no restrictions! Our float is called A BAD 'UN .... Everyone dressed in Arab clothes. To this day I cannot work out what we were portraying. Each year wearily patient Cape Townians put up with mad students begging for money on their floats parading through town, all for good causes, naturally, like helping colored people. I am the 'freshette' chosen to go and chat up the Mayor of CapeTown to buy raffle tickets during Rag week. Why me, I wonder when I see my picture in the 'Cape Argus'.

My parents in distant Walvis Bay are amazed and proud.

Cape Town University had always been liberal and emancipated, compared to others in South Africa. Totally un-awakened politically, I had no views on the lot and lives of other races.

Nuns never spoke of such things, nor did my parents. When other students asked me if I would join various action groups I always refused. In my closed-in way I needed all my time to myself. I had also learnt to be wary of 'being German'. Looking back I would say I had the social conscience of a twelve year old. This comes of spending four years under the tutelage of nuns. History was a collection of stories in a book. The ancient Greeks, the French Revolution, the Boer War, all good basic events to learn about, but I don't remember ever learning how to assess and judge anything. "Never talk about religion and politics", was what our 'etiquette nun' had advised. This suited me just fine. I was used to that!

Kolbe House, Rondebosch.

One of my first brave ventures was to find this centre situated down a steep hill from my new 'home'. I walked into Kolbe House noting times for Sunday Mass in the chapel and other activities which sounded like fun, the first one to attend was a tea party on the lawn under a venerable tree. Mrs. Spring, the housekeeper, had prepared a lavish spread for about twelve of us and I offered to help pour the tea. It appears this immediately identified me as 'a leader' and soon I was roped into all manner of things I really didn't want to do at all. Moral: never offer to pour other people's tea.

Sunday Mass in the chapel turned out to be a very good way to befriend other students.

In later months I heard a strange tale from twins called Helene and Therese : "our brother mentioned he'd seen a 'freshette' at Mass and that he just knew he would marry her one day. Only seen, not even spoken to her! Imagine that!" I thought this was very romantic.

I had settled into Botany studies with great gusto. It was even moderately interesting. Months later, during a practical in a laboratory I noted one of the demonstrators peering down my friend's microscope. Inside his tweed jacket I imagined broad shoulders, bearing silent witness to protective, caring kindness. I cooked up some question to ask him, hoping he would peer down my microscope as well. He did look vaguely familiar. Later, strolling down the steps in front of Jameson Hall, to the residences, where he'd parked his car, he told me he'd seen me at Mass, that he had graduated from Science last year,...and that he was now studying for a BA. Impressive! A tiny gold crucifix on his lapel told me he was very religious. He had beautiful dark eyes with enviably long eyelashes. We both felt very shy.

I signed in, went to my room, and thought about 'my' demonstrator.

Another nice boy, also Catholic, seemed equally impressive. This one was a redhead, with sticking-out ears, studying law, very witty and amusing. I liked him a lot. He never so much as noticed me, he was obsessed with another girl. I began to think I liked him even more than Pierre and more than the very rich Jewish boy, who also had a car and stood to inherit South Africa's major Peanut butter industry. Now this one was very earnest indeed and decided I had to meet his parents: "they are curious about you", he told me.

In Bishopscourt, one of the poshest areas in town, in an intimidating mansion, over dinner, they questioned me about my parents and the War. They seemed satisfied with my account. Once their son had me back in his car to take me out some place he became somewhat demanding. I was very unfriendly about even a kiss.... so this little episode came to a sudden end. I had hurt his manly feelings. How difficult it is to get these encounters right! I didn't mean to hurt him, only to wriggle out of any sort of physical stuff ....this seemed top priority in those truly innocent post-convent days. And yet there was a bit of lust...like when I saw my Botany demonstrator Pierre in a tweed jacket! How does one describe such virginal, innocent 'lust': no more than a wish to be noticed and admired and perhaps, held, briefly. Perhaps I was just a tweed fetishist, unknowingly. Somewhere in this new phase of existence is a first year science student, trying to keep up and feeling, surprisingly, in control of her social life. Those three years ahead,at that time, seemed like an eternity of new delights and experiences, all waiting to be lived.

Soon I signed up with a venerable teacher, Maria Neuss, who in turn had studied with the great violin pedagogue Carl Flesch. This means a great deal to a violinist! To me it was a passport to violinistic respectability. When I presented myself at the College of Music the authorities decided Neuss would be my teacher; a great honor. Unforgettably, she always had a cigarette between her lips while demonstrating; the ash would become longer and longer until it fell on her instrument and slid down into the f-hole. All her students were waiting for the day her valuable instrument went up in flames. This riveting lady was the wife of bushy-bearded conductor Fritz Schuurman, in charge of the University symphony orchestra. My place was at the back of the second violins, a case of sink or swim. I had never played in a 'proper' orchestra before and found it very hard. 'The Mikado' in George did not count. This was terrifying, the steepest learning curve, ever.

To be honest, the thing I loved more than anything was walking down the hill to attend the rehearsals, to be part of the magical atmosphere in the venerable building and the feeling of being accepted by all the music students and teachers who were part of the 'band.' No doubt they despised me, a mere science student. One learns to keep ones head down in such a group.

Those were the days when it was still safe for a young lady to walk home alone in the dark after rehearsal, all part of being 'free' and grown-up. The fact that my path home took me past Kolbe house, where Botany demonstrator Pierre lived, became an added pleasure. I could call on him, he would walk me up the hill. The road between the College of Music and Kolbe House was aptly named 'Lovers' Walk'. Now don't get this wrong ....I was a convent girl!

Pierre quickly brought me to a part of life that was completely undeveloped: literature and theatre. He already had his B.Sc. and now was his time for English literature. His tiny student's room was full of books, both French and English. He was fluent in French and eager to involve me in all his experiences. I assumed he had French origins. First he made me read Baudelaire and then Graham Greene. The days were not long enough to fit everything in. I wondered about his father, who allowed him to stay at university for yet another three years! "He must be so well-off," I thought. Pierre even had a car! He loved all theatre and took me to the Labia Theatre (named after its patron, Count Labia) to see the controversial new play called 'Waiting for Godot', puzzling but material for much speculation. Pierre was always taking me out, we were getting fond of each other. There was so much to talk about.

When the time came to visit Walvis Bay for a few weeks I had already become a much more conscious creature. Strange, my parents seemed to disagree with me a lot! Stuck in Walvis Bay for six weeks, what a punishment!

Pierre and I wrote each other many letters. My old friends were still about, but I felt I'd moved on, being with them seemed different now. "Unspeakably hideous, smelly Walvis Bay," was all I could think, so I consoled myself listening, endlessly, to a recording of Bach's Chaconne for solo violin. I was obsessed. This was music for being alone, for dreaming. I was also committed to play a Mozart Divertimento for an event in our Common Room in Fuller Hall, at the beginning of next term. It gave me something to do. Other students got themselves holiday jobs to earn pocket money, but this possibility had not yet dawned on me. I must have been a real drag, mooching about for so long.

Fortunately I was not alone getting to Walvis Bay and back to CapeTown by old-fashioned steam train, other students joined in Windhoek and places further along the tedious treck southwards, with endless stops for picking up more coal and water. Sun beat down on the carriages and dust and soot flew into the windows wide open because of the uncomfortable temperature. We consumed vile food and prayed for nightfall, when the cooler air made it possible to collapse on our bunks. Needless to say, depending on the company, there were raucous goings-on.

Tucked up with Graham Greene and Baudelaire I remained one of the quieter passengers. Was it four days and three nights, or the other way round? I can't remember. There was a lot of Africa and it all looked the same: dry shrubs, dust, small flat-topped hills and distant karakul farms, the odd small dreary town...poor ragged black children running along the tracks, shouting, begging.....

On arrival the first thing is a hot bath. I have no memory of being picked up by anyone at the station. How did one get back to the University on the other side of Table Mountain? There is no memory, besides I would not have liked anyone to see me after such a trip.

The only thing in my cubby-hole: a letter from Pierre, what joy!

Ndola, Northern Rhodesia.
January 16th 1954

Dear princess, I want this letter to be waiting for you when you arrive. I so look forward to see you; my so-called holiday, as you know, has been quite demanding ...Dad seems to think I need to know more about the business. He insists I stay as long as possible, which is why I can't pick you up from the station. No doubt your father has managed to send one of his friends in CT to get you back to Fuller Hall.

As soon as I arrive I'll take you out and we can have a long talk. How about the Drive-in at Sea Point? We'll have our favorite: Banana and Bacon toasted sandwich! Love from Pierre   Ps It's my birthday today!

After this separation we both realize how much we care about each other; our delightful round of cultural explorations continues.

• • •

Soon exams were hanging over us: hard grind was now the only way forward and studying together was at least more fun than swotting alone. Armed with lecture notes, books and rugs we set out whenever we could to combine duty with enjoyment of beauty spots around the mountain, and on rainy days, Pierre's digs were an interesting prospect.....

This was a tiny cottage in the gardens of Kolbe House shared with a troubled fellow student obsessed with issues of race and injustice, an Afrikaaner who carried South Africa's pain on his shoulders. One day we found him staining his skin brown and getting together torn and filthy shirts, trousers and worn out shoes, in order to be like a poor colored laborer, looking for work. He then set out for the harbor to do research on the treatment of blacks and how it felt to be one.

I didn't know what to think. No-one else I knew wanted to do such a thing. Pierre stood by, concerned, interested, but mainly with the worry that all this would backfire in some way like the police finding out ...perhaps the greatest fear in apartheid South Africa. Leanings of dangerous sympathies for colored people were the perils that got one locked up in prison. It was all terribly hush-hush, best not talked about: there were spies about. We were sworn to secrecy.

My own awakening about bigger issues was a long time off, absorbed as I was by, lectures, laboratory practicals, lessons at the College of Music and the attentions of my devoted boy-friend. Still only friends, physical proximity began gently, slowly, surely. He confessed to being an 'experienced' man, who had slept with prostitutes in Beirut, and this information I, an innocent convent girl, took on board with due interest and curiosity. Both Catholics and wary of getting into 'trouble' Pierre hinted darkly on several occasions that we had to 'talk'...that there was something I *really* needed to know...and "why yes, of course," I said guardedly, not knowing what he was on about. Perhaps he wanted to get engaged? Perhaps he had some ghastly disease? What could it be...was there someone else? When he finally worked up the courage to tell me what was troubling him I was still none the wiser!

We'd devoured our favorite Banana and Bacon toasted sandwich at the Seapoint Drive-In when he revealed he was not French, as implied, but... *Lebanese*. Uncomfortably embarrassed, (I had never heard of 'Lebanese', and there were so many things I'd never heard of) I said: "I don't mind, honestly! But what exactly *is* 'Lebanese'?.."

I'm not sure he believed me.

Nevertheless, I was given a long spiel about 'Liban', and the Cedar of Lebanon, and Phoenicians, and Arabs... and how his family always spoke French. Somehow he managed to convey that there was something wrong with coming from Lebanon, and that I, being German, would mind, would think him an Arab. Feeling deeply sorry for him I was only at the very bottom end of a slow learning curve about such things. All I knew was that I cared about him very much. At that point I still had no idea that *anybody* would 'mind'. "Why did you say you were French?" I wondered, and his reply was: "because I speak French, because I love the French, and Lebanon belonged to France once." What he could never bring himself to say was: "I could pass for a French, Italian, Greek or whatever Mediterranean you'd like, but please *don't think of me* as an Arab, or Syrian, or a Jew." He needed that little golden crucifix on his lapel, he needed his golden-eyed German girlfriend, he needed his Belgian cousin (*his* uncle Mansour had married a Belgian woman, Marthe, their child was therefore 'Belgian...')

It was a case of racial inferiority-complex and I began to understand how he saw me, on some sort of pure-race pedestal. All this brought out my maternal / missionary instincts. He was so vulnerable. I would help him, be his crutch, and to hell with all this meanness and incomprehensible thinking. For a long time we avoided this topic. It was deeply embarrassing, not just for him, for us both.

Little time was spent with his twin sisters Helene and Therese, tall, gaunt, olive-skinned girls with short wiry curls: Therese the outgoing amusing one and Helene very serious. I began to feel Pierre did not like to be seen with them, by South African standards they looked a bit 'colored'. He had a problem with all this, perhaps? I was too cowardly to confront him and besides, I didn't want to upset

207

him. They also lived in the official residence on campus.

Year One of B.Sc. studies flew by and I found myself sitting the first University exams in Jameson Hall, or 'Jammie' as we called it. Pierre then flew off to France and Belgium to spend time with his cousin while I trecked for four nights and three days to languish in a Namib desert dump called Walvis Bay. Not fair, I thought.

The results, mercifully, only arrived in January, because they would have ruined my holidays. I had failed Physics and Chemistry, and the re-sits were scheduled for March. For the first time I had to eat humble-pie, never before had I failed so spectacularly.

1954 turned into a year of wrestling with fate, the odds against me: even though Pierre returned from his holiday in Brussels and Paris laden with gifts of French perfume and frilly sexy knickers I felt crushed by my efforts to keep up, on all fronts. I was certainly kept out of mischief trying to pass *two* failed subjects, without help from anyone. I did manage Chemistry but to my dismay Physics was a write-off, even the second time. Another year then, of my least favorite thing, and no escape!

Soon after I had to dissect the arm of a *real* corpse for the Zoology course in the famous Groote Schuur Hospital! Awesome!

Pierre of course passed everything and was always there for me, taking me to shows and Balls and lovely drives all over the Cape Peninsula. We were known on campus as a 'starry-eyed' couple, madly in love. I was still a virgin, and remained one for another year at least, but cut off from real life, politics, the big world. It was like living in a bubble. Inevitably, they have a way of bursting. You can't see it coming, but it's a foregone conclusion.

I think it was an unglamorous year, but in the end I managed to get on to the final year of Microbiology, which was what I had been aiming at all along. One so loses track of goals when one has to take so many small difficult steps.

Pierre and I had become secretly 'engaged' by the end of this time and somehow this closeness and security superseded all the science I was trying to absorb. I was still only 19 years old. My trouble was that I had absolutely no vision of what I really needed or wanted. That 'violin'-thing, that great passion, had died down. The 'science' thing was an unequal struggle, and there was no love at all. Pierre? Well, he was a rock. What other reality was there?

By this time my parents knew all about my French / Lebanese boyfriend. Prudently they said very little, but the implication was that they'd had experience of Syrian traders during their many years in Accra, mostly wealthy diamond smugglers, or at least shady in some way. I suppose they were trying to influence me and that they hoped this was a passing infatuation.

It never occurred to me my parents might be even remotely xenophobic. They'd lived in the *native* town of Accra, *not* with the whites in their own township, they had many Jewish friends, my father had enjoyed the favors of a pretty black mistress in his bachelor days, ...

By the time I started my third year my parents came to CapeTown and took us out for a drive near that spectacular bit of beach facing Table Mountain. I believed he'd won them over. Little did I know that, behind the scenes, there was an exchange of letters between the mothers! Pierre's mother had invited the Ihlenfeldts to visit Northern Rhodesia for Christmas, to break the ice a little. The reply, although polite, was utterly negative. The Ihlenfeldts had no wish to build any bridges; a marriage between a German and a Lebanese was unthinkable..........

Romantic Interlude in the Namib Desert

(a *true* story.) .....one of those interminable journeys from Cape Town to Walvis Bay a dusty, tired girl student is accosted by a boy student from Stellenbosch University, both going home for the holidays. He'd spotted her violin-case; he enquires about her studies and destination and then ends up having dinner with her as the train chugs slowly towards a tiny station in the middle of nowhere. The sun is setting fast. "Tot siens," (until I see you again) he mutters, looking deeply into her eyes... and when the train stops, those who are watching see him being picked up by a farmers' truck. He turns, he waves.......She slept badly, it was hot. Waking up early to stand in the corridor she gazes across the morning expanse of dusty dried shrubs. In the far distance is a horse and rider, trying to keep up, or even trying to catch up... puzzling. He gradually becomes larger, in fact, he is now quite near... waving his hat and shouting. Goodness, this is the student with whom she had dined last night! "Ek kan nie eet nie, ek kan nie slaap nie" he shouts,(I can't eat and I can't sleep) Will you let me visit you in Walvis Bay, or in Cape Town...? She shouts back that he should forget her: "I have a boyfriend already".....and sees him kick his horse hard ...to keep up. Poor thing, it was exhausted. She waves and waves become smaller, receding into the dust. What an opportunity missed...

Pierre and I survived another two longish holidays apart and I even got myself my first job in a fish meal factory in Walvis Bay. The work was measuring the percentage of moisture in shipments of fish meal in a special laboratory: if any sack of the stuff was too dry it might ignite in the hold of a ship and cause death and destruction, perhaps the most boring and smelly way to earn some cash you could ever imagine. There I was in my white lab coat piercing every bag of odorous fish meal with a special hollow needle containing a hygrometer, and then recording the result. Every single bag, and there were many hundreds, had to be pierced and accounted for. My parents seemed to be proud of me. I can't imagine why.

In Cape Town, working in the Groote Schuur Hospital laboratories was part of the Course: mainly testing Petri dishes full of bacteria and working with Xrays during microbiology practicals. The most interesting part of my three-year course was potentially the most dangerous; now there was little time left before our final exams. Suddenly three years of study had become ridiculously short.

As far as the great love affair went we had, after some discussion, decided to take a very big step: I was to 'lose' my virginity. It was I who wanted this..."we just can't go on the way we have for so long. We are grown-ups," ......and so on...

Why we decided to do it the way we did is a mystery now. We went for a walk at dusk along a private mountain path, behind the University, somewhere below the famous Rhodes Memorial and, standing up, resting against a sloping bit of 'Devil's Peak', Pierre 'deflowered' me. It was cold, calculated and painful, for both, and quite scientific really. No mindless passion, nothing sexy at all.

We both missed supper that evening.

Another dusty, interminable journey to Walvis Bay, more 'work experience', and, after six long weeks of so-called holiday I had a secret arrangement to meet Pierre on the train journey back to CapeTown, stopping off at a ghastly railway junction called De Aar.

We so needed to be together, alone and far from prying eyes. CapeTown to De Aar must have taken at least a day by car, and Pierre had arranged for us to stay the night in De Aar's 'finest' hotel!

One never forgets high emotions. Both exhausted, he from the long drive, me from the filthy train, our happiness to find ourselves together and completely alone in the middle of 'no-where' was overwhelming. We frolicked in a hot bath, dropped into bed and slept, intermittently. We were indescribably happy. It was our honeymoon, really.

September 1955. Help!....,my periods, they seem to be late! It's probably because of all this travelling... and being in Walvis Bay. My body reacts to everything. Even at school I sometimes missed periods, like in George, only every three months. Perhaps I'm just exhausted and also worried about Pierre and all that.... If they don't come soon I'll find a doctor...I know, I'll ask Mrs Emmett to tell me the name of some-one. No, what if I'm pregnant....I'd be kicked out of residence, and where would I go..., I'd better tell Pierre.

A medic confirmed there were signs of early pregnancy. To be certain he'd do another test and let me know, in a day or two. (Oh God!) I said I'd call back...I didn't want him phoning the residence. Two days later: the results are 'positive.' Pierre, solicitous, strong, collects me in his car and we drive up into the mountains to Bain's Kloof, where UCT's wooden shack for Botany student research is home for a night and a day. I wonder if the bumpy road might solve all our problems. We discuss our options: abortion, unthinkable, getting married at once: what about our finals, parents, where would we stay? I can't think at all, let alone 'straight'. Poor Pierre abandons me to 3rd year Botany students, hard wooden bunk-beds in a log cabin and the 'convivial' evening around the log-fire. The course will begin as the early morning mists lift. My closest friend Marilyn becomes my confidant. I am devastated. As I lie sleepless I consider gin and jumping off a cliff. It's all too humiliating...............................

"Please God, let me have a miscarriage." I wanted to be an unsullied, un-pregnant me again, studying for a B.Sc.

Just like dissolving morning mists, the shock of what I'd got myself into floated away, to be replaced by acceptance and courage...I made an appointment to talk to Mrs Emmett, our warden.

She was charming. I was embraced, congratulated and advised to send a telegram to my parents, not to be dejected. "You can get married, quietly," she said, "and stay in residence until after the exams are over, in nine weeks' time." I was surprised, suddenly everything appeared quite straight-forward and natural.

Mrs Emmett had only one request, that it should all remain secret. Whom had I told, only Marilyn? Then she too must be sworn to secrecy! I could have one night out, on the day of our wedding and was to sign back into residence the day after, and return into the fold as if nothing had happened. If the news got about it would have set a precedent.

The telegram arrived in my fathers' office; he left work early to break the news to my mother. She passed out. The doctor was called...It doesn't bear thinking about, their disappointment, shock and disgust with me and their shame at having to tell friends and family. I knew how my father felt, he'd made it all quite clear one day when he explained that "when different races mix the end result will be an unhealthy, unattractive, half breed, just look around you, look at all these poor coloreds in South Africa." He knew no better; it was the handed-down wisdom of his age, he'd never studied biology or science. I was shocked by his ignorance and saddened to realize he would never understand. I despised him then, and ignored him. He had no insight into the appalling state our relationship was in. My mother, more cunning and less outspoken, never came out with unscientific twaddle such as this, and eventually managed to put on a brave face. It was a learning curve for my parents too..... It is fair to say that I felt totally distant, for a very long time. At first, I admit, I hated them.

The hour of reckoning was on its way: first a 'quickie' wedding in the Catholic church in Rondebosch, with a tiny gathering of close friends, and Pierre's best man, followed by supper in a restaurant on the Main Road, on the corner to the church, but only the two of us and Father Fortune, the Jesuit priest who had married us. After that we drove to the "Red Sails" in Hout Bay, a small hotel near the beach, where we spent the night, listening to the waves and the wind. I was depressed and silent; to my surprise all joy and pleasure seemed to have vanished.

We were a married couple for one day, then it was back to 'swotting' for our finals, in separate lodgings. What a relief to get back to Fuller Hall. Life continued, almost as if nothing had happened, even after such an upheaval. Poor Pierre, he must have wondered what he'd let himself in for: an unresponsive, depressed 'wife', furious in-laws, another six weeks of studying and then...?

November and December flew by. I failed my finals, Pierre passed his. He, the practical one~ and the person with funding, rented a tiny house in Pinelands, a windy, bleak suburb; we moved in for a few weeks, to learn to live together and to meet our respective parents who had all decided to come to CapeTown. It was our first Christmas together. I had never cooked before.

This was the very least of my problems. Parents: when they arrived from Walvis Bay they took the line it was their duty to kit me out for my role as a wife...the trousseau, in other words. My mother dragged me around CapeTown's Adderley Street to find a flowery dressing gown and some respectable nightgowns. I was already blossoming and needed a loose-fitting maternity smock and one of those skirts with a hole cut out in the front for the expanding tummy. How ridiculous, how unglamorous! My mother was at least trying to make things better for me, but the tension was indescribable. My father offered us £100 pounds, to help with the expenses: my dowry! I suppose this was the equivalent of £1000 today (2007).

Pierre's stepmother Josephine was a woman of great warmth and poise. She showed no stress or doubt when *she* dined with us and with my parents, in our little house in Pinelands. With great sweetness she made light of everything I had produced, either burnt, overcooked or not cooked enough, but the wine was good and so the ice broke, just a little; my father even took a photograph of the occasion, a sign for sure that he had been won over by Josephine's undoubted charm.

For me this was the start of ten years of trust and affection for a   lady, who really understood what being a wife and a mother was about. We called her 'Nana', and she looked after me as if I was her own daughter even though she had two of her own: the toddler Danielle and Jacqueline, a convent-girl in Southern Rhodesia. I learned from Nana how to be practical and positive and to have standards in home-making I'd never come across before.

Pierre surprised me too. He returned from some outing with a very large sack of bran which he deposited on the kitchen floor. "This is for you" he said," my mother says pregnant women get very constipated and I wouldn't like that to happen to you, so take at least three large spoonfuls every morning!" This would be sufficient for the rest of my living days. I had never tasted anything so disgusting in my life. I was already hiding my stomach inside a smock. I was not even half-way through my pregnancy and strictly speaking the birth date *should* be in July....since we'd got married in October. I made suitably vague replies when I was queried about this. In the fifties one minded about such things. I tried to consume less, so the baby would remain small and not want to get born in a hurry. But I knew well enough when it was due.

Soon we were to leave Cape Town for good and settle into our real new life in Ndola, Northern Rhodesia. Still on my father's German passport I now received my own and it was British. Pierre, a resident of Northern Rhodesia, had a British passport. I became British, by marriage. Nothing to it, I thought, just strange: by marrying a Lebanese, who wished he were a Frenchman I, who had been an under-age passport-less German, had become British!

My new name Attala meant nothing less than att-allah....'gift of God'.

We flew, of course. No more god-awful train journeys for me! I had felt the baby 'move' once or twice in Cape Town, and so now there were the three us, in the clouds,.......for a while.

1950's Ndola was a very small place indeed.... nothing more than a shed for an airport, a few small shops, one hotel and the 'Bijou' cinema. At a rough guess there were no more than 3000 whites, who lived with Indian and Colored people in town. The entire country had a population of 37,000 Europeans. Some 2 million native people lived in townships, or out in the country, 'elsewhere'. Some came to work for the white man in the towns, some were employed in homes.

The Attala home was a stately double story mansion, with a tennis court, swimming pool and terraced garden and several servants permanently on duty; they lived in small quarters in the back garden.

• • •

Pierre and the 'new missus' are welcomed as befits the only son of the house. Two Siamese, 'Emir' and 'Emira', purr around our feet as we are led upstairs to a large bedroom overlooking the tumbling terraces of flowers in the garden. Intimidating, everything seems groomed, richly luxurious, foreign, substantial, outmoded.

There is a grand piano downstairs and a ping-pong room. Two black men in starched white uniforms take orders from Pierre as to time and extent of dinner later on. I have nothing to do, other than put my swollen feet up, or wander about, inspecting the pool and the plants. Nana has an excellent vegetable garden, which she tends herself, along with the Northern Rhodesian gardener. The rainy-season is well underway... earth and air has a muggy, damp smell. Now tired and looking forward to getting into that huge, satin-covered bed I note all opened windows have metal gauze to let in the air and keep the 'bugs' of central Africa out. A good idea! Unpacking takes less than five minutes. I own very little. There is a new green leather vanity case, a gift from Nana for Christmas; apart from a gold necklace, given to me by Pierre, and some modest baubles collected over the years there is little of interest in it; needs are minimal, no pills, no lotions... just a comb, a tin of Nivea and a tooth brush. After a wonderful hot bath and some creme on my face I pull back the blanket to find an enormous spider crawling from underneath a pillow. I scream.

My knight in shining armor is not far off, advances fearlessly brandishing one of my new slippers. The mood of enchantment (if there is any) now somewhat diminished, I insist on stripping the entire bed, just in case of sibling spiders. Not an omen, I hope!

• • •

The days were long. Pierre went to the office after breakfast and I looked around for things to do. I had been allocated a small car....Pierre had taught me to drive in CapeTown; life might have been intolerable without that skill.

Northern Rhodesia gets to be very hot during the day, despite its altitude walking about was no fun. There were really only two roads I needed to know: 'Broadway' for going down hill to the family firm, Border Motors, a General Motors agency with numerous branches on the Copperbelt, and 'Cecil Avenue', cutting across to the right. This is where there were several shops, a Post Office, one small supermarket, and a tiny dress shop 'Rivoli,' run by an Italian lady. It was all quite primitive, but then it had only been founded in 1900.

My new husband behaved strangely, once he was back. Driving me around he immediately had a never-ending list of things he personally wanted to build, change and develop in the area. He had great plans, nothing he saw was good enough. He made me dizzy and weary with all his energy. Always glad to be back in the big house or to float about in the pool, I thought about nothing at all. I *did* practise the piano every day, in a desultory way, Chopin Nocturnes, Haydn Sonatas. After some weeks away 'Nana', tiny Danielle and Pierre's father Antoine, returned to their splendid home.... so Pierre and I made plans to set ourselves up in a small flat in 'town'. A second-story flat in a newly-built complex of offices was soon ready: a black sofa, black curtains with some abstract flower design, an armchair and a pine bookshelf. Why did I choose so many black things? The view from the window was terrible: glaring sun on a dusty road and a large yard full of second hand cars, further along was a dam, where I had spotted a small crocodile crossing the road, scuttling back into the water.

Nest-building is fun; I used up my dowry on whatever was needed. Nana gave us quite a few things from the big house *and* we employed a delightful Bemba called Tom to come in from the 'township' each day to clean and serve lunch, kitted out with a tassled fez and white gloves, whenever we had guests, Tom did the work while I learned to become a proper 'madam'.

What *did* these black men think of us white 'madams'? I cringe with hindsight when I remember the fez and the gloves but Tom seemed pleased enough with his uniform at the time. He was gentle, discreet, polite and kind.

My twenty-first birthday was celebrated by a gathering of Attala cousins during which I was presented a gold ring with a big ruby by my father-in law. "Your eyes are the colour of 'jaune caca' "he told me, gazing into them,this is a Lebanese ring, for you, *specially* from Beirut". "How touching" I thought," such an exquisite ring...perhaps I've won him over." I was aware he wasn't *too* keen on a German daughter-in-law!

My father-in-law was portly, short, with a very long nose, spectacles, close-set intense eyes, dark skin....a chiselled Arab-looking face. His white hair brushed back over his large head, he had to inhale medication from a bottle with a pump; he carried it with him all the time. A nervous man with troublesome asthma and it seemed he had plenty to worry about.

His favorite place was by the phone in the garden room. Here he made contact with all his friends in Johannesburg. On Saturdays he was permanently by the phone, placing bets on horses or dogs, or whatever it was possible to bet on. Betting was his passion. He both won and lost large sums. I was in no position to be judgmental but could not help remembering (and instantly repressing)....my own father's so-called 'shady' Syrians.

Nana introduced me to her numerous lady friends and one of them, hearing me practise, announced she knew a ballet teacher who needed a pianist... would I like to have a go? A small door had opened, allowing me to start an independent activity in a field I *should* have been pursuing for the last three years. There I sat, fat, hot and sweaty, with swollen feet, gazing jealously at dainty bodies, kicking and jumping in time to my piano skills. For three months there was something else to do, something that took my mind off my strangely constricted life and my hideous expanding shape. It was a lifesaving thing and I resolved to take up ballet as soon as the baby was born. In the meantime I waddled about with swollen feet wearing Pierre's shoes. As the months passed I felt more and more bovine. The heat in the flat was intolerable. "Why don't I run myself a cold bath and lie in it for a very long time, to gaze at (and shrink) my disgusting, swollen body.... aha, I felt a twitch, 'it' likes being cool, just like me!" This was unusual....'it' hardly ever moved.

Our only cinema, the Bijou, was on the other side of our road and quite well served with the latest films. We went there often. But that really seemed all there was to do in Ndola. Pierre, not into drinking in bars or playing sport, preferred reading or writing poetry or listening to a few records we possessed. He taught me to love the French chansons: these were played regularly...*and* he taught me the words. "We'll visit France and Beirut one day soon, *and* we'll drive to Elisabethville just across the boarder, where Uncle Mansour and his Belgian wife live. French delicacies are flown in and there are nightclubs; life in the Congo is nearly like that in Europe! Imagine....all this, I promise...just six hours away by car!"

Pierre wasted no time and bought some land in and around Ndola. One was a corner plot just five minutes away from the office, up a hill called Northrise, the other some 10 miles out of town. He wanted to create some wonderful place, somewhere, somehow. He was bursting with ideas and with energy and creativity. He loved driving out there armed with hat, sunglasses and a spade, to turn up the baked earth and study plant life, drink from his thermos flask, making plans. I'd stagger along, wearing *his* shoes, because of horribly swollen feet, just about dead from the heat, hobbling about unhappily in fear of snakes and creepy-crawlies, not knowing how to survive until he'd had enough. It... and I... were no fun at all.

He wanted me to enter into his plans; I couldn't keep up. There was an uncomfortable feeling between us at this time. I was not at all sure who or what I was, or who I was becoming. Still kidding myself the baby wouldn't arrive until July I found myself, on the 29th of May, in hospital, with a long lonely night ahead. The timing was absolutely right, perhaps a few days overdue. Was it customary then to get on with giving birth on ones own? Or perhaps, being me, had I requested it? I *think* Nana suggested she'd stay with me. I can't remember now. I clambered onto an uncomfortably high, hard, clinical bed and was left to it. A nurse said she'd look in from time to time. "Fine", I thought," I know what happens next, soon I'll be a mother. And thin again." I thought I could do it, just like everybody does. It was a lonely night. By 2am I was screaming loudly, waking up everyone in earshot. The Ndola hospital was tiny, perhaps twenty patients, if that. One patient told me later that she'd been kept awake by my noise for hours and that she had prayed for me. The nurse kept herself to herself. I couldn't understand why she was unable to do something, anything, to make it better.

I began to call Pierre's name, but no-one seemed to hear. From two until dawn feels like a long time, when you're alone on a high hard bed, screaming. Eventually the doctor arrived and sliced whatever needed opening: a huge baby boy emerged. I lost too much blood and needed a transfusion.... it was horrible, all of it... when I'd been so confident before. Now I was like a dead thing, for many hours. Later Pierre arrived with flowers; the room and the corridor outside already full of bouquets from all of Nana's friends; I had never seen such flowers! He sat with me, our son in the nursery cried a lot, I was told. Maybe that was a good sign, a boy who made a lot of noise. I was curious to see him.

"He is big," Pierre told me proudly, "a new Attala, a 'gift from God'."

On day two I got up, trying to go to the baby, but collapsed in the corridor. Nana had just arrived, she helped to tuck me up again. Then my baby was brought to me and encouraged to suckle, but he just wasn't interested yet. I stroked his large head, his black hair and looked into his blue-black eyes: a real Attala. But most of the time he cried, or whimpered. Nana and the nurses felt there was something wrong; no-one knew for sure. The baby lay very still. Could he be exhausted just from being born?

On day three Pierre and I had a good look at 'Luke', who for once was peaceful. He gazed at us as we undressed him, we wanted to see all of him. I was startled to see his huge genitalia. He still refused to drink.

Nothing changed. I remained in my flower-filled room, Pierre and Nana came every day, the baby was examined by the doctor who had several views... that he might be 'mongoloid' as there were slightly slanting eyes, or that there might be some internal problem. An X-ray was scheduled for day five. The result: Luke had broken bones all over his body, even his skull had broken and reset, in the womb. He would never be able to walk, he would be a cripple. It was thought to be an extremely rare condition called Osteogenesis imperfecta.... Perhaps one baby in 20.000...or something like that.... Brittle Bone Syndrome.

He cried so much because he was in pain whenever he moved. We were devastated. I wondered how it would be if he lived ....and felt it would be better he did not. At the end of day five he was in an Oxygen tent, after that I never saw him again. Nana took care of everything: she visited us throughout, she informed everyone, she consoled Pierre and got all the baby things out of our flat. She called the priest to baptise Luke before he died, and on day six she dressed my dead baby in one of his baby outfits, for the funeral. I remained in my room, still bedridden, and was told later about the tiny white coffin carried by Pierre to the Ndola graveyard......

There was plenty of time to reflect while I was recuperating, but I could not cry. I seemed to be an onlooker in someone else's show. Nana had kept my parents informed by telegram. It was now up to me to come up with some views and feelings that I could readily share with them, without allowing too much bitterness to creep in. What had caused this sad event? I remembered my father's nauseating views on 'mixing' races. What were his thoughts? "I told you so?" On a more scientific level I remembered my work in the X-ray department in CapeTown, wondering whether this had somehow managed to damage to my ovaries. This was also the time of several atomic bomb tests in America...had some harmful fall-out landed in Walvis Bay? No-one knew the answer.

Recent research (2006) on brittle bone disease has identified a new gene known as the cartilage-associated protein or CRTAP that, when mutated, is likely to prevent fully functional collagen from forming. Collagen provides the framework on which bone and collagen are built.

Re-installed in our flat, the nursery completely cleared of baby things, Pierre tried, with infinite patience, gifts and kindnesses, to cheer me up. I had been ordered to remain in bed a little longer (sitting down was excruciating.) He played me all our French chansons, read to me and brought gifts and food. Never ever had such a fuss been made of a young wife. Soon the whole sad business began to fade and I focussed on re-inventing myself, my figure, my hair and my clothes. Hideously stretched and marked I was a mess whichever way you looked at it.

As always, Nana acted far beyond expectations, in touching ways: she took over our flat with four or five friends, to give me a massage, to wash my hair, bringing exquisite handmade Lebanese chiffon nightgowns, flowers and magazines. To cheer me up I was presented with a five carat diamond ring, which had belonged to Adèle, Pierre's exotically beautiful mother, who had died when he was born.

I set about becoming a new person. This involved dieting, dyeing my hair, re-discovering my violin, taking ballet lessons, and .... accepting the fact that my parents wished to visit us! This was a shock at first. It also provided some incentive for turning the nursery into a guest room, trying harder in the kitchen, and generally learning to become what felt like a 'grown-up'. I was twenty-one, after all.

The Ihlenfeldts arrived and were made welcome, first by the gracious Nana and later by Pierre and me, in our little flat. We drove them all over the Copperbelt showing off what little there was to see, anthills, the copper mines, the business branches, and somewhere, en route, we collected an adorable white kitten from friends. It was almost a substitute for a baby.

My parents never said what they thought of my new life; an equilibrium had been established. My father resumed his careful letter-writing with endless, meticulous accounts of their dull social life or plans for retirement. I replied, but not as frequently as he wished. My mother's illegible scribblings were witty and amusing: I much preferred those. Time had come to enjoy being young, and to learn new things. To expand in new and unheard-of ways!

Even with my body trimmed down several sizes, my hair dyed, I was still in greater need of 'stylishness'. Soon followed a series of journeys: first by car to the Belgian Congo, to meet Pierre's uncle and family and to learn how far Africa had 'come' under the Belgians. I found black men wearing shirts and ties and working in offices! What's more they spoke immaculate French, miles better than mine! The shops were tempting, with imported goods from Europe and all this only a few hours by car from the Copperbelt....Unlike South African Apartheid the Belgians seemed to have got it right. Or so we thought at the time! I liked being there very much, but for the fact that I was acutely conscious of being a 'Pomeranian Peasant' compared with Tante Marthe and of course Miriam, a beautiful Belgian girl, married to Jacques, Pierre's cousin. The Elisabethville Attala's had a different feel to them,...one had to be on one's toes all the time: not unlike visiting an embassy! Tante Marthe, dressed in the latest from Parisian couturiers, drank nothing but champagne, even for breakfast, Miriam ate only the daintiest morsels of fillet, smoked salmon and asparagus, in order to be as slender as a pencil. I tried not to get depressed.

In no time at all I was discreetly told off for wearing 'unsuitable' garments. At first it didn't seem too bad, as it was all in French!

For an official opening of a new motor agency branch in Salisbury (now Harare), where we all met up some weeks later, I was reminded again that there seemed to be rules about what one wore and when. I had bought an exceptionally pleasing dusty pink slim skirt and long-sleeved top for this representative event, with Pierre's approval. Tante Marthe, however, took me to one side and lectured me: "mais Evelyne, tu dois porter a tailored suit, avec un hat et gloves...and what about your shoes and bag...they don't even match!"....well, both crushed and resentful I fled to our hotel room for the rest of the evening. Pierre offered practical help. In future I would receive, from Paris, a monthly fashion magazine and he would help me whenever I bought anything, or had things made. This was nice at first.

It was at this time, I realized something had gone wrong with my insides: months passed without periods. Even worse, I was growing little hairs in places I didn't care for. I was not pregnant, besides

I lacked all desire for procreativity, which left Pierre disappointed.

Nana insisted I saw a lady doctor, a friend of hers, who diagnosed, with much psychological insight, a female complaint which manifests as a thickened covering of the ovaries, thus preventing female hormones to be released. Her theory was that I'd been traumatised by events and that my body said: "no more of this!". Nowadays ovaries can be put right with a course of hormones, but in the 1950's it meant: 'the knife'!

A Lebanese specialist in such matters was found in Johannesburg and poor Pierre took his non-functional wife to be repaired. The surgeon removed two thirds of each ovary, as well as my appendix (just in case) and wished me luck. "There are no guarantees" he said, "you may or may not conceive again". Nana wasn't going to take this sitting down! She set off to Lourdes in February 1958, to pray. She was staunchly Catholic.

Soon I was pregnant again! The next nine months Pierre and I began to live life to the full. How unbelievably fortunate we were! We were making a new start. The big black cloud had gone. Pierre amused himself with a new hobby: he took flying lessons. One afternoon each week he did the required number of hours to obtain a pilot's license. I stayed on the ground and applied for work in the hospital laboratory. To my surprise I was offered a part-time job analysing blood and other bodily samples; someone actually taught me to extract blood from people's veins! (The hardest thing is getting the needle in . ....)

While spending several hours a day in a white lab coat again there were many chances to observe unusual events, like an autopsy on a youngster who had killed himself on a motorcycle, by not wearing his helmet. The sight of this vulnerable-looking corpse having its skull sawed open caused me to pass out on the floor. It soon dawned on me that working in the hospital was something I could do without. A much better idea followed.

There was nothing in our way: we employed an architect to design a house for us up in Northrise, so as to get out of our hot flat, and out of town. A young South African arrived from the Congo, where he had been working for Pierre's uncle, to meet us and to discover what sort of customers we were. Here was a meticulous man who needed to know every detail about our likes, artistic leanings and our philosophy of living. How very pleasing to be taken so seriously!

Do all architects take so much trouble? He was a Corbusier fan who showered us with pictures of the latest developments in Europe and America, while cleverly forming his own plans. After several consultations there was a spectacular end result. Money was not mentioned; this creation was one of the most involving, bonding and fulfilling in our lives, a pleasure and a joy.

Wallpaper, fittings, furniture, all was ordered from various parts of Europe and shipped with astonishing efficiency to this distant part of Africa....just for us! J. and Pierre became close friends and Pierre invited him to live and work in Ndola. A delightful old house quite near to Nana's place was offered to J. and his family, also to an assistant. The population of Ndola was growing rapidly, almost trebled, in ten years. Soon J. was getting work all over the place.

While J's amazing design of a pre-cast concrete roof was under construction I tried to keep myself amused by teaching infants at the Ndola Convent; it has to be admitted I showed little ability and even less affinity to small people who were to learn to count and heaven knows what else. They were noisy, they wriggled about and I had no idea how one copes with six year olds. I lasted about three weeks and declared myself defeated. The nuns seemed to understand and were reasonably gracious.

Instead Pierre came up with the splendid idea that we should go abroad to Rome, Venice, Brussels, Paris and London, before we became parents. He arranged everything, as always. All I had to do was pack, and go.

The Grand Tour was to begin in Venice.

In June we experienced a whole week in the most romantic city in the world. It rained mercilessly, every day. Pierre, the tough rugby player was determined to visit everything of note, happy on foot from morning to night, dragging me along, mostly full of complaints. I was after all, three months pregnant. How could I possibly match his energy? Here was a handsome, poetic, unstoppable, dynamic person, bubbling over, off-set by a solemn, cool, Nordic mother-to-be, who needed to sit down and take it easy! I did what I could but tended to retreat to our little hotel quite often. Once, walking about in the rain on my own, I found a tiny boutique catering for pregnant ladies and bought a lovely orangey-red broderie anglaise 'tent' attached to some slightly stiffened frame. In it I resembled a large vibrant traffic-cone, successfully hiding any bulge, current and future. It was dramatic enough to wear when taken to La Fenice to hear Maria Callas sing in "La forza del destino"....a lavish show with real live camels (or was it horses?) on the stage. We emerged somewhat dazed at 2 am.

Next stop: London. This was when I first began to realize how much Pierre loved the theatre. He knew about the latest, most up-to-date trendy plays and managed to get us tickets for any work that came from the pens of people such as John Osborne and Arnold Wesker— 'angry young men' ...and Pierre was one of them, I suppose. How had all this scorn and disaffection managed to reach us in Africa? Newspapers, perhaps? Pierre had British papers flown out to Ndola each week. There was no television yet, nor any radio worth listening to.

In Harrods I purchased a maternity garment, an elegant voluminously-shaped coat, a 'Givenchy copy,' no less.

Even in June London seemed a chilly place to a person from Central Africa, so I trudged about gazing at the usual things like Buckingham Palace and St Paul's, wearing my expensive coat.

At Liberty's in Regent Street, we bought a Danish white leather sofa, to be delivered to Northern Rhodesia, as soon as possible.....hardly realizing then quite how posh we were! London seemed grey and serious but I had high hopes for Paris, our next stop. His cousin Jacques with Miriam were to join us there making a cheerful foursome, albeit with one small snag: my French had a long way to go. I made great efforts to keep up. We saw films, plays and went to the 'chansoniers', where the sharp and smart French kept up with the latest in politics and gossip. It was all fairly impossible for me. I did the best I could. Jacques, Miriam and Pierre were well used to the French, I was on a steep learning curve even when it came to food. Only the very best and most rarified would do for the Attala's!

Unforgettable: a Rabelaisian restaurant which made sport of serving up dishes in shapes of male and female anatomy along with life-like imitations of indescribable human excretions, all edible of course. We laughed, pretended to be shocked. If you kept your eyes shut it was all quite delicious.

We also touched down in Vienna, where Pierre was introduced to *my* delightful aunt, Dagi who took us to a wicked nightclub, even more evil than those in Paris! Eventually there was the daunting task of facing my grandparents in their castle. They were charming and it felt good to know Pierre had been shown to, and accepted, by everyone in my family who mattered to me.

Rome was hard work, hotter than hell. I couldn't wait to get home.

By the time Pierre and I returned to Ndola our new house was nearly ready, causing a stir amongst the white population on the Copperbelt, and in architectural magazines world-wide. The precast concrete roof hovered over the second story like a nun's starched hood and our talented architect and builder kept their fingers crossed. All timber and fancy interior fittings arrived in good time: we were able to move in a few weeks before I was due to give birth.

One week before the birth, Pierre's father Antoine ('Tony') was killed in a car crash.

Pierre was now in charge of the entire business .

He could afford to be lavish.

Gabrielle Toni, born a week earlier than expected, on December the 24th, weighed about 7 lbs and was a misery. The nurses put some sparkly Xmas decorations on her crib and on two other Xmas babies...After three days we came home. Gabi cried and cried. Nana assured me she'd settle down and recommended gripe medicine. The screaming continued and I became afraid of this very hungry baby and gave up on breast-feeding. A 'trained scientist' needs to *know* exactly what was going *into* such a permanently screaming open mouth. "Why do women want babies?" I wondered. It seemed no fun at all.

Wisely the new Dad flew off to Johannesburg on business and left 'the women' to sort out all problems. He returned with ever more special Lebanese gripe medicine, used by Lebanese babies in Johannesburg! Gabi took time to accept life in her lovely new house, with her lovely new parents. Pierre was a proud father.

1959, a predictable year, in comfort, even luxury and yet another steep learning curve: I was not used to babies and turned into a fastidious 'according-to-the book' mother. Dr Spock was the fashion in those days so I got by without asking too many questions. Our by now bottle-swilling Gabi soon did what was expected, enjoying mashed bananas, fresh vegetables, sitting, crawling, walking and learning social skills when other babies came to call. We had a large circle of friends by then, who invaded our lives every weekend and there were other mothers and babies to compare ourselves with. The big draw was our lovely house and glamorous swimming pool.

Pierre's mother had invited the Bishop of the Copperbelt to come and bless our newly built home. This picturesque event, with a bishop in full regalia, incense, Holy water splashed about in generous quantities and much muttering in Latin, made the house-boy and the cook very anxious. I was already sensing that Catholicism was much like the 'Ju-ju' in African villages and when I was asked to go to church with my new-born to be purified, (some ancient practice of the church I knew nothing about), I bristled with indignation...I mean, what was there to be purified? Once the bishop had left and I'd dried up the splotches of holy water I began an inner dialogue with God, made a deal with him even.... he could strike me down if he wished but I could no longer continue with all this mumbo-jumbo. I refused to go to Mass from then onwards.

God didn't mind. Instead of Mass, every Sunday there were guests with prams, children, towels and picnics and we all became very attached to each other. The men, architects and lawyers and the wives 'just' wives, still young and pretty and enjoying colonial life, such as it was: lovely weather, servants, tropical fruit and good vegetables. We didn't know it yet, but the daily existence under these very pleasant conditions made us restless and, in my case, bored. It was all quite delightful. It was the 'sixties'....a time of some notoriety! We partied, drank and danced into the early hours. When it was hot we swam, also at night. Sometimes naked. Daily life was easy, too easy. The men talked about politics a lot, but somehow parties and babies won every time. I did pause occasionally, to worry about Africa and the reality of being there. It felt wrong somehow, and now there was all this talk of 'independence'.Once or twice, when I was shopping on the main street,

I was jostled and even pushed off the pavement by young black men.

I hardly gave it a thought.

The most unsettling time was early morning, often it was not yet light. I remember despair and loneliness, sitting by the window, seeing the early morning foggy garden of the rainy season, the birds pecking on the lawn, the anthill still just a faint outline by the pool.... while Gabi drank her bottle. Mothers are supposed to feel fulfilled and content. I can't describe my misery. During the long hot afternoons, minding Gabi in the garden, I was bored and lonely and wished I could be doing something else.

CapeTown! My retired parents now owned a house very near my old university and had invited me to come and stay, anytime! Was this the answer? Why not? My mother would mind Gabi; I could have a few lessons at the College!

I got my violin out of some recess and started practising. I'd almost forgotten how to play...I was twenty- four years old. In 1959, with a one-year old in a carry-cot in one hand and my grotty violin-case in the other I flew to CapeTown to be welcomed back into the bosom of my family .

Our great estrangement was not discussed; Gabi, a perfectly normal blonde baby basked in their attention. My mother loved having her around. My father invited all their German friends. We were on show! It made a nice change, for a few weeks. Soon

I started missing Pierre, and the house, and all our trendy friends. I'd had a few lessons at the College of Music where Stirling Robbins, former leader of the LSO worked me very hard for a very short time with, among other works, the Bach Chaconne, my great favorite.

"If only I'd got my hands on you five years earlier" he said. "I could have done wonders with you."

After a month of this, I felt ready to cope with returning to the Copperbelt...but now with quite a task! I bought a beautiful large vase in one of CapeTown's most elegant shops, to be shipped back to Ndola, a gift for Pierre. It arrived safely, some weeks later. Pierre thought it was not the 'right' sort of vase and J. the architect agreed. My beautiful vase was put away. I could not understand...I thought it looked perfect.

Ndola was not such a backwater after all: a shining cultural beacon appeared in my life called Mrs. Elsie Fraser-Munn, who ran the Central African Conservatoire of Music. Once she realized I was someone who could actually play a violin I was immediately invited to take part in all manner of delights, like perform, with organ, the entire Handel's 'Messiah', as solo violin. As I had never done this before (had anyone?) I entered into the spirit of things and survived the ordeal. It probably did me good.

I was assigned to teach at the conservatoire (a private house with a large drawing room containing a grand piano) and roped in to take singing lessons myself. Mrs. Munn was an irresistible force who never took 'no' for an answer. The fact that I had little more than a 'rusty' Grade VIII diploma was neither noted nor discussed.

When you live in Central Africa different standards apply.

"Do you realise, my dear, you would sound just like Kathleen Ferrier, with a voice like yours....all you need is to train for a while, here you are, listen to these exercises"..., which she then proceeded to demonstrate. After 45 minutes of excruciatingly embarrassing vocal gymnastics I fled, promising to think about it.

Obediently I returned for another lesson and was given various important-looking books, including Schubert Lieder, and sent off again, feeling hopelessly trapped, with a strangely sore throat.

My doctor saved the day by writing an official note to Mrs. Munn certifying that I had fragile vocal chords and should not be made to sing under any circumstances. I suppose she must have seen through that! But it was the end of my 'singing career.' Mrs. Munn insisted however, that I begin work on a Diploma from the Associated Board, but for the violin. Wise woman.

Pierre was also getting involved in the Copperbelt cultural life such as it was. His passion for theatre was fired by local amateur dramatics and he began directing shows, most memorably Wycherley's Restoration comedy 'Tis pity she's a whore', which was entered for adjudication in an all-Copperbelt competition.

The adjudicator was Peter Hall, flown in from London, just at the beginning of his now illustrious career. We did not win, of course, but theatrical events can be a lot of fun. We invited Peter Hall to dinner and he took me into a quiet corner and asked: "what on earth is a person like you doing in a place like this...why don't you live in London?" It was plain he was not taken with the delights of Northern Rhodesia.

I thought about this more than was good for me.

Most days I was alone. Pierre, a night person, who liked to go to work very late was usually out or up until 2 a.m., rehearsing amateur groups or 'working'; I never enquired. He wrote poetry and also a play, which I remember not liking. In it was a line I recall to this day: "I smell Negro sweat"... uttered by a white person who sensed he was about to be attacked...just a small hint of the fears of the white man in those days!

He got into a rhythm of sleeping until late morning while I did what mothers do from six or seven in the morning,...until he got up and by then I'd probably taken my car to go shopping or visit a friend. He would return late for supper and disappear again. Obviously there were days when we went out together, but leaving Gabi with a babysitter was always more my concern than his. The days were long..... It was in this time that a fondness began to develop between our architect J. and myself. He dropped in once for some reason, heard me practising and said:" I wouldn't mind having that noise going on while *I'm* working," or words to that effect. On Sundays, when all our friends drifted into our garden to swim and hang about J. and I spent time on our deckchairs talking to and gazing at each other. At parties we danced a lot; Calypsos were all the rage then, and sparks began to fly, as they do.

One afternoon, during Gabi's siesta time I heard the familiar noise of his Volkswagen parking on the driveway and knew at once why he had come. No one disturbed us and this time of day became dangerously ours, for months. He taught me to like my body again. But such things are painful and cause pain to others. When J. told Pierre that he loved me Pierre replied: "yes, I *know*. So do I....

J.'s wife was not as benign and came to call for a woman to woman talk. It did not go well. My excuse was that I had no wish to take J. away from her, just to 'borrow' him for a while. "Why not borrow Pierre, he's nice too"...was all I could come up with....

This worked for a while. Pierre and H. appeared to get on famously and for several months everybody enjoyed the ongoing social events without turning a hair. There were other people involved in this miasma of behavior, but it becomes a bit dull to go on about it. I became pregnant. It was my secret hope then that my next baby would be J.'s.

Pierre knew about my doubts, but he was completely in control, as always. "I will love it, even if it is J's"... he said, knowing there was a strong possibility it was his own. What an admirable and splendid man! How could I have been so ungrateful and disenchanted with all he had to offer? Our closeness seemed to have vanished as far as I was concerned; he was a great believer in 'freedom' and put no pressure on me.On the plus-side was Pierre's back-up of kindness and generosity, on the other was my immaturity, no grasp what life was about. Life felt all wrong. I was spending too much time navel-gazing. I would not like to admit, even to myself, that my parents may have been right. All I knew was that I was twenty-five years old, having my third child and 'knowing' two men.

I was tormented with *who I am and what am I doing.* A hand-writing expert informed me I was suffering from a "Madame Bovary" syndrome. As I had not read the book this did not mean too much. One day, at a party, a woman who read palms announced I would leave Pierre and be very rich one day. This gave me a jolt: up to that moment I thought I wouldn't ever do such a thing.

As soon as 'we' were pregnant Pierre and I left for Europe once more, to enjoy a last chance of being free enough to get away. Gabi stayed with a Danish friend, Birte, a few houses away, whose small daughter was Gabi's closest friend. I set out on an earlier flight so that I could visit Salzburg, a place I'd always wanted to see, and then took the train to Klagenfurt, to stay with my grandparents in their castle. My own mother would be visiting at the same time, as well as all her siblings, who were scheduled to appear from Vienna and Italy. What a to-do: The entire Ragg clan assembled in Schloss Mageregg! After getting to this ripe old age of twenty-five without ever spending time with my family I would suddenly be surrounded by them. It was summer 1960.

One hot morning, shopping with my mother in one of Klagenfurt's busiest roads by the famous dragon in the marketplace I slid to the pavement, unconscious. My poor mother! When I came to my senses I was put in a cab and taken to the nearest doctor. I began to realize there was bleeding, some sort of painless miscarriage.

When the doctor was told I was three months pregnant he was reassured...".some hormone tablets and three weeks in bed should bring all this to a satisfactory conclusion." Three weeks in bed.... what sort of a holiday was this going to be?

One month passed. My only cherished memory of this time is being driven up the Loibl Pass in my uncles' car surrounded by my mother and her sisters right up to the Yugoslav border, where we stopped to drink Slivovic and gaze across to the mountains and valleys where the Raggs originally came from. We were on the famous Karawanken, last mentioned over one hundred pages ago.

Meanwhile Pierre had postponed his trip so that I was fit enough to accompany him for a few days in Nice and later on to Denmark to look into the furniture business he was hoping to set up.

When we met at the station in Nice he had rented a snazzy sports-car and smelled strongly of sweat and perfume. I remarked on this and he confessed he'd spent the night with a girl he'd met in a nightclub the day before. I was intrigued, but that was all. Nothing Pierre did ever made me jealous. We were both like that. Wherever we were on this holiday Pierre went out to nightclubs and amused himself and I went to bed early. A strange set up really. We still liked each other. He said I was 'completely free, he believed in this. But I don't know if either of us were happy. The innocence of our great love at Cape Town University had slipped away and left us as friends. Liberated ones.

Poor little Gabi: when I returned she would not leave my side, even when I went to the loo. She was plainly disturbed by my two-month absence and it took at least three months to reassure her. I had no idea children minded being left so much.

Locked into pregnancy, life proceeded gently, inexorably.

There wasn't much to do, other than keeping everybody fed, clean and happy. Did I read? I can't recall. When Gabi had her nap I did too, when she watched the Flintstones, so did I. Having a television service in Northern Rhodesia was the very latest addition to our rather spare cultural life, if one can call news and adverts and the Flintstones 'culture'. Our black and white TV set was no bigger than two shoeboxes on top of each other. We had a record player and a small pile of records. These things helped to pass the time: even knotting a dreary beige bedside rug helped, for a while. We saw our friends socially.... but the mad parties had ground to a halt.

J.'s wife was also pregnant. There were three of us 'Sunday swimmers,' all with big bellies.

When Pierre was away on business trips he left me with a small white pistol by my bed 'just in case'. There were many reports of crime in those days. He taught me how to use it. I was scared. One night there was a prowler in the garden. I observed him.... peering out from the dark bedroom, armed with my pistol and a beating heart. Would I have shot him? He sloped off undisturbed.

In these changing and troubled times the white population of Ndola was delighted to have access to such wonderful things as were now available in a very classy bookshop and a smart outlet for imported Danish furniture, thanks to Pierre's good taste, high standards and astonishing energy.

In February 1961 Lucienne Erika made her first appearance. One careful look and I knew she was Pierre's.

• • •

The early sixties were a time of unrest and steady erosion of colonial rule in many parts of Africa. Northern Rhodesia, neighbor of the newly independent Congo, had its share of protest against Federation with skirmishes and attacks on whites and Pierre, along with other liberal-minded young men, did his best to steer a course by taking part in political gatherings of black party members and leaders.

One of these was Kenneth Kaunda, then a charming man in his twenties, who came to our home on several occasions. He strummed on Pierre's guitar and played with the children. Having been recently released from prison he was now the president of UNIP (the United National Independence Party) and with civilized black persons such as him about there was surely little reason for unease. But needless to say, many whites were beginning to feel and fear the famous 'winds of change.'

Uncertainty grew in September 1961 when Ndola got into the world headlines: Dag Hammerskjoeld, the secretary-general of the United Nations died in a plane crash just outside the town. He had been engaged in negotiations in the Congo crisis, across the border. This political affair was revealed some years later to have been caused by a fighter plane attack but it was hushed up at the time. Hammerskjoeld's coffin was placed in a church in Ndola for viewing when Belgian families poured across the borders in convoys to pay their respects, filling up the town. There was a photograph in the Northern News, of Pierre and me walking solemnly past the open coffin. I had seen corpses, but never one in a coffin.

Motherhood was so much simpler the second time round...I knew how it all 'worked' and Luci soon turned me into a doting mother. With the appeal of a tiny mischievous monkey, clinging, loving and quick and I adored her....while Gabi had some adjusting to do but was soon won over by this quirky new person.They became the best of friends, in a funny way. As soon as I felt up to it I took them both to CapeTown, to show my parents.

Why am I going into so much detail? To show, even to myself, how curiously, laboriously, a relationship changes until one sees only ONE way out. What Pierre and I had was so very strong at first, strong enough to cut me off from any feelings I had towards my parents. And now? We seemed to be able to manage without each other. After only six years. I planned to return, of course. But not until I'd had some more lessons. I certainly had no plans to leave Ndola for good. My new baby helped to fill my fairly vacuous existence....I missed J. if I missed anybody, but even that was tailing off .....to be honest.

The Marriage of Figaro.

Mozart took over our lives in 1962: the Central African Conservatoire had mustered sufficient singers and musicians to give a run of performances, after many months of rehearsal, all over the Copperbelt. I had engaged a nanny, so that I could devote myself to higher things! The wondrous Elsie Fraser Munn ordained I should 'lead' the orchestra which consisted of piano, 2 violins, a cello and a flute. All missing parts were incorporated in the piano score, so no worries there.

The Conservatoire was agog: the large living room filled from one end to the other with chorus, soloists and 'orchestra'. It was a hot, humid day, after heavy rains all morning.

"A tight squeeze," I thought, as I tried to get in, with my violin case, "wish I'd tried harder to arrive on time... and what a racket, with everyone either chattering or warming up. How am I supposed to get into the orchestra area and who on earth is *that* ....why has he spread all those magazines around himself on the floor, ...he must be the flutist Elsie found in Luanshya....he's looking at me ...*and* he's just winked. Well! No-one has ever winked at me like that before..."

His music-stand was behind my back and once settled I turned around to greet him and take another look, noticing his scruffy clothes and dandruff covered shoulders.

"I'm Evelyn," I said "and you are....from Luanshya?" We looked at each other. "Charles Chadwick", he mumbled, removing his pipe from his mouth. "I suppose I'll have to put this out now...."

Mozart's Marriage of Figaro needed many rehearsals and I was frequently prodded in the back by the flute with a quiet hiss: *"help, where are we?"* Plainly Charles' 'counting' was even worse than mine! How delightful; here was a character unlike no-one I'd ever met before, casual, nonchalant, funny. He was British, I liked his voice and his devil-may-care approach. He mentioned he was a District Officer, working for the Colonial Service. I only had the haziest idea what he was talking about. We had plenty of time to get to know each other, even with my back turned to him for hours and hours. Meanwhile our producer and musical director were driving themselves into darkest despair. Opening night was only a few days away and both stage and acting were laughably dreadful, so bad in fact the director resigned, saying he had his reputation to take care of. The orchestra crept off home. Later, soaking in my bathtub, staring at the turquoise mosaic tiles, while Pierre, for once at home, was taking a shower, this cosy setting triggered a useful idea:"how about *you* offering your services to Elsie Munn, you're always going on about the theatre? *You do it...Mozart needs you!*" To my surprise Pierre agreed at once.

Another late rehearsal and some of us dropped in by the only hotel, to have a drink. Pierre, still busy with the sets, stayed behind. It was somebody's birthday and there was dancing in the lounge. Charles danced with several young ladies and finally got round to me. After he brought me back, politely, to my seat, someone whispered in my ear: "do you realize Charles has a wooden leg?" I had noticed many things about Charles, his shabby clothes and unkempt appearance, but I thought people were teasing me. He was witty and made me laugh, he was tall and handsome. I have a weakness for tall men. My theory is that women who had insufficient fathering always look for tall strong father-figures to make them feel safe and looked after. Charles was very sure of himself and his posh British voice pleased me enormously. I knew nothing about public school boys in those days!

In the meantime my not tall but oh-so-dynamic Pierre came, saw and rescued the 'miscarried' Figaro. What he achieved in three extra rehearsals was little short of a miracle. I felt so proud of him. Hundreds came on the first night and on the second night people had to be turned away. The Northern News wrote enthusiastically and the phone went all day; the show was re-scheduled for another event in Mufulira, the entire Copperbelt agog.

After the final performance Charles offered to run me home. As he pulled up outside our house I looked at him closely and stroked his face...in a tender sort of way....just for one second. At that moment the big front door opened and Pierre, who had got home earlier, stood there, lit up by the lights in the hall. I wondered if he had seen us. I felt guilty.

Charles and I arranged to meet in the Ndola Park, to talk more frankly and unobtrusively. Nobody in their right minds went to the Ndola Park, which was hot, sandy and bleak, so I felt safe there. I had Gabi and Luci with me, just so Charles would know that they existed. He was a natural with children, doing with them all the things people do in parks: swings, slides...that sort of thing. I'd never seen a man do things like that! Was I beginning to fall for him? After two or three more innocent meetings, once, at my house, when he looked around proclaiming I was *not* to take him too seriously, he was just a 'ladies' man', having recently recovered from an affair with another married woman, I became determined I would conquer him,....it was almost a challenge. With great ease I entered into the world of lies and deceit but also of fabricated dreams, full of new hopes.

At the same time there were further theatrical events at Ndola's Lowenthal Theatre: Menotti's Telephone, Bach's Coffee Cantata (presented as a mini opera in costume!) and TS Eliot's 'The Wasteland', all produced by Pierre with sets by our architect. I was to recite T.S Eliot, sitting in a rowing boat on stage.... and remember feeling acute embarrassment. The Bach was more my style and Charles played his flute again. We were all in it, together! Hilarious. This triple bill took people by surprise. It was of a standard never before achieved and described as "worthy of the West End". For another cultural event, more sobering, I had been cast as an ant, in a play called "The Sycamore Tree". My costume consisted of a green swimsuit, tights and a green bathing cap with much boring sitting about in dressing rooms. This was definitely not 'my thing'.............

• • •

In 1963 the Federation of Northern and Southern Rhodesia was dissolved. It was the year of breaking free: a person who had been kept and led and cosseted and overwhelmed became a person who no longer wanted all that passivity. I needed a new identity. I prepared myself for a Licentiate examination by passing, first: the general Paper for Teachers' licentiate and after that, the practical of the Associated Board. I was well prepared. I had visited London and taken lessons with two well-known British players, David Martin and Frederick Grinke, both teachers at the Royal Academy and alas, fairly non-committal about my talents, I thought.

Charles wanted *me* to visit his mother; a very English lady, bemused by my background, but nevertheless, kind. It was all beginning to look like a serious step - in the right direction! Her husband, Charles' stepfather, flirted with me. I was used to that. Most men flirted with me. I took it for granted. Perhaps it happens to all women? Even Charles' *god*-father took me out to dine and propositioned me. I'd heard that English men were somewhat repressed but maybe I was giving out the wrong information? Perhaps he was just out to test me...did I live up to the highest standards to enter the Chadwick clan?

Back in the safety of Central Africa I was asked to perform on Northern Rhodesian television, some unaccompanied Bach: a nerve-wracking experience, but there has to be a first time for everything. Soon after came the important examination and I certainly was well-prepared for that. My examiner, visiting Africa for the Associated Board pronounced me a 'sensitive player, with 'a sound knowledge' that should make her a delightful, sympathetic teacher.' I was chuffed.

During this time there were frequent trips to Luanshya, to spend time with Charles, who managed to slip away from work unnoticed. Or so he thought. It was a poignant time; overwhelmed with loving and protective feelings for him, I tried to leave my mark by sorting out his home and his clothes and by admiring the novel he was writing. We even had a little dinner party for his friends. Our tiny Central African mini-scandal got about and before we knew where we were Charles was 'posted' to Mwinilunga, some godforsaken village hundreds of miles away. Had the District Commissioner heard about Charles' affair? Did the Foreign Office have 'emergency moves' up their sleeve when staff got into trouble? Whatever it was, we were separated. Letter writing was our only life-line, for months and months. I opened my own post-box in the main Post office, just for Charles' letters. I sent him parcels of nice things, even a record player, as he said his had broken down. It cost £15! He sent it back, saying it was not the sort of sum a District Officer could spend on such luxuries. I was dismayed.

He was then removed even further, near the Caprivi strip next to Angola. I fled to CapeTown with my children and we planned meeting there. When he came to the house my parents were not pleased with this pipe-smoking Brit. "What do you think you are doing? Remember you are a Catholic, Catholics do not divorce"...that sort of thing. I didn't have a leg to stand on. In the past they'd always said I should marry a German or an Englishman. Yet here was an Englishman and they disapproved again? Charles and I spent a week together; he stayed in a hotel nearby and we went out with the children every day. Gabi and Luci adored him.

For some reason he became involved in an ongoing debate I was having with a fellow violinist, who had offered me her fine violin to buy; she was upgrading to an even more expensive one, which she needed for her increasingly professional playing. Charles insisted I should have her instrument and that he would buy it for me. I suppose he was showing his commitment to me, why else would he have done this. We're talking about a lot of money here... enough to buy a sensible car! Remembering the fuss he'd made about the £15 record-player I should really have asked Pierre for the money, but couldn't, under the circumstances, and my parents even less. So Charles paid for my first 'good' violin.

He had to return to his job a week later, this time to Lusaka, but I stayed in Cape Town for three whole months, thinking, scheming, planning and practising...and learning to touch-type and tabulate. "Perhaps, soon, I will need to earn some money to keep myself and my children..............."

Returning to Ndola I discovered Pierre had given many parties, other women had worn my clothes, even slept in my bed. I threw a plate of hot tomato soup at him, in fury. I minded only because he'd let them wear my clothes...the rest didn't matter. It was time to consult my mother-in-law. Standing in her bedroom, while she was getting something out of a carved, scented Cedar-wood trunk at the foot of her bed, I gave her a somewhat sanitised version of the truth. We stood looking out of the widow. She advised, with her lovely French accent: "Evelyne,...men *are* like that...just *let* him, why not, what does it matter...?" Although I had not disclosed *all* scandals, nor my relationship with J., I did tell her a little about Charles. She showed no sign of discomposure, gave no reproach, to my surprise. After that I loved her even more!

Only a month later Charles was recalled to London for a course at the Foreign Office. I asked Pierre if he would mind if I went to London, with our children of course, and he said, "why should I?". So I flew over, first on my own, found a basement flat with the help of an agency, arranged the delivery of an upright piano and a little teak desk from Heals' and then returned to Africa to pick up my clothes and my daughters. Sounds easy, and in some ways it was. Apart from the fact that Pierre supplied the funds I was *beginning* to think for myself. I had left Pierre, for a while, I thought. Who knows, perhaps for ever.........

Having gathered together a few pleasing objects for 18 Hillfield Park, Muswell Hill, the place soon felt more homely. By Attala standards, my chosen flat was, well, not exactly a slum, but a little depressing, if it hadn't been recently painted and cleaned up.

Just outside the window was a pile of rubbish, (which remained there for as long as I did) and the garden in the back was completely neglected. I was not used to such things, but somehow it was all part of a big adventure. It was England. It was real! My mother had been born just a few miles from here, imagine that.

The owners, a Cypriot architect with his good-looking English wife, were incredibly welcoming and I soon had the tiny basement flat looking more to my taste with the help of a couple more extravagances from Heals. I could make my own choices, at last! Pierre dispatched one of our Persian rugs, as well as my favorite painting of an old fashioned girl, bought in Hamburg. More importantly, he was generous with a monthly cheque, to pay for everything. I had all I needed and could afford a good private school for Gabi and Luci, just around the corner, as well as ever more music lessons, this time the piano. I would be able to keep myself teaching piano *and* violin, if necessary......Never had I felt more carefree and independent. Guilt? None at all. Missing the luxuries of home, pool, friends, not for a moment. Twinges of regret about Pierre, about Africa,...... well no, nothing.

But then, who was I kidding. There was this Charles, who had not yet 'declared' himself, other than buying me a violin and presenting me to his mother. His stepfather had actually warned me against Charles, saying he was moody and unstable and not a good bet at all. I did not believe it.

Everything in London appeared more interesting than what I'd left behind. Dirty, grey, busy, wet, teeming with life, but such a thrill! The children were cheerful enough and only occasionally asked about Pierre. But Luci had started wetting her bed, I knew that was a bad sign. The headmistress announced she was the worst-behaved child she'd ever had in her school and also the only one who ate her meals *under* the table. As Luci was only three and a bit I didn't take this too seriously, and hoped the bedwetting was a consequence of the school rather than the new life in England, away from her father.

Behaving like an independent spirit gives one a great buzz..... I hardly worried about a thing. I never considered how lucky I was Pierre was so generous with his money, nor that I was *stealing* back my freedom. Charles was established in a small rented room in town, but at first we saw little of each other as he was on a course run by the Foreign Office, to do with staff-training in the newly independent Zambia.

His step-brother, a well connected ex- BBC man and took a great interest in Charles and his new lady friend. We were frequently invited to glamorous parties in Kensington and before I knew how it came about I had been invited to submit an essay on "Women in Africa" and a polemic on "Race relations in England" to the BBC. What little I knew about the woman's role in Africa was discreetly added to a learned piece written exclusively by Charles' pen. But the one about race relations was a different tale: It was noticeable, when I made calls in London, that mentioning my surname was not a good idea. People on the other end were suspicious of foreigners. I was not divorced and reverting to my German name seemed even less wise. I noticed other things, mainly to do with black or brown people. It was *not good to be anything other than properly English.* Xenophobia?

A 'class' thing, perhaps,.....the less travelled, less educated, less worldly Brits were suspicious of foreigners. It took me a while to gather some facts; the piece, part of a program with Enoch Powell, the 'wayward wizard of Wolverhampton,' was broadcast from Bush House to the world. I managed to catch just the last bit of it, clutching a portable radio to my chest. I had to stand outside to get a better reception, a bizarre moment, hearing my own voice! Recording this was not a problem, I did rather enjoy the novelty of finding my way about in the warren of corridors in Bush House, but when I was asked back, for a live discussion at a later date, I sat silently, frozen in terror of saying the wrong thing. I was never asked again.

Yvonne, my land-lady from upstairs, had two small boys of her own. She seemed to like my girls and generously offered help with baby-sitting whenever required, so I was soon busy spinning a great web of connections and events, all of my own doing.

I had been given the name of a modeling agency in Shaftsbury Avenue, by a distant acquaintance in Ndola and when I turned up there, as suggested, I was immediately taken on as a prospective model! All one needed was a set of photographs called 'contacts' and once I'd survived that........ my face could be seen in a flashy magazine called International Model, for the benefit of...I'm not quite sure now, advertisers and filmmakers, I suppose. All this was very surprising, gratifying, but not quite what I'd come to London for. Just a little bonus, perhaps.

Someone advised me to go to the City Literary Institute, to sort out my piano playing. This venerable institution had provided adult education, with excellent teachers, at a very reasonable cost for about twenty-five years and I was immediately placed in a class with earnest amateurs wanting to become more accomplished, just like myself. Our lecturer, a pianist of stature, assigned each of us to learn a Mozart piano concerto, as well as the piano reduction of the orchestral part to accompany another student. My concerto was the "Coronation", and we were invited to return the following week, having learnt the first movement. I was willing, I tried,.....it was a struggle. Despite his high standards the teacher remained charming. He wanted to help. I was questioned, "why was I doing this, what was my background", and when he knew the lot he suggested I try a private teacher, a Canadian, who lived in Swiss Cottage. This was the best thing that could have happened; I cleaned up my act and soon I was practising works for the Royal Schools Teaching diploma, as well as taking lessons in theory and counterpoint.

Why is one so happy when there are things to overcome? Why did I not enjoy my Science courses, years go? Something had changed. There was huge motivation to be a musician, even though I was nearly thirty and had produced three children. Now I burned to improve myself, to be somebody.

None of this could have happened without Pierre's money. He came over at one stage to see his children, even took them off to Torquay for a few days. I bought them smart little 'going away' pleated skirts and jackets, with matching hats, for this great event. He invited me out to dinner and a show. While we dined he grinned and said I still had no idea how to put on make-up correct. I was instantly cured of any residual friendliness towards him. Ironically Charles was babysitting for me, that night.

Not long after there was a call from a law firm. It was to do with divorce proceedings. "Well, now it is happening", said my inner voice, "be strong, be calm." Inner voices keep one on track in times of stress. When I opened the door to the solicitor he looked at me in genuine surprise:" I thought you were a black woman, because of your name !"...

We sat opposite each other and I filled in the papers. The man kept looking at me, sympathetically, then ventured: "if I had a wife who looked like you I definitely wouldn't let her go." The only kindness he could offer was a little flirtation.

He also brought instructions: I should go to an address near Regents Park to return the five carat diamond ring I was still wearing. It was the London home of my Ndola doctor, a friend of my (now) ex-mother-in-law. She would carry it safely back to Africa.

"I guess that's it," I thought, "closure of a decade as an Attala."

How curious it seems now, by any standards life with Pierre had been remarkably privileged. When at first I knew his weaknesses, very soon he became my rock...arrogantly sure about *almost* everything. I did *so* care about him. Why on earth then did I need to get away? All those new beginnings there had already been, throughout my life...never before had I spent ten whole years in *one* place,.....spoilt, cosseted, indulged...what finally prised me out of all that, and above all, out of Africa?

In the sixties there was much talk of freedom. Not only black Africans but also whites hoped for just that: hippies, suppressed Communists, artists, architects...shackles and constraints were falling everywhere, while all became bolder, looking for greater fulfilment and wider horizons. A white skin in Africa began to feel uncomfortable; being stuck in my golden cage had begun to pall, even to scare me. A white woman was burnt to death by black men, on the road to Luanshya. I was not far off thirty years old and there surely was more to life than feeling trapped, or terrified.

How to get back to Europe, *with* my little girls of course, perhaps, one day, to make it as a professional violinist, became the seemingly impossible dream.

Then, out of nowhere there was this 'new' man, with his roots in England, his lively literary mind, his wit and charm. *And* he liked my children. He worked for the Foreign Office, and that too, was surely a very good thing! What could possibly be wrong with that? Not that he'd suggested marriage.... but I had *some* faith in my ability to bring him to his knees!

Once in London for one whole year I turned, every day, a little more, into a would-be British person. In January 1965, when Churchill's funeral cortège was shown on television, (those cranes in the Thames harbor bowed in mourning...) touched and saddened along with British people I caught myself almost forgetting I had been on the 'other side' during the war. Where were my loyalties? I wasn't sure. *I suppose I never quite knew my own identity, where I belonged. I would re-invent myself. All I had so far was a new sense of freedom.*

Charles, the most archetypal Brit I'd ever come across, his family and friends, knew exactly who they were. My own parents said nothing about Germany; whatever thoughts they had about Germans, other than their relations, seemed to be suppressed, kept to themselves. They had a huge number of friends, German, English, Afrikaans, who all wanted South Africa to be their home.

In London I swiftly, bravely, made contact with musicians, teachers, BBC people, fashion and modeling agency persons, several famous photographers and people from the world of film, actors and dancers..... as well as ordinary folk, such as the milkman and the hairdresser and so on, all Brits with their revealing voices and views of one sort or another.

My own accent, still the well known South African variety, I became increasingly aware of ...while hoping that lying on the same pillow as Charles might have an improving influence. But there is more to becoming British than sorting out an accent: I knew practically nothing about the English, their history, their class system, their political parties...all the subtle distinctions.

Those few months we had together, before his return for the next tour in Africa, were packed with (his) family events, and I was included in them all. It seemed I was accepted, just as I was, glamorous, ignorant, different, naïve. We were going to be married! "You do realize, Evelyn, Charles will never have any money,"......my kind prospective mother-in-law was obviously testing me. "I will try to earn some too," I replied, "besides, I really don't mind! Soon I'll have my diploma, follow Charles to Lusaka, fully equipped to teach and play both violin and piano....I will find pupils... "

If only Lusaka were a little further away from Ndola: we would be only six hours drive away from my former life. My heart sank, the idea of returning to Africa drove me to despair...still, "my future is with Charles; we will not be there for long, surely, in a year or so we return to London, become Londoners, and never, never, never have to live in Africa again!" Those were my thoughts.

Then came the doubts...on more than one occasion: Quite early on I had sold a diamond necklace, a gift from Pierre, in order to kit myself out in some expensive clothes: a tweed jacket with a fox-fur collar and a matching hat, mainly to look smart whenever I 'play-acted' being a London model, calling on my agent for example. How unwise of me, to go shopping in Bond Street, of all places, for such things! And when I was about to live in the middle of Africa! Charles had agreed to meet me for lunch and when I arrived in this new outfit he became offensive and hissed at me furtively: "take off 'that silly hat, and *why are you dressed like that?*" I thought he'd be proud of me! How wrong can one be....

The second occasion seemed more serious: after another glamorous Kensington party I drove him back to his rented room somewhere near Oxford Street...he was very drunk, I was quite glad to see the back of him. No sooner had I got into bed in Muswell Hill the telephone rang...it was Charles, in a pitiful voice: "Come and get me, I've locked myself out and I really can't wake up the landlady". I took a dim view of this. It was 2 a.m. The children were asleep. "Find a cab", I suggested.

"I have no money in my duffle coat..." "I'll give you some when you arrive..." I sat up, half asleep, waiting. He arrived huddled in his coat, without trousers on, in fact, quite naked under his coat. Never did you see a stranger thing than one skinny leg and another 'artificial' limb sticking out of his shabby duffle coat. He stank of vomit and of whisky. I was disgusted. There were *some* explanations...how he'd got undressed, been sick, and how he'd suddenly remembered to put the milk bottle out, accidentally locked himself out and did not like to wake up his landlady, how he'd phoned using a few coins in his coat pocket from the phone booth on the corner. I listened, eyes shut, very weary, crept into bed: "Have a bath, for God's sake"....was all I could think to say. When he got in next to me, still disgustingly smelly, I *did* think "I can *never* marry this man."

Had I been less earnest I might have seen the funny side. Plainly I was a bit low on the humor stakes. My German side, perhaps?

Another moment of pain - certainly nothing to laugh about - occurred one afternoon, in my miniscule kitchen. The brothers were making preparations to leave London again, Charles to Africa, William to Canada. I heard a strange sobbing noise and found Charles, with his back to me, leaning against the sink, weeping in loud frightening gasps. I could think of nothing other than to put my arms around him: "we'll soon be together again", I tried, but he pulled free and said, with real venom: "you stupid bitch, I'm crying because of my brother, because I will not see him again for years... you think *everything* is about *you*!" Stung, I walked away, to hide my tears. My new world had just collapsed. How was I to know he was sobbing about his brother? Why did he need to lunge out like that? Had he been drinking...? No-one had ever called me a stupid bitch before.

A pleasing interlude cheered things up a bit: a call from my agent, assuring me I'd hit the jackpot by being chosen for the 'Drinka-pinta-milk-a-day' girl. Such wholesome looks and clean complexion! They would send me the dates for filming in a few days. "And congratulations" they said, "this is the Big One!" My picture would be *everywhere*. Great! But also embarrassing......

No sooner this was in the diary a letter arrived from the Royal College, confirming my Diploma Examination.....on the *same* day as the filming. Sods Law. No one would budge, I tried both sides. Despite my agent becoming steely and unpleasant Charles' view was that I should forget about the milk-ad and do the Diploma; this surely was more important. Then we could be together, in Zambia. Well, he was right, of course......With considerable regret I cancelled my brief near- encounter with fame.

Shortly after he left I did my piano diploma...and failed. Sods Law, again. Candidates were encouraged to try again, three months later. Not the end of the world. Once again alone in London I was able to work a little harder at my piano, under the vigilant eye of the excellent teacher who was also very sharp. We changed the program: a different Haydn Sonata, a different Brahms Rhapsody, a more pleasing contemporary work. "You might be able to *fool* them into believing you're a pianist" she said. I *tried* to enjoy her laconic style.

The agency forgave me when further jobs came in. One was for Eno's Fruit salts, when I had to be attentive to an executive wracked with indigestion, the other to impersonate a Persil Mum, with two little boys. The only reason I was chosen for the latter was because I was a lot *less* glamorous than the other much younger ladies who had lined up at J. Walter Thompson, the famous modeling agency. A 'mum' with two little boys, hanging up her washing, has to have a slightly withered look. I fitted the bill. It's what happens to you when you get divorced, practise all day long.... and fail examinations. But that brand-new life in Zambia with Charles was within reach now.....

One <u>unusual event,</u> the kind one might perhaps see in a film, stands firm in my memory: a young black actor - dancer, whom I had met at the afore-mentioned glamorous parties in Kensington had telephoned repeatedly, I tried not to encourage him at all, but he would not give up, pleading to see me again. He knew I was 'engaged' and shortly to return to Africa and still he telephoned. "I want to know more about life in Africa", he said. In the end I gave in and went to his very 'arty' flat, where he had prepared a meal for us. He asked many questions. We listened to music from various parts of Africa I did not know. He was extremely likeable. We talked, we ate and listened and when the conversation dried up I made a move to go home.

"Why not dance with me first"? he asked. I assured him I was a poor dancer. He then suggested he'd like to dance *for* me, and turned on some special lighting. His room was large, decorated with exciting masks and ethnic objects; everything happened in it, cooking, sleeping, eating...and dancing. I sat on his couch, expectantly: soon he emerged from behind a screen, ...completely naked. Here was a very beautiful man, and, with a huge erection, he danced in a trance-like state, for a long time. I could not believe this was happening. After a while he danced nearer to me and then even nearer, until he lay down on the couch and begged me to sleep with him. I must admit I was tempted. He tried to remove some of my clothes, tentatively, gently, perhaps he hoped I wouldn't notice...he moved seductively, silkily, to make our bodies touch. I'd had wine and was 'entranced', but...I *did* notice. And thought about poor Charles, lonely in his little government house with a corrugated iron roof, in Lusaka... I had to tell this unreal, seductive creature that I wanted to be faithful. Even though he was probably the sexiest, most beautiful man I'd been with, ever. I kissed him, chastely, *with care*, then dressed and walked away, with a tortured smile. Virtue triumphed. We were silent.

He didn't follow. I wish I could remember his name.

Three months later I managed to fool the examiners of the Royal Schools of Music, just like my piano teacher had suggested. With an ARCM added to my LRSM I was equipped to do my thing, wherever

I might be, an 'associate *and* licentiate' of the Royal Schools of Music.

Zambia, Lusaka, 1965 .

I have joined my chosen English-man. A small voice in my skull drones on, assessing, understanding, remembering: .... "here a week now. Getting used to all this will take a while...that pong of wood-fire... still, I've seen and been in such places before,...the corrugated iron roof, the polished red floor and the government furniture,...just hadn't really imagined actually living like this......oh well......Kitchen? Primitive, massive wood-fired stove, hot as hell, no fridge, just a wooden box with gauze-covered doors for ventilation. Come on, get a grip: my mother had one of these in Walvis Bay days, so if *she* could cope....

...I do wish he hadn't bought these terrible curtains for the girls' room, awful cartoon characters in tacky colors, what will it *do* to them! And the curtains in the living room are ghastly too; his mothers' hand-me-downs...I'm not going to let myself crack up now....Charles seems very pleased to see us and goes about admiring, as he puts it, 'all these female things', meaning my toiletries in the bathroom and some of the objects from Muswell Hill... These are *little* things that can be put right.

That *bigger thing* has been upsetting, disgusting, but perhaps we've sorted it now.....a Zambian woman who seduced him, 'a parliamentarian' he says, while I was stuck in London. I don't think he has crabs anymore, the oil is working. He says she is *not* pregnant........I still want him and love him, just as before, but if he still wanted her, if she *were* pregnant...... ...."

"...Lusaka only has one main road, it feels slightly more important than Ndola... layout is better, the buildings are bigger, it is the capital, after all. Hot and dusty. I wonder if Kaunda, now he is the President of Zambia, still has contact with Pierre?

Pierre comes here often enough, to oversee the running of another large General Motors outlet and, I have to admit, a *most* appealing shop full of wondrous things from Denmark.He has been in touch, to see his children He took them up to Ndola for a few days. I've asked him for my piano. He said he would like to keep it but would let me have a smaller one from a local piano shop instead. No point in quibbling, I haven't a leg to stand on! Charles cannot stand Pierre, he doesn't want me to have *anything* of Pierre's, flattering, in a way, but unreasonable ......

.....there is a huge Mulberry tree in the garden, a dry dusty plot of dismal neglect... hopeless I should imagine, but then I'm not a gardener. The wood-fire smoke emerges from the servant's shack. Charles' peculiar ancient car, or rather, a van called the 'Old Lady' and also a beaten-up Hillman, are parked there. He is fond of wacky, tacky things, or I assume he doesn't mind. His factotum, called Morrison, has been all over the Copperbelt with him; he tolerates my arrival but takes a dim view of changes. There is also 'Blotto', a mad Dalmation, who loves everybody, likes chasing cars down our road. Gabi and Luci are taking all this very well. Soon they go to school, Charles will drive them there on his way to work. I have nothing to do until they return. I could practise...find pupils, go swimming somewhere? Or shopping?

'Wer A sagt muss auch B sagen' (who says A must go on to B) is one of my mother's sayings...and what about 'Plus ça change, plus c'est la même chose'?.... I have asked Charles to wait a bit, before we *actually* get married. *Just in case we are making a big mistake.* I do feel a bit ill-adjusted after the revelations and the blazing row we had. It seems right to 'just live' for a while and see how it feels......... Life in Lusaka isn't so bad really, considering. There is an ex-pat population of pleasing cultivated folk, and there are even some musicians of quality".

In no time at all I am fully engaged in the most delightful way: not only is there a first-rate cellist two houses down our road, but he comes rushing round when he hears Charles practising his flute in the lunch hour, and then discovers, with delight, my skills on violin and piano; he is quite bowled over! Arnold Zelter, the enthusiastic cellist: an anchor in my new life! He knows everyone in town, and through him we are instantly part of a new circle of persons and, as happened later, life-long friends.

His parents, (Arnold is still living with them, has just finished his studies in England) are the kindest, most gentle, thoughtful people, the kind one often finds in Africa, emigrated from Europe before the war, and who had entered into the spirit of Africa in their youth. First settled in Southern Rhodesia, the older Zelters have a deep involvement with black Africa. Known to be Communists, personal friends of Doris Lessing, they are liberal, enlightened company in every way. It is an honor to be with them. Zelter senior owns a fairly ramshackle import/wholesale/retail business of bales of material in one of the dusty back streets of Lusaka. What fun to drop in and purchase materials....I make good use of his shop. Within two weeks I have bought some thick brown-red denim and constructed curtains for our front room.

What a difference! I find some marvelous African prints and make cotton frocks for my daughters, and a matching tie for Charles. Creativity, always a good *sign*, seems a cure for all ills. Gradually life in Lusaka becomes and stays a good time, a happy time.

The talented young cellist is also interested in wood work and creates a fancy music stand for us, under somewhat bizarre circumstances: Pierre had suggested I take my former dressing table from Ndola off his hands, he would send it to me in a van. I was delighted......The van, not in the best condition after the long bumpy journey from Ndola, turned into Surrey Road, drove too close to a ditch and turned over in front of the Zelters home: out, and into the ditch slid the dressing table and disintegrated into a heap of firewood. But such exquisite firewood!

Arnold gathered it up and amongst other things, made a fine double-sided music stand from it, for flute and violin duets!

Well, it has to be said that Charles and I were playing marvelous duets, ... not necessarily musical ones.

But we had not yet 'tied the knot' officially. Charles' father, who worked at Oslo University and who had also married a German, some years after *his* second divorce, now took trouble to write to his son with some serious advice: "*do* get married in church", he said." it's the *only* way for a good marriage." I was particularly touched by that; however neither of us was inclined to much 'holiness'. Besides, in the eyes of the church I was still Pierre's wife, until death do us part. With assistance and encouragement of new friends, who were in Africa working for the British Council, (whatever *that* was?).....we decided on a date and made arrangements for a simple registry office event. For some reason Charles didn't even want a ring, but I insisted he bought me one.

An old Etonian with a crumpled, bespattered tie and an even posher accent than Charles... declared us 'man and wife.' Witnesses were the British Council representatives and his wife, Hugh and Elisabeth, the latter a violinist like myself. My daughters, aged seven and five, in special garments with matching handbags, were our bridesmaids. It was all over in a few minutes. We drove on to the hotel to celebrate with a modest luncheon and chilled champagne. I felt overdressed in a white silk coat, bought specially in London for this great day.

There *never* was another opportunity to wear such a thing.

Now, after my very 'British' wedding, celebrated on a steamy hot day in the middle of Africa, I had a *real* British name to put on my already British passport. From *that* point of view an historic day.

Not long after my parents arranged to stop off in Lusaka on their way from CapeTown to Austria. We put on a magnificent show for them: the children sang a song or two, Charles and I performed flute and piano duets, some of Charles' raciest Badineries and Sicilianos from the repertoire; my mother remarked we were 'absolutely listen-able to'....a grand compliment coming from her.

On the second evening my father invited us to dine at the hotel and we dressed up for the occasion. I recall wearing a somewhat fancy pink chiffon number, which made Charles feel uncomfortable; still, it was a lovely evening, being wined and dined, and seeing my parents gazing at us with approval. It had been ages since I'd been taken to a smart place to eat...to see, to be elegant, to *be* seen. Whenever, in much later times, I suggested to Charles we do it again, his standard reply was always: "when we have something to celebrate..."

There would have been only one thing worth celebrating in Charles' life and that was to become a published author, his one obsessive dream. He and his typewriter were 'an item', it went wherever he did and life was incomplete when he was not working on something.... I suppose it was one of the few things that had kept him sane when posted to the outposts of the Empire in his District Officer days,... his own special "something to celebrate", constantly in the back of *his* mind. Out in the bush he had cleverly taught himself to play the flute, and later, while on leave in London had even taken lessons. But *there* was no big dream, just talent and pleasure. *His* field was literature, his great joy were his books, his pipe and his writing. A self-sufficient man.........and why not?

While Charles and I were getting used to one another a huge historical event occurred on our doorstep. Lusaka is not far from Southern Rhodesia and this is where Ian Smith was causing a stir by announcing his Unilateral Declaration of Independence. It was November 1965. The response was swift: Rhodesia was placed under the first United Nations Security Council sanctions. These forbade most forms of trade and financial dealings.

Within weeks we felt the effects in Lusaka, even though Northern Rhodesia had become the fully independent Zambia in January 1964. Planes which used to bring goods to Rhodesia, no longer landed in Lusaka either, and trains stopped running, shops became empty. Bakers had no flour and soon we were all baking our own bread, and eating extremely healthy local produce! Where did *we* find the flour? Did the embassy provided it? At first it was frightening, but we soon adapted and anyway, one of the most pleasing things is baking your own bread, with that smell wafting through the house. Later, before Christmas, I baked traditional German biscuits together with a new Swedish friend, who lived just around the corner. Why was this was such a pleasure,....the smell, the giggling, the end results... we felt like a little girls again!

It was becoming very hot. We finally decided to take a week off, while my daughters stayed with their father. We had planned to fly to Malawi, get ourselves up Zomba mountain to a famous guest house, the 'Ku-Chawe Inn,' to celebrate a belated honeymoon.

Up in the cool fog and forests of the mountain life turned into a picture-book of delights. One morning we bumped into a fellow walker, just as it began to rain. We followed him to a shelter; he was a pleasant older man, who revealed, casually, that he was Glyn Smallwood Jones, the Governor General of Malawi. He omitted the 'Sir'. "Do come and dine with us, our lodge is not far, I'll send someone to pick you up," he said. We set out; I was on my very best behavior. Silver, crystal, and liveried servants, even in their holiday chalet! Charles held the fort, talking politics, while I managed some small talk with Lady Smallwood Jones. "My first brush with diplomatic life", I realized, "quite intimidating..." wishing the evening to end. One can only hope the Governor General and his wife were pleased to have company, stuck up there in the damp mists of the mountain.

We walked a great deal, reading wonderful novels in our log-cabin and drinking hot chocolate every night. It was then and there a tiny embryonic creature began to take shape.

The following nine months were well spent. Elisabeth, the British Council friend, who was a somewhat better trained violinist than I, became a regular contact, someone I was always delighted to visit and play music with. She was not as keen on performing in public but we did nevertheless put together several events in churches and at the University, and most memorably a 'run-out' to a place called Broken Hill, home to a lead, zinc and silver mine opened in 1906..... several hot, bumpy and dusty hours away from home.

(Broken Hill is where the eponymous skull was found in 1921, now   known as Homo Heidelbergensis, said to be 130,000 years old.)

We had worked hard preparing a mixed program of solos, duets and trios, with a pianist to accompany us... something to bring 'culture' to the hardworking miners and their womenfolk. The performance was arranged in the local theatre, the posters were up.

Bach, de Falla and Bartok, they proclaimed.

On the big day, after a filthy journey (no such thing as an air-conditioned car in those days) and thankful arrival in the darkened theatre, slightly cooler than outside, we began to rehearse. Halfway through the 'run-through' our organizer appeared, wringing his hands: "we've not sold a single ticket so far, I'm so sorry....."

We, the hapless musicians, looked at each other. "Perhaps they'll come flocking tonight?" he suggested, crestfallen, but admitting his doubts. "Still, I have just had an idea" he mumbled and shuffled off.

Apart from our loyal husbands, hanging around in the auditorium, and a couple of cleaners, there seemed to be no music lovers in this miserable, un-prepossessing dump. We gritted our teeth and said: "the show must go on, after all we've worked hard for weeks and weeks."..."it keeps us off the streets" as Charles liked to say.

At the appointed time we walked onto the platform to gaze down at a sea of cheerful black faces. It appeared there had been a change of heart in Broken Hill. But there were armed guards by the exit doors. Our audience was the Broken Hill Prison, its inmates the most attentive audience we ever enjoyed! We did so hope our music-making was no worse punishment for them than languishing in a lonely cell. Halfway through one of my solos the power failed and there we were in total darkness, surrounded by 'wicked' jailbirds. We tried, for a while, to continue in the dark, feeling rather nervous, but memories failed and so we left the stage. The audience never stirred.

However, the British Council was pleased with us.......bringing German, Spanish and Hungarian culture, as we had......to the masses...just one of the things they did in those days, although they would have liked British composers better. But from all this came an excellent idea.

Zambia, about twice the size of Britain, with a population of only about 3 1/2 million Zambians and 74,000 ex-patriates, had a flourishing broadcasting station. With the help of Zambian Jazz musicians who had been coming to me for lessons in note-reading and basic harmony, I got myself an introduction to the Zambian director and tried to plead a case for European classical music. Luckily the man in charge of cultural matters had been to London, by courtesy of the British Council perhaps, and had received training by the BBC. When I told him I'd broadcast (*once*,.. but I didn't mention that) from Bush House I was offered a weekly slot of 45 minutes of classical music, to be discussed and introduced by myself. What a coup! Provided with a typewriter and a stack of vinyls I could set about bringing classical music to all of Zambia! My aim: to win Zambia over and away from all that dreadful pop stuff everyone seemed to like so much.

With borrowed recordings from our friends this wonderful Odyssey began, and lasted an entire year; a nice way to keep my own memory alive in Ndola, given that many former friends there would take note of this wheeze of mine, and what a great way to pass the long months of pregnancy. Charles, the writer in the family, corrected and advised me on my scripts and we both learnt a great deal: there was the timing to do, and of course my own 'delivery' to rehearse. As for my English accent, it *must* surely have been improving. One has made a great leap forward when one says 'Bayt-ovun', not Beethoven......'Mow-tsart' instead of Mozart, and then there is 'Baark'.

The nine months of this, my fourth pregnancy, were certainly not dull. Charles fell ill several times, with Pneumonia and Tick fever, but he was strong and recovered well. It was his task to de-tick that impossible Dalmation from time to time, which caused the fever.

Blotto was altogether more trouble than he was worth. He was genetically programmed to adore all persons, good or bad, and to hate cats or cars in motion. If a burglar attempted entry at night (as happened often in those days) Blotto's tail beat the floor in delight and anticipation of a 'visitor'... and the robber was left to do as he pleased.

One night a burglar actually entered the bedroom, ...I woke up to watch him rummaging in my handbags, lined up neatly on a shelf. "Don't move"

I thought, (too terrified to move), while Charles snored beside me, but as soon as the man crept out with several bags I flew into an indescribable rage, put on my slippers, and tore off behind him in a flowing white nightgown, using my remaining shoulder-bag like a lasso swirling above my head. A Valkyrie could not have been more terrifying, while one-legged Charles managed to hop to the open window shouting the loudest and most terrifying curses, shattering the sleep of the entire neighborhood. The burglar ran faster, dropping the bags as he fled. There had been no cash in them anyway. It was surely Blotto's job to see off burglars, not mine!

However, Blotto *did* have a 'thing' about departing cars and the unforgettable sight of Charles, on many occasions, chasing the enraged beast down Surrey Road, dog barking, his master shouting loudly and waving a walking stick aloft, is etched in our minds. He would beat the silly animal mercilessly; the children were distraught. That dumb dog wasn't worth having!

Like all expectant parents we had fun discussing names. "It's a boy this time, I'm sure" I said, "'John and Thomas' sounds nice together"...puzzled by Charles' grins. One has to be properly English to know such things. *He* was keen on 'James', and as my grandfather had recently died in his castle in Austria I suggested 'Manfred' for a second name. James Manfred has a manly ring to it, I thought, although it was a small reminder that my British son would have *some* alien genes. Besides, it would please my mother. We were already planning to spend Christmas in CapeTown that year, with our as yet unborn child, while my daughters were to join their Dad. We were 'doing' alternate Christmases. They loved going to him and always came back full of news of the wondrous goings- on in Ndola, and brought back new toys and clothes....and ideas! I did think that having two very different influences was surely enriching their perceptions. "Daddy said we can do this and that, and daddy gave us"...and so on....well, to be honest, it was hard sometimes. By far the worst occasion came when they returned with a cage containing two white rats. Charles, who was never at his best on Sundays, usually recovering from a heavy dose of whiskey on Saturday evenings, took one look at these creatures and said: "Out, out, out! They are not staying in this house, I will not have rats here." The children began to cry. "But we love them, they are so sweet and they won't bite you...and Mr Kaunda gave them to us...".Pierre had been to visit the President, with his daughters, and Kaunda had indeed bestowed the rats. But Charles was adamant. *Whose side was I on?* My daughters said they hated Charles and wanted their Daddy. I was trapped wanting to please everybody.

In the end Charles got his way. I've suppressed the fate of the rats. Guinea pigs, a cat and a dog had been part of the household for many months, but the decision over the white rats was the start of a very 'twisted road' I should never have taken.

One can never, never, please everyone; it takes time to learn this.

Again and again I reminded myself that my children had every right to enjoy their fathers' largesse, that I was behaving according to the wisdom of King Solomon, remembering that Charles and I (and the new infant) would, could... shortly become a separate family. There was also an element of selfishness; I needed Charles all to myself. It was self-preservation as well as a hardening of the heart mixed with the need to 'wipe the slate clean' and start again. He was such a very *good* stepfather, with his stories made up specially, like 'King Murgatroyd' and reading to them at bed time,... they so loved his ability to engage with them, to make them giggle, to stimulate them. He was much better at parenting than I was. I was almost jealous. Well, just a little. All this was the first part of the 'twisted road' mentioned above.

I was barely conscious of it at first. The girls were away more and more. I did my broadcasting, prepared some successful concerts with Arnold the cellist and a superb American pianist, and, not noticing, became extremely pregnant. One concert, a trio recital of Beethoven's 'Ghost' and Schubert's marvellous 1st trio, took place only two days before the birth of our son.

James Manfred was a skinny thing, about two weeks premature and delivered in the record time of twenty minutes. The doctor never even made it to the hospital. Poor baby, I was ashamed to show him to anybody, with those stick-like arms and legs. Charles was very happy. He said "I love you" and drove off in a trance of joy to see our friends and celebrate being a father,...having a son.

Two months later we took our infant to CapeTown, to experience a German Christmas with my parents, while my little girl-VIP's flew to Ndola. It all felt quite normal..... but it was that twisted path...........

According to Soeren Kierkegaard *'life can only be understood backwards, but it must be lived forwards'*.

It is easier now to see where and how I began to take the wrong approach to my daughters. Like all children they wanted to be the centre of our lives but they gradually fell between two stools: the VIP life in Ndola and the ordinary family existence with Charles and me. And now there was a little baby, which added *some* interest to their lives, but also took the focus off them. They gave no impression they felt left out.

Of course life was much simpler when they were in Ndola. With a new baby there is much to do. I moved out of our bedroom, Charles should not be disturbed in the night..."the sleep of the breadwinner is sacrosanct" I thought, and he never demurred........ I *did* wonder about that.........

After the short holiday in CapeTown we were informed by the Foreign office that our time in Africa was up, next step was a 'home-posting'. My broadcasting, concertizing, having servants and lounging-by-swimming-pools life had come to an end.

London, 1967.

April Fools' Day: is this a joke...it is snowing at Gatwick airport! A few bumps on landing....our five month-old grins toothlessly over my shoulder, at least amusing the fellow-passengers.

Packing and travelling almost over now; tired thoughts flutter about: "my girls abandoned in Africa, this time for longer; while Charles and I become Londoners...they might not even *like* to be with us once we are organized...just look, rows and rows of identical homes, how *do* people find their way about in a place where everybody has the same houses?..., poor Gabi-Lu, (as they are increasingly called by us) at least they are safe for now in Pierre's beautiful place,..."

However much one looks forward to a new life, the change-over can be disconcerting. We are creatures of habit: moving into a dingy flat in London feels like yet another come-down. Charles' brother had booked us a temporary home in a basement in Belsize Village, just to get started. The corrugated-iron roofed 'government' house in Lusaka has now assumed a glow of exotic splendor.

"No-one here to help carry our cases....., someone has left milk and teabags... that Asian shop, just five minutes from here, I saw it, it was open when we passed... oh well, here we are then. England! At last….. "

One needs a knack for nest-building: just one or two deftly placed familiar objects, a vivid tie-dye painting, a potted plant, some bright cushions help to distract us from a depressing, hideous flat. Once the tacky window-less so-called kitchen has a brighter bulb and I've scrubbed down the sticky equipment the first visitors begin to call: William and family, Charles' father from Norway, his stepbrother, his mother. Not at the same time, of course, so I can enjoy them all, in their different English ways.

Charles' father endears himself by calling me 'a slip of a girl'. I've never heard *that* before, it sounds so slimming and lissome, all the things I wish to be, so that no-one will think of me as a post-natal mother of three...well, four actually, counting the first baby.

My man had much on his mind; he seemed depressed. What followed was no help: within a few days of her visit Charles' mother tried to commit suicide, taking an overdose. An ambulance was called, just in time, her life was saved. Charles did not say much. I never found out why she had done this; it was not talked about, just a veil drawn over the happening, a dense tactful silence. English people tend to be like that. Why would she do such a thing; this elegant, lively lady, with seemingly no care in the world? She'd looked so pleased to welcome us, to inspect her new grandson. I felt close to her, because I loved *her* son so much. Years before, when I first discovered Charles had lost a leg in Korea aged only nineteen I was appalled, just imagining *her* feelings at the time of her child's amputation.

Our numerous tasks were challenging, stimulating, enlivening but also exhausting. Apart from entertaining placid James, the easiest-going of my children, there was much to do: getting him a cot was pretty urgent, he was doubling in volume every day, or so it seemed. In the baby-shop our eye was caught by a new contraption into which you harness your infant, suspend it in a doorway to allow the happy creature to bob up and down, thus strengthening its leg muscles. There he was, our son and heir, limply dangling and staring in a helpless way. "Jump", we cried, demonstrating, to the best of our ability. We got ourselves a good aerobic workout, but our son was not amused. Despite all efforts he never got 'the hang of it'…. a picturesque way to describe the problem.

However: hanging over *me* was a black cloud of worry…. it would not go away. With some difficulty it was all spilled out before a friendly doctor in Belsize Village…the perplexing fact that my lovely new husband seemed to have no desire for physical closeness any longer, that he had 'gone off me' as they say.

The doctor's theory made *some* sense: that a new father would see his partner in a different way for a while, more as a mother figure, and that she might find herself on some pedestal, to be loved in *a different* way. I tried to settle for this, but the worry remained; after all, it had not been my experience with Pierre.

After much determined house-hunting in the Hampstead, Highgate and Belsize area we found a modern 'chicken coop' on Denning Road, over four floors, with a large basement leading out into a narrow garden, just a few paces from Hampstead Heath. It was brand-new, light and *clean*. How fit I was in my thirties, up and down the timber stairs all day long..... so house- proud, polishing them by hand, all thirty-six of them. The girls shared a room on the ground floor. Pierre had brought them to us, they settled into our simple lifestyle without any problems. The convent school was 15 minutes walk from home and Charles, as before in Lusaka, dropped the little uniformed girls off on his way to work.

The older one, now a small maternal figure, (just like Cölestine and Erika had been to *their* sisters) guided her little sister through the terrors of nuns and their restrictive ways. Just contemplate all those nuns casting spells over generations of females in this family!

My role was to pick them up each afternoon, wheeling Jami along in his pushchair, often in the rain, and then to do all the things my servants in Africa had done for me for so many years. Where did time go? In this pram-pushing, nappy-washing phase my only relaxation was shopping for groceries with James, who, furiously sucking a dummy, would be buried under a few days' provisions in his pushchair. Once we got as far as Selfridges in Oxford Street, using public transport, but the sheer physical effort was too much; I knew I'd never try that again.

I had certainly become a Londoner now...washing nappies in the old (second-hand) twin-tub was the worst thing, then drying them, draped all over the music room, weather being the way it is in England. One Saturday afternoon Charles set out and returned with the latest thing: *disposable* diapers, what seemed like a year's supply of them, the entire back of the car...piled up to the top. No more nappy-washing! How remarkable was that!

But the novelty was wearing off. I began to look around for something outside the domestic sphere, like opening my violin-case, trying to play something, anything! More sensibly, I went for violin lessons, which could be done in the evenings, with Charles baby-sitting. He was good about this, generously forking out the going rate, £2 an hour. I recall feelings of guilt spending all this cash on myself. Two well-known professionals got me started with a new regime of serious work on my technique. Our neighbors, a French couple, must have been less than thrilled to hear my never-ending practising through inadequately thin walls. Taking up space in the basement was a jaundiced Canadian Maple baby-grand, an even *more* noisy instrument to torment the persons on the other side. How musicians and their neighbors suffer *in semi-detached houses*, the only factor we had failed to consider when we bought the place.....Only one more year, then James could be started off in a nursery school; I'd at least have the mornings to myself.

• • •

What does it mean to 'become a professional', being an 'amateur', having a 'calling'? With 'a calling' there is the implication of something not of your own choosing. It also implies a gift, something you carry around with you, use it or lose it.

Let's assume an individual has this gift, has a reasonable desire to perfect the gift, but has not been blessed with sufficient training. This is the province of an amateur, who is not judged, nor needs to earn his bread with this underdeveloped skill, who is nevertheless content with what he has achieved and sleeps easy in this knowledge. He is fortunate. Then there are those who have this *calling*, who get to the right teacher at the right time (for violinists that is about age seven or eight), who learn to practise correctly so they pass through the early grounding, say to Grade Vlll (the British system of gradation) by the mid-teens and who are then admitted to advanced studies, to absorb advanced technique, repertoire, performance. The next step is Music College and going abroad for further studies with famous teachers and performers, competing with other whizz-kids in international competitions.... only such players *may* become professionals. Working single-mindedly for a good ten to twelve years, strong, with healthy nerves, the constitution of an ox, and *if they still actually enjoy music after all that*, they will earn their bread with fine orchestras or as soloists, if they are very special, have exceptional gifts.

By the time I was thirty I was probably half-way, perhaps not even that. With dogged perseverance I did all I could to advance my skills. *Unlike* that Great-Uncle Sepp in Neumarktl, the zither virtuoso, a Wunderkind! In those days I knew nothing about him. I was no Wunderkind, only a hopelessly late 'starter'. Nor had I any concept of the distance still ahead of me.

If any well-meaning person had told me straight that my obsession was just too late, that there was no chance of getting to the top of the tree...would I have believed it? Probably not.

The sixties. Everything was changing, Africa, Europe, the world, was changing. Britain too, with Harold Wilson newly at the helm, was a country in crisis. Even so, many ex-pat British were cutting their losses and returning to England. In Pierre's case, he still kept the magnificent house in Ndola and of course the business, which was run by two of his cousins. My 'ex' remained a 'bwana makubwa', which is Swahili for a big or powerful man. Now, owning a new home in London meant he was near enough to see his daughters whenever he came from Zambia. He had custody over his children and continued to pay a monthly allowance for their upkeep and schooling; according to our divorce I had been assigned 'care and maintenance.' Fair do's. That's what Welsh people say. It was rather nice to have his cheques every month!

It was the time of 'Oh Calcutta', of the 'Hippies'.... wherever you looked, and of strikes and demonstrations. On the news was a battle outside the American Embassy, policemen on horses fighting demonstrators against the war in Vietnam. I felt sorry for the horses and also pleased I lived in the safety of Hampstead while observing the goings-on in central London. Mr. Wilson was not popular and his policies generally led to severe restrictive measures.

Not knowing much about British politics I found myself confused. I'd got the idea about Empire, and how it was all falling apart, but Charles' view of his country seemed to me quite different from the reality. "The British value black and brown immigrants", he said and "Unions are good"...and yet, looking around, there seemed to be nothing but trouble. I still see and smell the mountains of rubbish bags on Denning Road, waiting to be collected by dustbin men who had a grievance and never came. There seemed to be strikes everywhere. In Africa nothing quite like this happened.

"Well, it takes time to understand British ways," I thought; not that I understood anybody's ways then. Charles, whenever possible, was pleased to spend whole days watching cricket, another mystery. Poor man, he explained everything patiently and probably became resigned to be living with a person blunted by living in Africa or generally from some other planet. Glamorous, perhaps, but I needed a lot of help to keep up. Shakespeare, the latest plays and novels, politics, sports, very little seemed to 'hit the spot'. I tried to become, at least, a domestic goddess of sorts.

As we settled into life in England there was a chance to join an amateur orchestra in Highgate. I also found myself a competent pianist with whom I patiently waded through mountains of repertoire for performances in music clubs, here and there, paid 'gigs', even.

By 1968 and 1969 we had taken trips to Stratford-on-Avon, abandoning James with his grandmother, and later on to Margate with James, where it rained every single day. I even dragged Charles over to Hamburg and Eutin, determined that he should see a little of my homeland and believed he quite liked that. We lived it up on the infamous Reeperbahn in Hamburg and Charles flirted with the kitchen help in Eutin so that I began to feel life with such a good-looking man, smoking a pipe all day long, was proving to be a trial. The ladies noticed him, of course he responded whenever he got away with it, as men do.

Once I spotted him leaning out of our bedroom window whistling appreciatively at a girl on the road. She was, apparently, someone who went on the same bus route as he did occasionally. "What is he doing, flirting with young girls.... when I've given up a life of luxury for his sake and am now his drudge in England," I sulked and said....constantly on a knife edge with jealousy. He liked talking about the 'typing pool' and watching the 'dimpled thighs' of the young girls playing net ball in some park, near his office in Holborn. I felt threatened. "You're ridiculous," he'd say ....in a huff.

Why was I so unsure of myself? He made me feel old and undesirable. Perhaps I really was? Here was that black cloud again. My mother's advice had always been: "never show a man how much you care, he'll only take advantage of you." The idea was to have some pride and self-respect. Did my Mum learn that from her Mami, and did Mami glean this wisdom from Josephine?

Well, I wished he did take advantage of me, but it was a rare thing. What exactly did 'advantage' mean, in this context?

"More than likely it is a case of the 'mills of God, grinding exceeding fine...' my punishment for having broken the rules," I reminded myself. In the eyes of the Church I still belonged to Pierre.

When our podgy son turned two I persuaded him to chuck his dummy into the bin, for ever, and took him to the Tom Thumb Nursery, where he was as happy as can be and, under the eye of a stranger, became potty-trained, overnight!   My regained freedom turned into a frenzy of practising, inspired by the handsome teacher's ravishing playing. In Hampstead there were famous people and musicians wherever you looked: one bumped into Jacqueline Du Pre and Daniel Barenboim regularly, the cartoonist Hoffnung lived opposite and wherever you walked you heard voices of singers and players at work; just the inspiration needed to get my act together.

When I'd heard the Dvorak Violin concerto played by an Austrian girl in the Queen Elisabeth Hall... I so wanted to do that too, more than anything else ....I'd close the music room door and enter into my all absorbing task. My poor neglected children were beating their fists on the locked door, pleading for food and love and attention. I cared only about myself..... Pure fantasy, but I have been accused of it. Still in my early thirties, I worked as hard and long as I could muster.

Memorably, but only once, I did abandon the entire family to go all the way to Aldeburgh for a lesson on the Mendelssohn concerto. My teacher was working there at the time of the Festival and I was dedicated enough to travel that far. Charles dined out on the tale of his dedicated baby sitting, which included taking all three of them out on the Heath and later, cooking fish fingers for dinner. How gratifying to get away for once, have a Sunday to myself. Not many husbands would offer themselves up in this noble way in those days? I don't suppose he got much writing done that day. He'd already had the bitter taste of rejection of some of his work but, like myself, his determination knew no bounds. Not just dogged determination... obsession as well. We were both driven and never questioned our pursuits.........

If a man could walk on the moon, as had indeed just happened, then so could we succeed in our chosen crafts.

• • •

By the time we'd become used to life in London a bombshell fell in our midst: we were posted... to Nairobi. "Back to 'bloody' Africa". My words, not Charles'.

"I've said goodbye to Africa for ever,...we *can't*, surely not, we'd even asked for 'No More Africa', how can they do this to us, and anyway, what about the girls, can they go to school there?" I was beside myself. "I'll have a word" said Charles, grandly, you *know* we are 'globally transferable' and have to go where we are needed, but (chewing his pipe) I'll get advice on schools, don't worry".......

The Foreign Office informed us that Nairobi schools were of a poor standard, the girls would be best left 'at home', especially the older one, in a boarding school. Would we consider separating the girls? "There is a special advisory body for parents: ask for an interview and they will offer many options to suit your children."

The Advisory Body quizzed us about our children's abilities, interests, talents and hopes for the future. At the tender age of eleven and nine one can detect trends, not much more. We said we were looking for a *happy* place, with a bias to the humanities and arts and, most important, enlightened kindly staff, who would take great care of them, *just like a family*. Nowadays all this would have been fed into a computer and out would come the requested establishment. After some thought our experienced advisor told us he would send us the prospectus of a place called St Christopher's, run by Quakers. "Your daughters will love it", he promised," we have excellent reports, it absolutely fits the bill. They will learn to be truly independent, challenged and stimulated."

Their father was informed; we all studied the prospectus, Charles drove me there to see for myself and to meet the staff who would be taking care of my children. It seemed fine, in a mouldy sort of way, to me the British boarding school ethos of plain living appeared depressing, it all looked so shabby and Spartan. Charles assured me that *all* British boarding schools were like that; I tried to imagine how my girls would react.

"They've never seen such tatty furniture before, they'll hate the place", I thought. It would take some getting used to. I felt uneasy. "Thank goodness they have each other.... and now there is a good chance they will see Pierre more often..."

I thought of them a lot at first, clinging to the idea that the older, the sensible one, would help the nine-year old through this huge adjustment. I tried to overcome my own resistance to yet another stint in Africa..... here was more of my twisted path, yet again.

• • •

It is 1969. Of seven generations under the magnifying glass there are now four living, (Mami, Erika, Evelyn and daughter), one gone to another world (Josephine) and two further links in the chain, yet unborn. After the sale of her castle Mami lives in Vienna in a fine Old Age home. Erika only rarely comes all the way from Africa, a fact that tears her apart. She adores, misses her siblings and her mother for whom she has nothing but the tenderest feelings. Is this deep affection born out of being separated such a distance? Just the words 'Mami, Papi, Klagenfurt,' cast a magic spell on Erika. 'She certainly never gave up her German passport (by marriage) for a South African one. Until her death she received a small pension from the German government.

2 generations are in Britain, getting to know the British, not quite taking in that it really is becoming 'home'. There is no way to knowing if Grossi's move to Hollabrunn had caused her any angst, one

suspects she was too grounded for all that. Mami on the other hand, returning to Neumarktl only once, after it had become a part of Yugoslavia, found it so painful, that she decided never to go again. She could not bear the memories. In earlier years she was glad to leave Sandefjord, England *and* Nazi Germany, later she was even content to be rid of her castle. Living in so many places, some not even mentioned yet, has turned me into a melancholy thing. Constant change means pain, again and again. One tries to become 'new' and whole... and then, after embracing a new place one wonders where one is coming from.

My eldest, only a teen-ager at the time, complained that 'nothing ever stays the same', coming to that conclusion long before I did. As we moved from home to home, never *quite* belonging, just like wild geese, the irony was that each painfully acquired new home.... would have to be lost eventually.

One day we will learn to let go.

Kenya, 1969.

This was perhaps the start of my 'Wanderjahre', Goethe's famous concept of getting out into the world to learn, understand, and 'find yourself'.

Nairobi, one of the largest, fastest-growing cities in Africa, was a very pleasing place indeed, 'home from home', like all ex-British colonies. In the fifties Kenya had been in a state of emergency arising from the Mau Mau rebellion against British colonial rule. By 1963 the country was independent, with Kenyatta at the helm, all was well.

When we arrived for our first British Council posting we settled happily into a flat-roofed house with a large garden, employed a Kikuyu maid 'Njere', and adopted a Collie called 'Cavalier' and a Siamese cat called 'Roundhead'. To my greatest delight there was a nursery school two houses down and the homely Lavington shopping centre just around the corner, a motley collection of Asian-owned one-story buildings, arranged in a U-shape under tall Eucalyptus trees. They offered all that was necessary. Soon I could say "Jambo" and "habari" and "asante sana." This is Swahili for hallo, how are you and thank you very much.

Daily life thus completely organized I had time to devote myself to my violin. Still inspired by London, with ambitious works to be practised and performed I was absorbed by the 'right' musical circles, all expatriate then, (with the exception of two Kenyan trumpet-players) in the Nairobi symphony, a decent amateur group. There were several good pianists, and in no time at all I was taking part in improbable events all over the capital. There's nothing like being a big fish in a small pond, it gives tremendous courage. Soon in demand, even with a chance to perform the Mendelssohn concerto with the Symphony Orchestra I took part in never-ending events, all of some quality. The Goethe Institute, roughly the equivalent of the British Council, was doing its bit to bring German culture to Africa also latched on to me, an 'ex-German', involving me in several interesting projects, such as performances with Franz-Peter Goebels, an eminent pianist from Detmold, Germany.

It was lovely to be with German people again, to speak, dine with them and be re-acquainted with a part of me which was quietly slipping away. We gave numerous dinner parties; the term was 'being representative'. Our silver wine goblets did look very splendid on such occasions, so much so, that Franz Nagel, the Goethe Institute representative, raised up his goblet...and then broke down, revealing he had been a Jesuit priest some years back. A profound silence followed! Playing reams of Telemann on the recorder, with or without other players, was *his* hobby now, and he was a dab hand at arranging impressive cultural events. We liked him very much. Later there was just a small snag: I had made an unexpected and unwelcome conquest. I received an embarrassing call from his wife: "do you realize my husband is obsessed with you, writes poems for you and is completely miserable. I don't know what to do........" Poor woman, I had no idea. He pulled himself together and recovered...as one does.

Becoming more ambitious than I had been in London I persuaded one of the local pianists to work with me in order to present ourselves at Nairobi's National Theatre: my first solo recital! Hard work of several months practising together paid off, the hall was full and the audience generous with applause and praise.

But, my pianist had also fallen into a passion; *his* distressed wife, traumatized, came to Charles, to cry on his shoulder at the British Council office... while I fled back to London to have some more lessons with the handsome teacher, who had come to mean rather a lot to *me*. Again, something I did not see clearly at the time: the smitten pianist resembled my violin teacher in London, who in turn resembled Pierre. All three had black hair, beautiful eyes and medium build. Does one have genetic predispositions that get one into trouble from time to time? There was something 'in the air' in Nairobi, the wonderful climate, vegetation, gracious lifestyle......

In 1971 the Lusaka Musical Society, in the form of our dear friend Arnold, (the cellist who lived on our road in the Lusaka days) sent me an official invitation to return to Zambia to give a trio concert with a young, imported Czech pianist called Ivan Klansky.

I was delighted. The only snag: four-year old handful James, who would take care of him for a whole week? He and our collie, Cavalier, were inseparable. In the end his father took time off work and stayed at home while I had this unique opportunity to fly to Lusaka, rehearse with a superb pianist and cellist and give a pretty good performance in the Charter Hall. What a privilege! (The young pianist was to have a big career and is now someone of great eminence in Europe.) On his way home to Prague he stopped off in Nairobi and performed on our grand piano, a house concert for a few select guests, inviting me to come and see him in Communist Czechslovakia. Flattery, for sure, and I tried to arrange something, but just getting an entry permit proved to be impossible.

Many have fallen in love with Nairobi and with Kenya. The haunting beauty of the Rift Valley, Lake Naivasha or Mount Kenya, all accessible by car, got us out of town, especially at the start of our 'tour'. From time to time we drove to the Ngong Hills just outside Nairobi, linked with the writer Isak Dineson, who made her nearby farm famous in the novel 'Out of Africa'. We'd stand up there in the tall, dry grass and gaze out toward the Rift Valley; my constant fear, being unarmed, was the possibility of a stray lion wandering about. Or Charles' pipe dropping some ash in the breeze and starting a bushfire of unmanageable proportions. There was nothing to fear. Our lives were pleasant enough although... even *there*... were those 'black clouds', following me around.

Charles, a loud snorer, kept me awake most nights. Since he showed no interest in me I began to sleep on the veranda. By the time I came to life he was already on his way to the office. Other husbands would spend Saturdays and Sundays at home, going shopping with their wives or making trips around the country, but Charles *had* to go to the office every weekend, or so he claimed. (In retrospect I think he must have gone there to do some undisturbed 'writing'.) I resented that and felt he was avoiding being at home. Somehow the boss got wind of our estrangement. He, and his wife, urged us to take a weekend off, to visit a swish hotel near Mount Kenya, where we enjoyed the sight of white peacocks on the lawn, a log-fire in our bedroom, even an attempt at horse-riding...in short a romantic time together. Did it work? I can't remember. Did he snore? Probably.

It is true that I seemed to attract male admirers. Even the ten-years-younger cellist in Lusaka had presented me with a gold brooch, his soulful eyes professing helpless devotion. But it was Charles I *really did* want.... he however appeared to fancy everyone *but* me. I was nearly forty by then and although he was proud of me, of my music, my presence, other things drove him away: my jealousy, my aversion to cooking and entertaining as a British Council wife, and, I suspect, the absence of sound, literary conversation. Charles and I were, allegedly, 'larger than life' and much admired by everyone. This was nice of course; lucky no-one knew what was happening or *not* happening, behind the scenes!

One day the still smitten pianist invited himself for a coffee and a talk. Would I marry *him* if he divorced, would I divorce Charles? I told him I'd gone through all that once before and that divorce was horrible and that I had no intention of doing it again. He dissolved into thin air. He wrote poems. I still have one, written in great pain, just for me.

My daughters came to stay twice in the three years, on their way to holiday with their father in Ndola. It was always fun to have them with us although the space was tight: they shared Jami's tiny room and slept on a borrowed bunk-bed, on loan from a kind Asian family across the road. We made a point of taking them to see some of Kenya's splendid sights, the Rift Valley, the game and the Indian Ocean. They were so very close now, endlessly entertaining themselves (and us) by singing pop-songs in the car ....James adored them both. We stayed in a memorable hotel, old colonial style, on the shores of Lake Naivasha, saw the pink flamingos and also spent Christmas in a hotel on Mombasa beach, where the heat and humidity were unbearable. Charles suffered on the veranda with his typewriter, being creative, as always.

Although the ocean looked spectacular we all preferred the pool; the beach sand, glaringly hot and full of prickly things, sea water a tub of tepid bathwater, with prickly *plus* stinging creatures, menacing in equal measure. Everyone, apart from Charles, were in the pool from morning to night; James learned to swim, thanks to his sisters. It was difficult to work up any sense of Christmas, despite the visitation of a special hotel Santa, complete with white beard and hot red coat and hood. James, five years old by then, was agog. The girls made the children's room 'Christmassy' by decorating palm fronds with cotton-wool 'snowflakes'.

Christmas doesn't really 'work' in Africa. Well, just once it did: when Luci clambered up on the roof armed with wrapped presents for James and dropped them through the chimney.....Jami was so excited he never even noticed Luci's temporary absence.

When 'Gabi-lu' left us only Luci was in tears. But her tears, hard to take...were for our collie, Cavalier, whom she loved more than any of us! I remember feeling sad: she loved the dog more than me, us,.... that's how it felt. We were becoming estranged. Did they weep when they left Pierre? We discussed this with the boss, whose wife was extremely concerned and puzzled we saw the girls so little. Her husband tried to convince the British Council in London to pay airfares for my daughters but step-daughters were not entitled to taxpayers' money. If Pierre had not retained his home in Zambia I suppose Charles would have had to pay the fares himself. Fortunately for us Nairobi was not very far from Zambia.

Again, the 'twisted road' from earlier times: we accepted certain facts...that the girls were Pierre's responsibility, certainly financially. He was, after all, 'the richest man in Zambia'. They seemed very happy. Why complicate things? When, to my greatest surprise and dismay we received news of our next posting, to Lagos, Nigeria, it never occurred to me that headquarters had discovered a way of economizing on air-fares for my children: we would see the girls since they were coming to Africa anyway on a regular basis. No, surely not, there must have been some other reason they needed us on the West Coast. My destiny...yet another three years on the continent I so wanted to get away from, the only chink of hope was that one got 'home leave' *every* year, for one month, since the climate on the West Coast was so appalling. 'The white man's grave' is what people used to call Lagos in the old days.

Once again: *reconsider* the generations currently (1973) enjoying their lives: <u>Cölestine</u>, has befriended an elderly gentleman; they go for walks and have long chats over dainty Viennese cups of coffee. On the 9th of July she dies from a cold, turned into Pneumonia. *Two of the seven women are gone, ... two are, silent, unborn.* <u>Erika,</u> in Capetown, rushes to Austria for Mami's funeral, desolate to witness the body of the ninety-year old buried in the same grave as Papi, up against the wall of a tiny, ancient village-church. "Schrecklich," she whispers. Erika's misery is slightly dispelled by the realization she is about to inherit one quarter of the proceeds of the castle...and quite a bit of family silver. Carried back to CapeTown, it is polished every week by the colored maid, Abigail. <u>Evelyn</u>, beginning yet another 'new' life, this time in West Africa, hears about her grandmother, feels vaguely sad. Memories of those first four years with Mami are based on hear-say, photographs and old letters. There only one recent memory: a very good recipe for Strudel, typed out on Mami's rickety old typewriter in Mageregg, where all the family met in 1961. <u>Her</u> sensitive, budding, colorful <u>teenager</u>, jets about with her 'other' family to visit either Beirut, where they now have a handsome house quite close to Pierre's twin sisters,.... or to Ndola, still an option in those days,...or just the two girls, to Lagos, one of the least acceptable African cities. Normally she is still at the boarding school recommended by the Foreign Office, along with her sister, whom she has learned to control and manipulate, taking on the role of a mother-substitute......"All is well," thinks Evelyn. It is the time of sexual freedom, drugs and wild music, the time of the Hippies, but "my daughters are *safely sheltered* from all that; no doubt their father makes sure they are doing well....."

Nigeria, 1974.

Charles flies ahead, James and I remain in Nairobi for another week; I am involved in one last Goethe Institute concert and there is the packing to supervise. Yet again! Friends and colleagues remind us that we are 'so lucky' to be posted to *such* an interesting part of Africa, a place with a history and culture..."never mind the awful climate, everything will be air-conditioned and there is the sea,.... of course."

For James the hardest thing is parting from his dog. Cavalier has been his best friend for three years; they're found wandering about together....there seems to be a strong bond between them. Now the dog lies by our collection of suitcases, head on paws, thin and miserable, refusing to eat. He 'knows' all about suitcases: he's been left before. We stroke him, try to make it better...his tail registers our love, but so weakly......it is heart-rending. Both pets will be allowed to remain in their home, with a new owner. We're not so worried about Roundhead, the mad cat, who is really an acrobat.... *disguised* as a cat. Mostly found on top of doors or shower-rails, he gazes down at the passing show, taking a philosophical stance...............

Lagos is located on a group of islands, endowed with creeks and a lagoon. In the 1970's it was already an overcrowded, shambolic city, now, thirty years later, the population is 13 million, second only to Cairo on the African continent. In the 15th century it had begun as a small fishing and farming settlement, a Portuguese trading post. By 1862 it was a British colony and in 1960 it became independent.

Unlike Nairobi there seems to be nothing British about it, as far as I can tell. It is chaos from the very start: the first hurdle, the infamous Ikorodu Road, a dusty artery leading into the centre from the airport. Our haphazard and sporadic progress is impeded every few yards by traders, often young children, determined that we should buy, or at least haggle over a huge variety of goods. They just about climb onto the bonnet to get the driver to stop: imploring faces, young and old are squashed against the car-windows. I am terrified. Our driver, arm dangling nonchalantly from the car window, contemplates his road, there is no other route into town, the crawl is hot, slow and for-ever. Everywhere, tumble-down shacks, squalor, poverty, litter, nervous skinny goats and scrawny dogs, dust and dirt... lorries covered with colorful pictures and curious injunctions appear to be bussing people. These are 'mammy-wagons', informs the chauffeur. To add to the chaos drivers have one hand on the hooter at all times: desperate cacophony for miles around accompanying the dismal scene. There is no alternative: we adjust to this novel experience, ...Charles takes it in his stride; he's already been in Lagos for a week!

The first days we spend in a block of flats, on Ikoyi island where newly arrived British Council Officers stay until their prospective homes are ready for habitation. From a veranda can be observed the comings and goings of a fleet of six or seven Mercedes belonging to a rich Nigerian, a man with as many wives. Lagos has many such resplendent people, in impressive flowing embroidered robes, fingers weighed down with heavy gold rings, but in even greater numbers are beggars and cripples..... often missing limbs and creeping around in the dusty dirty roads, hands stretched out. They are sometimes treated in a kindly manner by locals but more than often I see harshness, kicking and curses.....

My violin 'fame' had travelled ahead: I am immediately involved in a concert in the cathedral, arranged by the organist Ken Jones, an Irish builder of organs and harpsichords. When I return from this event my family has disappeared. Neighbors inform me that James has fallen off a swing .... nothing serious then! Father and son re-appear from Lagos General Hospital, after a long wait for an X-ray and the inevitable plaster cast at two a.m. full of horror stories about conditions in Nigerian hospitals, with rats scuttling about under the chairs.

Our spacious, 2-story house is newly built, on Turnbull Road, Ikoyi Island. Not far is Ikoyi Park, famous for a sign near some soggy ponds which read:

DO NOT SKATE ON THE ICE

Ha!...How consoling such miniscule remnants of British colonial humor, from times long past, what pleasure to read this in temperatures never below 30 degrees Centigrade and 100% humidity day and night! On the paths bask ugly blue-y pink lizards, doing never-ending push-ups in the sun. We only go there once, maybe twice...walking in Lagos, with clothes sticking to one's back just isn't very pleasant. Generally a smelly place, with open sewers and drains running by the side of roads, occasionally the dumping place of corpses, we see beggars and deformed, helpless people and wherever there is a space, a stall with some hapless trader, mostly women, selling whatever comes to hand.

Within days we learn that officialdom and most, if not *all* problems, can be solved by way of 'dashing'. This is a system of bribery: exchanging a desirable thing such as a bottle of whiskey, or cash, for a service which you would not normally receive without a very long wait,...such as having your air-conditioner fixed or your tire pumped up.

Society was totally corrupt in the 70's. Organized crime seemed part of life... all homes employed night-watchmen, poor fellows armed with machetes, threatened with all manner of evil if they did not stay awake all night. Also in our employ were a large cook who lived on the premises with wife and sons, and a 'houseboy, who cleaned up after us all. The garden was so new there was nothing to do or look at. A gardener did get a coarse stretch of lawn going after much travail... I took no interest until we'd rigged up a net for the occasional sweaty game of Badminton.....

Indoors, praise be, was air-conditioned in every room, except the kitchen. Generally avoiding activities in it, I once entered the cook's domain, and found him almost completely naked, glistening from the heat, stirring something...I never cooked a thing in three years. Eating wasn't such fun either.

We lost weight. "Chop (eat) small"- "no quench" (die), was our motto......the Brits had left their lingo alright! And the hoover was called "dem snake dat chop dem dirt"...

How delightful to have air-conditioners: with a normal 18 degrees and tolerable humidity indoors, things like books, shoes and other leather-goods were preserved from growing moulds and disintegrating completely.   It was not unknown for violins to dissolve into 92 separate parts, when left in their cases unused for a while. This actually happened to my friend Elisabeth, who was holding the British Council front in Accra, Ghana, the friend who had played concerts with me in Lusaka, with whom I enjoyed a friendly rivalry, when it came to violin technique *and* life in general.   We kept in touch. Hilarious correspondence kept us amused during our West African postings, comparing hardships, the odds this time *truly* against us.   With the humidity outside so very high, condensation formed on the cool windowpanes,.... as if it was permanently raining, while one felt safe, dry and cool, gazing out.

In order to play a violin in hot churches the trick is a generous heap of Baby Powder on your left hand to facilitate moving about, otherwise you'd be stuck to the fingerboard from the sweat.

Wearing anything other than cotton or silk is a punishment. The direst punishment is when the electricity supplies fails, especially in the night. This happened with maddening regularity, ... a sudden silence as the gentle hum stopped; you'd wake up at once, "oh no, the power...please God, let it come back" ... instead there was an instant, insistent whine of a mosquito searching for a gap in your net. None of us had learned to fall asleep without that reliable hum which promised gentle, cool, dry, sleep, minus mosquitoes.   This became such a need that even babies could not sleep when taken back to England, without something droning on for a while. Silence meant suffering, sweating, misery and ....no sleep!

The British High Commission dominated our social life. Staff had access to the swimming pool and that included us, the British Council.. We did spend time at the beach, during Gabi-Lu's visits, but the sea was dangerous so no-one went in properly and besides, more often than not, there would be corpses carried along on the shoulders of bearers, rolled in sisal carpets with feet sticking out...this tended to dim any flickering enthusiasm. James was haunted by the sight of a dead body he'd seen floating in the harbor by the embassy.

There was a bad feeling at the beach; everyone knew it was the place for public executions... allegedly to teach the 'criminal element' to reform. My father had once attended such an event, in his younger days, working in Accra. Carrying his camera with him he was able to capture and describe the feelings of the assembled multitude, all taking a keen interest, listening to the last words of the miscreant and the officiating priest. There was a cheer, when the deed was done, when the 'price' was paid. It *must* have been a learning experience to some. Apparently Lagos too found these hangings a valuable deterrent to increasing crime in the city.

The embassy launch took Brits out to another beach, across the harbor to a remote place, quiet and safe, where picnics and social life thrived in a more British way, with umbrellas, cool boxes, gin and tonic. Entertainment could be found elsewhere: an adventurous embassy official got hold of old films and created events on his spacious lawn, under the African sky. A lovely idea, but sabotaged by the insect life! I regularly emptied out giant cockroaches from my handbags. They liked crawling *into* things.

When we came home in London one evening, after a night at the theatre, we learnt the insects had outwitted us. Before our eyes were crawling beasts, scurry-ing off into corners and *under* things, as we turned on the light. 'Rentokil' informed us that we had imported eggs and larvae in our suitcases, having recently arrived from West Africa. We were evicted for a day, while they did clever things to free us from these unwelcome immigrants.

Lagos ex-patriots stuck together. So it was refreshing that one of our neighbors, employed by EMI, was on friendly terms with one of Nigeria's most famed musicians, Fela Ransome Kuti, the pioneer of Afro-beat and known to be something of a maverick, as far as politics of his country were concerned. Having studied at Trinity College in London his music was a fusion of Jazz, Funk and African chant. He was revered by a large international following; he created a concert hall known as the Shrine, and started a commune of like-minded musicians, with a colony of nubile women, raising eyebrows of the uninitiated. He went a step further and created the Kala Kuti Republic, with its own laws, which needless to say, did not go down well with the Nigerian establishment.

We would never have dared go to the Shrine if it had not been for our EMI friend, who made it possible to find it, in a part of Lagos one was unwise to visit without a local guide. Pointless to say it was hot, because it always was, but inside it was even hotter. Surrounded by a heaving mass of excited fans, assaulted by the sheer volume of Fela's band, I sensed the vibrations beating against my ribcage, I could barely breathe... It was unbearable. We didn't stay long, felt we'd heard all we ever needed of this *so* famous person.

Lagos also had a symphony orchestra; it was like no other. I first heard about it well into our appointed three years, because of members of my audience at a recital I was playing with the famous Franz-Peter Goebels. (We'd met in Kenya. He re-appeared in my musical life by inviting himself, not only to stay with us, but also to play three joint recitals in Nigeria. He was a marvelous pianist.) A program was devised and rehearsed for a concert in the Italian Embassy; they had a hall with a good piano and an assured, appreciative following. As I stood before my audience I noticed four Nigerians, close enough to be looking up at me, sitting by my feet... seemingly studying my armpits. I began to worry about the sleeveless evening gown "have I shaved my armpits? ...These people are intent on my every move".......

After a successful evenings' playing they came to meet me and tell me about their Apostolic Faith Orchestra: "please come and hear us play... we so need somebody to help the string section, we have no teacher..."

• • •

Picture a hangar the size of Heathrow's Terminal 3, then a symphony orchestra on a platform at the far end, dressed immaculately in formal black and white evening dress. Seated in the auditorium, eight hundred Nigerians, all in their best exotic finery, an impressive audience.....we are guests of the Apostolic Faith Orchestra, but we'd been delayed along the Ikorodu road and now, a little late, having missed the overture, we are escorted to the front of the hall, disturbing everybody,....the familiar rhythms of Beethoven's First Symphony...."but, is there some distortion,...what on earth are these strange sounds... still, it's just recognize-ably the First Symphony....they *look* good, seem to hold their instruments correctly,".....we are dumb-founded: is it possible to perform such a work, without anyone having learned to play in tune? The audience loves it and roars with pleasure. But the players *know*.

What does one say afterwards? I had been invited to help, now it was over to me. I followed up initial cautious praise with an offer for violinists to come to our house, for a 'sectional' rehearsal.

At the appointed time two vans full of musicians piled into our front room, bringing music stands and music. In no time at all I had discovered that none knew how to tune their instruments, nor could many of them actually *read* the music. They must have learned the entire concert by rote. With such numbers of them I soon felt the only way forward was to take a few of the better players and teach them individually, in the hope they could then teach the others. The instruments and music books had been donated by the Apostolic Faith Organization in Portland, Oregon, who had dispatched everything to Lagos but had forgotten the most important thing: a teacher.

Wind and brass were rather more advanced and I forget how this had come about, but I did feel helplessly 'up against it'. The orchestra's gratitude was overwhelming. I was touched.

The recital with Goebels was repeated in <u>Ibadan</u> at the University, and yet again, further north, in Kano. I believe we flew the rest of the way, as <u>Kano</u> is almost up in the Sahara desert, indescribably hot and more exotic than anything seen so far: small thick-walled mud houses, camels, turbaned men in long dresses ...... very little vegetation, and vendors selling marvelous objects like pouffes made of camel-skin, and heavily embroidered gowns.... temptation at every corner. Speaking of musical events: an invitation arrived to present myself at yet another university, this time in Enugu for once *not* under the auspices of the Goethe Institute. A friend from Nairobi, who had taken up a teaching post at <u>Enugu</u> University offered me two concerts, one mostly for his students and another, more prestigious, in a concert hall, or was it the local town cinema?

The Governor of Enugu Province was to attend.

Having just experienced 'fame' by recording a performance on Lagos television, (a dire event, which took all of seven hours to get done, due to technical problems to do with power cuts, machinery not working, miscalculations in the lighting)...I was feeling good about my playing and decided to offer two programs, one of shorter works, typical violin repertoire and another: *three* violin concertos, accompanied only by piano, (alas). I had been working for ages on the Bruch, the Mendelsson, had even performed them in Nairobi and now felt the urge 'to do it again'! Preceded by a short Vivaldi concerto I launched myself into this, for me, dizzyingly huge concert....and got away with it, a resounding success, with all the trimmings, flowers, photographers, the 'media' taking an interest...there was a broadcast the following day, to perform live and to be interviewed by ferocious Nigerian lady, who questioned me, mercilessly, as to the relevance to Nigerians, of events such as this performance.

I tend do go into 'over-drive' when pushed into tricky situations. Here I was, a British Council wife, 'live on air,' in the middle of Africa, having to defend King and Country, Mendelssohn and Bruch. I surprised myself... as if someone else had taken over my mind I came out with overwhelming evidence that *all* culture was relevant to the brotherhood of man, to the enrichment of our souls......and other eloquence I had truly never thought about before! It was almost like being momentarily 'possessed'.

Possession of another kind overcame us all during one of the holiday visits of my teen-age offspring from England: they mentioned, in passing, that one of their classmates had a Oui-ja board, allegedly useful for fooling about with 'spirits' enjoying the afterlife. There was not a lot to do after supper in Lagos, and for want of entertainment we found ourselves around the polished surface of the dining table with our fingers lightly resting on an upturned glass. Luci was appointed 'scribe' while Gabi and I felt the glass pulling towards the alphabet in a circle; we'd written the letters on cardboard and cut them out. There was a flickering candle in the centre, James was in bed and Charles upstairs with his typewriter...all normal activities...the cook gone home to sleep.

At first I felt bored, telling myself to relate to my visiting daughters somehow... "what harm can it do, it's just a bit of fun?"

Before long Luci started complaining the glass was too fast, she couldn't keep up. So we stopped to look at her writing. We saw lines and lines of letters, without divisions into words. "It's all rubbish", I proposed, "let's read books instead."

Then one of us mysteriously began to see some sense by clustering letters into words,...then phrases,... which in turn seemed to become someone else's thoughts, instructing us how to proceed! At this point Charles appeared, wanting to know what was going on. He disapproved, said we were mad, all three of us and "stop it at once, you surely don't believe such nonsense."

But we tried again, on another evening, and begged him to join in. Protesting, he did. Soon he too felt that strange surge under the fingers. Luci remained the scribe, did her best to keep up. We did not look at the letters, just allowed ourselves to feel like zombies in a trance, while the glass whizzed about. We were hooked all right: in our midst there seemed to be a character called Ted Bolkin, a postman from St Albans, who had died in a car-crash, who was (dead) keen to answer any questions we might have. We had many..... Night after night 'Ted' instructed us about the future and especially about life after death.

We accumulated a great wodge of papers, and without wishing to appear too eccentric, even told some ladies at the British High Commission about this. After the school holidays had come to an end, when Gabi, by then miserably in love with the High Commissioner's son...(who barely knew she existed...) was back in her boarding school, several of these ladies came to the house for a coffee morning and wanted a demonstration of 'this Ouija thing'. So I set it up, though it's not quite the same at eleven a.m., without a flickering candle, and servants wandering in and out,.... but after an initial embarrassing refusal to move, the glass began to spin about; soon two of the ladies took fright and begged to be excused, one of them very pale, saying she "didn't like it".

There was some talk in later weeks, with looks askance, was 'I still *doing* it?' The answer was 'yes', with a neighbor, a beautiful and rather fey lady, with whom the glass went completely wild.

Well, the long and the short of all this was: whenever I had to perform I would call on 'Ted Bolkin' for super-human energies and there's nothing like a bit of 'juju' to lift the spirits and one's skills to a higher level. The human brain is a wondrous thing. At the time it worked for me. I got in touch with the *Society of Psychical Research* in London and read a huge amount of extraordinary literature. Sadly it gets one nowhere, remains a tantalizing mystery.

One statement from 'Ted' was that Charles' novel would be published *one* day, when we queried all the rejections, and, when pressed further, Ted stated: "ten bird pecks end midnight". No-one has managed an explanation for that prophecy. Thirty years had to pass before the book finally appeared in print. So what is all this about: is extra-sensory perception something to be cultivated, something useful? It certainly passed the time in steamy West Africa.

• • •

Colleagues, hearing about the wonderful French cuisine of Dahomey, suggested a convoy of Brits drive up to the neighboring country about 100 miles north of Lagos, for a long weekend.

The Kingdom of Dahomey had been a powerful and extraordinary West African state, founded in the 17th century, surviving until 1894. It borders on Togo, Nigeria and Burkina Faso, the seat of government in Cotonou. From 1960 - 1975 it was the Independent Republic of Dahomey, then renamed Benin. Everyone has heard of the famous Benin Bronzes, now to be found in the British Museum. In earlier centuries Dahomey expanded and flourished with the slave trade and was very unpopular with neighboring peoples because of its extremely cruel practices.... it was the home of human sacrifice and 'fetish'. The Yorubas from Nigeria were pleased to assist in bringing on the Kingdom's collapse in favor of French liberal rule, but despite the disappearance of the Benin kingdom the Yoruba people continue to produce art-work inspired by the royal art of Benin.

Our goal was to get to the lake-village Ganvie. This lies in a lake near Cotonu, and now has a population of 20.000 people. We were taken around in a boat, carefully navigating through the stilt houses or pile dwellings. Thought to be the largest lake village in Africa it was established three, possibly four centuries ago. We learned that these were dwellings like those found in the Neolithic or Bronze Age in the Alps, or in South East Asia. Needless to say the main industry is fishing and fish farming. The lake is shallow. One is more likely to get stuck than drown. To James' delight we bought a large, ornate tin sword in a scabbard, both lethal and decorative, and a fearsome grass mask, from a trader with an eye for the tourist trade. I wondered about the bacterial cocktail in the waters all about us. How it all works is quite beyond me. One hopes there is a river flowing through. Still, an unforgettable sight.

We flew to and fro between London and the west Coast every year...a real plus as far as I could see. In London my small, blond, sun-burnt son would be sent up the hill in Hampstead, to school, while Charles could write, or watch cricket and football and I could take lessons and 'keep house', something one tends not to do in Africa! This I found pleasing. So much so that, when Charles went back to Lagos early, James and I stayed behind, to enjoy life in England a few weeks longer.

It was during such a spell that I succumbed to the charms of my favorite violin guru, an emotional upheaval all of my own doing, which gave me the energy and inspiration to continue battling with my endless quest to become a better musician. I did not feel guilty. My feelings for Charles remained as strong as ever, although tinged with a kind of doubt and wish that we could be closer and more romantic together. Ironically, we were...for a short while, after our reunion. I kept my infidelity to myself though.

On another return trip, this time all three together, we stopped off in <u>Accra</u>, to call on our British Council colleagues, the Crookes. I was tremendously excited to return to the place of my conception and of my parents' happiest days; their house was still standing, and easy to find. Near it was a European-style church. We headed for that, to get out of the hot sun and also out of curiosity, noticing an elderly Ghanaian up a ladder, cleaning a window. He climbed down, greeted us in a friendly way and I told him we had come to find the house of my father, who had lived here in the 1930's. The man took my hand and said, warmly:" aaah, you must be Mr Ihlenfeldt's daughter." He'd instantly made the connection.

We were haunted by this. Forty years had passed, since my father left Accra and here was the *first* black man we spoke to...*and he actually remembered my father's name!* Too dumbstruck at the time we did not think to enquire how he knew. I've kicked myself for years. Still under the spell of our encounters with the world of the spirits, we believed we had been guided *to* this very man, by some friendly other-world being.....

We liked Accra, envied our colleagues their posting ......it was a less stressful place than Lagos, somehow more settled and bearable. After the return to Lagos we began to feel the time was coming for a renewed move. What did headquarters have up their sleeve this time?

But first there was another memorable evening at the British High Commission: a huge reception for Harold Macmillan, by then retired from government, but 'doing business' for his family's publishing firm.

At one stage we had both fled outside to the cooler air on the veranda, where I found I had sole responsibility of entertaining this venerable personage. It wasn't too bad: his next stop was CapeTown and I could at least be knowledgeable about that, besides, he seemed well pleased to be gazing down my decolleté, while chatting about this and that. Such occasions were the most worrying in my 'British Council wife-career' ... I never quite knew how or when I'd put my foot in it. Some high-powered diplomat had said to Charles that I was 'enlivening' company; I wondered for weeks what on earth I'd said.

• • •

Soon the news came: we were to fly directly to Brazil, destination Sao Paulo, a place with both hot *and* cold weather, a country where one spoke Portuguese. This sounded promising. There was only one problem: we had no language training, and only the flimsiest summer clothes. Charles refused to make a fuss, he couldn't bring himself to badger headquarters. He'd rather pay the fare himself, so I was sent off 'home' to England to bring out required warm clothing, to take across the sea to South America. I felt pretty cross he refused to speak up, but in the end it was *his* problem. Having no Portuguese was a real pest; I felt resentful being sent to Brazil without at least *some* language preparation.

The saddest persons in Lagos were our cook, our cook's son, who was James's best friend and the Apostolic Faith Orchestra. The ladies of the string section surprised us with handsome gifts of black velvet garments, shirts for the boys and a long kaftan for me, richly embroidered in traditional white embroidery. Without taking any measurements they had cleverly judged our heights and widths. They also appeared en masse at the airport to wave us good-bye. I never thought I'd feel so melancholy leaving Lagos.

It was the one place where I'd had nothing else to do but practise my violin. For three years my technique was pushed to Paganini Caprices, Concertos, unaccompanied Bach, struggling with 'impossible' feats in order to expand my range of skills. But I was already pushing forty!

Brazil December 1975

Any melancholy thoughts evaporated as we landed, early in the morning, in Rio de Janeiro. The bay with the Sugar Loaf, jutting out of the sea, the beaches and the inviting lay-out of the city nestling against the low hills, made an overwhelming impression, and as we landed I could see at once that this place resembled Europe.....not at all like Africa. I was instantly in heaven!

The local representative put us up for a few days while I wandered about with my son, taking in dazzling sights and the general atmosphere of colorful, inviting, pulsating life. Here it was, the famous Copacabana beach, a great playground, physical perfection on show, where drinking just one 'Caipirinha' sent me into a state of spectacular intoxication and confusion....the 'cidade maravilhosa' instantly more divine, the giant statue of Jesus on the mountain more terrifying.....

Charles took a day off work and up we went in the cable car to the famed Sugar Loaf to immerse ourselves in spectacular views. I wanted to stay there forever. But no, on we flew, to the most populous place in the southern hemisphere. As we approached I could see the surrounding mountains enclosing a vast grey smog- filled bowl: our new home!

Sao Paulo is indescribably vast, unknowably, mind-bogglingly gigantic, in all directions. We needed a chauffeur throughout our stay; getting to know such a city takes more years than we had to offer. Rotten timing: we had arrived on the 23rd of December. Our house was not quite ready and on the advice of colleagues we were packed off to a hotel in the surrounding hills, to spend Christmas as best we could. Fortunately I'd packed a few gifts for James and a tiny collapsible Xmas tree for 'festivities' in our room, a dismal start to our new life. Not being able to communicate we sat or wandered about in the gardens, feeling cut off, un-Christmassy, unsettled. The only entertainment was a masseuse, attached to the hotel, who, for a pittance, offered a whole body massage... so for want of anything else to do both we 'treated' ourselves to a relaxing pummeling, not without much prior to-do from Charles, who had never heard of such a thing. Imagine the raised eyebrows when he wrote home to his mother!

The British Council, dealing as usual with scholarships and cultural exchanges was linked, in Sao Paulo, with an organization called the Cultura Inglese. Charles' official title was the Superintendant General of Cultura Inglese: a powerful man called Pinheiro Neto was the President. Right from the start this was a testing arrangement. Charles felt uncomfortable with Pinheiro Neto and their dislike was mutual.

A shame really, the Cultura Inglese, a South American institution, was a massive enterprise, with at least 12.000 students of English enrolled in Sao Paulo alone. The accent was on British culture and in the time we were there we had visits from Sir Michael Redgrave, and the Actors Company with several top-notch British actors performing Pinter, Shaw and Ayckbourn to overflowing audiences. Pinter was treated with special enthusiasm, as son of a London East-end tailor of Portuguese-Jewish ancestry (da Pinta) the Brazilians considered him one of *them*, not a real Brit at all. They loved his verbal acrobatics, his inconsequential everyday talk, easy to follow but nevertheless conveying much sinister content.... Just the thing, especially if English is a second language. Not to be outdone, the Cultura in Sao Paulo put on a show of their own, with Stoppard's 'Rosencrantz and Guildenstern are dead', and Charles, a magnificent performer of Polonius, led me to believe I was married to a man of hidden talents.

To me, our tour in Brazil felt, at first....lonely, isolated. Our nice little house in the suburbs, reasonably close to the British school, allowed James to be transported on school days by the same chauffeur who took Charles to work. Thus abandoned each morning in the daily company of a wiry, hyperactive Brazilian maid, I communicated in sign-language at first, gradually picking up essential phrases. She was an obsessive cleaner, who shone copper pans with lemon and salt until they looked like new, and hosed down the tiled bathrooms from ceiling to floor every other day, literally. With greatest difficulty I was able to persuade her once a month was more than enough for this upheaval. Even once a year, or once a decade would suffice. But no, she'd strip, first herself, then the room, down to bare essentials and got the hose out, again and again. "Something to do with the air pollution in Sao Paulo, she explained, "it sticks to wet walls", or something. In the meantime I 'fast-tracked' basic phrases in Portuguese, and other survival skills. With a small car and a map I was left to get on with shopping and finding my way about; a challenge and I was not too pleased at first. Much of my time was spent practising, and keeping James amused after school. I gave him piano lessons. The local Brits were helpful, friends were found and James was quickly 'in' with a gang of Brazilian boys at the end of our road, all budding Pele's of course. In fact, James could get about in Portuguese in no time at all because of his new pals. He'd bring them all home and served refreshments, with his enviable ability to communicate. I stood by, half amused, half glaring at the mess and spillage.

I forget how it came about.... some helpful person put me in touch with a young pianist who had been studying in London. Paulo Gori, an outstanding talent, already taking part in international competitions but also messing up his life with drugs, had been sent back home to Brazil to 'chill out' and to practise. He was persuaded to play a recital with me, he needed the money. In some ways crazy, but also splendid to work with, we decided on a sophisticated program, Debussy, Prokofiev, Mozart and Beethoven.

The venue was one of the most prestigious in Sao Paulo, the Musée d'Arte, an art-gallery with concert hall attached. Here was one of those occasions when I did not quite realize what I had let myself in for. Not only was there a second concert, in a nearby town, _Campinas_, but also publicity, TV and general hullaballoo when a young star is made a fuss of. Let's get this right: HE was the star and I was, at most, a vapor-trail, doing the best I could. As far as I could assess, the first performance was as good as I was able to do, being swept along by Paulo's incredible playing. However, a BBC producer in the audience came to see me later enquiring in a somewhat underhand way whether I had ever *seen* myself play.... on film? Did I realize I had no *presence* as a performer?

I had been totally eclipsed by the splendidly-trained piano wunderkind. I was competent.... but outshone. The review said as much. I had much, much more to learn (and suffer), as an 'artist'! But the Brazilian audience was so warm and wonderful, all trying to embrace me (and him) and emotional about the concert..... the greenroom full of bouquets and cards and excited chattering. One gets a taste for all that!

After that, before further concerts, I took to performing to myself in a mirror, just to get a measure of what was coming across to the viewer. Learning to believe in oneself is the hardest thing of all.

There were other pianists I performed with, but in the end Isabel Mourao became the most important. "What, you have not performed in the Wigmore Hall in London?" she exclaimed, "that's terrible, why not"? To her it seemed the most natural thing... "just *do* it", she said. It was *her* doing then, during a short leave in London, I presented myself in the Wigmore Hall, in January 1977...

None of my family could come: Charles was needed back in Sao Paulo, James was with a friend and my daughters lived with their father, now in Canterbury. Only Charles knew what this event meant to me and how important it was for my future as a violinist. My agent (this sounds very grand) had invited fifteen critics. Not one came. Just as well. I'd put together this event in only three weeks, with a pianist recommended by my latest guru, Emanuel Hurwitz. He'd said kind things about me in a newspaper, "that I would have had a very big career had I started a bit earlier", which was a *fairly* pleasing way of being damned with faint praise. Some one at BBC Radio London got wind of this 'human interest' story and came to interview me at home about my 'debut 'at the age of forty. Almost forty-one, but I kept dates to myself. Fate and Fortune were kind and had kept me looking 'youthful.' I saw it as an initiation into the rigors of becoming a pro...not unlike killing one's first lion, if you are a Masai.

• • •

Despite advance publicity, an advert in the Times, an interview by BBC Radio London, an article in the 'Ham and High', the audience was small, just about 100 persons. Charles lost a lot of money. Playing in London is expensive; an altogether questionable thing to do without a sponsor. Apart from that it went well, considering. I was scared, not *quite* out of my wits but exceedingly brave. Good friends came to support me, although I'm sure they thought I was not brave, but foolhardy. My teacher's wife, also a fine musician, gave a positive report to her husband. Later, when he'd listened to the tape, along with some other 'eminent' violinist, whose name he could/would not reveal, he told me it was decided I was 'no ordinary violinist.'

I still have the recording of this event. For me there was always that nagging doubt: am I good enough, can I really play the violin like a pro? Have I caught up? What a hopelessly self-absorbed person!

I so needed to be alone,... to such an extent even, that when my daughters arrived to see us, while on leave in London, I can honestly say I have hardly any memory of them. The fact that both of them were wearing a lot of make-up is the only thing I took in. Gabi had just turned eighteen, Luci was nearly sixteen. As far as I knew they were happy and I saw them as practically grown-up. I'd last seen them over a year ago in Lagos; there had been little communication since then. It was that 'twisted path' again.

They must have stayed with us, as did my parents, who had carefully planned a holiday in England to coincide with our leave. They inspected the Wigmore Hall with us, when I was trying out the accoustics, with various splendid violins on loan from the famous Charles Beare, London's top dealer.

In Sao Paulo I played the tape to my pianist; she was delighted. Now my most loyal and helpful advisor, Isabel Mourau got us a run of concerts funded by Sao Paulo State. We worked up a program and flew about performing all over the place. One of the last concerts with her was in Salvador, where a local violinist / teacher from Russia informed me my playing 'resembled that of Yehudi Menuhin.' Now that was a very kind thing to say and I lapped it up. On the other hand...Menuhin was known to play out of tune...perhaps he was telling me my intonation was questionable?... but I'd had a standing ovation....? So you see, an artist is never sure, or satisfied, and the smallest remark could knock me off my pedestal, shatter my confidence, for ever.

As far as shattered confidence goes, in our private sphere we were going through a strange time too, trying to liven up our 'interplay' with dressing-up as people other than ourselves...anything, to bring *some* enthusiasm. This was not quite my thing, but 'what the hell' it seemed to bring *some* results......

Still, in very many ways, being a 'British Council wife' had huge advantages. Like the visit of one of Britain's greatest pianists, John Ogdon, which led to an informal luncheon in one of Sao Paulo's superb restaurants. This gentle shambling giant was accompanied by his wife, who had the responsibility of making his concert-career possible at all: he suffered from a condition which made him turn in on himself, locked into an interior world, where no-one could reach him.   At certain times one could get some response, but mostly his form was present, his 'person' elsewhere. It was a surprisingly difficult situation especially for his long-suffering, devoted wife, a pianist of note herself. We lunched and chatted with her, while *his* head hung down close to his plate, seemingly asleep. Occasionally he took a bite of whatever was put near his mouth. I don't believe any of us had realized he was in this parlous state. It seemed improbable he could play the piano at all. And yet, as he ambled on to the stage in the evening, took his bow and sat down to play one of Beethoven's monumental works, he transported us all with him to another plane, transfixed by the power of his vision and abilities. I wept, it was an experience I can't describe. Afterwards, thanking him for his playing, I took both his hands in mine, wanting to make him feel how I revered them, and him, so hoping he could feel something outside of him. He smiled, I think.....

Other luminaries from England visited Brazil adding further dimensions to our privileged lives. There was a great deal of cultural activity in this crazy city. There were no dull moments. The Cultura Inglese kept us all on our toes.

Once or twice, when I could prise Charles away from his typewriter, we took off to see other places, like Curitiba, Santos and Brasilia, the latter a surprise to even experienced travelers like us. When you fly over central Brazil you will see it, shaped like a large butterfly, in the savanna below. A planned project, and built in 1956, it had led to intense debate on what modern urban life should be like. Some of the world's most famous architects were called in.

We felt dwarfed and estranged from real life being chauffeured from one splendid building to the next. The distances from one place to another were huge and living there must surely be a nightmare as far as petrol consumption is concerned. It could not have been more different from Sao Paulo, like landing on the moon, strange and unreal; I certainly longed to get back 'home'.

One unfailing delight was going out to shop, back in our part of town. Brazilians know how to enjoy themselves: they serve free 'cafezinhos' in supermarkets, in order to make shopping an almost 'air-borne' activity. Having drunk a small sweet cup of strong, hot coffee, shoppers *fly* around the place, buying everything in sight; all the while their ears filled with enlivening hip-swinging Brazilian popular music. I too was carried away, aroused by permanent caffeine overdose. Many people were poor, out of work, yet un-usually smiling, easy-going. It must have been the coffee!

One day I took my cleaning lady home to her 'favela' after she'd finished her tasks, so I could learn a little more about *her* life. It was suitably chastening to see the conditions in such a township: slightly more substantial 'dwellings' than those of South African townships and better organized, even so, primitive by any standards. Yet she appeared clean and cheerful each day, and above all, I believed, honest and very wise. Everyone was Catholic. She had children, but no husband. While my servant earned the money, her mother took care of all their own domestic tasks.

There were some men about, mostly sitting on their doorsteps, doing tapestry....a favored male pastime in Brazil. Unemployment was huge; men played 'futebole' or did tapestry. I too became hooked, not on football but on tapestry: one could buy all requirements in the famous supermarkets.... crazed by a 'cafezinho' there was a wide choice of vibrant designs and colored wools,...irresistible. One of my creations has accompanied me in my violin case since 1977, now thirty years old it protects my instrument while reminding me of the excitements of Brazil.

Language skills had got me far enough to understand that *all women* regularly had massage in saunas and that it cost almost nothing to do so. My maid showed me where to go and soon I became a regular, just like her. Less pleasing, she took to 'borrowing' my clothes. I had lent her a special garment for a wedding she wanted to attend, but as the months passed she started helping herself, without telling me. When this came to light I realized I'd become too easy-going. There was now a tiny dent in our relationship. But exchanging language skills was indeed a strong bond. We survived amicably, until the bitter end.

This surprisingly, came all too soon. Charles had aroused the displeasure of Pinheiro Neto over some financial matter and headquarters put an end to the posting and sent us back to London. Whatever it was, we were all pleased, if somewhat surprised to be 'home' so soon, having stopped off on the way in Lisbon, just to see how Portuguese *really* sounds when spoken in Europe. For a few days he and I could test enough of our Brazilian Portuguese to feel we could get by. How nice. And how different it all felt, compared with my meagre little memories from 1944, when, as a nine-year old, we went sight-seeing during our repatriation as 'prisoners- of -war'!

Curiously, learning Portuguese had totally wiped out my fairly adequate French. I kept hoping it could be revived: but no luck...it was gone.

And (I believed) I had made it (sort of) as a serious violinist.

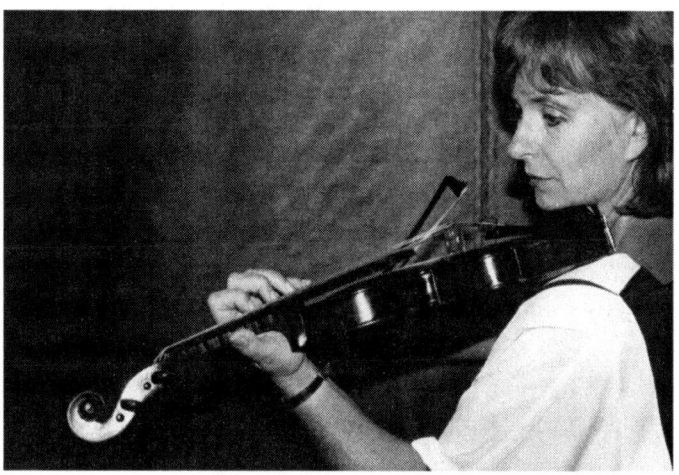

Evelyn in Canada 1984

England, 1978

We're home, Charles in a somewhat parlous state. He's exhausted, I think. Various plans come to light: to find *and* settle James in a boarding school. Our stroppy ten year-old seems quite in favor of this idea. We also consider taking 'leave' (let's *see* England, I've never been further north than Nottingham...) and above all, let's enjoy life a bit, let's *talk*.....we really *must* talk...

First we dropped the restive offspring at a summer camp for young musicians; he was to improve his piano skills while we would be able to talk, undisturbed. There's nothing like a long car journey, sightseeing aimlessly, in the Lake District... balm for the soul, stimulating, and also soothing. We spoiled ourselves, staying in a luxury B+B, serving gourmet food, all for £25 a night, a huge sum in 1977,..... called in at Wordsworth's house, saw all there was to see. I was happy. The only nagging doubt was the usual problem.....impossible to put right, it seemed: How was Charles?

Standing on a hill with a sweeping view of beautiful English countryside, I put my arm round him and, full of affection, pleaded for more physical closeness. Embarrassed, annoyed, I couldn't tell, he shrugged me off and made it clear there was nothing to talk about. An ominous and threatening moment..... I sensed for the first time a real danger, the situation was certainly out of *my* control.

There was only one way forward: both of us had to get on with our 'efforts', now that we were home. He had his job; I so wished I had one too. With the help of various contacts I wrote the usual letters, applying for auditions, for concerts at music clubs, for anything at all that would further my non-existent career. A promotional leaflet with photograph was designed and printed for this purpose. It's what one had to do to 'get on'. Charles helped me.

All I could do for *him* was clean, shop, cook and hide away his rejected manuscripts which flew in and out of the house. I felt compelled to do that because Charles became so deeply upset every time the rejections arrived. Stupid really- he had to have them sometime....I'd choose the moment carefully.

But the time for rejection is never right. In despair I telephoned one of the agents, without Charles' knowledge, to have a longish chat with some friendly man, about "my husband who is not able to find a publisher," what exactly did they think was wrong with the manuscript? I had no idea how ridiculous I must have sounded, and how angry Charles might have been, had he known. The literary person on the end of the line offered this pearl of wisdom: 'if the manuscript comes back more than twenty-five times it is best to *give up*, as there must be something seriously wrong.

Or words to that effect. Once there *was* a reaction, and Charles found himself invited to lunch with a very reputable publisher, who began to talk about 'film rights' and such matters. But time and time again the verdict ended with "very well written, but not commercial enough." Poor Charles. I went up and down the emotional ladder with him, and he did the same for me. I sort of believed in him, but wasn't *quite* sure ....and I truly doubt he was in any position to believe in me. Neither of us had a clue, really.

Matters became more serious when I began to present myself at auditions for major orchestras, like the BBC. The big hurdle was sight-reading, every time. Nobody wanted me. An hour spent playing to Harry Blech, the conductor of the London Mozart Players, also led to a non-committal reaction. I slunk away with my tail between my legs, so to say. I had neither pupils, nor a job, the only thing that kept me going was learning new repertoire with an elderly scientist, John Bateman, also known as 'groper' Bateman, who insisted I perform difficult contemporary music with him in various venues such as the Oxford and Cambridge Music club, a grandly-named amateur organization in London. This stylish host, for he had regular concert-parties at his home, kept me sane, when my mounting disappointment in London got the better of me. I was so desperate I began to find little things on pavements, several silver pendants: these I interpreted as omens of my impending better fortune, little silver horse-shoes, suns and stars. Why were there so many of them, lying about? Nine fruitless months in London, it was the black night of my soul, the 'The Slough of Despond.' I was going mad!

One morning I was caught wheeling a trolley out of a department store, laden with two bags of groceries paid for earlier, next door, plus a diary, a *fitted* sheet and a blouse for my mother, *not* paid for. My husband was complaining about our sheets, always having to be tucked in. Why had shoplifting become an option? I was clearly out of my mind. The fine was £75 and I had to ask Charles for the money. It was mortifying. I had to ask him for money every month, ("what, again...?") but this time he was kind and concerned and decided I needed my own account, with a steady income from him. I blush to my roots just remembering, alas, it is true. How humiliating to be forty, to have to ask for money, even more so, to pay a fine for stealing. I still don't know why I did this. The lady judge said that menopausal women often found themselves in this situation, offering me a glass of water when I broke down sobbing. I do believe she was trying to console me. Besides, I didn't think I was menopausal yet. I think peri-*menopausal* is the term used nowadays, even that was a way off.

Life is strange. Just a few days on there was a call from the 'fixer' of the London Mozart Players, they needed a deputy, for a three-hour rehearsal in Kensington, with a concert in the Queen Elisabeth Hall. My lucky break, the day my life changed! On a late summer afternoon, taking a rest from rehearsal in the gardens surrounding the Brompton Oratory, I became a *new person, content to be alive.*

• • •

Music comes from what is in your heart...I believed, naively, in those days.....and as a soloist this may be partly true. Sadly, and importantly, in professional music-making what is in your heart is second to what technique you've acquired during years of training.

Playing with other precision players I managed, but only just, to keep up. It was a case of being totally focused on those little black dots in front of you, and God help you, if you were sticking out of the body of sound created by the orchestra. The London Mozart Players were a tiny group: I started as a 'second' violin and there were sometimes only four players in the section. My blood pressure was probably rising to dangerous levels, knowing that one mistake too many would ensure I would not be booked again. And the boss, Harry Blech, believed in challenging his players to keep up the standards. During a casual chat on the telephone he enquired which *concertos* I had performed so far, and since the Sibelius was not on the list: "would I like to learn it and come round to play it to him?" Not one to be intimidated I took advice from my guru Manny Hurwitz. "It'll take you two months to learn," he said. Spot on; taking an accompanist along, I performed the Sibelius to the conductor in his home in Wimbledon. He was appreciative and later told the leader of the band how well I'd played. My confidence grew, I enjoyed the feeling of being accepted without any criticism....besides, the cheques were, to my mind, very handsome. My account was building up pleasingly.

Charles had worked hard to find the correct school for his son, subjecting him to all sorts of IQ tests because he was not progressing properly,...then finally discovered what seemed the correct place: 'Broomham', near Hastings, would help James to prepare for entry to secondary school. He would be a boarder and, to be honest, I looked forward to that.

It *was* a wrench, Sussex was two hours away, and when it came to the crunch my son wasn't brave at all; we *all* suffered, tearfully, in our different ways. James, a puzzling boy, was wise, lazy and not academic; neither of us knew how to get the best out of him.

I never got the 'dedicated parent' thing right. I needed to be alone, with my new music life. All my children had to let go; was this a case of 'man hands on misery to man', as Larkin proposed ?....I abandoned all three of them, for *my and their* own good, as my mother abandoned me for nearly five years, as Grossi abandoned her little Cölestine in Neumarktl. And 'abandoned' is ridiculous. I truly believed everyone was in good hands.

My big daughters certainly astonished me. Appearing occasionally from Canterbury I would pick them up from Kings Cross station, two bouncy, lively, affectionate young women in colorful clothes and full of chatter and laughs. The younger one did a cartwheel on the pavement; I could hardly believe it, such extrovert behavior! She was still at school, distinguishing herself with A's galore, in everything. What was to become of such a talented young woman? The indulgent elder sister was ready to go to University. Life seemed one big excitement; they made *me* feel very dull, staid, old and uncomfortable, perhaps it was more jealousy: living with their father had turned them into such unusual, exotic creatures. My influence on them was plainly zero. Just as well. I remembered how they'd used giggle, in the past, when I tried to speak German to them when they were little: "don't talk funny, Mummy", and "your name is *in a bog,*" *(Ingeborg).*

They had shown little interest in the rigors of classical music. Now, ten years on, they were intimidatingly up-to-date, in fads, fashion, pop music, TV programs, while I still felt I'd dropped in from another planet. My British-Lebanese-German daughters! Were they Hippies, or what? They were fun alright. But, we were 'estranged'....a strange word that, to be e... stranged. They had turned into two exotic birds I had to capture and get to know. We tried the ouija-board again, but they now seemed timid and refused. I thought I detected them looking at us in a disapproving way, as if we were either dull or mad or just plain old-fashioned. Their father was filling their heads with all manner of interesting concepts, like FREEDOM, and ADULT CHOICES, and somehow I felt *we* were being examined and judged. Charles took the easy way out...... flirted with them; I became jealous, wary, weary and confused.

On one of their visits I suggested a visit to an art gallery in Hampstead, feeling conscious of our dull life, hoping to entertain them a little. The gallery, attached to the Hampstead School of Art, offered courses in 'Life drawing' and, contemplating this poster.... I said to them: "Gosh, I'd love to do that, what fun it would be." Their reply, very matter-of-factly: "well, why don't you," led to instant signing up, opening a Pandora's Box of delights, the start of three years of developing my 'other' talent, modest, but liberating in so many ways!

Whenever they left I felt they were pleased to escape, as exotic birds do.

Once or twice they re-appeared with young men in appalling jackboots and other frightening punk gear, which led to tension, stress and revulsion from me; I had only one wish and that was for them to go away. I *should* have been asking questions, about drugs, about birth control pills, about their euphoric states of mind. And about their future! Like a coward, I remained silent. Once they'd gone I felt safe again, eagerly waiting for the next phone-call, from them, but even more, to be quite honest,... from *anyone* who had a 'job' for me.

• • •

For the first time in my life there was a diary, filled with dates that got me out of the house and into the world of London classical music.

Once I was accepted by the LMP other doors seem to open without me having to do a thing. I was soon invited by other orchestras such as the New Mozart Orchestra and the English Sinfonia, meeting and performing with illustrious musicians, people whom I had only ever seen from a distance or on record sleeves. It surprised me to find how many of my orchestral colleagues admitted to feeling bored, tired and underpaid. "Oh, not that again", said one of my desk partners, when Mozart's G-minor symphony stood on the music stand, or the general groan at yet another concerto, recently performed in some other city. We travelled a lot, mostly by car, sometimes by train, or coach, all over England. The soloists were inevitably famous musicians, but the hours were long. Just a few names, to add glamour to this account: Henryk Szering, Paul Tortelier, Cristina Ortiz, Mayumi Fujikawa, Alfred Brendel, Janet Baker, James Galway, Iona Brown, Nigel Kennedy...... one needed the constitution of an ox to recover from one 'gig' to the next.

After only a few months I was struck with the fact that orchestral musicians were very dreary indeed, the conversation mostly about fees, overtime, mileage, and the weather. Life, darting from 'gig to gig', can be, *was*,... stultifying, and the glamour of full evening dress on the stages of fine concert halls became, like everything in this life, a routine to deal with in the most efficient way possible. Returning late at night, from wherever I'd been, Charles would ask me if I'd enjoyed myself and I had to admit the truth was "not *really*." Of course there were lovely moments, fleeting ecstatic phrases, sublime soloists, and we all supported each other, getting to the performances and back late at night, but it was hard work. Inevitably men made advances, some people had affairs, but I kept clear of any entanglements. Looking back, I was very lucky to have experienced it for three years, but the glamour of such slavery is overrated.

Other surprising events kept me working hard at being a good musician: I had fairly eminent relatives who lived in Lübeck and they had heard me play privately, when I visited Germany before. Not exactly household names, they lived as professional musicians all their lives, he a flautist, she as pianist. They also ran a concert series in the beautiful ancient St. Annen Museum in Lübeck and decided to invite me as 'guest violinist from London'.

This was a step in the right direction: I performed a concerto by Tartini, with members of the Nord-Deutsche Rundfunk Orchester from Hamburg, and on a later occasion, some unaccompanied Bach; we also did various trio concerts in other towns like Bremen and Bonn, even crossed the North Sea to Heligoland.

Now these were unusual concerts, and a lot more pleasing than being a small cog in an orchestra! The fact that I had to go abroad, to play concertos in Germany, resonated well with the 'fixer' of the Mozart Players and my prestige grew,....especially when I had been booked for a trio concert in

Detroit, America. Just imagine: "Evelyn has to fly to Detroit to play a recital...." my colleagues looked at me with renewed interest.........

Somewhere, in the midst of all this busy-ness we moved from our 'chicken-coop' to a basement flat up the road. I'd spotted the FOR SALE sign, and as the relationship with our neighbor had become too strained because of her booming quadraphonic speakers at 2 a.m., night after night, and threats of court cases and police intervention made no difference, we sold the place and had an architect re-design a neglected Victorian flat, for a *new beginning*.

What a shame this flat was not filmed on first inspection: to find a dwelling in the middle of London's fashionable Hampstead, in 1980, in such a derelict, foul and primitive condition was truly worth recording. The 'poor old thing' who had ended her days among at least a dozen cats had obviously escaped the notice of social services.

By the door hung a romantic bell-pull and as you crossed the thresh-hold there was a coalhole, still in use. The potentially handsome front room, with a boarded-up fireplace was dark, damp and foul with broken old chairs and filthy objects. Nowhere was there any sanitation other than an outside loo, the kitchen a tiny corner on the way out with a miniscule brick-oven, and a small tin basin, with one dripping cold tap;   the garden a formless thicket of impenetrable weeds under a tall ash tree. Plumbing? Whoever had lived here was still a Victorian. There was *no* bathroom. One very small inside room, without ventilation, was filled knee-high with discarded junk, even a WW1 helmet. The smell of pee (cat, human?) was rank, the grime indescribable. Small wonder the place cost only £15,000. Puzzling, no-one had helped this old person. Didn't she have children, did no-one care? Perhaps she was bad-tempered, feral. We discovered later that the entire house, built 100 years earlier, had belonged to Mary Stopes, the pioneering family planner and eugenicist. Our basement was where the servants had lived; perhaps the former owner had been a parlor maid, who served Marie Stopes, and had never got away.

Originally, what had *actually* caught my eye, was a sapling, about five feet high, growing out of brickwork next to the bay window. I marveled at its ability to grow, out of a hole in the plaster. Each time I passed I admired its will to live. And then, unexpectedly... there was the FOR SALE sign. I'd already bonded with the place, because of the plant. I suppose that old woman was rather like the plant, hanging on, surviving on very little. I wish I'd seen her, taken her in; there *were* such bent old neglected women, struggling along on Hampstead's arty pavements.

We spent a lot of money on renovating, the flat became beautiful, in a dark, old-fashioned, classy way: two and a half rooms, a kitchen the size of a broom cupboard where the coal hole had been. But we loved it and it was a bonding experience, a happy upheaval. I sold my nasty Canadian Maple piano and used the proceeds to find a Blüthner, with an exquisite tone.

Charles used to play some works by Chopin and Mendelssohn so well in those days, that once or twice I thought his performance was a recording on the radio. He loved that piano. He also loved good pianists. There was one on our road, you could hear the endless practising as you passed. Hampstead was like that.

At this time my black clouds were to become even blacker. How confusing it all is, looking back, memories tinged: my own niggling dissatisfaction with my violin technique and with the even stronger sense of having failed in other important ways. Underpinning our uneasy relationship was *his* frustration with *his* writing and also with *my* reaction to *his* work. Not having any experience or training in literature, apart from reading and usually enjoying, *some* authors, Charles wanted feedback from me, whenever I was asked to read the novels he wrote. I was terrified of saying that I found them 'pastel' colored, a bit quaint, possibly boring, ...floundering about, but always of course 'how well he expressed himself, such marvelous prose, so sensitive, so cultivated'. Somehow, as the years passed, his inability to find a publisher seemed to become *my* fault, a result of *my* negative views.

Had I just simply said "how wonderful" and left it at that we might have been happier, closer, who knows?

Charles was away often, never happier than when he was packing his case to travel to distant countries as an 'election supervisor'. He'd whistle cheerfully just before he left, something that never happened at other times. When the Southern Rhodesian elections took place in 1980, he was away for three months. During such absences I always hoped things would improve between us.

Quite the opposite: much given to visiting my favorite fortune-teller in Camden Lock I was dumbfounded by his pronouncement: "I see your partner, desperately involved with someone, it could be a male person, it could be female...I can't see this clearly, but it is a very young person, jeans, a bike..."..... and I thought, for once, the fortune-teller was surely completely bonkers, Charles was much too busy with his job for such a thing.....but my antennae were out, I began to see how thin he was, always in his garden hut, scribbling away, looking pale and wan. One morning I found some partly burnt love-sonnets in the garden. I then began to remember people's insinuations: the old Irish woman upstairs who had said, out of the blue: "but Mr. Chadwick is a GOOD man, isn't he...such a good man...?", looking straight at me in a curious way, and a well known agony aunt, Anna Raeburn, who lived two doors away, had stopped me on the road asking what were my views on 'male fidelity'...

I'd just returned from a concert, carrying my violin, and felt too tired to get into a long dissertation on the topic. All these (cowardly) ladies were trying to tell me something that I was not picking up myself: Charles had been seen with *another* woman!

Nicola, a piano student at the RCM, *always* wore jeans, *always* travelled on a bike, which explains how the fortune-teller had picked up the 'androgynous' signals.

Explains? It really wondered about such things: how does fortune-telling come into being, what do these individuals do, to 'read' such information? I knew nothing about Nicola when I went to Camden Lock. I had hardly noticed Nicola, she lived in a basement flat and somebody's bike was always tied to the rails of the gate on the pavement. I did however know Anna Raeburn upstairs, just from one or two neighborly chats. All this remains a mystery. I truly don't see how the fortune-teller could have been reading the 'Nicola topic' in *my* mind.

This was when "the shit hit the fan". What a terrible and corny way to describe what follows:

I had returned triumphantly from Munich, after three successful and well-reviewed recitals in Germany.... Charles announced we had been offered a posting to Canada. Did I want to go? I said I wasn't sure, there was my 'work', my pupils; how about his own feelings? He hedged for a while. For some days I managed to keep quiet, but soon I could bear it no longer: I told him I'd found partly burnt pages

358

of his poetry and tried to get him talking,... had he fallen in love with someone?

"What's it got to do with you...a poet needs some inspiration, it's not serious....".but yes, eventually he conceded he was *besotted* with a little piano student two houses away, and they had been 'seeing' each other, but it was entirely platonic. I said I understood, and of course, "this happens", mentioned the fortune-teller episode, and finally confessed my own infidelities, with assurances that I had never stopped loving him and "what about us?....we've stuck it out for over fifteen years, and what were his thoughts about that."

Well, he just couldn't help it, we had been together for so long, and of course, he loved me, but "that sex-thing....well, try to understand and stop worrying", he suggested. I even enquired if he was perhaps homosexual, but he didn't think so. He was so *not* jealous about *my* confession, it was puzzling, even hurtful. Suddenly a posting to Canada seemed like a very good idea indeed. I could think of nothing else but my husband's infatuation, as he played it down and even became amorous with *me*, for a change. Nice as that was, it made things even *more* trying. It was so very easy to imagine how he felt about such a beautiful and talented young thing, and the fact that he was simply transferring his pent-up passion to me instantly put me into a state of feeling 'second best'. I couldn't eat. My colleagues thought I'd gone on some terrible diet; both of us became haggard and wan, from all the stress.

But we had opened up and, at last, able to talk. With such tumultuous emotions the only trouble was I couldn't believe most of what I heard him say. He was too quick and slippery with words. Round and round we went, trying to sort out our feelings and our future. He was 49 and this was his mid-life crisis.

My colleagues in the orchestra suggested I stay in London and send him off to Canada on his own. After all, it would be hard, even impossible, to get back into the profession, if I went away for several years. "Goodness, you must love that man", opined the wife of our concertmaster and I remember thinking how strange it was to be seen as a 'tragic' figure. But I was not tough enough to be parted from him. Besides, with all the excitement of packing, and buying new things for our next posting, and having somehow, at last, found a way to be closer and more open with each other, Canada appeared to be our salvation.

Before we left I confronted my demon(s) by calling on Nicola, the pianist who had bewitched my husband. She looked quite uncomfortable when she let me in, fearing perhaps I'd come to make a scene. I offered her my piano students, and mentioned, in an offhand way that I had been out of London quite a lot, giving concerts, and that it was obviously not a good thing to leave one's husband alone for too long. Just to show her I had a sense of humor. She was extremely beautiful.

• • •

There is a sub-plot to all this. It has to do with my daughters. It's quite difficult to remember what they were up to; a sign no doubt of my inadequacies as a mother.

Gabi must be 21, super-clever Luci is 19 and refuses further studies.... She, plainly in a state of anarchy, her young man in Punk boots, want to rebel even more and see the world...travelling and busking with a group and 'being free'. But they must have money, they need a 'home'. What they have is sexual freedom, presumably drugs and wild music... nothing but negative thoughts from me ...as far as that goes.

Charles says "wonderful" and gives them £2000, a down payment for a little cottage, somewhere. Good move. They buy a double-decker bus instead. A 'mobile' home. I'm not amused. It's the busking idea that gets me down. Putting a hat on the pavement and hoping for some cash to appear in it. It's not 'begging', it is 'giving a performance', they say, to be rewarded with money. This is their view. "Just like gypsies," I think....

Do 'Flower People' radiate love and compassion because they are permanently drugged, I wonder. What about the £2000? "Ah, we will sell the bus and buy a home, later." Charles is less fazed by all this than I am, perhaps because Luci is not *his* child. I am furious with him for trying to keep on the right side of my childrens' views, instead of playing the strong step-father figure. What does Pierre think? Not wanting to antagonize *everybody* I keep my mouth shut.

Gabi, still a student, seems more staid, less faddy. Why can't Luci be more sensible, like her sister?

Ottawa. 1982

I've stepped off the plane, straight into The Future. Just look at the 'Pomeranian peasant' now: new full-length sheepskin coat, fur hat, dark glasses and dainty boots... I pick my way through the snowy, icy landscape, feeling like an actress on a film set. Everything is larger than life...the roads, buildings, the shopping centres and cars, you name it...what a shiny, clean wondrous planet am I on..? Except for the telegraph poles, anomalously primitive, crooked logs, straight from the woods, all shapes and sizes.

Mogs, the inherited cat in 215 River Road is at least five kilos heavier, six inches higher, than any British moggy. Canadians are cheery, friendly, even the taxi-drivers, who compliment me on my 'lovely' British accent ("only my second language" I stop myself saying). French Canadians have an altogether peculiar accent, something from another age, another place.

Our house looks out across a road, over a strip of now bare park, on to a frozen river. There is a distant bridge. The view is gorgeous. Charles declares the place has 'no ghosts,' and is plainly not impressed. His view of it is colored by the fact that he studied Literature at Toronto University, after his leg was blown off in Korea; he feels he knows Canada well enough. Having turned down a place at Cambridge to come here, he *must* have liked it then....

Such abundance, opulence even.... Brent Cross in London is a poor wee thing by comparison. And he's so wrong about 'no ghosts'...there *are* historic buildings in town, near his office on Elgin Street, and some remaining 19th century architecture in Sussex Street: one still, just about, senses the fact that Ottawa was once the centre for the Canadian lumber, milling and timber industry, for the whole of North America. It might even explain the poor-quality telegraph and electricity poles. The place is full of rivers and canals. It is small enough to get to know well and I am so happy to be here. We are making a new start, all is well.

A new American Steinway baby-grand is on order, and our house, large and beautifully heated, comes with a Portuguese cleaning lady and the larger-than- life stripy cat; both of them very assured and on the bossy side. The cat comes to the bedroom door at six a.m., makes a huge fuss trying to open it. Apparently our predecessors allowed this. Well, Mogs, think again: we are locking you into the basement tonight.

The social round begins, one dinner party after the next. I will have to invite all these persons back in due course. The Portuguese ambassador, a keen music-lover, is already planning a soirée with classical music...he knows a good pianist and a cellist. This is the way forward: meeting musicians.

Mogs' resting place in the basement is declared my music room, where I keep all my books, stands, instruments and where I can practise undisturbed. Mogs loves the metronome and sits on the table, with his paw stretched to touch the moving inverted pendulum. Once the Steinway is installed upstairs Mogs shows he understands about such things too and sits patiently next to me while I play. Then it is *his* turn, he tries one paw, then both and eventually walks along the keyboard daintily, considering his massive frame. It sounds suitably '20th century' and New World. Mogs, my first Canadian pupil!

In the basement is a ping-pong room, where we have a television and a big cosy couch, and also buried below the ground-level, a huge guest suite, bathroom.... and a tiny bedroom, for James, when he appears for school holidays. Upstairs are two large bedrooms, bathrooms, a grand suite of drawing-room, hall and dining room, the biggest kitchen I've ever seen apart from the one in Mageregg... and a tiny study, for the smoking, typing, poring-over-Canadian-Literature man of the house. After our modest basement in London this place seems quite over the top. One soon grows into such a space....we already have. We've also acquired two second-hand bikes and some ski's, the cross-country variety! I will learn......

Canadians understand heating: downstairs rumbles a vast boiler, big enough to fuel the Titanic, the heating is always on, night and day. Thank-you, the British Taxpayer! While Charles drives out of our double garage each day, across two bridges, to his office in town, Mogs and I are as warm as can be. A huge cosy bubble is forming around me. In some ways I have never had it so good.

"Have a nice day", is what everybody says, where-ever you are, in a smiley, open-to-chat kind of way. Why are they so friendly? I was told Canadians were boring, but no-one mentioned their kindness. Our neighbors come over with a 'welcome' potted plant, they are Quebequois, and offer help and friendship. He is someone important in Parliament (Ottawa is the capital of Canada) and she is a university lecturer at Ottawa U....that's how they say it here: *ah' dah' wa' yooh*. I find myself trying to pronounce things in the Canadian way, feeling laid back. "In the summer you must come and swim in our pool", they say, "we have no fences in Canada, please come over, anytime. And we are used to looking after Mogs whenever you travel."

It's all too good to be true. The sun shines, icicles glisten and Mogs frolics in the snow. The cold air makes us frisky. I have seen icicles the size of elephant tusks. No, really! They sort of build up, over time. No sooner are we all settled than we pack our bags to take a week's trip across Canada, visiting some major towns, and while Charles calls on Universities and Council representatives I lounge about in 5-star hotels and explore, on my own. I learn to have eggs 'sunny-side up' and note the joys of blueberry muffins for breakfast.

The best way to get to know any place is to walk about and just look. A bit lonely sometimes, but there is always much to talk about later, when Charles returns from work, if we are not invited out.

Vancouver, named after Captain George Vancouver RN in the 1700's, has everything any human could want, mountains, the sea, beauty and wealth; apart from numerous Chinese I am struck with the comical British-ness of Vancouver Island, Union Jacks on display, London buses for transport.

Elsewhere Canada has a neutral orderly feel to it, plain and good. <u>Winnipeg</u>: dusty, bleak, wind-swept in a primitive wild-west sort of way; <u>Edmonton,</u> more groomed, <u>Calgary,</u> flashy. The big surprise are <u>Montreal and Quebec,</u> two bustling French cities of elegance and style, very different from the rest. Even Ottawa has a totally French twinned city on the other side of the Ottawa river: it is called Hull and I am finding out about the two unhappy factions... French Canadians and English-speakers, like two jealous siblings, vying and quarrelling endlessly, while they try to define their identities. By the time Charles and I return to Ottawa I have seen much of the country, apart from the North, the famous <u>Banff</u> in the Rockies and Newfoundland.

We have bought two power-steered cars.... no-one in North America bothers with gears - and special tyres for the winter. I can barely believe the amount of snow Canadians put up with each year. In Quebec City it is piled so high along the roads that the houses behind are invisible from the road. As soon as the stuff floats down the snow-ploughs come out of no-where, de-snowing every road. All shopping centres, both above and below ground are fantastically heated, in fact if you don't fancy being out you need never venture into the cold. Temperatures of -10 to -25, even -30 degrees Centigrade are quite normal in January and February. The condensation from your breathing turns into tiny ice crystals which settle on your eye-lashes and eyebrows. The cat reappears with snow-laden whiskers; he seems to like the great outdoors, at any temperature, but not for too long.

An Ottawa violin teacher has died a short while before our arrival and some of his pupils are finding their way to me. Within weeks I have a budding musical life. With the prospect of professional fees I gladly relinquish my 'diplomatic status' and scheme and plan, how to fill my days for the best. Like in London this means 'auditions'. The most prestigious orchestra in Canada, based in Ottawa at their National Arts Centre, is my first target, they hear me but decline...possibly because they know I am a diplomat's wife and will not be there for long. This is a blow: it is the best group far and wide. I soon meet many of their players, in other, less prestigious smaller orchestras, but not being with them on a regular basis rankles.

Having set the scene for life in Canada the problem now is how to deal with seven years of events: two fat diaries about the ups and downs, the myriads of memories, without becoming tedious. It also dawns on me that *capturing reality* is an illusion. Whose truth can I tell ...only mine? Even *that* shifts and moves about. How about Charles', or my childrens'? How depressing, how frustrating!

Somewhere, while all this is going on, Erika, my poor little mother and my father are beginning the run-up to the end of their lives. I never thought of this at the time; one believes parents will be around forever and both seem hale and busy and taking a great interest in our new life, even threatening to come over to visit! Erika's youngest sister lives in South Bend, which as any Canadian crow will tell you, is due south, not far from Ottawa. Canada= "kann er da?" (can he, there?) was my mum's little joke, not that I'd ever let her in on our marital problems. Who knows what she was alluding to, she was quite fond of making rude or plain 'dirty' jokes. Austrians are like that, scatological. See Mozart's letters!

As for my daughters, ...a somewhat delicate issue, with the eldest living first alone, then with a friend, after she'd spent a few weeks with us in London...we'd sort of pushed her out into a state of independence, and it was plain from the start she didn't like it at all. To cope with life I once found her locked in the downstairs loo, on the floor, chanting 'Om, Om, Om', which is allegedly a form of eastern meditation. Without this she felt she could not cope. She'd found a secretarial job with a handicraft magazine, she had to get to her office in Soho by Underground each day, she found it stressful.

The younger one, infected with the wish to be free, to rebel against society, and totally under the thumb of her boyfriend, the one in the 'bovver' boots, was travelling without any funds, busking her way across Europe. This was, to me, so unthinkable, so shocking, that the only way forward was to suppress the whole idea and get on with my own life. What did Pierre think? Was he still endlessly 'on' about freedom? He, by now, had so many other children, he was probably quite pleased to have shed the first two, according to my calculations, 24 and 22...or possibly 23 and 21 years. They were much on my mind, entering the school-of-life, doing it the hard way. It was only a matter of months before the eldest had ditched her job and joined the Punk buskers. I could hardly bear thinking about it. Just imagine the dainty teacups, coffee-cups clattering at Ottawa diplomatic ladies' coffee-mornings: ..."and what are your children doing, Evelyn, also at Oxford ...or still at school......?"

I got out of 'telling all' by changing the subject, even better, by not attending coffee-mornings: I had to 'practise for recitals', or 'go to rehearsals', any excuse would do to get away from diplomatic ladies. In their company I did tend to feel like a 'Pomeranian peasant' anyway, even without revealing my children's peculiarities. It's not as easy as it seems, being properly British. With a treble-whammy of being German, brought up partly in South Africa, divorced from a Lebanese, it is definitely easier to suppress matters with such potentially explosive backgrounds.

A Woman with a Mysterious Past, indeed, 'representing' Britain, abroad! On top of that: Hippy children. Representing Britain abroad is not quite like being an ordinary Brit...say, at a football match...one has to 'try harder', put one's best foot forward, wave the flag.....*all* the time.

On April the 2nd, 1982 Britain sent a Task Force to the Falklands.

A group of Argentinian scrap metal merchants raised an Argentinian flag on these islands, which was considered an offensive action and the now famous amphibious attack launched patriotic sentiments and much debate everywhere. Not usually deeply involved in world affairs, Charles and I became hotly embroiled in our snowy Canadian outpost, so much so that I began to feel divorce was the only solution for us. As time passed, I began to realize how very *many* views there were on this episode, and yet another storm in our relationship passed, ebbed away.

Everyone has heard of the iconic Glen Gould, Canada's starry, eccentric pianist. He stands alone, completely special. On the way to perform my first public recital in Ottawa, on October 4th 1982 there was an announcement on the radio that Glen Gould had died from a stroke. Canadian musicians and lovers of music must have been stunned. By some bizarre chance I had included an Elegy for unaccompanied violin by Stravinsky in my program, dedicated to the memory of a French musician. I was able to make an announcement....and played, with real sadness. This first recital in Canada was a successful start to seven fulfilling years. At the end of 1982 I began recording each day in my diary.

William, Charles' brother, the drama professor from Waterloo Ontario arrives for the first of many Xmases, bringing along one of his students, a silent twenty-year old. They are in love; he wants to 'shed' his wife.......

On the 25th December my diary says: "We are learning to play darts. It seems one has to look hard at the target and then allow the dart to fly to it. Perhaps all of life is like that: *know what one wants... then,...relax"*.....

Canada provided me with two roles: that of the British Council wife, helping her husband do his job...(why, *some* of us asked ourselves, should we have to be involved in this way...being 'representational', which meant official entertaining and let's face it... a lot of work...) and the secondary role of continuing to be a violinist. While, to his credit, Charles was always supportive and eager that I should have every opportunity I could get, he really needed another wife to do the 'representational' bit. Occasionally, when I was really tied up in a run of performances for some show or other, I arranged for expensive caterers to come and take over. This would use up rather more of the 'entertainment allowance'...not good! I returned from a performance one evening to be told the salmon I'd bought had been only large enough to feed twenty of the twenty-four guests....

Such minor but unpleasing events added more strain to our already frail relationship. I was alone at least two weeks in any month, while Charles travelled all over Canada, at first taking me with him. I visited <u>Toronto</u>, and Newfoundland, landing on Prince Edward Island covered in snow. On the way to <u>Charlottetown</u>, by car, we walked (briefly~brr~freezing in the wind) up a brown sand-dune to view the sea, that is, the ice, solid waves and drifts.... no water visible! Cute shingled houses painted in tasteful pastel shades, a tiny quaint town nestling in the snow...a Hilton, surprisingly sleazy-genteel, grace this little island. Confederation Centre, with art galleries, theatres, a library and restaurants,... could this be the 'saving grace' of the place? After a five-hour drive to a ferry-ice breaker on which we travel, crunching and churning up the frozen sea ..., cracks like flashes of lightening cut across the white expanse, and the shattered ice thickening and piling up, the ferry gets slower and even slower... we do eventually make it to New Brunswick. Again the pretty, undulating scenery, pines, snow-covered farms and a glorious red sunset, to pick up a flight in <u>Fredericton</u>......

Such experiences were the perks of life abroad, and Canada provided many.... getting to know the territory was part of 'being representational'.

Frozen rivers and lakes are challenging prospects in Canada.... apart from the obvious ice-skating and encampments over drilled holes for fishing.... one could wander among fantastic ice sculptures each year, some of them works of art, created in a competitive spirit to be awarded prizes just before the weather changed.

Shortly before we had witnessed an annual event which scared me out of my wits; we'd been told the Rideau River, just 25 meters from our house, would have to be opened up, or else the force of flowing Spring water from further up country would break the ice causing flooding all over *our* part of town. Early one day I woke to explosions, not unlike the sounds of the Russians advancing during the war... and leaped out of bed.... to find Mogs cowering behind the sofa, his hair on end: outside were municipal workers in special orange gear cutting small squares into the ice, then dynamiting it all along both banks so the water could flow freely down into the larger Ottawa River. This usually continued for three days at twenty minute intervals. Our cat could not endure it and encamped behind the furniture. Nothing had prepared me for the shaking walls and rattling windowpanes of 215 River Road. On the plus -side..... this was always the sign that Spring was near.

Canada *has* no Spring....it seems to go straight from 'covered in snow' to 'covered in filthy sludge' to 'covered in Dandelions'. These plants became the bane of my existence. They have roots the size of healthy carrots and I developed an obsession about pulling them out and admiring them. They must have been lurking there, under the snow, for weeks on end. I spent hours on my haunches, in the hot Canadian sunshine, ridding the lawn of these evil villainous weeds. Mogs took a keen interest, as did an elderly retired gentleman, a former military man who took regular walks along the river and decided he was in love with me. I called him the "spy"...he told me he'd once been one, and took to bringing me flowers. In Canada there are no fences, no garden gates. If you are gardening you are fair bait to any passers-by. Still, it was nice to be admired, even if by a relentless, ancient, lonely "spy".

All Canadian cities have a unique flavor, the loveliest of all is surely <u>Quebec</u> City, the only North American fortified city north of Mexico. It is one of the oldest towns in North America. The aboriginal Algonquins gave the place its name, "Kebec" ... meaning "where the river narrows", the river being the great St Lawrence. The Old Town, its restaurants and lifestyle and above all the history, make it a truly memorable place.

Not too far away is <u>Montreal</u>, nestling at the foot of 'Mount Royale', also on the St Lawrence; it is now one of the largest French-speaking cities in the world, after Paris. In the northwest of the city is 'Hampstead' where the nouveau riche live and 'Westmount,' where the *very* rich live. Also up there is a famous Oratory, festooned with crutches donated by persons who had been 'cured' by Brother André, a French-Canadian holy man. They are very Catholic, the French Canadians. The Confederation of Canada remains bi-lingual and I loved that, it added so much color, stimulation and interest, but alas, also a fair amount of bickering and distaste, distrust. There was this endless 'thing' about the 'Canadian Identity'...and scoring off each other.

The St Lawrence Iroquoians had a settlement by Mount Royal at least 2000 years before any Europeans got there. But in 1535 French explorer Cartier claimed the St Lawrence Valley for France and needless to say, as the decades, centuries passed, the settlers from Europe had much to fear from the Iroquois wars and raids.

• • •

Even further a-field, in April 1983....it seemed like halfway across the world.....we found ourselves one night on Hudson Bay at a place called <u>Rankin Inlet</u>....a small shack- airport decorated with antlers, and signs in Indian writing,.... outside a glowing full moon and lots of chattering Indians in soft sealskin boots and parkas, carrying away large cardboard boxes or relatives on 'skidoos'.....motorcycles on skates. Incredibly, this tiny spot has supported a population for about 4000 years; it is mentioned in Norse Sagas as Helluland, the 'land of the flat stones'. We were on our way to <u>Yellowknife</u>, arriving there late at night ....the capital of the North West territories. 400 km south of the Arctic Circle it was famous for its goldmines, now closed. Instead, diamonds were found. Covered in snow, even in April, I saw nothing at all but a few buildings sticking out of piles of snow and snow-mobiles.

Other high spots were two visits to Banff, both unbelievably glamorous: one for several days of an international Quartet competition, where we feasted our ears on the best young string players from all over the world, and the second event a TV film festival, in June 1985, during which we stayed in the ultra glamorous Banff Springs Hotel, the place of stars and royalty.. Strange how all these events have become so extraordinary in retrospect, at the time the reality was quite ordinary.... I was becoming incredibly spoilt and unquestioning. What had I done to deserve all this? Charles and I usually had lots to chat about, but there was always a distance, an invisible fence around him.

<u>Niagara</u> Falls, a one-off visit, regular trips to Toronto for cultural events - often of the literary variety that most pleased Charles (he had carefully read all the Canadian authors and truly relished meeting British and Canadian writers whenever possible).... our calendar of events was endlessly, gloriously and improbably interesting. Should I rattle off lists of *some* of the famous persons we had the honor

and pleasure of meeting in those seven years, from Prime Minister Pierre Trudeau to Maggie Thatcher, Princess Margaret, Gillian Weir, Margaret Drabble, William Golding, John Mortimer, Hanif Kureishi....Yehudi Menuhin....Trevor Pinnock, David Willcocks, and many, many more....?. All in a day's work, but seriously, it was good. No, better than that, it was marvelous. And, talking of 'work'...I actually performed in front of 1000's with Bob Hope, Dionne Warwick, even two lavish gigs with Liberace, using electronically amplified instruments in vast Conference centres. This was 'big-time' stuff. I was high on adrenaline.........

Through the sweltering summers, the frosty winters, the opulent travelling, entertainments and lavish shows and my own delightful 'business' of teaching and performing, there were three overall concerns which changed both Charles and me, *and* our expectations: *my* music, *his* writing, *our* children. Then there was the fourth, unspoken one, and the most frightening...our relationship.

However, what 'exercised' me on a daily level, was the never-ending wish and need to push my violin-playing way beyond what it had been. When I began lessons with the now famous Mauricio Fuks in Montreal, who diagnosed the need for a fundamental change of my bow hold, (a very hard thing to do when you are nearly fifty,) the struggle paid off, after a while. In the past, I had got by with my inadequacies...I was 'easy-on-the-eye' and could put on a good show.....but finally I had a better grasp of tone production, and from this gained security both as performer and teacher.

James was sent to see us during summer and winter holidays. He too was grappling with his instrument; to become a classical guitarist requires hard work. We had 'in-house' competitions to see who could play scales better and faster...he won! But his schooling in Henley was causing problems: the only activity he truly enjoyed was football, or going out with girls. None of us knew quite what we could expect of him, least of all he himself.

Occasionally the telephone rang, or a letter arrived, with a cry for financial aid from either Gabi or Luci, still swanning around on a bus, busking and, as the years passed, parading around their baby daughters on the streets of Spain. Luci had produced a daughter, and Gabi, not to be outdone, did the same a year later. Both daughters, unmarried, no money, no homes and no prospects, had given birth to my first grandchildren. There were two letters and once even a phone call from Pierre; I think they were about our daughters' latest escapades.

With no more than a fleeting acquaintance with Luci's partner and no idea about Gabi's man, I was horrified.

I wanted *no-one* to know. I wished I hadn't even told my parents: they were equally dismayed. On this first stage of grandmother-dom I could not connect with either Gabi or her sister..."they are grown-ups" I kept telling myself, "this is what they choose to do and it is not my business..." while a niggling little voice was saying: "is this all my fault? What does Pierre think of his daughters now?" It never occurred to me he was the ring-leader. I was so ashamed of their hippy-ness. I really didn't understand. I had frightening nightmares about them, strange sinister dangerous scenes, described in my diaries in those times.

Now an Interlude......we fly across time and land on the 24th October 2007, at 14:37...when Gabi tells me in the course of a flurry of emails:

"I'm fascinated by your 'hippy-children-shame', what a huge thing for you, not to mention us....Poor you, poor us...it all seems so crazy in retrospect but the feelings, they are very real. I'm so interested to know more. It's odd to have lived the other side of it. Your reaction was something rather abstract to us. Strange, being older now, having lived that experience and now seeing it from a different perspective. To us it was something to be proud of if you can imagine that. We were identifying with a whole generation of people, not just Dad, but songs, books, plays, films, it was a whole cultural movement. Remember the musical "Hair"? We knew every word by heart!

Dad wasn't the only idealist. There were much worse ones than him roaming the planet, longer hair, smoking pot! Now it's a piece of history, all that... some of the old hippies are very creative and productive on all sorts of green issues. It is probably all those ex-hippies that will 'bust a gut' to save the planet...."

I tried to consider a more flexible approach. It was hard, if not impossible, for me. I was not moving in circles that were exposed to hippy-dom. We never saw 'Hair', but heard about it. Goodness, what will the young get up to next?

To me such things were not *real* life. *Real life was still about 'trying hard' and 'getting somewhere' in life. Hopping about naked and being generally rebellious was not for grown-ups. Well, you could see this in nightclubs........And these 'flower-people', making LOVE not WAR....* yes, they were sweet, but this was not 'real' either......

By then James was about to go to Music College in Cardiff and needed sorting out, so I flew over, rented a room for him, set him up with the necessities of student life. He'd never lived alone before. All in all I had little faith in the activities and choices of my children, but who knows, maybe James would become a 'normal' chap.

Serving for so long in Canada we were present to see two High Commissioners take office and became particularly friendly with the second couple, Sir Derek Day and Lady Sheila. There was hardly a month when we were not invited to Earnscliffe, a Victorian manor overlooking the Ottawa River, since 1930 the home of the British High Commission. Lady Day had a butler called Mr Dear; she would call for him during posh social occasions, "could you bring the Port, Dear. And some more coffee please, Dear", which never failed to amuse the guests. We saw a great deal of each other. I felt accepted by them, more than by many of the other 'higher echelons'. They were lovely, warm and understanding, not even remotely pompous. They appreciated my musicianship and asked me to perform on numerous occasions, even for the Canadian representative of the Queen, the 'Governor General'. It is fair to say that I was beginning to feel very much part of the British establishment in Canada; this was pleasing. The Days knew nothing about my 'anarchic' daughters.... although I don't suppose they would have minded. Everyone loved Charles... I tagged along. When, in 1985 he was awarded an OBE, I was disappointed he wanted to be given his 'gong' by the Governor General in Ottawa, gone was the chance to go to Buckingham Palace..... Charles had turned it down! How much more British could things have been: a face to face with the Queen...and now this turning *down* 'turning up' at the Palace. Too bad ....

This leaves me with my flickering flame of a marriage: we could have been so very happy I always thought, we had so much going for us. But Charles had observed and absolved his brother divorcing and marrying a much younger woman and I felt all the time that he had simply wearied of being *my* partner and that he too longed for a change. Perhaps, without realizing he needed a more literary, more truly English person by his side. I had no idea he was still in touch with Nicola. To me, she stood on a pedestal, radiating youth, beauty, talent, and I was 'old hat', just a friend. A housekeeper-friend, a sister..., how can one tell what was really the matter. Not that I was undesirable...I had numerous offers and opportunities for going 'astray', and indeed, on two and a half occasions.... I did.

One half-an-occasion was my sex-crazed dentist, and the memory of that is merely sad, if not comical. The other two were one very old and famous person about whom Charles was apprised.... and a young man half my age, so very touching, if not flattering.

My husband never ever showed any sign of jealousy. This was quite painful.... he just didn't seem to care. To me this was worse torture than if he'd beaten me up. I *wanted him to care, I wanted him to want me. He could not.* He just laughed when I told him...then asked: "does he want to marry you?" And at the next opportunity, went straight up and shook the man's hand. As if to say: "well thanks, mate, why don't *you* just take her off my hands and look after her for the rest of *your* life....

Beside regular and stimulating trips to Toronto and Montreal we also managed one 'home leave' with a visit to Vienna and Milan, and for me, two weeks in CapeTown.

This time my father wept when I left, something he'd never done before. By then Head Office had informed us that another, final posting was being planned, this time to Poland; when I told my father he instantly mapped out *his* visit to Warsaw. I had mixed feelings about him coming to see us there:

as an elderly German who had lost his beloved Pomeranian homeland to Poland after the War he would surely forget himself and come out with something tactless...I kept my thoughts to myself. Dark as they were they proved to be unnecessary: three months later he was dead.

"I'm going to be 100 years"...had been his mantra but, his time was up.... aged only 88; he had been a heavy smoker for much of his life. He'd recovered from an aneurism *and* from prostate cancer...were his tears at the airport some sort of premonition of this very sudden and brief lung cancer?

Handel's Largo, played on the organ during the cremation service had made me sob on cue beside my Mum who, with a sideways glance of her pale-green eyes surreptitiously slipped me her handkerchief, as if to say " I didn't think you really cared?..."

Later the Lutheran Pastor invited everyone present to come to tea in the Ihlenfeldt's garden on Paradise Road. Erika Hermine Josephine, by now a shrunken, scatty, brave person, was, as always, able to put on a show. She did not believe in public demonstration of tears and sorrow and managed, graciously, to host the reception. *She* should have been a diplomat's wife!

A few days on we took his ashes to a rocky beach near Clifton on the southern side of CapeTown and, clambering over the rocks, I was to throw them in the sea, as designated by my father. For a few moments time seemed to stand still. Some flecked foam flew up onto my black skirt leaving a permanent white mark on a prominent front pleat....no doubt a reprimand from my Dad for not checking the direction of the wind.

"Schrecklich, schrecklich"...I heard my mother say, again, quietly, to herself. I imagined how frightening, how terrible the reality of it all must have felt: her big, strong, good-looking Reini turned into ashes in a cardboard shoebox......

Now, for the first time, Erika was in charge of her own life. It was 1988, she was 81 years old. I suspect, secretly, she was quite excited about this idea. For a while.

I felt so responsible for her. Even though Erika still had many good friends, all were elderly and kept doing that 'disappearing trick', so the only people who could offer advice were her sister in Vienna, and her daughter, halfway between Ottawa and Warsaw.

We both visited and stayed for longer spells, trying desperately to get her out of the house and into a place where she could lead an independent but more sheltered existence. Erika was as stubborn as a mule. Nothing seemed to suit her and we simply had to wait until she saw reason.

After a year's struggle, the 'mule' was won over by a posh establishment opposite the President's residence, Whitehall Court. Erika Hermine Josephine felt she could settle for leading the existence of a 'dowager duchess,' surrounded by other elderly folk. There were even some lonesome gentlemen lounging about! She always noticed them...

There followed three weeks of mother-and-daughter team-work: we worked out exactly what she needed just for herself in her New Life, then announced a Big Sale, to friends and former colleagues. For three weeks, I trimmed down her possessions; a painful, terrible time for her. Once, getting it really wrong, I cleared out a drawer in the bedroom, which included what I assumed to be my fathers' false teeth. Within a day or two she was asking for her 'spare teeth'. I had no idea she even *had* false teeth! The rubbish bag had been picked up the following morning. I never had the guts to tell her. Fortunately she had become rather forgetful. While she slept I stealthily emptied possessions into black bags and hid them in the garage, or even out on the road. Car-loads of books and records went to the German Old Age home, also shelves of kitchen stuff, items accumulated over the decades, bedding and all my father's clothes. She quite liked it when she got a good price for her furniture, she loved having money and enjoyed adding up how much she'd 'earned' so far.

"You can afford some nice new teeth," I ventured. She looked pleased. In the meantime my father's banker had come to call, to explain to her she was now a wealthy lady and could have anything she wanted. Erika, the arch-scrimper and saver, survivor of two world wars and one major recession, showed nothing but dignified delight. Eventually she was settled in style: a one-bedroom flat with a tiny balcony...viewing the Presidential gardens and the back of Table Mountain. Surrounded by her best things, her Persian rugs, favorite pictures and her silver, with china and glassware in a smart little kitchen for private entertaining,...we had done really well! She owned a car, in garage no. 23. There were lifts to the elegant dining room and the place was full of very friendly retired persons. She had to 'dress' for dinner! She quite liked all that, at first...

• • •

After seven years on the North American continent came the pain of packing up again, and even worse, by the fact that no-one wanted to take on our ten-year old furry personage: wise beyond the usual, the only cat I knew who would go for stately walks with me, who attacked children dressed as mice at Halloween events, a cat who thought to bring me exotic birds dripping blood over the marble floor and who recognized the image of himself on the lid of a butter-dish. Standing on his hind-legs, paws on the table, he'd gaze at this striped pottery cat, make pitiful sounds, his tail swishing to and fro. When a vet was called to give him an injection, I held him in my arms, with a strip of his favorite mozzarella cheese near his nose; he kept very still. He knew. He was carried off in a black bag. To think how I deceived him!

Sandwiched between seven years in Canada and a 'New Life behind the Iron Curtain' were those few months of preparation for the final posting, back in London. Charles took special lessons with a Polish teacher, but, equipped with Linguaphone cassettes already in Ottawa, (we feared the challenge of a Slav language and its complex grammar....) we hoped to become better and cleverer than ordinary mortals if we started in very good time.

The opinions of a Rumanian violinist, a Polish cellist and a Russian violist, with whom I had shared numerous musical events, were: that we would detest it... warning, in heavy Slav voices: "don't go, Evaleen, you cannot 'leefe in Kommunist kahnntry...you ahrr meking Beeeg Mistake...daire iss no foot, eet iss daark and daire iss no vork, de shops ahrr embty....

However, the very first phrase of Polish Pavel the cellist taught me was: "dsijai jest wadne, sloneszcnie dzien".. (today is a lovely sunny day)......"it will be useful" he said, "it will cheer you up...." He corrected my pronounciation, patiently, for several weeks; he was, as in everything, a perfectionist. Charles and I vied with each other, repeating such phrases as "kwiaty na parapecie" (flowers on the windowsill) and other amusing Linguaphone offerings. "When will we be able to say *that* to anyone?"..... we giggled about that.

I got into the habit of telephoning my mother every other day. She kept asking me to come and stay with her: "what shall I do all day", she asked, like a child. I was conscious of having to 'mother' her, so depressed, confused, and helpless. The business of getting her settled, learning Polish and of living in London again while darting down to Cape Town from time to time, allowed little time to worry about Charles. I had to be away quite a lot. He claimed he was no longer interested in Nicola and like a fool I believed him. Once our time in Canada had ended and we were back in our basement in London, Erika treated herself to a visit to London to make a pilgrimage to Woodford Green. Dewy-eyed she claimed to 'remember' the roads,...we found Snake's Lane, but the house of her childhood memories was no longer there.

"I wouldn't like having to keep an eye on *him*," she stated one evening, completely out of the blue..... when Charles had gone off for 'Polish lessons'..... she still had an eye for a good-looking man. Did she sense, with a mother's instinct, what *we* were going through? After London she flew to Vienna, staying with her sister in an apartment on the seventh floor of a building with no lift. These were two fit old ladies! A bit muddled, asking the same questions over and over, but really well in other ways. Eventually, when Erika returned to CapeTown, all alone, the scenario changed. She began to withdraw into her flat, unable to make contact with her new surroundings. She blossomed only when her sister or her child came to see her...and when she could lure old friends to her flat, but somehow, living alone, became a huge problem. Not only for her, also for everyone who cared about her.

There was no way I could have taken her to either Canada or Poland. And there was no way Erika could return to Vienna....she was too much an 'African' by now. Feeling her fate closing in on her, sensing the misery of a lonely Old Age she was becoming an eighty-five year old 'Poor Thing'.

I was truly missing Ottawa. Then, gradually, Poland became a reality. Someone 'in the know' had arranged for us to meet Adam Zamoyski at a luncheon.

This distinguished historian and internationally best-selling author just happened to be a Polish Count from a family which for 400 years, had been one of the most glorious and influential in the country's history. Tall, slender, distinguished, in a black coat with velvet collar and a flashing diamond ring on his hand, he told us some of the more relevant facts we would need to understand Polish ways.

"What a burden", I thought, "to have to come to terms with such a history." Educated in England, studied at Oxford, despite such a back-ground his immersion into the thousand years of conflict in Eastern Europe was what *he* was all about.

After this meeting we realized just how much *more* reading and learning lay ahead for us.

• • •

Where is the Truth? I've studied the diaries and they are full of complaints, miseries and disappointments. Why have old memories   assumed a golden glow of happy days, good fortune, gratitude, twenty years on?

Perhaps current contentment has an effect on past sadness?

Poland 1989.

Over the Baltic, the island of Rügen, just a few moments before Swinemünde...and there it lies, just like the page of my Atlas: through scattered clouds I see Pomerania; an isthmus, lakes...then down another 200 miles in the direction of Warsaw, ETA is 4 pm and this time there is no great adjustment, the so-called Pomeranian Peasant comes 'home'... correction: once this was home; my *new* home is London.

"Don't kid yourself, get real...just because the Ur-Ihlenfeldts were fashioned here, grown from this earth down below, were buried in it....it's never been home...this is the dreaded Communist Poland." Maybe I just *want* it to be home. 'Po mare' in Polish means nothing more than 'by the sea'. My father's beloved Pomerania, and the Baltic: this he regarded as his very own land and ocean.....he was devoted to it all, many of his ancestors tilled this earth, spoke the dialect and knew the customs...he loved it, but not enough to stay ...in fact, he thought of it with a mixture of fondness and distaste...the small-mindedness, the backwardness.

Church records show the earliest *Ihlenfeldts* were laid to rest more or less where my flight is crossing right now. The unusual name may well go back to an ancient Knight in Mecklenburg or some Nordic invaders: there are *Uhlefeldts*, *Ahlefeldts*, and *Ihlefelds* in Sweden and Denmark. Swedes occupied and terrorized this entire area for at least one hundred years. Poor Poles, poor Russians, poor Germans, everyone being pushed around and made homeless, over and over again. For 100 years there was no Poland whatsoever. At the end of the Second World War Stalin was granted much of the borderlands in the East of Poland and instead Poland received a large chunk of East Germany, including my father's homeland: one of the reasons we had to flee, when the Russians were coming. Only half of me comes from here...I remind myself, the other half, from the west side of those very high mountains, that go pink in the setting sun, a happier, sunnier place.

28 May. Hazy sunshine on arrival. On the runway militia with guns and *bayonets* are waiting for us; "is this how it will be here, with *the Communists?*" I haven't yet disembarked, am bristling already: I was seeing things: the supposed bayonets were walkie-talkies with long *antennae,* how silly of me. I remind myself: "stop seeing problems when there are none."

Being diplomats usually has advantages but no, we are not exactly *whisked* through Immigration; under dimly-lit neon tubes sour-faced officials in the dismal, peeling building make heavy weather of the formalities. First impressions: tall Linden trees along the roads into town, drab, dusty high-rise apartments absolutely identical, everywhere,... further in, more stylish, but neglected European-style architecture, wide roads and pavements. Cars seem to park *on* the pavement, diagonally, side by side, so they can slip out backwards into the traffic.

Quite clever, that, if you are careful! You could easily bump into the wobbly, antiquated trams, if you are not. Pitiful window displays remind me of Ndola in the 50's. A sinking of the heart: I hear the warnings of my colleagues in Ottawa.... this is dreadful, not unlike black and white films about the War.

Sunset is the time when new places look hostile.... the 'unknown' brings a sinking feeling. This is why Brit's invented the sun-downer: a good dose of gin and tonic unlocks the flow of positive thoughts and adds delightful release, blissful relaxation......

......from a window on the 13th floor of the Forum Hotel I confront the Palace of Culture, built by the Russians for the Poles as a peace offering. It dominates everything. Roads are being dug up everywhere...Warsaw will have a Metro, to be finished in about five years, in the meantime it looks a mess.

We've been granted an hour from arrival at the hotel before we are picked up to dine with our predecessors. They return to Britain in two weeks, their personal belongings already packed. What we see in the house is what we'll get, along with our own sixty packing cases from Canada. Our *final* new home, before retirement.

Not much to say about that: an ugly, grey, three-story building, on a road called Ro ana, in an area known as Mokotow, adequate inside, plain furnishing and some valuable paintings on loan from head-quarters. My heart is not 'singing', but, as Charles was given to say 'in for a penny, in for a pound.'..... We talk about the hand-over, both official and domestic, the only amusing thing is their Corgi, wearing a large white cone around his neck to stop him biting or licking or something. He barks non-stop. Charles wittily calls him a 'pièce de resistance', but this joke requires knowledge of Polish (*pies*=dog) and French (*pièce*=object) *pièce* has same pronunciation as pies... oh well. (dog of resistance= a watchdog)

We are told we are watched and bugged, *all the time*.... across the road there are antennae directed towards this house and that whenever we go out we will be followed. We'll get used to all this.

29th May, 1989. Swarms of shifty men hover around the hotel entrance. We are being followed. Charles falls for the pestering Pole who is offering a favorable exchange rate, and we *do* need some zlotys! "7000 zlotys to the £" we hear and there is a great flurry of zlotys for the £20 pound note we offer....we should have had fourteen 10.000 notes. Feeling guilty....it's all so quick, and under-hand, we don't dare check. But when we do- we have *one* 10.000 note on the top and all the rest 20 zloty notes! This supposedly illegal act is the quick way for Poles to get their hands on foreign currency which they can then use in Pewex shops where western goods are available. We are learning!

The Deputy Representative takes us sightseeing round the Old Town, completely reconstructed after the War. This is the lovely part of Warsaw. Like a film-set in its perfection.

At the end of the day we decide Warsaw is not unlike a grey, derelict Vienna, almost totally without any niceties,.... alien, not to be trusted. Speaking of niceties: In Poland one *always brings flowers when visiting and gentlemen kiss the hands of ladies on arrival and departure.* This is the first custom in Poland I warm to.

As our baggage from Canada and from London will not arrive for another five days we are packed off to do a reconnaissance trip from the top of Poland (Gdansk) to the bottom (Wroclaw).

30th May, 5.30 am: Warsaw Central Station, a cavernous, clean place right by the famous Palace of Culture. We don't have far to go: Warsaw is clean, the roads, the subways, no litter, no graffitti, noticeably so after the filth of London. There is much scaffolding, apparently not so much for repairs, more for keeping rubble from falling on your head as you walk. From the platform I see two Russian trains, dark-green, old-fashioned, complete with lace curtains and fresh flowers by the windows.........

We settle into our compartment and gaze at Poland, flat, some oak-forests and primitive farms with horse-drawn ploughs and reapers with scythes and horse drawn carts. I've returned to another century. Charles notices him too: at a station there is a man who resembles my father...same shape of head, same hairline. I'd never considered my father as 'Slav'. Am I 'seeing' things?

Wroclav (Breslau) It's difficult to think of Breslau as anything but German, as if one had to think of Köln as French or Hamburg as Danish. It used to be the capital of Silesia, situated on the banks of the Oder. A terrible battle in 1945, a three month siege during which something like 29.000 civilians were killed, apart from military casualties and 40.000 prisoners, estimates vary, but these are the events to think about now.

First call is a wondrous late 17th century building, the University. Students are on strike but the Rector entertains us with a multilingual luncheon during which we 'glitter' in French, German, English. For once even I am useful: there are two German publishers at the table who speak only German. We are shown the famous Baroque Hall, the Aula of the university, where Brahms conducted the first performance of his Academic Festival Overture. Poles play down any German history, but even the Rector speaks passable German and we hear a lot on the streets, when we wander about in the old city with its beautiful Gothic buildings and Protestant churches, now converted to Catholicism.

After a mere 24 hours we have convinced ourselves that Wroclav is a very pleasant place, *much* nicer than Warsaw.

Another train journey brings us north to Poznan. Our hotel is out in the fields, near a wood. I am woken by the local cuckoo, on a warm sunny day. Didn't some relative of mine come from here? I must find out. I feel good here and yes, I know, it's all in the mind, this thing about 'belonging.'

The freshly painted Orbis Hotel,(a chain of Polish hotels) seems more prosperous than Warsaw, which is stuck in its dingy, neglected image, as I think back. Someone explains that this town has a groomed appearance, attractive shops, because it is near the German border and the prosperity is due to the annual Poznan Fair. While Charles sees to his work I visit an 'Instrument Museum' with impressive old clarinets, oboes and forte-pianos, also some named stringed instruments and two of Chopin's pianos, used by him in his youth. There are many folk fiddles and I learn that Poland considers itself the *land of the violin*; the folk fiddles are crudely carved and hugely in demand...I have no idea what they sound like.

June 1st. In Gdansk one smells the sea air. From the window on the 8th floor of another hotel I see the distant shipyards. Last night we took a post-dinner walk around the block, through some dark streets and past St Brigid's church where Wallensa goes to Mass. The place is deserted, lifeless, no sounds, no pubs, no traffic; where are the Poles? The hotel dining room is filled with Japanese, Germans and other foreigners, like ourselves. I eat pork knuckles and sauerkraut, like other Germans, Charles averts his gaze. Polish beer is alright. But Gdansk looks rundown and neglected, like Warsaw, dusty and dreary. What Poland needs is a Paint Factory..............(When you go to a Polish loo in a public place such as an hotel you have to pay the attendant 30 zlotys who will tear off a modest length of loo-roll, then you may proceed.)..... Plainly, a toilet paper factory is needed as well.

After Charles' official duties with charming Rectors in old-style Universities and Polytechnics we are free to inspect the mostly reconstructed Danzig, the ancient Hanseatic Baltic town, full of heart-rending, moving tales of the distant and not so distant past.

There is the lovely old Mariatzki, the most beautiful of many 'old' streets with below-street level shops selling Baltic treasures, art and amber in every shape imaginable.... cavernous brick churches, just like the ones in Lübeck. It is impossible to know what is Polish,what is German; a touchy subject. I object to ancient inscriptions on German grave-stones, deliberately made illegible by Poles. If *my* great-great grandfather, an admiral in the German navy, had been buried in a local church and commemorated with a carved stone on the floor of a church I would surely be allowed to feel aggrieved, if *his* dates and name had been removed. He *did* work in Gdansk. He died somewhere in Pomerania in 1882, long before the Nazis. Charles reminds me of 'collective guilt'...... I don't like it.

This is where it starts, that 'guilt thing': It is hard to be a German *anywhere*, but even harder in Poland. Warsaw and Gdansk have shrines on every street where candles are lit and flowers are left on a daily basis, to recall the murdered Poles during the War. At first I am amazed, then shocked, then tearful, finally resentful. I am truly sorry that German soldiers did brutal 'unforgivable' things, Russians, as well. Should I put a candle down? *I'm collectively guilty.* I honestly don't feel guilty but I am supposed to. How does one handle all this about 'the sins of fathers visited on their children'......who said that, anyway? I don't want to know and yet I must. *I must.* I try to imagine these cruel events. But guilty? If my father had committed crimes, would I feel guilt? I think 'uncomfortable', certainly. Wondering why he'd done it, wishing he hadn't. It would have been *his* decision, not mine. Anyway, he was in no-one's army and lived, locked up in an African Camp during the War. Thank God, at least, for that. So I walk past sad flickering candles and try to focus on other things. Like the wars over this ancient Hanseatic town.

Being here is having a disturbing effect on me.

2 June. Non-stop from breakfast till dusk: first a call on yet another Rector and the usual chat, seated on old carved chairs...charming, they always seem to be. He gives us strong coffee, delicious poppy-seed cake and I have time to enjoy his beautiful clear Polish; even *I* can understand. Later we see the Old Town and then lunch in a grand hotel, memorable for the scooped out ice cream containing a lump of glowing sugar. (sugar-lump is soaked in brandy, then lit).....

At dusk we are taken to Gdynia, the harbor area and to Sopot, with its elegant pier and holiday hotels, the Baltic turbulent, the swans looking uncomfortable. Swans? Strange, I don't associated swans with waves and oceans. Do they like salt water? Perhaps the Baltic is not salty, just polluted. Bathing is forbidden.

Another early start, we must catch the train back to Warsaw at 6am. We look forward to a sturdy Polish Peasant breakfast during the journey: bread-rolls, with ham, cheese and coffee.

Blearily, taking the briefcase, so my husband can deal with the small suitcase, I enter the carriage, vaguely aware that he seems to be held up by a sudden knot in the flow of human bodies trying to board, I hear shuffling and "przeprasczam" (excuse me, sorry) and a few calls from men to one another, it all takes a while before Charles appears, sighing, bemused and ruffled. Already settled for our three-hour journey I have placed his briefcase on a seat. The train moves while we discuss the commotion and discover to our delight there is an English-speaking Pole sharing our carriage. He is a guitarist. We chat and when we are asked for our tickets Charles feels first in the usual pocket, then the other, then searches his briefcase... the wallet...where is it ....he had been robbed, in broad daylight, and hadn't even noticed.

We'd been warned *not* to speak English in public places, and obviously forgotten to keep our mouths shut. The Warsaw/Gdansk train-robbers are famous for their skills; the Polish guitarist saw it all, telling us about their cunning wickedness and offers to make a written statement to the police at Warsaw station and also to the police in Gdansk. Later I wondered if he was perhaps part of the gang, the man who soothes the ruffled feathers with his excellent English? Never have three hours on a train passed more rapidly...it was not so much the cards nor the money, more the fact that we never even cottoned-on to what was happening...two of the three men still on the train protesting innocence, the third vanished of course...very clever. On top of everything, no breakfast, 'skint' as we were!

"Mother-hen" British Council is almost directly opposite the Station. We rush back under her wing, are plied with coffee and reassurances..."it happens to almost everybody, don't worry, we'll take care of everything".....cluck,cluck.cluck......I had not yet been to the office...a magnificent place, easily the most impressive I'd come across, with a hall for receptions, a small cinema, a large library with reading room. Tomorrow is a very Big Day!

June 4. The Polish Elections. The world is watching: this will surely be the day Communism is vanquished? Having passed muster we've re-located to the top floor of our new home; our predecessors are still living down below, about to return to England. I stare out of a window hoping to see crowds on their way to vote, but Warsaw is quiet, deserted. To see some action we are taken to lunch at the British Country Club, but there too all is quiet....

dark clouds, mosquitoes, later some drizzle. In the evening we are treated to a visit to the theatre: two amusing short plays by Vaclaw Havel, enjoyable,... we needed 'help' though: actors speak faster than Linguaphone tapes ......

5 June. With some help from our predecessor's wife I am learning about useful shops on our road, and how to get onto wobbly, antiquated trams: incredibly cheap, 30 zlotys, about ½ pence a ride in any direction, that's Communism! We call in at the Embassy shop which measures 5x3 yards and stocks sensible British basics ...enough for very lazy British staff to survive if they are too scared to look around Warsaw markets. Our Ambassador is paying for a packet of Aspirin at the till......

Markets are out in the open, a huddle of covered tent-like stalls where you find fruit, flowers, smoked eel and imported goodies from Germany, cheeses, olives, biscuits and other luxuries, costing 1000's of zlotys, in line with prices on the other side of the iron curtain. Colorful, full of life and surprises, but very few Poles can afford this; one feels guilty buying things here.

Back home I am introduced to the cleaning lady 'Dorota', who is not only intimidatingly lovely but also speaks a little English, enough to break the ice anyway. She used to work for a Warsaw newspaper, now does house-cleaning to supplement the family income with dollars. If ever there was a so-called 'representational' female, she is the one....*she* should be married to Charles and I should be doing the dusting. She has promised to help me with my Polish...... Then on to the Embassy Club to meet staff, followed by a dinner party at the Deputy Representative's, with a wondrous collection of interesting people, ministers, poets, a conductor and a flautist...people are elegant... I shall have to try a lot harder.

6th June. Have trammed and walked over huge tracts of this city. Typical on every street-corner are the Ruch Stalls. 'Ruch' is Polish for 'motion', 'traffic' or 'movement.' Here you purchase newspapers, stamps, tram-tickets, matches and shaving cream as well as the more intimate necessities of life; also typical are the columns with little red domes, displaying posters of cultural events.

Mysterious archways leading to courtyards are a common feature of architecture here, an endless delight; what is it about a dark tunnel leading to unexplored territory? It is quite usual to find nothing but overflowing dustbins, but often there are little gardens around a religious statue or benches under a tree, in bigger spaces perhaps small shops like milliners, shoemakers or silversmiths. Bras and corsets can be made to measure, judging from the stunning Amazonian encasements with stout circular stitching in a shop-window behind the British Council. Out in the residential areas it is still usual to have frames in these courtyards for carpet beating. In the early evenings, after tired wives return from work one can hear the thumping of rugs being beaten, reverberating between the surrounding walls. Or is it the Polish husband who does the beating? Large overflowing dustbins, usually left overturned, while cats, immense black crows and pigeons, rummage peaceably together, the cats skinny and feral, no cat-lovers here. Pedigree dogs are the thing, not a mongrel in sight. Dogs on the street are always muzzled.

Some things have not changed in Poland: an ancient horse and cart frequently pass the house, delivering coal or soil, or whatever. Coal is dumped on the pavements in front of apartment blocks and eventually shoveled into basements to fuel collective hot-water systems for the entire building(s), socialist style.

I actually bought chives and cottage cheese (we are instructed *not* to buy Polish milk products but I reckon if Poles live, so will we) and also a huge tin of Greek olive oil, a real bargain....On closer inspection, at home, it proved to be Russian oil and not much better than cat's pee, no wonder it cost so little. The cottage cheese was delicious. Big reception at the B.C Office for us...not at all dull and food from the Country Club.......

7th June. Blackest rain, non-stop; just what this place needs; a good wash. Appalling to see so much evidence of the last War, walls riddled with gunshots, so much neglect. The war ended 45 years ago! Pavements are hazardous and such bleak empty shops.... In an underpass in the town centre I come across five cheery old men on accordions and violins, playing pops from the 20's and 30's. They are very good but their hat is empty. They must be the generation that knew the War, perhaps fought in the uprising. I am so moved by them. If they knew I was German.......?

We are still caught up in a social whirl: dinner at the Embassy's second in command, where we meet, Count Zamierski, a Princess Radziwill and the author Kapucinski, famous for his writing about Africa. There is an impressive mountain of caviar on the table, I've never seen anything like it.

8th June. Last big drinks party for a while. We still haven't received our air-freight luggage, nor the crates from Canada. Even worse: part of my tooth breaks off while eating in a restaurant. So much for that Canadian dentist.......I must have swallowed it; I did think the rice a bit granular, however everyone here says local dentists are not recommended. I must fly to Berlin, or Vienna, or back to London to have it seen to.

9th June. Knowing the luggage has not arrived and that my mum is in Vienna I have hopped on an Austrian Airways flight to kill two birds....see my Ma...get that tooth fixed. It makes sense. Departure from Warsaw airport worse than arrival.... Lengthy and suspicious scrutiny by guard, along with arguments and queries about a piece of paper which had been removed by the first one, while I am stuck between two hostile Poles..., it's awful not to be able to talk...I thought they were supposed to be so nice. Not on this level, they're not. I must be honest I was glad to be out of Warsaw and back in civilization. My cousin Fritz brought Erika and Dagmar to meet me, but had to rush off, so a rented limousine got us back to Vienna's District III and we talked and talked and had tea, and supper and then my aunt walked me round the block to a monastery, where I slept under a huge crucifix in a monastic cell. "What's happened to the monk who normally lives here? And how do I get across the corridor to the loo and shower in my flimsy gown without frightening a holy person? Can my aunt mobilize a dentist?"

10th June. During an enlivening breakfast seated opposite a music critic from Tel Aviv (whose surname is Frankenstein) my family comes to pick me up. I'm told they have made numerous calls to dentists who simply do not work on Saturdays or Sundays. I will just have to give up smiling, until I find someone. (Why is Frankenstein sleeping in a monastery...? I am resolved to find out...) We walk through some of Vienna's smartest streets and visit an exhibition of Klimt, Schiele and Kokoschka. Klimt is and always will be my favorite artist. After a treat in an elegant ice-cream parlor we take the U-Bahn to Heiligenstadt, where my beautiful cousin Hanna drives us up the mountain to view a Polish church (in honor of my visit!) It was built to commemorate Sobieski's famous victory over the Turks 300 years ago. He came to Vienna, like good neighbors do, along with Polish troops to help get rid of the infidel.

11th June. Sunday. We go to the Augustiner church and hear Beethoven's C Major Mass, followed by an open-air lunch. I've had plenty of time to study my mother: she is reasonable in the morning, but by late afternoon her perceptions become unfocussed. She's not on drugs, she's not drinking... she's not even sure if I'm her child or her sister. By nightfall she is mad. I am alarmed, frightened even. Has she come to the end of her usefulness? Dagi admits she hopes her sister will die rather than live on in a state of madness. Eka asks the same questions over and over. We talk behind her back, aghast. How can she even travel alone?

12th June, sunny in Vienna...raining in Warsaw. We are just 55 minutes apart. It appears our air-freight from London has finally arrived, after two weeks transit. Even an oxcart would have been quicker. Still, here I am, brooding about my mother, also unpacking, with the first stirrings of home.....I've carefully smoothed my chipped tooth with a nail-file.

13th June. Rain....taken by charming young Poles from the office to the Customs shed where a huge amount of time is spent hanging about, waiting. It is chilly. There is nowhere to sit. Eventually our boxes, packed in Canada and in storage ever since we left, are weighed, unpacked, examined by unimpressed officials. It takes hours and is 'bardzo nudny' (very boring). I imagine Charles, warm and dry in his smart office...why do I have to be doing this...surely it's 'men's work'?

14th June. And here they are, all fifty-seven boxes, some of them already in the rooms where they will be needed, kitchen, dining-room, many alas, on the landing...total chaos. Canadian packers have wrapped every single object in at least one square yard of white paper, every book, each spoon, imagine the work and I've been at it all day. *Alone*.... But nice to see my things again. The big wooden head from Nigeria nowhere to be found. This house still feels strange.

15th June. More and more of our things emerge as I slice open cardboard crates and plough through mountains of white paper. I'm collecting the paper to give to the little shops when I next go shopping... surely they'll be delighted to use it.... instead of newspaper. Meanwhile it feels like a nightmarish, solitary Christmas: ....a new iron, new kettle, dishwasher, dryer, washing-machine. My Polish cleaning-lady is helping.

I'm supposed to be going to the Queen's Birthday party at the embassy, so I try the tiny hairdresser around the corner. She uses beer as a setting lotion. No–one speaks a word of English .... I experiment in Polish, no choice really! My hair looks good. Smelling of beer and ready to go to the embassy, it seems the office has forgotten to pick me up. Dorota calls a cab, tells the driver where to take me.

16th June. My wondrous machines are hooked up and humming; the embassy electrician has had a busy day. I'm setting up a music-room in the basement, rather like in Ottawa, but with a higher ceiling and better acoustic,...sorted out and filed all my music...to think I've played all of this stuff. We've bought a monstrous turn-of-the-century upright piano from our predecessors, it's huge and black and Austrian...someone will bring it down into my den. Haven't touched my fiddle sinced May 26th, is this a record?......... finally got rid of that mountain of white Canadian paper; at first the greengrocer seemed non-plussed, even a little hostile... then graciously accepted one half and sent me to his friend up the road, who sells groceries, with the rest...I'm so proud of my Polish!

17th June. Warsaw's telephone system is totally antiquated: one can hardly hear what is being said...we make an agonizing call to Cardiff. It takes hours to get connected ...it's so crackly, apparently not overhauled for half a century. At noon our first visit to Lazienki Park: what a marvelous surprise, gorgeously varied landscape, very close to where we live. (Actually there are many lovely parks here, although not as groomed as we have come to expect in the West. I do believe the lawns are mown with scythes.) Transcendental delight: to be drawn in by the strains of distant performance, open-air, of Chopin's piano music...to find, in an expanse of red roses, under a huge improbable *stone* willow, next to an artificial lake.... an amplified grand-piano. Each Sunday under this statue, celebrating Poland's greatest hero, Warsaw's best pianists sit for several hours, playing one Chopin work after the other... 'free' music, in the fresh air, dogs barking, children trying to be quiet and adults sitting or walking in a state of quiet bliss. How well-dressed the Poles are, even the children, all in their Sunday best! And the birds are joining in. I feel as if touched by a magic wand. And tearful.....*this is the moment I'm totally won over.*

19th June. First the ecstasy...now the agony. I speak of my first experience of SUPERSAM, a caricature of a supermarket, unimaginable in the West. One must line up for a small basket. (Oh my...there are roughly 60 persons ahead) Never mind, I advance towards the baskets, becoming aware of security cameras, directed at the queue, every 5 feet. The hall is dingy, with a dark brown ceiling...possibly designed by the same architect as the airport. From where I am I see haphazard and rickety grey metal shelving, carrying rows and rows of the same stuff: pickled cucumbers in glass jars, shredded pickled cabbage known as Sauerkraut to Germans, small grey or brown paper packages of unknown things... lentils perhaps. I have not brought my pocket dictionary, feel nervous about picking up a package and looking inside. Those cameras are probably checking my every incredulous move.   I find small cardboard boxes containing a semblance of cornflakes. Here is fresh brown bread, without any packaging. For dairy and meat products one joins a different line-up, to be served individually. I have done my homework and know what to recite. I have eggs, bread, pumpernickel, 1kilo butter, buckwheat groats, a Swiss roll, sour cream, one jar kefir, no fancy packaging, just brown bags and everything laughably cheap. My Polish shopping spree adds up to roughly 50 pence. Not bad! I am very proud of myself. Cakes in Poland are outstanding and so cheap I am constantly shaking my head...there are *some* plusses when it comes to Communism.

I prefer to remain car-less and use trams, except on *serious* shopping days. On Fridays I run Charles to the office, then drive to the Embassy shop and from there to the 'diplomatic' gas- station, where there is no queuing. There are hardly any petrol pumps in Poland and those that exist have long line-ups, except late at night or at 5 am.

We're settled now, I think. I must stop this blow by blow account of first impressions. Everyone is kind and helpful, my cleaning lady, for example. It is her day off. A great relief not to have to appear fully dressed and made up, to play my role as lady of the house. The gardener is very gentlemanly, he talks and I nod, smile winningly and say 'dobrze' ('good') from time to time. He knows what to do.

Keenly aware of the huge barrier, due to lack of communication- I am determined to learn more by watching childrens' TV with a dictionary in my lap. Watch, listen, write the word down, find it in the dictionary.... I am keeping a record, also alphabetically. How anyone can come here and not learn Polish is beyond me, but people do. As there is nothing to do apart from walking about on the streets I make great advances stumbling about on my own; the pavements are not the most even in this place. I hunt for interesting things in little shops, trying out my best 'shopping' phrases. The other day I found three smoked ducks on display, so I bought half a one: it was delicious, I rushed back, but they had gone.

Poles stand patiently in long queues, nearly every small shop has several persons hanging about outside; perhaps it is a form of social intercourse, or just a way of making sure they are not losing out. Totally startling: a farmer selling a pig's head, amongst potatoes and cabbages...it was propped up on the pavement, flies buzzing around it. How would it feel to boil such a thing? You'd need a huge pot. What would it taste like?

Pan Paderewski, a pianist who lives nearby, has been recommended as accompanist. (Pan= Mr.) He appeared, and stayed a very long time; this was hard work as we spoke mostly in Polish and broken German and English; I began to fear he'd never go. We will play next week, on a trial basis. It is an honor, of course, he is not only the grandson of the *great* Paderewski, Poland's famous concert-pianist and composer (as well as Prime Minister) but also the Head of Chamber music at the Warsaw Academy. This will get me practising again. How exciting!

A few days later he calls again, this time with two well-behaved spaniels. I have noticed how frequently Poles walk their dogs, all of them the most pedigreed creatures. Today the animals sit quietly while we play through a few things, feeling our way musically... he's very good, has made numerous recordings with 'prizewinning' violinists. He suggests we prepare a recital for October, to take place in the Academy Concert Hall and wants to make a recording of my party-piece, the Elgar Sonata. This sounds good to me...we'll see. First he has to go to Europe for two months, for some concertising and for a holiday. I am both re-assured and intimidated, but try not to show the latter.

• • •

Things are not going well. This account of the lives of _seven women_ is turning into a manic account of travels and experiences of just one of them. The others are there, of course, in the background: poor _Erika,_ now totally in limbo, on the verge of dementia; her loneliness does not allow her to enjoy her wealth or even what little there is to be got out of life when one is eighty-two years old.

Ingeborg or _Evelyn_, or Knups, the Pomeranian Peasant, is caught up on an undertow of madness. _This madness rests on many things: beginning to understand the horrors of European History, of German iniquities, gradually seeing, accepting, the ever-widening gulf of_ *relationships going wrong, the feeling of estrangement from her children....realizing the finiteness of Erika's life, ...*

Time is passing quickly. There is much loneliness.

<u>Gabi</u> appears to be a mother. Little Polly, a grand-child, has appeared. There is no announcement, no warning this will happen. When Ingeborg, Gabi and <u>Polly</u> meet, for the first time it feels strange and strained; the younger generation has brightly colored red hair ...everything about them is colorful. They live in a slummy rented house in a village in Kent, looking cheerful. They have no work, no income, and no future, just happy hippies who need *our* money and ask for it. Polly, almost three, is a wise and completely enchanting creature. I wonder what she will do with her life.

The madness described earlier is not unlike the start of a new but painful love-affair: the total involvement with something new... the realization of the terrible suffering that had occurred in this part of the world and learning about Slav culture and language. Shorter mad surges of 'love' can come from everyday, often ridiculous experiences, even from finding a small corpulent lady dentist in Warsaw who had 'access' to American materials and needles. Having inspected my nail-filed tooth she sent me off to an instant X-ray, a Dickensian attic up three flights of bent wooden stairs to a dingy, cluttered flat-let housing a retired doctor with ancient 'retired' apparatus. I had the X-ray in half an hour, the entire process cost 10$, then having proof that the remaining tooth was sound, repairs with good American materials could take place. A case of *very good* "Polnische Wirtschaft," a contradiction in terms of what this famous phrase really means. An adventure, a delight!

After only two months in Poland we had seen Poland from top to bottom. Now we drive to Radom, one of Poland's oldest cities, and Sandomierz, also ten centuries old... then down to the Ukrainian border, roughly an eight hour journey. When you go on a journey in Poland you are wished a "szerokiej drogi" which means a "wide road". I love that ... it makes extra good sense here, where it is unwise to be in a hurry because of horse-drawn carts or even the odd combine harvester. You even see old-fashioned motorbikes with side-cars like in old war- films.

In Sandomierz we are taken around a re-built market square and an old vicarage-museum, filled with a hotch-potch of treasures, catalogued and lit, of course, but it does feel like stumbling into a dusty old attic. Then on to Lancut, where we attend Summer master-classes for violinists and a guided tour of the Palace with an incredible inlaid parquet floor and a dream library for the count-of-the house.....even the latest English, French and German papers and periodicals....all poignantly coming to a sudden end...at the outbreak of WW 2. In Poland it is never far away, that terrible war.

Only two hours from Warsaw is Poland's most eastern city, Lublin, on top of a hill, looking down on a former suburb called Maydanek. The old town, partly restored, has an Austrian-Italian feel, the rest is a crumbling ghost-town, laced with tacky new high-rise buildings. Below the hill is the Memorial Museum of Maydanek.

The first thing you see of this former concentration camp is a concrete monument by the roadside, the eye is drawn along a path behind this to something resembling a huge chalice, silhouetted against the horizon about ½ a mile away. Between these two structures are the now familiar barbed-wire fences, observation towers and rows of low wooden barracks. We wandered about in this area and imagined, or *tried* to imagine, how it felt to be trapped, branded, de-loused, de-haired, de-humanized, terrorized and starved....until you were shot or gassed. Three successive barracks filled with hundreds of thousands of blackened rotting shoes collected by the Nazis for re-processing become part of this sickening experience. Eventually, having forced ourselves to look at absolutely everything, we get close to the vast concrete chalice seen on arrival, from the roadside. It stands next to the crematorium and has an inscription in huge letters:

OUR FATE YOUR WARNING

The chalice contains ashes, found on the site. We are stunned, drained, tearful and tired. Through no fault of my own I am part of this inhuman crime. Not Charles, just me. How must he feel, married to a German.... I am at least able to hide behind a mantle of British-ness, my English name, my husband's work. We drive back up the hill to Lublin and sit next to a fountain, eating our sandwiches, without enthusiasm. There is no consolation... unless one counts driving home. This has been only our first viewing of such things.

On Sunday the 20th of August Poland has its first free parliamentary elections. Everyone knows how it will be: the Solidarity-backed candidates win 99% of the seats in the Senate. There can be only one man for president and it will surely be Walensa, even though he is only a 'lowly' electrician.

The British Council is up to its ears in the 'Know-how Fund'...Britain's contribution to helping Poland on its feet. Charles has never been so busy. I hardly see him, we sleep in separate rooms and he leaves for work very early. This is nothing new... we've slept apart for years. He comes home haggard and drained, to change and then out again for receptions, dinners, concerts, films, a busy social life. At first I try to keep up, later I often stay at home. I am good at being alone: it comes from being an only child. Sometimes, on week-ends, we do things together. We take walks through streets and parks, I show Charles around, like a tourist guide...the sight of battle-scarred buildings still unrepaired since the War. I show him our "own" little park in Mokotov, with two monuments to the slaughtered dead of our suburb just south of the city centre. It is close to the 45th anniversary of the Warsaw Uprising, an event which caused the total destruction of the entire city; currently all memorials and shrines have fresh flowers and candles. Now, almost 50 years on, when the rest of Europe is all done up again, Warsaw still festers in its peculiar way. The wounds will not heal.

Don't misunderstand, the Socialists have done their bit, restoring the Old Town; they've built their Palace of Culture, and much of the centre of town is respectable, there is also the handsome ceremonial route along Lazienki Park, the road of the embassies. But traces of World War 2 are everywhere.

One can of course, go to Poland, and try not to think about the appalling events of sixty years ago. Some people make that choice. I needed to absorb these distasteful events, caused by persons similar to my father, my uncles, my grandfathers. Somehow the mind falters with such thoughts. It is completely real, yet unthinkable. What a thing to inherit.

We visit <u>Auschwitz</u> near Krakow, we visit <u>Treblinka</u>, just one hundred kilometers from Warsaw. Ausschwitz, the Nazi's Final Solution for Europe's Jews, gives an unsuitable first impression: a *pleasant* modern building offering refreshments and ticket counters... modern and westernised. This feels all wrong. However much you need a cup of tea or an ice cream, you should surely not be having them here, on this damned spot. Everyone has seen this camp in documentaries and films, but despite any inner preparation the reality hits hard. You can't 'shut down' to protect yourself and it is best not to try to speak, because you will be weeping.

Treblinka was a more 'internalised' experience. Situated in the countryside, amidst woods and shrubs... one sees a railway track, which ends...then a small field with smallish rocks, standing upright, like so many calcified persons...and there is no-one to be seen anywhere, the place is silent, even the birds are silent. It was a grey day... misty, drops of rain... if one had not read the history...well, one might not understand. I tell myself nature itself is eradicating the loathsome acts that have taken place here.

To grow up with this history must have a powerful effect. It may explain something about Poland's visual arts. Remembering cultural events of the late eighties, early nineties,...installation art, paintings, theatre, posters- there is an over-all memory of primitive, basic, hard-hitting and utterly brutal realism... making one feel one had never understood, or been honest, about life before. This art oozes straight out of fear, pain and cruel suffering. Nakedness, sack-cloth, blood, destruction, filth, chaos, silence, fear, darkness, deception, raw cruelty, often with oblique reference to the political yoke of Communism, this thorn in the flesh, now falling away, had been overpowering: there was an urgency in art I had never seen elsewhere: sickening, frightening and shocking. The shock of change after seven years of suave, bland and blatant luxury in Canada could not have been more extreme.

There are other places of pilgrimage in Poland but nothing can be more Polish than the 'Black Madonna' of Czestochowa.

According to legend St Luke the Evangelist painted this picture on a cypress table-top of the Holy Family. There are frequent miracles attributed to the 'blackened' portrait of Our Lady; just like Lourdes it is a 'Must See' for any Catholic in Poland. During one of our son's brief holidays from his Music College we took him for a drive south and stopped off to join the throng of visitors swarming to catch of glimpse of the famous painting. He stood before it for a few seconds and probably requested success in his chosen career. No doubt his father had similar thoughts: in *his* case she's done him proud, he can't complain.

Doing the whole tourist 'thing' included the Salt Mines near Krakow. These were up and running in the 13th century. We began to appreciate their awesome-ness after a descent of 200 meters by stairs to a chapel carved entirely from salt by the more dexterous miners themselves. Old pictures show hooded figures at work, a reminder of the Seven Dwarfs of Snow-white fame... the entire experience quite like a fairytale. Later, getting to know the lovely old town of Krakow itself, we found a town as glamorous as Prague.

The darkest, most magical place is in the Mariatzka, the Church of St Mary in the Market Place ...a chance to view a carved crucifixion by Veit Stoss, a

Nuremberg carver who came to work in Krakow for a while. Poles claim him as Polish, the Germans say he is German; I am troubled by these arguments..... but the dark blue ceiling covered with stars and chandeliers heavy with holy dust help to   feel uplifted and moved beyond all such pettiness.

Outside, the Clothmarket, the flea market, the flower-market, life overflowing, activity in every direction. Every hour, on the hour, a trumpeter plays a few bars high up on the church tower...he comes to an abrupt stop...a reminder of an arrow from some Tartar Invasion, hundreds of years ago. Having heard this event several times a day we decide it must be a tape, rather like the muezzins in Egypt these days,...the trumpeter's top A always sharp...yet strangely moving. We also study life as it is: a wedding party across the road with a Gypsy band, swarthily following the car, leaning right into the open car doors... horse-drawn coaches, making a racket on the cobbles and later a trip to the Wawel, the Old Castle (makes you realize what Mozart must have endured in his day, when *all* roads were cobbled).

After the first months in this strange country it begins to dawn on me that 'representational' life in Poland is even more fulfilling than in other places because of the writers, artists, musicians, film-makers, and journalists we are meeting.

However, a key-person for me, is a tiny, shrivelled old lady, Sofia Kaczkowska, to whom I had been sent with a gift from....oh, such a tangled story, I can't be bothered to tell the tale. I *find* the address I had been given: it is one of those forbidding high-rise communist-era-concrete blocks, just by the former Jewish Ghetto. There are three or four blocks, I find my way, warily, into one of them, (strange unpleasant smells of an indefinable disinfectant, soapy substance everywhere)... and when eventually, I locate her flat on the sixth floor she opens the door and so begins a three year relationship.

A geologist, now retired and in her eighties, she had lived in this 'shoe-box' flat for twenty years: one miniscule bed-sit with a corridor containing a hidden stove, counter, storage, plus a washroom. As I struggle in my faltering Polish she reveals a smattering of German and a tiny bit of English.... learnt from the British Council. She has no family, knew Austria as a child; her husband was killed in the War. She'd seen better days. In a curious way she felt, after a few more visits from me (she pressed me to come again and again) that I needed 'mothering' and help with speaking Polish. She made me read to her a Polish translation of Le Petit Prince: we drank cups of 'herbata' (tea) and I brought her little luxuries, which we then devoured together. I told her about my mother, now becoming more and more wretched in CapeTown and, each time I called on Sofia we managed somehow to create a bond,... she 'mothered' me, I looked after her, and felt admiration for her modesty, wisdom and resilience.

She told me her thoughts on Poland, on her life (refusing to talk about her husband, something terrible must have happened to him) as we became a 'support-group of two', getting together every three weeks. Even Charles was dragged along to see her, as was my visiting aunt Dagi, from Vienna. Poor little Sophia Kaczkowska, so tiny, so brave and resilient!

She helped me to come to terms. Thanks to her my Polish improved immeasurably, while I managed to bring into *her* life a little of the outside world, with stories of my family and my music. This relationship, so far removed from my otherwise glamorous life, made me experience a tiny slice of a truly Polish fate. It is exhausting, trying to speak sensibly in such a difficult language. Eventually, when we were about to leave Poland she gave me what was probably her most precious possession: a salt-cellar in the shape of a jointed silver fish. I cherish it. We corresponded for a while, but it was too difficult to keep up. She is surely dead now.

As summer and autumn passed life gradually settled into a pleasing routine: a few pupils, all children of foreign diplomats, a newly formed piano trio with two fine young Polish professionals, occasional concerts with players from the Warsaw Philharmonic, conducted by an American, (who was on to a 'good thing' since he got away with paying his players ten dollars a concert.) Dollars were still the only way forward in Poland, dollars changed into zloty's could buy many wondrous things.

There is no such thing as 'amateur music-making' in Poland. If you play a musical instrument it is because you have been chosen, trained and supported financially by the State to become a working musician and you will become part of whatever group needs your skills. Poland has special music-schools where children go to learn their 'trade' while also receiving a normal education. The standards are high and if you have a job in the music world there is no desire to fool around playing quartets or trios for fun, as one does in the West....when it comes to actual rehearsal with Poles the music-making is on a remarkable level of passionate commitment. I was the 'token' female, one of six firsts, playing with a fervor you just don't get in English or Canadian groups. I couldn't believe my luck; this was the kind of playing I love.

My 'big' recital at the Academy went well. Friends said kind things. But nothing exciting came of it.... after all that build-up there was the inevitable let-down afterwards. Why does one 'do' these things?

The Berlin Wall has 'fallen'!

I took my chances during one of Charles' trips to London and booked myself on a FIRST CLASS SLEEPER WARSAW / BERLIN RETURN, an adventure, all on my own. Once ensconced in a 'wagon sypialny' (sleeping car), sharing with a Polish diplomat's wife, there was little choice but go to bed, with space at a premium. I slept fitfully on an uncomfortable narrow bed, listening to assorted snorers and other noises, next door. Never again, I swore.

At 9 am. we pulled into Berlin Hauptbahnhof, but, alas I had *not* arrived. Having stood in line for a cab for thirty minutes I realized this dreary place was *East* Berlin. I had to retrace my steps, find a different train to Friedrichs-strasse, then stand in a massive throng attempting to squeeze through Checkpoint Charlie, the famous crossing point which had been opened on Nov. 9th. I became one of thousands of Poles and East Germans, patiently lined up as far as the eye could see while good-natured border guards hurried us along with: "was wollt ihr denn da drüben?" ("what do you want to go there for?") And yet, with the German equivalent of 'get a move on!' each and every face and passport was examined, slowing us down to a steady trickle...after about two hours of this I had arrived: there it was: the West, with lights, cabs, noise, shops bursting with Christmas treats..............

19th December. It's good to be booked into a 'Pension' just around the corner from the Kurfürstendamm, Berlin's 5th Avenue. 80% of Berlin's centre was destroyed during the War but this elegantly proportioned pre-war building with its elaborately carved stairs and the highest ceilings ever, is one of the cherished places just around the corner from the preserved ruins of the Gedächtnis-Kirche. Around its base a determinedly old-fashioned Christmas-fair is selling crafts, delicious smells wafting; I am engulfed with feelings of nostalgia for my childhood memories of Swinemünde and Eutin. I'm sad to be here alone. "If my parents could see me now," crosses my mind. Pulling myself together, I listen to the familiar sounds of Polish being spoken around me...Poles are flocking to Berlin and have made themselves unpopular by emptying the stores. Some shops have queues forming outside and only ten customers are allowed in at a time because of the overcrowding of persons from the 'East'.

During a two-hour coach-tour of West Berlin I find traces of World War ll: there are still pock-marked walls, but nowhere near as many as in Warsaw. The pre-war Berlin I had studied in a glossy anthology in the hotel has vanished; the four Allied Powers still have their districts.... with no noticeable mark apart from their be-flagged headquarters. Here is the dreary Rathaus where Kennedy proclaimed he was a 'Berliner' and we drive past Brandenburg Gate where a huge Christmas tree is hoisted into position. Just over there is a part of The Wall being blasted, so pedestrians can move freely between East and West...the bus stops and we buy a piece of 'wall'. Have East and West Berliners become strangers? Then on to the monumental Reichstag, sinister ... behind it more Wall and crosses marking spots where persons, trying to escape, were shot.

Nevertheless, a pleasant, modern city,... parks, lakes and canals; on every corner there are Wurstbuden (sausage-stalls) where one picks up a steaming bowl of pea-soup or a baguette covering one of the hundreds of varieties of sausages. I eat at street-stalls for three days, apart from breakfast at the hotel. Outside one of the supermarkets, joining the accumulated Poles, I wait my turn to push a trolley around for German Stollen, Marzipan and other delectable foods, the Poles mostly grumbling about the prices, but buying anyway. I visit galleries, museums, arcades and cinemas (The Rainman, with Dustin Hoffman 'speaking' German is one of my treats) and wondrous shops. In my alone-ness I speak to no-one for three days and on the third day decide it best to get to the station an hour earlier to be sure I catch the correct train back to Poland...."your train is leaving from East Berlin" I am informed, "just get on *any* train you can, we're adding new ones all the time to cope with the traffic." On the platform there is a heaving mass of Poles plus mountains of boxes and packages containing VCR's, TV's and other large objects. In the good old days it would have been chickens and geese.

The first train pulls in.... festooned with bodies. "How can I possibly squeeze in to that, with my case and two plastic bags"...my heart sinks.

A spotty German youth asks me politely if I need help. I nod and he grabs my case and clambers up forcing his way into the nearest carriage. I squeeze into the space he's created for me. Jammed in I then decide to squeeze out again. The whole thing is ridiculous.

This turns out to be the first of many mistakes. Had I persevered I might have reached my booked first class sleeping compartment leaving from East Berlin. Instead, I sit on a station bench to wait for a less crowded train. Here is my spotty friend again, settling down with a confident smile: "I'm here to look after things, I'm an *official*, you know!" He pulls back his lapel to reveal a pistol. He's a teenager... my thoughts go into 'over-drive'...while my mouth utters, "oh good," trying to keep on the right side of him, and to become invisible. Crossing my mind was: "should I give him my remaining DM so he doesn't shoot....will he do me in if I get up to go away, am I in big trouble......?"

"The bullets are in my pocket" he informs, "I use the pistol only to frighten people." I manage: "do you do that very often?" "Oh, hardly ever... he says, surveying the crowds milling about, "don't worry, I'll get you on the next train...." He gets up, bustles about, returns to smile at me from time to time.

Twenty minutes pass before the next train appears. I've lost sight of the teenage 'official'. I box my way past one overflowing carriage to the next. There, right at the front,...a first-class carriage with hardly anyone in it... what a relief, what luck and why so empty? This carriage is for Leningrad and is 'coming off' at East Berlin...

When the train stops, ten minutes later, the carriage isn't even by a platform...we have to jump from our Fool's Paradise onto some rough stones *way down there,.....* in the dark! I stumble, fall gracefully on my Christmas cakes...someone hands down my suitcase, then we grope our way past the hissing train, back towards the lights of the platform.

There stands a uniformed man fighting off at least fifty travelers, all with tickets to Poland. By now a ruthless and desperate liar, I wave my first-class ticket at him and 'explain' I am a British diplomat carrying important documents that have to be in Warsaw.... by morning.

"The situation is hopeless, gnädige Frau," he says, "you have missed your train, all trains are full, hotels are full, there are no planes, it is better you return to West Berlin..." I just looked at him. "I can't promise anything" he says, pityingly, as I stand, stare and note it is already ten pm. I have visions of sitting on this platform all night, waiting. It is freezing.

Thirty minutes later another carriage is added to an incoming train. I am escorted on first, hiding behind dark glasses from the stares of the other desperados on the platform. No more than five minutes later everyone else is on too, every available inch inhabited by bodies, boxes, backpacks. I see no women, only Poles of every age-group, all male. My five immediate fellow passengers, youngish with very long legs have to be carefully arranged as we settle down for the next eleven hours or so.

We communicate in German and Polish. By three a.m., becoming dehydrated, we share a can of warm coke, and take turns to stand up and stretch during dispiriting stops at sidings and a total of four passport and customs controls, unimaginably prolonged with all these imported 'western' goods in boxes. Any hopes of a visit down the corridor are shattered by putting ones head round the door: travelers and boxes as far as the eye can see. However, there comes a time when such hurdles simply *have* to be overcome. One friendly powerful Pole lifts me bodily over his precious new waist-high TV set. God knows what damage I do to other equipment on my way. Even in the WC there is a sleepy traveler, who vacates the premises with reasonable grace.

After Poznan matters improve, the corridor becomes pass-able, the train gathers speed, and the blackness outside turns to grey with heavy rain. Time has passed. I've not slept at all and think about these five good-natured men with whom I've spent the night, instead of which I could have been at the Embassy ball, dancing to a live band!

Warsaw: 11 am. A long queue, no cabs and a heavy downpour.

I drag myself to the other side of the station where the known-to-be bribe-able taxis are, counting their hard currency. Hair sticks to my skull and rain drips down my specs while I tear open a car door and ask "how many dollars to Mokotow..." in Polish, of course.

Family matters are becoming an increasing headache. Every three months I fly to Cape Town to be with my mother in her posh Whitehall Court flat; it appears mixing with new persons has become an impossible task: she wants her 'old' friends, or her sister, or me. Increasingly her mind and body are letting her down.

And then........my daughters.......

A mother's day greeting arrives from them on the 27th March,1990. "First time ever" it says in my diary "quite amazing..!"

Our 'connection' has been limited to their occasional requests for money and the usual Christmas felicities. Is it all my fault? The fact remains, I can't find it in me to approve of their vagabonding about, I see them as 'rebels' to society....giving birth to children without having proper fathers to provide, give them names...making use of the benefit system in the UK,..... "thank goodness my father does not have to pass comment on these things." My mother gets varnished versions of the truth...she would be horrified to see the way they are, what they do, the company they keep. I am 55 years old and feel, despite HRT, despair about the way life has turned out, the endless rows I am having with my husband, my children, also the loneliness of my day to day existence.

"If my mother were dead" I write in my diary, "I might just consider living alone." I don't stipulate where. I feel no great pull to London, nor to Canada, nor CapeTown. It is depressing to be me, not knowing who I am, what I am, where I'd like to be. Am I even 'British' now? I so *prefer* the *Goethe*

Institute events to the cheap and nasty attention-seeking over-the-top hyper-modern offerings of Theatre and Art that Headquarters sends out to Poland to impress. It's all tat, and I hate it. Maybe I'm German after all.............

My daughters are 31 and 29. Jim, the once so shocking 'bovver-boots' partner of Luci is now the partner of Gabrielle. I despair. It seems Jim is here to stay, when I'd so hoped he'd soon be 'history'. I have responded to this switch-over without any attempt to hide my true feelings, and receive, in return the following letter from Gabi:

August 17th, 1990.

Dear Mum, your idea of love stinks. If you can't love me for who I am then forget it. You are asking me to understand you without giving a toss who I really am. It's always been like this with you and Dad. Your love, your support is always conditional on me being who you think I should be, not who I am. You misunderstand me and it disgusts me that you judge and condemn Jim for nothing. He came to your flat in friendliness and you are a hypocrite to pretend all this time to tolerate him when you were seething with judgmental anger all along....

She continues angrily, and I am cutting a very long letter:

Charles made a decision -years ago, to withdraw from us because he thinks we are only after money etc. Even if that is the total truth ask yourselves WHY. The only thing you really offer is material things. Emotionally and spiritually it's always been put-downs, criticisms and sneers. You are nice to me when I give first- and it makes me feel really hurt........... I know you'll make some dismissive judgment of me, on reading this letter.....I'm tired and weary of your disapproval. I feel so uncomfortable with you both. Why should I inform you about my babies' birth when all I know I'll get back is disapproval and patronizing criticism

.....here she brings in her sister, who has moved on to a new relationship,...then:

I am manipulated by you....approval and love dependant on appearing to be the right kind of daughter. Your priority is always to appear normal..."do they go to school?".

(her children...she was teaching them at home)

I went to school- and it fucked me up. I've been unreal for years and so has Luci, ask her.... I think what I've been doing these last seven years is courageous and valuable... to undo my knotted-up personality, to allow my creativity to breathe again. It doesn't matter to you, or Dad. What ever I do I deserve your love unconditionally JUST because you are my parents. I'm supposed to accept any crud you guys deal out, but you can criticise me freely. The money isn't the issue, it's your attitude behind it... if you were unconditional you'd want to see me and give to me regardless whether you like my life, boyfriend, face, whatever..............

It is valid to attempt to find your own happiness EVEN IF OTHER PEOPLE SEE YOU AS MISTAKEN . There are thousands of tribes in this world who don't live as we do in the West. ARE THEY WRONG? Anyway, you are no model of happiness either. You may have material security, but does your heart sing ? Do you really feel love, are you scared of death, disappointed by lack of real intimacy and fulfillment? Hate me if you want, or more satisfyingly, feel 'sorry' for me because I'm so immature or whatever.... I cannot change you and probably never will. So if you cannot accept me say so and consider yourself as having only ONE DAUGHTER ... and a son.

We were spending three weeks on leave in London. I drove to Wales to make contact with both daughters and to see their offspring. But, after a bad row with Gabi on the phone, she was 'not there', so that was that. I put the letter in a folder full of letters asking for money, accounts of how much we'd sent to everyone and when...just a general file..... The thread between mother and eldest daughter was stretched beyond endurance. We had not put things right... a draining experience, even now, just writing about it.

I know of no other such set-to in earlier generations. I felt I was 5 billion years old. It overcomes one, that feeling of being prey to entropy. Is it true to say that the youngest-looking 50 year old has molecules the same age as the oldest-looking 50 year old...because their chronological age is, in both cases 5 billion years (the age of their component molecules)?

None of this is any consolation when personal relationships are so frayed.

I throw a big dinner-party to 'celebrate' 25 years of marriage. I beg my man to write a poem, which duly appears, 'totally incomprehensible', even to his mother. I dash one off in return, a sad thing, on the back-cover of my diary. I never showed him.

So here we were, Charles and Evelyn-Ingeborg, dining with princes (Prince Edward, Prince Czatoreski,) film-makers (Wajda, Ken Russell, Zanussi), authors,(Applebaum, Kapucinski), composers (Pendereczki, Lutoslawski, Panufnik) and all the while, behind the scenes, our own bleak relationship, makeshift, not conforming to the pattern one is supposed to follow.

The world is changing: we witness the end of Communism, an emerging New Poland. Sitting next to Prince Czatoreski, just an ordinary guy who enjoys boar-hunting and grows flowers for 'business' he informs me: "everyone at this table is tainted," (by Communism), looking about the glamorous assembly of ministers and artists during an embassy dinner, "everyone, without exception."There is a momentary silence, some mildly embarrassed smiling...then mute nodding and quick change of topic, in true diplomatic fashion. What does the man mean?

Mute nodding, I suppose, is about all I managed with Gabi. How unfair of me to expect *her* to understand my impatient disappointment with her lifestyle of political rebellion and social upheaval at that time, how I was governed by my own staid background, customs, and expectations of the people surrounding me. Mute nodding: yes, I was not a 'good' mother.

The new Poland under our very eyes is a remarkable thing. Spring sets in motion a big clean-up, mostly by elderly street-sweepers with twig-brooms, but also by brand new street-washing trucks, a gift from Nordic countries.Householders dig patches of earth on the edge of pavements and plant grass-seed, much appreciated by the Warsaw pigeons. There are Spring flowers everywhere. Nowhere else in the world have I seen so many flower-sellers. Poland is becoming more expensive and since private enterprise and 'market forces' have been unleashed there is constant wheeling and dealing. One finds, within 15 yards, spread out on the pavement, items such as Belgian coffee, Polish butter, tropical fruits like Kiwi, Cape grapes, pineapples, bananas, cigarettes from Albania, soap from Istanbul, dictionaries, toilet-seats, jeans and gym shoes, in every cranny of this town. All is fair in the price-war, stalls are set up in front of shops selling similar goods. Now that the West has come there are adverts on trams and walls, you can buy a coke to wash down your Zapiekanki (hot bread with cheese and spicy sauce) or your Hamburgeri or Hotdogi, you can contemplate buying electronic equipment or flying to New York, even to gamble in luxury hotels, if you have the cash. But petrol costs ten times as much as last year, nobody can afford it... how much new happiness and hope is there? A friend said she'd witnessed two separate scenes in our neighborhood...bodies covered with blankets, police and onlookers pointing to the windows above. I've heard people wishing the Communist days were back, when everyone had the same and knew where they stood.

And so the re-birth begins: a growing crime-wave, sprouting satellite dishes, cut-throat capitalism, bringing 'riches' and 'fulfillment'...............

The British Council was doing its bit to make riches flow into Poland. So were the Germans with their Goethe Institute, and the Alliance Française. My own *tiny* contribution came about unexpectedly: a school on the next block advertised 'English Lessons' in large letters on the gates, and there was that little voice in my head: "find out more, perhaps they'd like another teacher"...not that I had any idea how to teach English. "Still, I know how to teach violin, and it would be fun to pass the time usefully"... Having mulled it over I walked in and found the Head, who spoke passable English and looked extremely pleased to see me. As soon as he heard 'British Council' I knew I had a job: twice weekly I was in charge, for two hours, of a class of a dozen adult Poles, mostly men, who for one reason or another needed to advance their skills. Luckily the Council Library kitted me out with the latest teaching books used worldwide. My students were keen and quick and eager. I became as devoted to them as they were to me.

There was one last Big Adventure before our time in Europe came to an end: I'd longed to get to the Baltic to visit my father's beloved Swinemünde. Persuading Charles we needed this long drive north from Warsaw, was not too difficult ...first, to see the Masurian Lakes, and on the way taking in the equally famous 'Wolfsschlucht' and the ancient towns of <u>Torun</u> and <u>Olsztyn.</u> Copernicus, born in Torun in 1473, was the first to displace the earth from the centre of the universe, his calculations were a landmark in modern science. He also lived in Olsztyn, both towns have gorgeous mediaeval centres, badly in need of restoration. It was marvelous to drive through this region of forests and lakes, and, grandly, we rented a tiny plane for thirty minutes, to get an overview of the vast area, seemingly deserted.....I was expecting yachts and hotels and holiday-makers, but it all looked blissfully peaceful.

Much driving...my husband complains ...chest pains...and arm pains, and shoulder pains. I am more worried about this than he is. Is he all tensed up because we are together all day long? He'd better get used to that, with retirement looming. But no, we are getting along just fine, caught up in the imagining of so much history and now an interesting place: Hitler's military camp-hideout, the place in former East Prussia, where he and his generals plotted and planned the course of war, the 'Wolfsschlucht' (wolves' lair). It is hard to find in the dense forest...all that remains are huge moss-covered concrete blocks and remnants of buildings,

dark and silent, a spooky place, evil, by association...
we are keen to move on. Charles is continuing to
have chest pains. We share the driving and end up
in Sopot, just outside Gdansk, in the Sopot Grand
Hotel, where Erika and Reini had stayed about sixty
years earlier.

Now Swinemünde is only half a days' drive away.
Acting on advice from friends we'd booked to
spend two nights in a resplendently white place
called Hotel Amber, just opened in Miedzydroje
... our base for 'the great visit' to my grandparents'
home. First, I swim in the Baltic, which looks green
and feels toe-curlingly chilly. I do it again before
breakfast, then we drive to a ferry which takes our
car across the river; steeled for an emotional day we
drive into Swinemünde: the first landmark is my
father's Lutheran church, still with a model sailing-
ship hanging from the domed roof above the aisle,
even though it is now Catholic. Soon we find the
'Bollwerk', and the air-raid shelter...the one that
saved my life during the air-raid, looking half the
size I remembered, still useful for storage or perhaps
just too solid to knock down. There is no house...
just a bare plot of weeds. Why has no-one built on
it...perhaps the authorities think it still belongs to
the Ihlenfeldts? Dream on. I so wanted to talk to
my father about this visit. He had been back, a few
years before he died; he had come to terms.

Next morning an early swim, no-one else around, I
wade in three times, unable to say goodbye: it is *my*
Baltic now, and, just like my father, I feel distress

to be leaving. We drive non-stop until dusk; we are peaceful with each other, Charles talking about 'early retirement'. I would have been delighted to stay another six months, my Polish was terrific, ... my music had consolidated with the help of superb Polish musicians, I had a niche and dreaded going back. Charles, who travelled back and forth to London 'on business' constantly, could not wait to get back to England.

By this time I was being treated for high blood-pressure by Poland's most eminent expert on the matter. The drugs he prescribed more or less ruined a recital I was playing in Krakow, so powerfully calming was the effect! A valuable lesson just in time: I was offered one glowing farewell–to-Poland treat: the honor of presenting a program in Warsaw's Royal Palace. This could not have been more glamorous: a 'salute of honor' on arrival by the armed guards of the palace...and in the presence of two of Warsaw's most high-powered violinists, assorted diplomats, colleagues, friends and pupils, I had one last moment of happy elation: performing Schubert, Stravinsky, Richard Strauss in surroundings of immense beauty and prestige.

One of them, a dear friend, Poland's senior figure in the world of the violin, was also very keen on Astrology. While saying good-bye he felt I needed this warning: "don't go back, Evelyn," he pleaded, "I will find you work here, a future in England is not what is right for you." Not an 'old fool'.... he had held an important teaching post at Indiana

University, even in Communist times, he had studied my 'stars, he'd seen me together with Charles, and guessed, perhaps, what was becoming inevitable, more clearly than I did. But in January 1992 I returned to London to get the 'home-fires burning'. Charles followed, by car, right across Europe. He had been awarded a CBE and we were going to see the Queen.

Buckingham Palace, although a more intimidating place, also had its charms. While my son and I sat on small gilt chairs, listening to a band playing 'out of tune' popular classics, I watched my friend of over twenty-seven years, noted his stoop, his drawn pale face, (was he nervous?) and how thin he'd become in Poland. My heart contracted with the wish to protect him from sadness and disappointment. I had experienced so much in these years with him; he had taught me a great deal.

I was no longer afraid of anyone. I felt free. I was also conscious of the fact that *he* needed freedom even more than I did. On that day I felt as British as anyone else. Trevor McDonald, the Trinidadian newsreader, stood near us after the ceremony, proudly displaying *his* OBE to the photographers. How British was *he*? We'd had approximately the same amount of time, fossicking about, 'becoming British', shall I say thirty years?

It was a very British Day. I *did* think, on that day, I had made it.

The 'last chapter' begins with renewed classes, this time in portraiture, at the Hampstead School of Art. This was more than just pleasing...I showed some promise.

At that time, after much pleading for a bigger home, to end our lives in some comfort... builders were engaged to join our very small flat to the adjacent basement...to form a splendid space, now with a double garden (overlooked by at least a dozen other families peering at us from all those high old houses, but never mind).

I was occasionally involved with former colleagues, now in the English Sinfonia, which meant getting out and about. Charles occupied himself with becoming a governor at a local school and by going abroad to supervise elections in foreign countries. There was the continuing pain of never-ending rejection slips for his novel and renewed attempts at re-writing it and smartening it up. How many publishers had turned it down now, some ridiculous number. In so many ways Charles seemed a crushed man, despite past successes in his British Council career. We 'rubbed' along, as they say, it all looked normal....a distant, lonesome 'normal'...his feelings were elsewhere, all the time, if not with his writing, it must surely have been with other women.

This was the rawest of topics. One day, dusting the mantle-piece, I found a receipt for one dozen roses sent to Nicola, the pianist. I was devastated.

Eleven years had past since we left for Canada, and STILL he was in touch with her. I made a scene. That evening we had to go to a party given by the famous Anne Applebaum, who lived in a tiny flat in London. Sqashed body to body with journalists and literary Poles I observed Charles making a complete ass of himself, flirting with her in a discomfiting way. Was she the proverbial 'red herring'?

The next morning I got up, said "I don't feel well" and passed out. Taken by ambulance to the Royal Free, I was tested and released a day later, still living. "Not a heart-attack," they said, "but we'll keep an eye on you."

There were additional tensions. My daughters were on the telephone often enough asking for money. I had to go to Charles, questions were asked, accusations made and there was a very uncomfortable feeling about things all the time. James, the son and heir was set up without question in a house in Cardiff, but the girls.....'they have a father of their own, why doesn't *he* sort them out?" An understandable reaction of course. The requests kept coming. Cheques were sent. Accounts were kept.

What little we heard of their lives left us incredulous....where had it all gone so wrong? Grandchildren appeared in all directions; who were the fathers? What was the set-up?.....at least Luci was studying now........

Epilogue. 1992, back in London. I drove to Wales, making various attempts to put matters right with my daughters, performed with several amateur pianists...

....one of them, a physicist just retiring from the Open University, was seen in Denning Road quite frequently; he had an obsession with Walton and I learnt the violin sonata written by this composer specially to please the man. He was so thrilled by this work, it was touching to see. He had a paunch and holes in his sweaters, drove a battered old car and lived in a large neglected house, with a skeletal pedigree cat called Pushka. He was also an environmentalist, and a widower, the last bringing forth all my protective instincts. Charles encouraged me, ..."did I like him?"

"Well, yes" I said, "but, he talks too much..." The pianists I was used to got on with the job and collected their cheques before they rushed off to their next employment. This Walton addict had an awful lot to say, about everything, a real polymath. He had numerous lady friends, with one of whom, also a physicist, he travelled to exotic places like Moscow and to the French Alps, another he took to Prague and Barcelona, it was alarming trying to keep track of them all. "A bit of a Don Giovanni,...why doesn't he make a pass at me," I wondered. For someone so recently widowed he exuded a great deal of energy. He spent weeks at mysterious summer events called 'Music Camp'...he was music director of an opera company in Milton Keynes and he plied me with books on every conceivable topic...

He planned to sell his house and move to the country: "I'd really value your help with getting my house in order...to be sold," he said, surveying our newly refurbished Hampstead basement, the fine kitchen and splendid music room. "Do come and rehearse in *my* music-room, I have a nice Bechstein," he urged, he didn't care for my Bluethner.

It was 1993. By this time I had, quite unwittingly, got myself into a truly marvelous new occupation. One morning a cheque arrived in the post from a magazine called 'The Strad', which is read by the great fraternity of violinists world-wide. A few months before leaving Poland I had posted an account to the editor, about the important business of preparations for international violin competitions, with some 'insider information' of what was going on in Poland in this respect. I had no idea it had been accepted and printed. After we had left Poland the magazine managed to track me down in London. I called on the editor, casually mentioned my relationship with my ex-teacher, who was now 'Mr Big' at the Menuhin School, and was immediately invited to write an article about Mauricio Fuks, the man who was 'knocking the Menuhin School' in shape. He was in Paris at that time. I dropped everything to locate him, and got the story together in a few days.

The rest is history: the beginning of a mini-career as musical journalist and eight years of journeys, which got me to France, Germany, Denmark and even Japan.... and whenever I returned Charles was only too delighted to type out my handwritten notes and assist in turning everything into immaculate English prose. What a learning curve for me!

My mother-in-law came out with: "Poor Charles. I hope he's not too jealous *you* are the one who is getting published." But there was no sign of anything but generosity of spirit and much helpfulness. At last there was something we could 'do' together. A huge belated bonus, it was.

I flew to CapeTown often, to 'comfort' my poor demented mother, Charles flew off to supervise elections in other countries; he took two cruises on his own and once more we travelled together, this time to Uzbekistan. Interesting as this was it turned out to be a 'splitting-up' trip. Both of us were openly buying souvenirs for our new 'friends'... while keeping the peace and 'keeping up' with the stimulus of being in such a remote, strange place.

'East House', Alan's (the Walton addict)'s home, was having a make-over at his instigation, but using my 'expertise'. Frankly, I had never done such a thing in my whole life. Paint a room...... you must be joking? Practical by nature I found a handyman. Room by room the entire place was reborn. Alan and I were up those ladders, painting, renovating...throwing things out, a ritual cleansing of *his* past. I became inspired, re-created an awful brown wardrobe into something gorgeous decorated with Spring flowers. I discovered I could do things other than scratch around on a violin.

Alan's secret, totally walled-in garden was another place where we bonded.... sweetly trying to impress the other with our 'closeness to nature'. To be honest, until then I had not really considered gardening: but soon he did dazzling feats with heavy rocks and I cut, moved, dug up or planted living things. On a sweltering day we pranced around under a garden sprinkler hidden behind a shrub, completely naked. Innocence returned, but not for long!

When we were not painting a wall or planting a plant we were playing music together. Soon we bought a giant bed at IKEA, decorated the biggest available room in unusual colors, and turned it into our 'sacred space'. I went 'home' regularly to teach pupils, to help Charles cook a decent meal from time to time. He seemed perfectly content with all this, now totally free to pursue whatever he felt needed pursuing. We got on really well, as good friends should.

Wandering about in Hampstead I could not help grinning happily with the irrepressible thought that at last there was someone who really appeared to *want* me. I was female again and this felt so unexpectedly wonderful, my feet hardly touched the ground.

We hardly noticed the passing of four whole years... time spent learning to live together and time to sever the ties of thirty-three years with Charles who seemed perfectly well without me. I had no desire to inflict any wounds, I had loved him too much for that. Alan once revealed how devastated he'd be if I left *him* and I remember having to check with Charles what it meant, to be 'devastated'...one of those many words I'd heard but not analysed. When he finally landed himself with another partner, *and* discovered he was going to have a child, he suggested we divorce. Easy: in March 1998 I was free. But one truly distasteful moment came from an unexpected source: the Catholic Church. I was required to swear on the Bible that I had *'never been married'* to Charles Chadwick. Well, of course I had not, in the *eyes of the church*. But I had to *say it*, hand on the *Bible* ...for the sake of the new wife, who as a Catholic wanted a 'proper' wedding. Well, so she should, I tried to tell myself.

It 'pissed me off', though. Will I be forgiven my *one* lapse into coarse language? As I age I feel almost no further desire or need to impress others, but still relieved that my mother was no longer in a state to witness this shameful event. In 2003 my mother died. I tipped her ashes into the sea in CapeTown.

It broke my heart.

Now time is running out: I admit, try to come to terms with, accept, my many imperfections. Alan and I read, discuss, perform concerts, enjoy the seasons in our garden and we travel.

He is the most wonderful dynamic person to travel with, always so interesting and interested. We've criss-crossed the globe, the furthest places being Africa and China.

While roaming, learning, I have found one more treasure: the way 'back' to my daughters. It has been the longest and most unusual journey of all.

Gabi and Polly c1990

Polly and Leela 2007

Polly 2008

Gabi 2009

Part 3

Gabrielle's Story

(in her own words)

'Once there was a way, to get back home.......'　　The Beatles.

My earliest memory is writing. Sitting at a typewriter, three or four years old maybe, writing something about oranges. Could I spell? Could I write? I've no idea. Yet the power of the moment is still there. Things welled up inside as I wrote whatever it was, feelings of sunshine and joy that danced through and permeated my father's little study in our house in Ndola. Other memories are fragments of feeling and impressions; of life as kind and full of well being, dazzling sunlight on the water of our swimming pool, bright pink bougainvillea on warm white walls, teeny lizard's eggs in keyholes, brown/black children with ragged clothes, crunchy stones round our house; always, in all of it, my constant 'other,' my sister Luci.

Childhood hints of what people call the divine, that indefinable something that can be experienced when there's no separation between the self and life. It's one of its sweet gifts, simple 'being-ness', untouched by life experience.

Then comes the complexity that 'learning' brings, the scarier memories, experiences harder to understand or integrate. I'm older, hanging about in the doorway looking at my Mummy, in bed after an accident. I'm uncertain, wondering what to do, unclear, caught up in some nameless dread. She's in the little room, her recovery space, next to my parent's big bedroom. She has bruises all over her body. The feeling is trouble and turmoil, things not being ok. There are more memories. My Mummy is on the phone, crying, our puppy is dying, our cat ate one of her kittens, Nana is sad ...Where do you start when the memories flood in?

How to organize the fragments? The easiest place is where everyone starts: at the beginning.....my beginning.

My mother is German, my father Lebanese. He would now challenge this simple fact, seeing himself as Christian Maronite, a distinction he finds important. He has denied he is Lebanese, though the two seem interchangeable to everyone else.

Pierre Mansour fell in love, with a beautiful German girl, Ingeborg Evelyn. She had the right kind of looks, he had the hang ups. He was self conscious about his curly black hair and hooked nose, having issues about race. (He has issues about many things. His children had issues about his issues! But that is some time away.) During the years that he was a student in South Africa - years of the unjust system of Apartheid, the political climate was ripe ground for his paranoia. He was then and remains to this day uncomfortable about looking too foreign. Evelyn's regular features were an antidote to some of his fears.

Perhaps the cause of his insecurity lay in his own background. His mother, Adèle, died in childbirth when he was only three. There's a striking photograph of her, young and healthy, dark haired, exotic, dressed in white lace. She died young, poisoned by her baby growing for ten months in her womb. On her deathbed she called for tiny Pierre, who remembers her lying dying on purple velvet. She urged her small child to take care of his younger twin sisters, a heartbreaking scene and huge burden for someone so young. His new stepmother Josephine (Nana) brought him up as if she were his mother. Knowing her generous nature, she was trying to help protect the boy from pain. But Pierre was always proud that he never 'forgot' the truth: he knew who his real mother was and it wasn't Josephine. The white lie she told was not a kindness to him, but an injustice. He was unwilling to forgive this 'sin.' It's a tendency he has, not to see another's point of view. Just to hold on, attack and make them wrong. He has this trait to this day. Whatever his psychology, Ingeborg-Evelyn's parents, were not sympathetic to this foreigner who wanted to marry their only daughter. It was not a blessed start.

Evelyn, (who gave up the 'Ingeborg') and Pierre were an attractive couple. Black and white photos from their courting days show a fresh-faced young woman, a well shaved (no moustache yet!) sensitive young man. Good looking, sweet, vulnerable, their youthfulness shining out. Later photos show emerging glamour and wealth, sunglasses, designer dresses and suits, a young pair finding their style as they began to inhabit their new life together. After a modest start in a flat, their luxury home was built. It had every modern feature, a food lift from kitchen to upstairs, the latest furniture, gardens with swimming pool, servants' quarters filled with poor black Africans to service the couple's dreams. Pierre got busy building his empire, Evelyn adapted to this new world. She was straightforward, pleasing, accommodating, likeable.

It was not the complete truth. In those days women were expected to be attractive, amenable and undemanding. Hollywood's ideal women were gorgeous, feminine, spirited... but not assertive. It was a hindrance to finding direction in life, something Evelyn had yet to do. Books such as 'The good girl syndrome' a couple of decades later were to challenge these attitudes.

At this time Pierre expressed many ambitions, wanting to prove himself.....in later life his goal was simply "to be the best poet in the world." He used to say "one day you'll realize you were living with a genius." He was happiest changing things, which didn't bode well for us future children. He applied the same critical attitude to people as he did to current reality, working constantly to 'improve' things in some way. This made him exciting, charismatic, interesting.... and infuriating. We all worked hard for his acceptance, invariably failing to attain his idiosyncratic standard, especially as we got older. That is, when we were born, which we weren't yet!

So there was Pierre in Zambia, at the end of the fifties, with his brand new wife, in love. She was already pregnant. They lived in that small flat, hot and cheerless with an unattractive view, until their designer home was ready. They had bad luck in that flat, with a series of cats dying. An omen of what was to come?

Their firstborn, Luke, died at six days old. After that things were not the same. Evelyn coped with this sad event without crying, just went back to her wife-life. It began, slowly, to feel unsatisfying, something was wrong. She continued to look good, stylish, like everything around her, but quietly, insidiously, creeping like rot, estrangement was growing. On the surface things continued as before. There was no animosity. The couple felt the influence of the oncoming sixties, with its throw-away prosperity and focus on freedom and fun.

Then, about two years later when Nana prayed for the couple's fertility in Lourdes, a miracle happened! Evelyn was pregnant again! It was me, growing there quietly in the safe rosy-pinkness of her womb. Many years later, unaware of Nana's pilgrimage, I would visit Lourdes in a double-decker bus and experience first-hand, that magical atmosphere; people chanting in the streets, healing rituals, candlelight and imminent miracles.

A few months before my birth in 1958, Pierre's father Antoine died in a tragic car accident. A driver had fallen asleep at the wheel of a vehicle coming the opposite way. Antoine (Tony) was hit, his ribcage shattered, his lungs punctured. He died in an oxygen tent.

Pierre inherited Border Motors, the car company his father had founded in 1928. He had to work hard to learn the business, doing this successfully though his real interests were elsewhere. He was upset about the loss, as he'd loved and admired his Dad. Pierre had designed and built an outdoor chess table especially for his Dad's visits. He envisaged afternoon chess tournaments on the upstairs balcony, with a view of the gardens and pool. They were never to happen, the chess table was never used. I used to think about this wild granddad we never met when I passed that table and have a silent special feeling about him. My middle name Toni is in remembrance of him. Sometimes I feel superstitious about it, wanting it changed, in case it attracts a stray car...

Gabrielle Toni (me!) was born into this setting on December 24th 1958. I've been told I cried all the time for about three months, gulping down different formulas to try and settle me down. Photographs of me show a long skinny thing, with a worried face. Not a rosy cheeked advert-baby at all. There's an atmosphere in these early pictures of subtle stress. Evelyn was overwhelmed by the little screaming rabbit she'd given birth to. She chose not to breastfeed after one week. If I'd had any say I'd have yelled: "persevere please Mummy, it'll improve the bonding process between us. Plus it's much, much better for my health. Don't give up so soon I beg you! You'll get used to it!"

I sprang from the soil of an inexperienced mother, beginning to be bored with her role, unprepared for the demands I was about to make. Some mothers fall madly in love with their children. Others don't engage. Evelyn didn't take naturally to the little charge bawling its way into her life. No wonder I cried!

One of my later influences was Jean Liedloff's 'Continuum Concept,' 1975, which advocates physical closeness between mother and child. The book broke new ground in the seventies; arguing that infants should be carried and kept close to their mother's bodies as much as possible early in life, sleep with parents, breastfeed on demand as long as they want to be. Her observations were formed while living with the Yequena tribe in Venezuela. Their children, she noticed, are unusually self possessed, co-operative and secure. The child's self esteem is formed through the quality of interaction with its parents, not only mother, but the entire 'tribe' or extended family that should ideally be there for a child all its life. If a child has its real needs met, the outcome can be social harmony. Unmet needs create psychological problems that can result in mental and social dysfunction.

She argues that a bonded mother naturally, non-verbally, intuits her children's needs. It takes intention, commitment, as well as lots of honesty and practice. I chose to apply what rang true to me to my own children. It shocks some people to know that my eldest child Polly, now twenty-four, was breastfed until she was four years old! My youngest child Saba, sixteen, was breastfed for six years! My son Pablo, seventeen, lasted a year, stopping reluctantly because Saba came along. Liedloff argues that each child has a different rhythm and needs; mothers are encouraged to listen to and take their cues from each individual child, to trust them and themselves.

The simple truth is that children thrive on love, attention and focus, yet are often dragged rather than brought up, treated with shocking insensitivity without real understanding of their needs. We expect to create a society of healthy balanced individuals without knowing what we're doing. It's such an important subject. Often we're more sensitive to the needs of our plants than the humans we are supposed to cultivate and tend.

The urge for centrality is major in childhood. We all come in, feeling like the centre of the universe, born into other people's unfinished stories, in which each person is the centre. Like Russian dolls we spring from each other, entering a continuum that's never ending. To love is to make another as central as yourself. Like plants, we're reliant on the quality of our soil. But unlike plants, we're each defined by our relationships with others. All of us weave a complex and unique web of inter-connectedness. Plants grow best under optimal conditions and so do we, blossoming when we receive the right blend of emotional, social, physical nutrients. We can grow when some nutrients are lacking, but are more challenged to reach our best potential.

Luckily I was a pretty toddler. I'd have to be to win my mum over! By the time I was two I'd become the golden-headed advert child I'd failed to be at birth. Just when things were looking up for me, along came a threat: Evelyn was pregnant with her second child. She decided to go away for a couple of months leaving me with a family appropriately called the Cares. The father was Pierre's lawyer. Their daughter was my friend.

This is my memory: I am alone in a sandpit, holding some beads and becoming aware, slowly, concentrating on the beads in my hand, that my mummy is gone. Really gone, the kind of gone where she doesn't come back. Ever. Or so it seems to a small child, when time is long and two months a concept you can't grasp. I was only a toddler, strong in feelings, weak in the power to articulate. Children form identities, in part, by how another sees them. A child's identity can fracture or collapse when no one is there to mirror feelings, or support them in making sense of the world. Later, in my twenties, when I started Primal Therapy, this was the memory my body took me to, remembering something long ago forgotten, so clearly, felt to me as shocking as a car crash. My parents didn't like the sound of the therapy, it seemed suspect to them. However, the experiences I had doing Primal Therapy affected me profoundly, altering my life direction permanently. At first, just talking to my therapist about other things... then some skilful questioning and touch activated something I wasn't aware of. After that, the upset that came out of my body had to be experienced to be understood. As an adult I was taken over, sobbing with a long forgotten childlike rage and terror at my source of security disappearing. I felt an animal anger and distress, primitive and violent in its intensity. It was unimaginably life changing. For a couple of hours I physically relived what I may not have even expressed in the moment. This memory was somehow lodged in my body, connections I'd not made before lit up my being. I felt different. Some things made sense that hadn't before. I realized I was terrified of rejection and abandonment, feeling somehow I was so bad I deserved it: 'Mummy's gone. I'm all alone. She doesn't want me. I did something wrong. She doesn't love me. She wouldn't leave me if she loved me. It's my fault. I'm not loveable. Mummy's good, I must be bad if she doesn't want me. I'm bad and not loveable'. We are born narcissistic, interpreting everything in relation to ourselves. Yet our 'souls' are always awake even if our minds are not developed, our hearts and feelings are all there. Adult insensitivity to our needs really hurts. I was deeply hurt and confused by being left.

Young children are sensitive to change, needing preparation and support to feel safe. Some adults think because children are not verbally articulate they have no real consciousness. Pierre used to insist that children were not worth talking to until they're eight or older. We had arguments when I'd attend to my first baby crying. "You aren't going to be THAT kind of Mother," he'd say every time I went to her.

On February 20th 1961 Lucienne Erika was born. She found herself better received. To my chagrin, she took my place on Mummy's lap. Photographs showed me growing fatter; standing slightly to one side while Luci took central position. Evelyn felt more drawn to this baby, who was less miserable and stressed than I'd been. It was a self-perpetuating circuit, Evelyn was more relaxed and so was her baby. I'd become clingy when Evelyn returned from her trip abroad, terrified that she might do a disappearing act again. I wouldn't even let her go to the toilet without hanging on to her legs at first. I badly needed special attention and reassurance to feel secure again. It was not the best moment to have a rival for the precarious affections of my mother.

Luci's reign of power didn't last too long. After a while we became cute together. We began to discover the joy of playing with each other. She gradually shifted from threat to ally. 'GabiLu' was born, an alliance that lasted until our forties.

Evelyn had secretly hoped Luci might be someone else's daughter. She'd had an affair with an architect and Pierre knew about it. It was part of the 'open' marriage they had developed. Pierre also did his own thing, sometimes, when travelling, even visiting prostitutes, coming back smelling of sweat and another woman's perfume. They did all this without animosity, but things were changing. Conditions were ripe for new passions to emerge and they did. For Evelyn, it was not the architect but Charles; a tall Englishman she met through playing music, who brought that change. Charles's height was a factor in her attraction to him. Though Pierre had great charisma and drive, he was also one of those shorter men who make up for lack of height with personality. Evelyn wished he were different. Taller. There were jokes about wanting to stretch him. He could also be opinionated and overpowering, alienating traits that put some people's backs up. Gradually passion and intimacy began to fade between the couple as a result. Pierre was essentially an idealist; probably compensating for the inadequacy he carried deep within. To this day he is frustrated by unrealized potential and the gulf between his visions and reality. He was too busy bridging the gap to notice where his wife was bored and frustrated, or distant and isolated in their life. Charles appeared just in time and he was refreshingly different from Pierre. Evelyn was ready. She took the leap, into a new and hopefully more meaningful life.

"Daddy is outside next to the pink and purple bougainvillea, he's telling us we are going to live with

Mummy in England. He says they are divorcing. I feel sorry for my Daddy, he'll be all alone. I'm scared. I'm thinking about how sad and lonely he'll be. I'm going to draw pictures and send them to him to cheer him up. The wall behind Daddy, it's white with brown circles on it. You can put your hands on it and it's always warm. I'm feeling strange... like the whole world is cold and falling down. Mummy and Daddy know what to do, but it feels as if Mummy knows and Daddy doesn't. I have to help my Daddy, my heart aches."

ENGLAND My first impressions made me determined to hate it. First of all it was cold and grey. Everything was wrong. Traffic lights were a different colour. The birds didn't sing right. Where were the crickets, the swimming pools? Airport Officials were efficient and quiet. I missed the crazy black officials at Ndola airport, I wanted noise and chaos, dust, sweat and heat. That was home.

We lived in a flat in Muswell Hill. I tried to be good for Mummy. She had left me once before and now she's left poor Daddy. She might leave me again! I had a dim fear the divorce was somehow my fault. In London, we went to a nearby school, finding it difficult to settle, though there were compensations. Like the landlady Yvonne with her family upstairs, especially her son Kimon who became our great friend. We'd sit on the outside steps and sing the Beatles, "She loves you yeah yeah yeah," feeling expansive and free; happy to forget the oddness, newness of everything and how far we were from our Ndola. Kimon's family were Greek Cypriots. They ate 'weird' food, which we were reluctant to try. Despite our travels across the world, like many kids we were conventional about what we ate. Yvonne was surprised that such worldly children were so unadventurous. There were some things we had to hold on to, for our own sanity. Too much was changing too fast.

After Mummy left Ndola, and we went back to visit, our father would feed us fillet steak and fizzy drinks, chocolate galore, toasted cheese sandwiches whenever we liked, plenty of calorie rich rubbish prepared for us on demand by Andy our 'house boy.' Later, travelling alone on planes, (first class of course), we ordered burgers and chips like 'Jughead' in our Archie comics. Obliging air-hostesses scurried off to make them for us; just like the pictures. That was as adventurous as we got.

We missed Daddy. We had to get back to our old life. We missed 'Bewitched' on T.V, our black and white cat 'Top Cat.' We wanted our bedroom, our huge sunny garden. In London the houses were too close together, everything was small and squashed up. We came up with a plan. Stowaways on an aeroplane! It seemed so easy. We just had to get to the airport, sneak up the ladder to the plane and climb in through its underbelly where the luggage was stored. We had total faith we'd find it and succeed. After tying clothes into a piece of material for the trip, we sneaked off when Evelyn was doing her violin practice. We got as far as the top of the road by the Laundrette and felt hungry. We had no money, hadn't thought to pack something to eat or drink. A feeling of smallness, of powerlessness came over me. It was time to go home. We decided to try again some other day....

One day the ceiling fell down where we usually sat watching T.V. Luckily we were somewhere else that moment. The dust and debris was an eerie reminder that things could change in an instant. Perhaps there were things stronger than Mummy; now Daddy was gone we weren't quite safe.

Lusaka, 1965. Back in Africa again, it all felt strange. It was odd to have a new bedroom and to live in a house with our stepfather Charles. We needed reassurance and contact, but our Mum became more distant, her attention taken up by her new marriage. By the time her third child, James, was born, she'd made a choice: to let go of GabiLu and focus on her new family. Inwardly and outwardly, she handed over responsibility for her two girls to Pierre. The trouble was he didn't know. She thought he'd do the job better than her. He assumed she was doing it. As a result we fell into a kind of psychological no-parents land.

For a while we lived with Charles and Mum and went to school in Lusaka. I don't remember much, except the name 'Dominican Convent.' Until we went to boarding school there seemed to have been many nuns in our education. Years later we both did our First Communion in London, earnestly confessing invented sins to God, mouthing 'Hail Mary's' and 'Our Father's,' as penance. I lived in subtle fear of God's judgement; afraid I'd do something to displease him. Throughout the day I discreetly made the sign of the cross, making prayers to appease him, as a precaution.

Part of Evelyn's problem embracing us was Charles. He disliked Pierre, seeing him as an arrogant opinionated man. We were therefore Pierre's spoilt little brats; Charles was irritated by some of our attitudes and opinions. He wanted his life with Evelyn, not the baggage of her past life. We had no idea until we were grown up that he saw us like this. No matter how we seemed, we were just little girls who wanted love and approval wherever we went. If we had mannerisms that grated, we required guidance and compassion. We couldn't help what we'd been born into. Criticism and rejection were the last things we needed.

Charles seemed a kind man who gave us some of the normal attentions we craved as children: Simple things like reading stories and drawing pictures of his imagined " King Murgatroyd". We assumed he liked us. We both liked him. It was a blow in adulthood to discover how uncomfortable and uneasy he was about the 'princesses' invading his life. He had areas of low self esteem that we had no understanding of as young children. He could also be (irrationally to others but perhaps not himself) insecure and depressed. So for a while we were shipped off to Dad. I don't remember being sent to live with him. All I remember is being on holiday at his house and him trying to teach me the time, which mystified me. I do know that he treated us more like adults than young children. We didn't know until adulthood that we minded that.

We admired him, even worshipped him, despite his being too busy to spend much time with us. Luci and I were often left alone together, to invent our own little world. After Evelyn had left, there in our sunlit paradise, endless Coca Colas, Fantas, Seven Ups were available to us all day from our drinks freezer. All we had to do was grab one, click off its corrugated metal top on the special bottle opener, built in. There were no restrictions, we could grab two or three if we chose to. I'd drink seven or eight in a day. We'd drink them instead of water, taking them ice cold down to the boomerang shaped pool in our garden. We had a walk-in pantry stocked like a mini shop, full of, amongst other things, chocolate for us to help ourselves to. The result: I was a hefty eight stone at the age of ten. Our African 'servants' would ask us to slip them soft drinks and so on, some small compensation in servicing our luxurious lifestyle while they lived in relative poverty just across the garden. As children we were blind to the injustice in the situation.

Dad took me to his stepmother, Nana, to be appraised. She was a Lebanese woman with long salt and pepper hair worn in a bun, solid, reliable and generous always, ever loyal to my Mum even after the divorce. I trusted Nana and was asked to parade up and down in front of her. It seemed as if everyone was seeing me for the first time. She agreed sorrowfully that I appeared to have trouble breathing. I sensed her concern. Still nothing changed. Dad had other more important preoccupations than his daughter's obesity! I didn't really care if no one else did, happy to eat the same appalling diet that we loved, consuming vast quantities of sugar. Luci stayed skinny, but perhaps I was more of a pig! I was quite oversensitive and seemed to have an unmet need for reassurance and comfort. Food was one way to fill the need.

Dad had little modelling of family life, having been away at boarding school himself from five to eighteen, so our main contact with him became intellectual and verbal. He was not particularly demonstrative or affectionate even when we threw ourselves at him passionately for our bedtime kiss. If we squeezed too hard, held on too long, he'd push us away, embarrassed.

He did teach us to be articulate and sophisticated though. His passion was for ideas and action, creative projects, the arts, current affairs, theatre, music. There he was animated and interested in everything. He liked to be up to date, receiving boxes of singles to keep in touch with music in the charts and magazines from England. He disapproved of our Archie comics, trying to persuade me to read Plato's Republic when I was eight. I was an avid reader and did eventually find it interesting. He loved anything avant-garde, new, challenging, shaming the normal and mundane and encouraged us to be the same. We were allowed to stay up late and got indignant with lady-friends who tried to put us to bed. Dad would arrive home and give his permission to our resistance. We'd get back out of bed triumphant, to the bewilderment of his visitors.

One day he took us to a house to see his secretary. She had big blonde hair, a small waist and a little cardigan, buttoned up. Her daughter was our friend. This lady had a new baby over her shoulder, being sick down her back. "This is your sister," Dad told us. We stared, unimpressed by the dribble and sour smell of sick, accepting the statement as children do. We remembered this event, but Dad never mentioned it again.

We knew all our lives that this sister might turn up one day. We used to talk about it, it became a myth. When she contacted us in our forties it was as unreal as a long ago dream come to life. We knew it might happen but didn't believe in it, like Father Christmas or the tooth fairy. Dad's denial and deceit about it, the way he'd lied to his new wife about it, the way he forgot he'd once told us the truth...troubled us the most. Who was this man? This girl attempted to contact Pierre, but he'd have nothing to do with her, denying his paternity. That remains the situation to this day. We do know for a fact that Dad bought his secretary a house and gave her a generous amount of money at the time. That day though, back in Ndola, after we'd seen our baby sister, we just went home. We continued our life, staying up late, watching Dad have parties or chess tournaments in the living room. We swam in our boomerang shaped pool, ate what we liked, had racing cars from Border Motors that really drove, bicycles, everything we wanted. He'd say, "Remember, you can have anything as long as it doesn't hurt anyone." He promised us baby elephants, a Go Kart he was going to build himself, the world. When he bought a farm he planned to make a house just for the kids with their own pool. Some of it materialised, some didn't. All of it created a dizzying world without limits, full of colour and possibilities.

Dad ran 'Theatre Workshops' in the Border Motor building, another of his passions. He took us along, letting us play 'offices' at the desks. He also had a darkroom for producing black and white photographs. We knew fragments of his plays off by heart, such as 'Humbeat's Circle,' which explored black oppression. I loved the name Humbeat, it sounded like African drums to me! He used black African farm workers in that play. Their energy was phenomenal. I was impressed, excited and moved by their vitality and physicality. He had a verse in the play, which GabiLu knew off by heart and used to chant in unison:

"Let's sing the song of a glutton

Who took a large slice of the mutton.

He tasted the juice, the meat and the mince.

He ate and ate till he burst his buttons...

His friends were killed on the first explosion,

From that day on he ate alone.

For no more friends he ever won.

We had no idea what it meant. We never understood anything he wrote. He didn't help us. If we got him talking about his work, we'd end up bored and confused. Still, some pieces of his writing live on in my mind: "A man walking....Saw miles of teeth.... Under feet, biting...His eyes paralysed his nerves... Decomposed...Left his teeth in the sand."

They rattle around in me, together with unfriendly thoughts about his pretentiousness. I had many painful experiences trying to be part of his artistic world. For years he put me off 'creativity.' Yet I couldn't help it, it was in the blood!

Pierre was deeply interested in black liberation, talked to us with passion about apartheid and white oppression. I sensed the importance of the subject, trying to grasp, aged eight, what he was saying. It did leave an impression of scary injustice going on in the world, which shocked my young mind. He attended mysterious meetings at night where he was the only white man. He told us he was helping the Africans. He had some kind of connection with President Kaunda, in office from 1964-1991. The president came to our house sometimes and was received upstairs in the important room used on special occasions. My claim to fame is that the President of Zambia carried me up the stairs to that room. Once we visited a place of his in Lusaka, which had sweeping green lawns and beautiful peacocks. Dad had a meeting with Kaunda; we've no idea to this day what about. On that occasion we were presented with two white rats. We were thrilled with our rodents, Ruby and Vagabond. They had tiny pink noses, snow-white fur and seemed perfect. Sadly our red-eyed rats became 'the disappeared' along with other 'undesirables' of ours that Mum or Charles had to take on in Lusaka. Whatever else Dad got up to, it was his writing that was the most important to him. It began to become so obscure I couldn't relate to it.

Many years later when we were in our twenties he visited us in Rotterdam, Holland. He read his work to a group asking everyone for feedback and opinions. There was a silence. He was, could be, extremely difficult and confrontational if you volunteered a real opinion. Was it worth it? Everyone was weighing up the situation. My boyfriend broke the silence by denouncing Dad's poetry as "crap!" Dad leapt up, picked up a chair and shouted, "I put this chair between you and me!" There was another silence as we waited, the chair standing harmlessly and pointlessly between them. Dad seemed a cornered animal. It was fight or flight so he left the room, a 'Great Man' in a huff. As an afterthought he gathered anyone he thought supportive to him on the way out. Luci went with him. I stayed in the room with my boyfriend. Dad had little sense of humor about himself, little humility. He was very Mediterranean in that way. He sometimes recognized that his pride was a problem.

For years we laughed about that moment, away from him. We were members of a 'Kunst collectif' (Dutch Art collective) and becoming more independent of his influence. He no longer seemed as powerful and impressive as he used to. He was, at that time, younger than I am now. His marriage to second wife J was floundering. We were growing up, wanting to know him better as a person. Impossible: his pride prevented him being vulnerable, equal to others, hidden behind the role of 'Great Man' for so long.

Luci worked harder than me to be pleasing. She would have fiery arguments but in an almost intimate way, skillfully managing his   personality while striving to 'win,' yet maintain his approval. She acted as if she had a special inroad to his affections. I was more critical and cynical, feeling that being close to him was impossible. It was only after she left home and he'd treated her the same as everyone else she realized it had all been an illusion. She has never spoken to him or seen him since she understood that he favored her no more than anyone else, she was as rejectable as the rest of us. Dad's rejection of all his children has affected all of us in different ways. I've had moments in life, like most people, where anger and/or despair about the past has been overwhelming. Caring for my own children has made me aware of the neglect in our childhood. At times I've been very angry and upset. The neglect was not physical, but emotional, which is harder to see, but not to feel. Luckily, life experience can, over time, have a softening effect. As understanding of people's limitations and background grows, forgiveness becomes more possible. Having children helps. It's easier to see how hard parenting can be when you've experienced the daily grind yourself. I've used therapy many times, as a kind of re-parenting, to help me get clear on things that were hard to accept. Life is too good, people too precious, to waste time hurting. There's still a lot to understand, some of it may never make sense. 'GabiLu' weren't the kind of kids who had a say in what happened to them. We were told and expected to comply. We learned to soothe feelings of lack of control by uniting with each other, creating an independent unit 'us'. We needed something to make us secure in the world, big and scary out there. Soon we got used to travelling halfway across the world on planes, taking whatever crisis, bad weather etc. that life threw at us. Once, stranded in Dar es Salaam on our way to Ndola, a kind couple took pity on us. We'd been forced to spend the night in the airport lounge, sleeping anywhere we could find. We didn't really know what to do. This couple bought us dinner and as we ate, told us they were impressed at how grown up we seemed. It was only partly true. Really, most of the time we bluffed our way through situations, acting older and more capable than we felt. We were losing touch with what we really were, just two little girls.

Boarding School, 1969.

We had known we were going to boarding school, but not what that really meant. The day we were dropped off was a day like no other. I was ten years old, Luci was eight. Days your life changes can creep up on you without warning, the implications of that change can reverberate forever. Our significant day began with an uneventful car journey. I'm not even sure which combination of our then four parents delivered us. Was it Dad and J? Or Mum and Charles? All I know is whoever it had been, was gone. The next day they were still gone. Then the one after that. So it went on, without ceasing, the relentless 'gone-ness.'

Across a field in *her* new house Luci is biting and kicking her fellow inmates. I know about that. Now, ten years old, at my new school I don't even wonder how she is, or exactly where she is, even though we've never been apart. I'm too overwhelmed by my own experience. When I feel ready to take stock, it seems I am in a small room with five other girls. There are two windows, looking out on a garden. The garden looks green and inviting. I want to be out there, running away. But I sit still, looking at the walls and door. My eyes are fixed on the door but I am rooted to the bed. I notice my locker, a shabby little cupboard next to my bed. The room is small, painted some shade of light green. It's hard to find a place for me, somewhere away from the annoying noisy children I'm suddenly with. I stare at the bed, there are blue and purple striped bedcovers, thin cotton weave, the kind of thing Mum might have at home. The bed covers are quite nice. I don't really know what to do except stay on my bed with the bed cover, next to my locker, in the bit of the room that's mine. I'm drowning in a kind of swirling panic but act as if I'm fine because I want to be and really don't know what else to do. There are children shouting and lots of people I don't know.

There's no one to turn to. I'm just one of this crowd. I daren't move an inch. I've been left, they just left me here and they are going home. I can't go home. I can't think about it, I might cry, I don't want to cry. Everyone is saying things, shouting. I'm trying to be invisible, don't want anyone to see me but I can't hide, there's nowhere to go. I just have to stay here, if I move I might cry. Maybe I'll put something in my locker but for now it's safer to do nothing, just wait and see, try not to think. If I look at this bed cover long enough this might all go away and I'll be safe and back where I know things, not here any more, I don't want to be here....

They had those bed covers throughout the school, a positive memory. Somehow, to me, they were a link to home. Where that was I'm not sure, anywhere we had a parent I think! We were allowed to wear our own clothes at St Chris, as it was a 'progressive' school, a 'groovy' school. Luci and I had identical brown cord pinafore dresses, wool tights, pleated brown wool skirts. Combined with my pointed black-framed glasses, sensible haircut and overweight, whatever good looks I'd had as a golden haired toddler were more than obscured. This all went against me in the point scheme invented by merciless eleven and twelve year olds!

Luckily the situation contained its own solution. It was at St Chris I lost weight and ended up (at fifteen) a healthy eight stone.

Boy's rooms were the other side of our house 'Little Arundale.' Luci was a brisk walk away with her house parents at 'Arunbank,' different age groups housed in different 'homes.' Main school was a short walk for every boarder, there was plenty of fresh air and exercise. The school was vegetarian, much to our dismay. I craved sausages and bought tins of frankfurters to eat in the toilets, with my friends. Most of the time though, I had to eat what was there. It did me good in the end, even if at first I was oblivious to the health benefits of my new diet.

Already an uncertain little girl, boarding school plunged me into the unknown. I missed everything. The freedom I'd felt as a normal child was over. I was controlled by rules from morning to night. It didn't matter that it was progressive, co-educational and Quaker. It wasn't a family. All I wanted was some kind of real 'home.' We were forced to come up with survival strategies.

At school we immediately began disconnection from adults, identification with peer group. Adults were the betrayers. Many of us felt abandoned and rejected. Unless parents reassure you, it's hard to feel wanted when there is no real explanation or real communication with anyone. I pushed away normal childish longings for 'Mummy and Daddy', and distracted from the pain by comforting 'victims' around me; girls and boys who felt their parents didn't want them either. We were the lost ones, all together. That was comforting; to be in the same boat. As the relentless routine of the institution called school claimed us all, we began to build loyalties to each other. One day I stood up and announced a meeting "for kids only" at the back of the house. At least twenty accomplices turned up to plan a mutiny. We stole eggs from the kitchen and played catch with them, then refused to go to bed at night. "If we refuse," I said, "there'll be nothing they can do, we'll be free!" It seemed a way out at the time. Disrupt and take back power! There was perhaps some of Dad's non-conformist influence behind my great plan. I felt old and wise at eleven, entitled to this authority, certain that with team work we could build a new world! Eggs were 'nicked' from the kitchens and 'bunged around' the school grounds. Bedtime arrived and mutiny began in a fitful way. There were some shouts; lights went off all over the building. After five minutes I was standing alone with the light on in the middle of the dorm.

"What are you doing?" asked a member of staff. Minor disruption throughout the building had been effortlessly quelled by a few commands and stern voices from those in power. "Standing on the floor" I answered, trying to be cocky and savvy, determined to stay true to the spirit of rebellion. I was mildly amazed that everyone had gone down so quickly.

As ringleader I was made to stand outside the housemother's flat, supposedly thinking about what I'd done. I was cold. The house was quiet and peaceful, all dormitory lights out. I felt lonely, angry, determined and defiant. My housemother leaned into my face and explained I must see her as my second mother. If I had problems I must feel free to come to her. She had one fat arm and grey hairs on her chin. She was nothing like my mum! I was repelled, vowed I would never ever go to her for anything. She died some time later of the cancer that had caused her arm to swell, leaving a sad husband and two young daughters.

• • •

While I wanted my Mum, I didn't end up with many memories of closeness with her. One positive memory I have, was while holidaying in Mombasa. Charles was upset that day. He had his moods, which as teenagers, we tried to ignore. We decided to wade into the sea at low tide, to search for coral. Mum took off her bikini top, swinging it in one hand while we set off. With our bare breasted mother and the sun shining, we waded into the sea at low tide, a memorable mood of light-hearted intimacy opening up between the three of us. Charles, in a dark mood, had been left onshore, as we walked out to the dazzling brightness. Finding a live sea cucumber with its little dark green mouth just added to the hilarity and fun. We wanted life to be good and simple, full of affection and laughter, to forget our stepfather's confusing emotional swings and self-pity, leave adult complexity behind. For that moment all was right, we had our mother which was as it should be. It was a rare moment of belonging. Years later Luci and I both remember that walk.

We inevitably adapted to our situation, as children do. I discovered my rebellious streak. I had tried 'earning' love by being a good pupil, for a while going down that road. I'd do what I was told, then take my rebellion sideways, secretly angry at feeling powerless and unimportant. I was the good child first, keen to earn approval and positive strokes from those around me. But it was not enough; I was left feeling hollow and became an explorer of the forbidden. After the mutiny came kiss-chase, then cigarettes and alcohol. I was by now about thirteen. One day a group of us managed to get hold of sherry, wine and gin in the town, bought for us by an obliging someone the right age whom we'd asked in the street.

We drank our stash out on the fields behind the main school, mixing the alcohol indiscriminately. Gin was disgusting, like hot perfume, but I slugged it down without caution, my mind soon blotted out. I have a vague recollection of my clothes being too hot, wee-ing in the school bin, people cheering, walking back to my house, people laughing, falling asleep the minute I hit my bed.

Next day I had a terrible headache, combined with a sickening sense of creeping shame. I was naked. Some vague memories of ripping clothes off, leaving them back at main school somewhere near a urine filled bin in the library, swam around my aching brain. My friends had further cringe-making stories to share. Things kept emerging like fragments of a bad dream. It was announced in school assembly that someone had been sick under the school piano.

The experience at school and a few others put me off drink, but not off other things. I became interested in altered states of consciousness and trying all the fashionable drugs of the seventies. I turned on, tuned in, dropped out. In common with many of my generation, I felt let down by what the older generation had to offer. It felt hollow, empty and essentially meaningless. It seemed all they cared about was material things, not about how people felt, or who anyone was. I wasn't terrified of lack or insecurity like the previous war-traumatized generation. I'd had material comfort. What I'd had less of was emotional security or intimacy, nothing to depend on that made me feel safe inwardly, or significant to anyone. Like many of my friends at the time, I suppressed emerging upset at feeling displaced and without any consistent 'other'.... with 'pot,' then 'grass' or 'dope' to us, LSD, speed, barbiturates, Mogadon, Mandrax, uppers, downers, anything that was going around at the time. It was a way of belonging to a family, a family of 'flower children' who cared about each other (or so we hoped!).

P., one of our teachers, had several pieces of work published, and founded the Mandeville Press in 1974 in nearby Hitchin. He took a special interest in me, saying I could "write well about a piece of dust if that was required." Writing was just normal to me. It felt easy to turn out the assignments required. P. (we called our teachers by their Christian names) was a poet, a hunchback and a real character. He broke his wife's heart by having an affair with the drama teacher. He and his mistress took a flattering interest in my progress. My confidence boosted, I organized a speaker from Amnesty International to give a talk at the school, as well as one with the author Sally Trench, who wrote "Bury me in my Boots" about the homeless in 1968. The book had a huge impact. I felt passionate for both these causes, realizing I liked to help people. This was to prove a potential sticky place for me in later life, when I took this urge 'to give' beyond my capacity. I liked to make a difference to someone, to feel warm, needed and significant.

I also organized and directed a couple of plays and choreographed dances. As younger kids, Luci and I had made up lots of different performances and events. Sadly, over time I became disconnected from these talents. Even though I was singled out for my flair at English and Drama at school, at Art,

French and German, I became bored with academic accomplishment. I was looking for knowledge about relationships, psychology, intimacy. I had this inward looking streak, wanting to know more about being human, about real people's lives. I had too many questions, few real answers.

<u>Hippy Teens.</u>

By this time Dad had been through two houses, one in Ingram Avenue (one of the two hundred most expensive streets in Britain,) the other a restored and supposedly haunted ex-pub in Chiswick. His third house in Canterbury slightly resembled his house in Ndola, having a similar 'upside down' roof. He was still with J, and they'd had four gorgeous children. It was J. who encouraged us to change our image. GabiLu began to transform from 'nice' girls to longhaired hippy teens and to become more distinct from each other. I wore denim and cheesecloth, Laura Ashley skirts that brushed the floor, velour-paneled garments, John Lennon specs and patched jeans with inserts at the bottom...Luci had distinctive blue boots that she tucked in to jeans.

Dad's income from his business in Zambia became difficult to get out of the country. He wanted us both to leave St Chris to save money. I panicked. School had become home to me. I was scared to return to Dad. At St Chris I finally belonged, in a way. At least there I knew what to expect – structure, predictability, no nasty shocks that took me out of my depth. At home though, Luci had an advantage: she was bonding with Dad, J and the kids. They put her into a drama school, where she did well enough to land a part in a Shredded Wheat advert. Dad paid the term's fees with her wages, and then told her she had to leave. He gave no explanation, perhaps he had run out of funds. Sadly, that was the end of her career in drama, no one mentioned it again. I wonder what might have happened if she'd stayed. She did show real flair. Dad never encouraged his kid's talents, just seemed uncomfortable when others made an impact... he had to be the centre of everything, finding it hard even to make J. feel special. He used to say "I come first, then J, then you lot." We took that as the nature of things. It took me years to even question that.... it was so ingrained. I lost interest in achieving and began to decline academically. I cried often and didn't know why. Part of me no longer cared. I identified with the anti-materialist, anti- establishment, pro-people values that were the emerging hippy ethic at the time. It was now the seventies.

Mum and Charles seemed occupied with their own concerns, their marriage subtly stressed. Charles wasn't happy, she wasn't happy. He was quietly critical and terse with Evelyn, uncomfortable and constricted in himself. He dealt with his discontent by descending into the basement to work on his manuscripts, sending out finished work.... only to be rejected again and again.

Yet, he could be very amusing, becoming animated and witty talking about literature. He was also generous and good to us. We did like him, but thought he often put Mum down. He treated her as a bit stupid as if she didn't 'get' things. We didn't agree. She may not have always been knowledgeable, but her mind was all there. Sadly, with vitality missing from the marriage, everything was compromised. Charles had emotional problems that contradicted his more generous and expansive sides. Like many inhibited Englishmen he could become cold and dismissive.

Mum and Charles were by now critical of 'GabiLu', living in a different world. Dad and J. understood a little more about youth culture at that time. Easiest of all to relate to were our many siblings, I loved them; though we saw little of our stepbrother on mum's side. We also loved our stepmother, who tried hard with us. I didn't always like the way Dad treated us all, he seemed like a bully, had erratic 'scenes'. He was no longer king of his empire, but an uptight family man beginning to fear that he may not achieve his ambition (one of them!) to be the greatest poet in the world. He felt we didn't appreciate his genius but he would be validated after death. I began to find him tyrannical and ludicrous. Instead of feeling valued, I was put down, humiliated, and shamed by this increasingly stressed father. Intellectually he was as interesting as ever, we had many lively unconventional and challenging discussions at home, about politics, art, theatre, literature etc. I discovered I had a flair for drama and English as a result of that stimulating background.

Lebanon......Leaving Home

I left school aged fifteen and a half, doing GCE's early, as I was a year ahead. For the next few months we lived in Lebanon, in the tiny village of Ghazir, with Dad, J. and their clutch of children, Fran, Pebs, Clare and Doudy. These tiny tots ran amuck in sixties fashion through the attractive Lebanese home. J. was a true sixties chick, fairly wild, impulsive and freedom loving. She was also generous and extravagant, sometimes rumbled by Dad's discovery of items stuffed at the back of cupboards she was afraid to own up to, or worse, the arrival of his credit card statements!

The house in Ghazir was perched on a hillside with an extensive view of terraced land and a spectacular (especially at night) vista of the Bay of Jounie. It had wide spacious rooms, balconies both upstairs and down and was decorated simply with blown glass chandeliers and huge floor standing vases.

Once, during an argument with Dad (perhaps the items at the back of the cupboards?) my stepmother threw herself at the chandelier, shattering its blue and green glass globes all over the floor, then hurled the large vases over the edge of the balcony. They smashed satisfyingly on the terraces below. She probably cut up some of her clothes afterwards, she generally did! A bee went up my floor length skirt soon after that, which I ripped off, screaming, adding to the general mayhem.

Soon after this hysteria, Dad hired a Lebanese peasant woman, Hadla, to take care of the children. J. was exhausted! Hadla washed our faces with a flannel, though Luci and I were thirteen and fifteen years old. It was an affront to our dignity to be pursued by this tiny fearsome old hag in black flapping dress. Whatever she was really like, her shriveled leathery face and darting bird-like eyes filled us with revulsion and indignation. Shortly, after a fiery bout of our complaints, the poor woman was dismissed.

And then came our Lebanese admirers: Dad spent an evening humoring a local man who offered a dowry for my hand in marriage. Some fishermen on the beach wanted me to run away with them. Young bloods on motorbikes turned up to find out more about us. Beneath the house lived a young Syrian laborer Mahmoud, in a rented basement room. One day Luci developed mysterious blotches on her lip. After various alibis unraveled, it emerged they were love bites. I had been keeping watch at Mahmoud's door, but hadn't really understood what was developing in there.

Dad and J, amused and tolerant, welcomed Mahmoud into the family. The young Syrian assured Dad and J that he would never compromise Luci's 'honor;' to show his integrity he produced pills to 'suppress his desire.' When we returned to Britain he swept Luci into a Hollywood kiss, later he sent passionate love letters in Arabic that we had to have translated, but Luci never saw him again. We assumed he was called to enlist in the Syrian army as hostilities escalated in Lebanon.

Lebanon was becoming a dangerous place to stay, so the whole family, returned to the UK. Luci wanted to be left to attend the American school near Beirut, but Pierre refused. He was aware of the political situation and knew it was a matter of time before things got very bad. So the whole family went back to Kent. I was happy as my boyfriend from St Chris was back in Britain.

In Kent I got myself a job at the King's School in Canterbury, rather than continue with any more academic education. I wanted real experiences! I joined a bunch of much older women to clean dormitories, make boy's beds, set and serve the boy's tea. The plus of the job was the interest the King's School boys had in their new cleaner! The minus was the drudgery. Being one of the only young girls there, (apart from a pair who came in to help with cooking) I got plenty of attention. After too many visits to our house from more interested King's School boys Dad had had enough. He arranged an interview for me at the local college and I was signed up for A levels. These had to be done in a year: I dropped French to concentrate on Economic and Social history, plus English. A year on, after I'd left college, Dad rushed me into leaving home. He gave me a little talk one night, saying, "Fly girl Fly!" For some reason I felt so rejected and hurt that I 'flew' a few days later. I had no plan, no idea what I was doing.

So I went camping with my boyfriend. At Stromness camp site on Orkney, a wild storm blew our loosely pegged tent into the sea. A chance meeting in the street with the writer George Mackay Brown led to us staying in his house as his only guests. This lovely man introduced us to other writers and artists, including the composer Peter Maxwell Davies.

Maxwell Davis (as people called him) spent six months every year on the deserted island of Hoy where he drew inspiration for his work. My boyfriend and I camped on the impressive brooding island, near a lake where the last two children of the community had tragically drowned. Remaining inhabitants of the island believed the place was cursed so they packed up and left the Valley forever. We stayed a few days, the only people on the island at the time, soaking up the eerie atmosphere of the place.

After this, we ended up in St Albans where my boyfriend lived. He was soon off to University in Sheffield. I tried to find a place to rent; it seemed wise to get somewhere now I'd left home. I hadn't a clue what I was to do next. Perhaps it was no surprise that I was ripped off by a con man at the first (slightly) acceptable place I found, a shabby room in a house where a man with one arm lurked, leering on the stairs. Trains ran past the back of the garden at regular intervals rattling everything! The 'landlord' wasn't a landlord at all. He didn't even own the house, had just 'obtained' the key and was letting the room to two of us simultaneously, to get two months rent in advance and two deposits. He'd done this in several places and was finally caught and the police got us our money back. My boyfriend's mother felt sorry for me after she witnessed this abuse. She offered me a room in their stylish St Albans home rent-free for the next three years. It was an incredible offer for a student, so of course I took it. I applied for and received a full grant and never had to worry for money once in that time.

I was treated like one of the family and got close to my boyfriend's mother. She was a vivacious, Pre-Raphaelite-looking red head, a lecturer at the local art college. We had fun going to exhibitions and discussing art. I became a member of the Tate Gallery, travelling by train to London for private exhibitions and shows. Every night I was cooked healthy meals and really looked after, I felt lucky to be there. She encouraged me to sign up for a degree in Humanities at a nearby Polytechnic and I graduated three years later having specialized in English literature. The degree had five modules: philosophy, logic, linguistics, English and computer studies. I loved the course and was expected to get a first. My dissertation 'The idea of nature in Beckett' was considered so original that my lecturers urged me to sign up to an American University to continue doing research for a book. The idea terrified me. I saw the years ahead as a long grey road to a trap: academia. Even Dad and J., back in Canterbury, were doing degrees at the University: J. graduated with first class honors, Dad a 2:1. He hit the roof, saying only conformists and unoriginal people got first class degrees. After this I was struck by an overwhelming bout of resistance to doing research for my dissertation. With skimpy research I missed a first by three marks, to the lecturer's puzzlement and disappointment. I didn't care. I just felt overwhelming relief to escape Dad's wrath and the pressure to go to America. I was twenty years old and sad to say goodbye to my nurturing landlady. She was puzzled that my parents had never come to visit the whole three years, but I wasn't, we weren't that kind of family.

The Punk Period

In 1979 there was another short spell in Canterbury. For a few months I worked, first in a pop, then a classical record shop in Canterbury. Luci had met a 'punk' fiddle player, who she was excited about. We met in the Pub, where he sat surrounded by people, a kind of buzz around him, Luci's 'sister from London' did her best to look at ease: everyone else seemed to know each other. He told me later I had looked cool and unimpressed with the Canterbury hicks! Jim wore a pink knitted tank top, a leather jacket covered in badges, big black Dr Martin boots (that later terrified my mum,) spiky peroxide hair and ripped jeans. He was friendly, charming and funny, the life and soul of the pub, I liked him. Dad and J. did too, finding him a character. It wasn't long before he was Luci's boyfriend and my friend.

One day the three of us spontaneously jumped on the coach to Sheffield. We had no plan, just to visit my boyfriend. Sheffield was a friendly city, the University easy to blend into and get cheap hot meals from! We decided to stay a while, renting a couple of rooms; mine a single, Luci and Jim's a double in a terraced house.

My sister and I made Dennis the Menace finger puppets and colorful objects to sell at the local market, Jim played his violin and made far more money than we did. It didn't matter! We spent most of our time laughing, becoming a kind of performance because of the way we looked. In Canterbury, tourists often photographed Jim. In Sheffield the attention continued. We were labeled the 'Pop kids.' Jim attracted such crowds in the town centre that he was taken to court for 'obstruction'. He wore an oversized suit given to him by a barman and washed the blue out of his hair to be more respectable. The end result was an unthreatening 'fluffy chick' look that made him seem more innocent. The judge called him 'our wandering minstrel' and clearly amused, fined Jim five pounds for blocking the route, as there were 'mitigating circumstances'... people could get by at the back and he had caused no actual harm.

Punk was about being outrageous, challenging authority and doing things your own way. It was also an outlet for anger. We were more into fun and humor, but there was also anger. Some people were scared of us, especially of Jim. His own mother said she'd walk on the other side of the street if she didn't know him. When Evelyn met him she turned white with shock. She felt it necessary to wipe the chair he'd just sat on. We didn't intend to be frightening, just wanted to feel free. Yet we did identify with the feeling behind punk, the rebellion against something you felt had let you down. As with all youth movements you have to live it to really understand. Peer group was a factor and having an identity different from ones parents. It was also a statement, an identity, a rejection of certain values, an attempt to connect with passion, an expression of rage and outrage, as well as a refreshing change from studying.

After three months of fun we were ready to move on. I went to London, to stay with Mum and Charles in Hampstead until I found a job, Luci and Jim went back to his home in Whitstable where Luci did a secretarial course.

My job was at Marshall Cavendish on Wardour Street. At night I practised meditation in mum's toilet to cope with the demands of London life and living at home again. It was difficult to adapt to living with parents again. Later I moved to a flat in Kentish town, then another flat with a friend in East Finchley. Marshall Cavendish was a publishing company that produced part works: the magazine, 'Stitch by Stitch,' my role: editor's assistant. The editor, a lady, liked whole bottles of gin. I was too busy trying to bluff my way through the typing I'd lied I could do (secretly learning from the 'teach yourself' book under my desk) to worry about her tipsiness. Somehow we all got away with it! I left five months later to go travelling, amazed that the magazine had made all its deadlines on time. At my goodbye party I was given a cowboy teapot with hat and spotted scarf round its neck, many compliments and assurances I'd be missed.

I left my job with relief. It seemed wise to have the prospect of rising up the career ladder, but it wasn't exciting enough for me. My passions were not engaged by typing, and petty, stressful office politics. Instead I caught the famous 'Magic Bus' (a company providing cheap overland travel to students etc. throughout the 60's and 70's) to Perpignan, the south of France and also to Athens. I was enchanted by the beautiful city with such incredible light.

After eventful roaming I settled in the easy-going liberal city of Rotterdam, where, after renting a while, I ended up living in a squat rent-free. By now I'd met my boyfriend, a musician friend of Jim's. We began to live together, continuing this period of unstructured creativity and living on the edge. Luci and I bought a knitting machine and formed 'God Creations' a colorful clothing line making unusual knitwear. We'd also hand knit intricate jumpers or leggings on commission. I once made a couple of 'poetry' jumpers.

One client's poem was so long, I had to use the tiniest needles: the finished work was a work of art. I can see now, looking back, that we could have made a success of this, it was doing quite well, but we were casual about it. We then formed 'God Creations' and managed to get a buyer for our earring range with a chain store. Unfortunately we'd used weak glue and were embarrassed by our earrings sliding off their backs. Too full of other ideas, with too much success selling on the street and to our friends, we didn't persist in this effort. That was for capitalist entrepreneurs, not free spirits! Our talent was for living in the moment. We shunned success, boycotting the uncaring 'fat-cat' mentality responsible for producing greedy corporations that polluted the planet. We didn't want to strive for some elusive future, we wanted happiness now. To Mum and Charles this seemed irresponsible, immature and even deluded. Dad and J. saw us from a more artistic perspective. Dad was working at Canterbury Art College with young people just like us, which helped.

We spent that period of time playing, dressed in anything and everything. Fairy dresses with lace up boots, colorful dresses over trousers, patched jeans, jumpers covered in toys or knitted foetuses. We dyed our hair blue, purple, green, pink, half red and yellow. Jim wore a kilt, florescent knitted jumpers, patched jeans, things tied round his legs, the odd plastic fried egg from his belt, badges everywhere, my boyfriend had headscarves, pyjama trousers, pyjama tops. We'd chop up something during a conversation and wear it. Or find something in a second hand shop, flowery acrylic housecoats, things that sparkled, glinted, things eclectic and kitsch. We were walking art, a circus, theatre, a spectacle. My boyfriend played the accordion, Jim the violin, both individually and together, singing and attracting huge crowds. Our lives became a kind of street theatre; we had fun, having significance because of our clothes and the music. We laughed a lot! Humor, spontaneous experience was a large part of each day. We decorated everything we owned and also ourselves. Once, when my hair seemed dull, I grabbed a paint pot and dabbed dollops into my hair. It took months for the blobs to fall out.

We acted like children, on impulse. Perhaps tribal people know something of this urge to paint, decorate and parade the self. I don't know. Life was serious enough, why not make it fun? Perhaps we were just showing off. Whatever it was, we were enjoying ourselves! We were privileged to have the safety and freedom to live like this in a culture that was stable and relatively permissive. There wasn't much money but survival was never an issue. Ours was a spirit of optimism seen in some of the spoof 60's films, like 'Austin Powers.' All that was colorful kitsch and carefree; this was the path we took for a while.

Deportation and Childbirth

By 1981 Luci and Jim were expecting their first child: things got more serious with the arrival of Kizzy in 1982. Kizzy was a home birth, quite normal in Holland and born so fast she beat the midwife to it. Jim had to 'busk' the delivery, using a book and common sense. Apart from mistaking the black of her hair for something sinister, as the head crowned there were no complications. A little red 'Winston Churchill,' this baby was soon to become beautiful. I stayed in their flat to help out, knitting Kizzy a tiny baby jumper as a welcome-to-the world gift with "Do not expect a bright pink freshly shampooed baby!" on the front.

Tragically, Jim's mother had died of breast cancer a few months earlier: Luci had no involved mother figure to help. She had me and we did our best, but having a child is something no one is fully prepared for. We had to make it all up as we went along. Luci became stressed trying to respond to her baby's needs; maternal impulses weren't flowing easily. Gaps in her relationship with Jim began to reveal themselves, but none of us could articulate these personal issues with enough precision to get insight into the changes. We just tried to continue what had worked before. Only, it no longer worked.

Not long after Kizzy was born, we decided to form a busking trio, 'The Baby Cavemen.' We practised songs, worked out clothes for the act. Before we could try out our set on the streets, I woke to intense hammering on my bedroom door. My room was on the top floor of the squat 'Heemraadsingel', an empty house now filled with creative types. Walls and doors were covered with graffiti, there were improvised electrics, wires trailing up the stairs. We'd applied to the council for permission to pay rent on the house and this was their first response. Someone was shouting, urgently, "Wake up, wake up Gabi, there's an M.E. van parked outside (special riot police unit, equipped with tear gas and truncheons) the police are here....." It didn't take me long to realize I wasn't dreaming.

I opened the door. Whoever had warned me had gone: eight policemen and a policewoman entered my room. I stood there, foolish in my nightdress, trying to grasp the situation. A couple of them kicked a few bits of furniture around, while the policewoman photographed the result. The pictures were published in the papers as evidence of our 'living like pigs.' Though I was informed I had fifteen minutes to pack, I barely had time to dress, grab a small bag and a book, before time was up.

I left the building handcuffed, accompanied by a policeman who showed me to a police car. Riot police sat by, on the alert, in their van. There was a large crowd outside, reporters taking pictures. I was to be front-page news.

I realized I was shouting which I do when scared. If no one's listening, turn up the volume! Confused, stressed, in hastily grabbed fairy dress with rumpled purple hair, handcuffed and photographed, I was pushed into the car and driven somewhere I didn't recognize. Having just been asleep and without breakfast, it seemed like a dream. The journey through the streets of Rotterdam seemed endless, a stony faced driver ignored most of my questions. I asked if I could have a cup of tea when we got somewhere "You aren't going to a hotel," came the curt reply.

We arrived at a police building, I didn't know where, with no passport or valid papers. I kept explaining I had a valid passport; it was at Luci's house. All I needed was to phone, I could get her to deliver it. But the police were unhelpful. They'd already decided to make an example of the 'Engelse punk.' I was thrown into a cell with a thin stringy-haired heroin addict and some incoherent women. The heroine addict, who spoke good English wasn't encouraging. She understood the police better than I did. They had their own idea of what they wanted for me, which didn't include letting me get hold of my passport. I was denied that phone call no matter how much I shouted and banged on the cell door. What else was there to do? They'd taken most of my possessions on entry; pens, eye pencils, nail scissors etc. in case I tried to gouge my eyes out, break down the door with them, kill others or myself. They let me keep the book I'd grabbed as I left the squat, ironically Jiddu Krishnamurti's "The first and Last Freedom." Perhaps I could bash the door down with it! I had plenty of time to contemplate the concept of freedom, as I waited for something to happen.

I felt sick and dizzy, not having eaten that day. A plastic tray of grey meat and over-boiled red cabbage arrived, but suddenly I had no appetite. We were brought nightgowns and shown a room of identical grey beds with thin beige blankets folded on them. I tried to adjust to the horror of spending the night. Then a policeman came looking for me: he had a key! It was a miracle to walk through the door instead of screaming through it. I was led through a room full of police, one was the chief. He was a broad man in a lilac shirt and I made the mistake of looking at him. He ran at me, bashed me with his big body hissing "Get out of our country you dirty punk!" I was amazed. I wasn't dirty, except for not washing that morning! The clothes I wore were just fun to me. To this man they were a symbol of something dangerous, offensive. He hated what he thought I stood for. But he didn't even know me. I felt indignant, defiant and angry. Injustice makes me courageous. I lose all uncertainty in uncomfortable situations. Only when I am safe do I allow other more vulnerable emotions to emerge. I was taken to an empty courtyard and told to wait. It was a bit ominous to see the darkening sky. I just stood there, alone. Ten minutes later a gaunt Moroccan guy with several gold teeth joined me. He showed me some forged money hidden in his sock.

Half an hour later we were in a police car, driven to the nearest port. We were being deported. I began to argue, the more world weary Moroccan telling me it was futile. They hadn't let me get my passport! My sense of injustice was roused. I couldn't stop speaking, trying to justify myself. But the Moroccan was right: it made no difference. Before long I was on a boat heading for Dover. The Moroccan had his wad of forged money so he bought me a meal and a cabin. I slept after vomiting up the meal; stress had got to me. I never got to thank him, arriving in Dover penniless and hungry. British Rail allowed me a ticket, to be paid for later. It's not everyday you're deported. I met up with Dad mid-morning at the local school where he was doing some supply teaching; he drove me home. (Dad never walked anywhere no matter how near it was.) It was a beautiful day, England looking green and golden, bathed in sunshine. I spent the whole day sharing my story with people, so over stimulated and pumped with adrenaline that I stayed up all night writing down the details: it was impossible to sleep.

Next day Dad made a film of me talking about the experience. I'd rather have had some sympathy and a hug, but he wasn't that kind of a Dad. That was behavior for 'ordinary normal' people, taboo concepts in his world. The 'dramatic and interesting' event was a shocking trauma to me. I was naïve and sheltered about the way the world could work. One of the conditions of deportation was that I didn't return to Holland for six months. I returned within three weeks. Shortly after arrival I spotted a couple of the policemen involved, who waved cheerfully at me and carried on with their day. No further problems. Nothing much changed; only I chose to rent my next place to live!

Luci and Jim let me stay with them a while. They went off on a busking trip to Italy with baby Kizzy, I stayed behind taking care of friend's flats, watering plants etc, catching a tram around the city to get it all done. My boyfriend joined me. We lived at Jim and Luci's until they returned and then found our next place. Visitors arrived. Several crazy musicians who knew Jim and Luci called the 'We Don't Want The Peanuts We Want The Plantation Dance Band,' stayed with us a while, saying we were just like Jim and Luci. That's how much of a group we'd become.

First House and First-Born

My boyfriend and I moved to a damp flat and conceived Polly. The night of her conception I had a strange experience, hard to describe. I seemed to leave my body and was 'told' I was pregnant. My boyfriend had exactly the same experience. It was strange. Was it a double dream? We both felt our personalities 'lift' away and 'somebody' spoke to us. We called it the 'critter' experience for some reason.

I wanted to return to England to have the baby. My boyfriend's parents were kind but worried. They decided to help. His mum sorted out a room in their house for us to stay long as we liked. I spent hours sleeping, suddenly unsure I wanted to be with this guy. I was out of my depth, unable to imagine us living together with a child. My desire was to give birth at home, a normal thing in Holland but problematic in Britain. Unlike Holland, there's no functioning 'flying squad,' mobile units complete with birthing equipment, everything set up for hospital births. There was also the small problem of not having a home. My man's mother, ever practical, helped us sort that out. She and her husband would act as guarantors, enabling us to get a mortgage. It was a big risk to them and they had some sleepless nights. My child's future grandmother was determined we'd have a home for her unborn grandchild. My stepfather provided the deposit. We were thrilled!

This formidable and impressive future grandma came with us to look at houses, many of them awful. Then we found OUR house; a grade two listed building in Faversham, Kent. It was spacious, with four floors and a long, generous garden. Future grandma cooked us a casserole for our first night alone together and treated us to a week's worth of groceries! We were home-owners! My boyfriend was upset with his Mum though, feeling critical of her 'interference', but I knew we couldn't have done it without her and astonished that he could mind. I was so happy with her attentions, tireless energy, generosity and willingness to get involved with us. I developed a huge affection for both these parents. I had no maternity clothes at that time, just pinned a tablecloth a certain way and wore that with pyjama trousers. We had little money but were inventive and relaxed about it. It didn't seem the most important thing.

'At home' things were difficult. Dad and J. were beginning to show signs of trouble in their relationship. He became increasingly dogmatic, overpowering and arrogant, picking on us all. I stayed sometimes and got to experience a few of his dysfunctional moments, no one was immune from his attacks. Recently, J. said it was a shame he thought being frightening was a way to communicate. I felt more and more resistant to and questioning of his authority, all I really wanted was his love and approval. To this day I've never got it, but I'm not alone in that. He became more and more bizarre and abusive, causing unbearable scenes and bullying all his children increasingly as time went on. We struggled individually and together to make sense of him. His second marriage was going into crisis.

Once, pregnant and having dinner, I couldn't finish my meal. He got aggressive about this, J stuck up for me. I found it hard to judge portion sizes as the baby's head was squashing my stomach. Dad began to attack J. Something welled up in me, I'd had enough. I stood up and shouted at him, telling him he was a 'bully' and a 'tyrant' that he 'dominated everyone.' I told him to stop putting J. down, she didn't deserve it. I think I told him to 'fuck off.' He said I was a 'witch' and hoped I'd have a miscarriage. Then he left for Dover, 'forever.' The younger kids cried and turned on me, but I was unrepentant. Years later J. told me that was the night she'd decided to leave him. To the kids' relief he came back later, joking that he'd left fifty pence on his desk and didn't want anyone to have it. No more was said.

In August 1983, Baby Polly was born in Canterbury. Pierre let us use his house while he took his family to France on holiday. This was a compromise with the medical establishment as it was against their policy to allow a first birth outside the hospital environment. This was hard to accept after the laid back atmosphere of the Dutch. No one was willing to budge, so it was agreed: we had to be near Canterbury hospital. Pierre's house was five minutes away.

The birth went well. My waters broke first thing in the morning, giving off the sweet smell of amniotic fluid, like rosewater. It was a lovely summer's day, the sun shone brightly so I spent some of my labor in the garden. I had a great birth team consisting of Luci, Jim, my boyfriend, little Kizzy, plus the midwife. Everyone was efficient and cheerful, lunch (which I couldn't eat) was provided by Luci. Everything just happened. All I had to do was concentrate on breathing, going with the mighty energy gathering in my body. It would be easy to be scared, but I had a key: surrender. I told myself, don't fight, or tense against the natural process happening in your body, relax! I gave no energy to what might go wrong. The only hitch was the arrival of a chatty back-up midwife, who ignored me and got involved in conversation. Didn't she realize this was my day? My contractions stopped and we sent her off to wait in another room. She was not the first midwife we sent out over the years. Luci and I developed our own standard about our births. We were fussy and fierce, tolerating no fear or distraction that caused tension in the birth environment. I was out of bed the whole time, moving around until the last few minutes. Lying down, especially on your back, goes against gravity, it invites complications, making it harder for the baby to come down. Polly was born that night with a full head of black hair and an alert expression. Later Jim's auntie would call her 'the new Jesus', she seemed so aware and bright with her dark Chinese-looking eyes.

My man got himself into a musical circuit in Faversham, connecting with people and working at the nearby Arden theatre. He had unusual ways of dealing with life, getting surprisingly hung up and tense, making mountains out of molehills. He was extremely creative and perfectionist as well as an excellent musician and singer, but he wasn't handy with a screwdriver. Neither of us were. Nor were we domesticated, preferring late night discussions about the meaning of life to homemaking. We made an odd team. It became harder and harder to relate to each others' idiosyncrasies. Years later there was a suggestion he might have Asperger's Syndrome, a condition related to autism. This knowledge might have helped us make sense of some of our difficulties.

TENSIONS Things were complicated for me after we moved into our new home. Dad and J. came every Sunday for a while, bringing bottles of wine.

They admired Polly and were enthusiastic about the house, but I hated their visits. Dad terrified me with his irrationality. Looking back, it's touching that they came. I had no idea then how much upset I was carrying in myself after my rootless childhood. It was not the best foundation from which to build a home. My man and I didn't have the faintest idea how to be domesticated and settled. It seemed impossible just to sit in a house with one person and a demanding baby. We started to argue. During one of our exchanges he phoned his mother. I tried to stop him phone-ing, feeling his relationship with her was too dependent; after all I didn't need my mother! He pushed me away. In the scuffle I fell and tore a ligament. The result? Ten days of bed rest with time to think. A kind neighbor lent me a book about Atlantis, a primal therapy community on the island of Innisfree in Ireland.

I'd never heard of a place like it. As soon as I'd read the book I wanted to visit. It sounded exciting and radical, a whole new way of thinking about things. In many ways I'm typical of my generation, the so-called Baby Boomers. This era, from the mid 40's to the beginning of the sixties produced a generation whose thought processes were significantly different to the war generation before them. It is fascinating how kids are brought up differently from one generation to the next. As a loose generalization, the Baby Boomers had a distrust of systems, an interest in individualism, and in the 'real self' (vague as that may sound). There was a growing exploration of psychology, imagination, intuition, freedom, inner, rather than outer authority. Our generation had experienced more material stability than our parents and were now in reaction against their preoccupation with security. At this time emerged 'New Age' thinking, an explosion of ideas and alternative values drawn from a range of influences, spiritual, religious and scientific. The musical 'Hair,' on stage in 1967, was an example of the seeds of its emergence into mainstream culture. Its opening song 'This is the dawning of the Age of Aquarius' expressed the current astrological understanding that a new era was beginning. The media now ridicule the more 'woolly' sides of this individualistic movement, with its crystal reading and other wacky pursuits. Yet to many at the time, these numerous ways of exploring consciousness answered some of the deeper questions about life. I found it fascinating. As a twenty-something year old I threw myself head first into everything going, finding therapies and workshops that interested me. Some of it I rejected, much of it changed me forever.

With the next cycle of babies to be born it would all swing again. Values would change beyond recognition. Nowadays our children are looking for security, nice homes, being fed up with the spontaneity and free living that their 60's and 70's influenced parents had inflicted on them. They are still too young to evaluate the good bits and in many ways as reactionary as we were, but the other way! So it goes on. It cannot be denied that the time and environment in which you grow up influences who and what you become.

Typical of the 'New Age' movement was to value 'caring' and 'relationship' more than material security. To us, back then in the 'Age of Aquarius,' achievement was less important than people's 'being.' We watched the Beatles change with us, becoming psychedelic and cosmic. There seemed to be a sensitive balance to attain between the inner and outer if people were not to be neurotic and therefore destructive. In those days people were afraid of a nuclear war that would wipe out the human race. CND (Campaign for Nuclear Disarmament) was on the upsurge. The Vietnam War and subsequent bloodbaths had already horrified a generation. We wanted the bomb banned and everything put right! A culture that is fundamentally neurotic does not bode well for mankind, so we set out to heal ourselves and do whatever we could to change society for the better!

Sitting at home was not for me, I felt hungry for experience. There was so much going on out there, many things I'd never heard of. Fed up with bickering with my man, I decided I'd had enough domestication. Just six weeks after Polly was born, we were off! We left our house with a pram, a tent, a couple of rucksacks and sleeping bags. Neither of us could drive, so we took the train and headed for Hampshire, sometimes carrying Polly and putting all our stuff in the pram. The plan was to camp in beautiful grounds, where the Indian teacher

Jiddu Krishnamurti was giving talks in a marquee. A speaker and writer on spiritual and philosophical subjects, he spoke on human relationships, positive change in society, meditation, peace, awareness and had himself been proclaimed an incarnation of Maitreya Buddha. It was believed he was the 'vehicle' for a new world teacher and an organization, 'Order of the Star,' was set up to support his path. After being groomed for this destiny, aged 34, he shocked his followers by dissolving the organization and rejecting his role as a spiritual leader, asserting that truth was a 'pathless land.'

I loved his writings; he became one of my influences at that time.

Camping was tricky with a baby. Our little girl had to lie on my stomach all night to fit us in our tiny tent! In spite of the discomfort, we were happier living outdoors, with lots of people to talk to and good vegetarian food cooked by someone else....

During one of his talks Krishnamurti suddenly paused, noticing Polly, who was the only baby in the audience. She was the example of something he was talking about, so she was passed around the room, her tiny head of black hair moving away from us! She was happy, smiling obligingly at the cooing strangers, giving a perfect baby performance, centre stage, a typical Leo at six weeks old! We did get her back, eventually.

Luci and Jim were abroad, having their own adventures; we kept in touch. They decided to join us and experience something of Krishnamurti. Luci was not impressed by this serious man droning on about reality, truth and consciousness, though Jim was more interested. Later we all returned to Holland, where Jim and Luci had found a flat. My boyfriend wanted to busk around Germany, but I couldn't face it. My adventurousness had turned to tiredness; it was hard work being a new mum! I wanted to stay with my sister. It was not that easy: she had her own burdens, being a new mum too. We were overwhelmed by our own responsibilities. Little Kizzy, interested in the 'sparkle' in Polly's eyes, wanted to poke her fingers in them all the time. Luci was stressed with so many people in her house. After my man had taken some time out to busk for three weeks we reluctantly returned to England.

• • •

Dad had bought a studio in Canterbury where he did some of his work. Kizzy named it 'The Stripey House' because of its striking beams. While working there, he noticed his wife's car parked across the road a lot and wondered why. He chose to investigate, discovering J. was having an affair with a woman he referred to ever after as 'the Reptile.' Fidelity in marriage was by then a condition for him, things had changed since his Ndola days! At the very least he wanted honesty if there was attraction to another. There was a confrontation. He made the *entire family* come with him to 'The Reptile's' home. There we met a thin, plain woman with short brown hair, who stood quietly, saying nothing, just observing the raging husband and six confused kids. No matter. Dad had more than enough words for both of them! He wanted to show her the family she'd ruined. He also wanted our indignation, for us to back him up in his distress. We did feel for him. We felt for everyone! But we were unwilling to take sides, wanting the adults to communicate and work things out themselves. Pierre, his upset, became less and less flexible. He shut his heart and threw J. out, unwilling to examine any of the deeper issues behind this triangle. It seems our stepmother had become lesbian, we were not allowed to ask about her. 'The Reptile' bowed out gracefully and all the kids were left with Dad. Our ex-step-mother felt undeserving and incapable of motherhood. Confused, hurt, guilty and relieved to be free, she was too traumatized, paralyzed to take action around her children. So she just disappeared from their lives for a while.

Dad fell apart behind a front of competence. He would sit at the kitchen table for hours, drinking wine, ranting to anyone willing to listen. Our hearts ached. His wife had an affair with another woman: it was a lot to deal with. Dad had no time for anyone's feelings but his own, hostile and vicious about J., encouraging his kids to turn against her. Then he began to accuse Jim of having flirted with his now ex-wife. He became convinced Jim had touched her inappropriately and banned him from visiting. He would listen to no one and began to worry his four kids there was truth in this story. It was only years later they realized stress had brought on this paranoia, which got worse.

This period, when Dad was alone with the kids, is full of terrible stories. In particular the youngest experienced things that she cannot talk about even now. For a while it was she and another sister living with Dad, after the others left home: together they experienced serious neglect, the youngest cutting her own arm in desperation to get some real attention. Dad was too afraid to take her to hospital in case social services intervened. He doesn't really communicate with any of us any more. He has married a librarian, C., a strange, sour, hostile woman who pulls him away from people he meets in the street; she turns all of us away when we try to visit. They hardly ever answer or return phone calls, unless I do my 'technique,' leaving so many messages they have to call, just to stop me clogging up their machine!

Dad also changed his name. He has cut himself off from virtually everyone in his past, refusing recently even to see one of his twin sisters, who had come all the way from Beirut. She was very hurt. There is so much more: I got Social Services involved, after discovering Pierre had had a serious fall, perhaps a stroke. They investigated to see if C. had some kind of sinister intent towards a vulnerable man, but data protection does not allow intrusion. The doctor advises Dad is being adequately taken care of by this C.

Atlantis....And Luci's Second Child

Before things had got to this point, my sister gave birth to Minna, in the 'Stripey house.' It was October 9th 1984. This time a homebirth was allowed; she was the second child and the house was near Canterbury hospital. Minna had the cord wrapped around her leg, causing mild distress, until the midwife had slipped it off. She used to fuss and agitate about her socks as a child and we'd wonder if there was a connection! My boyfriend, Polly and I arrived late, just after Minna had emerged safely. Second babies are easier to relate to, not such a shock as first time around! We read stories to and played with Polly and Kizzy, so Luci and Jim could bond with their newborn. Our girls soon became like sisters. The three of them see themselves that way, so much of their lives have been linked.

In 1985 Luci asked Evelyn and Charles to match the deposit for Gabi's house to buy themselves a home. They needed a travelling home to fit their lifestyle, so they bought a Leyland PD3/4 Southdown 'Queen Mary' Double Decker bus! Jim wanted to work as a musician and be a hands-on father. Luci and I expected the fathers of our children to be involved with their offspring. As 'committed' parents, we believed our children should have what we hadn't. We studied books on nutrition and childcare, sharing ideas and tips with each other, and created an extended family, spending lots of time together. In 1985 we all decided to take a trip to Ireland to explore Atlantis, the community I'd read about when I'd hurt my knee. My relationship with my boyfriend was getting more challenging: a therapy commune might do some good. So two couples with three kids boarded the bus! It had a kitchen sink, working Rayburn, toilet and beds. Jim and my man busked through England on violin and accordion, singing and performing together, but my boyfriend and I were getting on each other's nerves. An argument began, Luci took my side and that was it. He decided to run away, jumping off the bus. The kids were upset by this drama; Polly losing her voice for a few days from shock. He reappeared some days later and we continued our trek west to Atlantis. There we explored Psychometry, that is, holding an object and 'picking up' information from it, then speaking aloud or acting anything that came to mind. This evolved to 'psychic readings,' holding a piece of paper with a name written on it and expressing in the same way. Most of the time these spontaneous 'readings' were uncannily accurate, seemingly providing a portrait of that person's inner thoughts and feelings. After leaving Atlantis we developed a craze for readings, doing them over and over with family and friends. Our kids loved this 'game,' they never got tired of it!

Throughout my life I've proved to have a psychic streak. This connection seems quite open with Luci and also with Polly. We know when it's the other one on the phone; sense each other's thoughts, that kind of thing. In earlier years when Luci and I used to do Ouija sessions with Evelyn, I would feel some kind of 'force' that ended up scaring me. I was too young and immature to know what to do with it. We stayed at Atlantis for two wild weeks, experiencing a way of life unlike any we'd known before. We joined in all their activities and were challenged constantly by their habit of communicating everything inside them. They encouraged us to do the same. They liked us, inviting us to join the commune and journey with them on a wooden boat to South America where they intended to settle. We were tempted, but not quite ready for that level of commitment. This commune moved to Colombia where they've been ever since. On July 9th 2000 guerrillas murdered two of their 18 year-old boys, Tristan and Javier. We read the tragic news and could hardly believe it, moved by the courage and guts expressed by the remaining communards and wondered what we'd have been like if we'd joined them.

In 1986 Jim successfully auditioned for a job with an animal-free circus, 'Circus Burlesque,' in Frome, Somerset. Of course we visited them, spending fun summer days with our kids playing inside and outside the brightly colored circus tent. At show times Jim warmed up the audiences by playing his violin, singing and playing the guitar. During the show he did the same again adding drums and playing his violin while riding a unicycle to packed audiences! Luci sold healthy snacks during the intervals.

FIRE!

At this time none of us wanted to continue with our lives in Kent. My boyfriend and I sold our house to do primal therapy, as championed by the Atlanteans, with a therapist in Brighton. Luci and Jim decided to go to Spain in their bus, to find a farm in the sun.

We got a good deal for our house and rented a flat on the fourth floor of a terraced house on Brighton seafront. Oddly it was the same date, mid March, as my deportation, that again I was to become front-page news in the local paper: First thing in the morning my boyfriend shook me awake saying the house was on fire. I thought he was joking until I looked out of the window: enormous orange flames were visible, licking outwards from the flats below us. A huge crowd had gathered outside to watch the drama. I had on a frayed white nightdress and nothing else, there was no time to dress. What I looked like vaguely crossed my mind but was erased by the consuming thought of getting us all out. We had to leave! The flat had a fire door which we opened cautiously to try going down the stairs. Billowing black smoke drove us back. Our fire escape was red hot so we couldn't get out that way. Promptly two fire engines arrived and we had a ladder to safety against our window! Polly was the first out, a tiny tot in a yellow 'teddy bear' sleep suit. She was totally obedient, sensing the urgency of the situation, going without fuss to the fireman. My boyfriend and I waited our turn to go down the ladder; worried the floor might give way under us. What a relief to go next!

I was embarrassed and relieved, going down the ladder in my nightdress with my protective fireman/hero behind me! I've loved firemen ever since. My boyfriend was the last to be rescued, each of us had to wait for a fireman to be with us in case we were disorientated and slipped or fell. Curiously, the night before I'd been doing an exercise from a book on free association. The idea was to write down all your thoughts for fifteen minutes. What came out sounded pretty crazy, I'd read the garbled result to my boyfriend: something about 'Nigel smoking' and a fire. Neither of us knew any Nigel, these fragments had seemed meaningless. We went to bed without giving it another thought.

When we reached the ground, during the fire, an ambulance was waiting. In it sat a dazed man with a soot-stained face. Introducing himself as Nigel... he explained with deep shame that he'd borrowed the downstairs flat for a couple of days on condition that he didn't smoke. He'd ignored the condition, had a cigarette in bed, fallen asleep and set fire to a pile of clothes left on the floor! We saw the second floor flat afterwards, black and eerie with melted phones like some nihilistic modern art piece.

Years later, when my fluffy long-haired cat Pickle disappeared, I felt her dying. In bed at the time, the feeling of her body convulsing in muddy water and leaves came to me. I felt a 'gold' light all around her and a very physical feeling that everything was ok. I was wide awake and said to Jim: "I know Pickle has died." The 'knowing' was strong. Some days later a friend found Pickle dead in a ditch, covered in mud and leaves.

Another time I woke having dreamt of a huge tree with an anguished face falling over and dying. I was telling the family about it and heard a massive crashing sound. We ran outside to investigate and found a large Ash tree, fallen over, for no apparent reason. There had been winds for some days, it might have had a disease, we never really knew why, nor did our neighbors.

• • •

After eight months apart, Luci, Jim, kids, my boyfriend, and I, all decided to reunite. We'd kept in touch but our various journeys had absorbed us. My boyfriend and I had been through many changes. Our therapist was surprised we were still together; he didn't expect our relationship to last. I'd had my doubts almost the minute I'd got pregnant, yet clung to hope that things might improve. Strange how life and fears can distract you from doing what might have been better for you. A lot of our life was 'going with the flow' making spontaneous choices without much thought of consequences.

Luci and Jim had spent much of their time in Spain, in Orgiva. Luci, ill with pneumonia, was treated by a French healer en route. They travelled with their children, enjoying the sun, being together and getting to know the locals. When they'd had enough they came to Brighton, parking their bus where they could, near the Steiner School in Hollingbury. It seemed an attractive place under the trees, but turned out to be surprisingly rough. Vandals had fun breaking in by smashing a bus window, then trashing it upstairs and downstairs. Becoming public property was one of the hazards of a high profile mobile home. In another parking place a business man got on, opened his newspaper and waited for 'service.' He ordered an egg butty, going through huge embarrassment when it dawned on him this wasn't a mobile café, he'd just gate-crashed someone's living room. We did offer to make him one anyway, but he couldn't leave fast enough!

Though we were still together, my man decided to move into a room of his own and despite all the hazards, I moved onto the bus. Our relationship was hanging by a thread. Polly spent time with each of us and we all still spent time together, but emotionally her parents were moving further and further apart.

The New Age

On August we all left in the bus (my boyfriend included) for Glastonbury, the 'heart chakra' of England, to be part of a New Age Spiritual event, 'The Harmonic convergence.' Groups were gathering worldwide at sacred sites and places of 'mystical' energy to experience a major 'energy shift' heralding a 'New Era of universal peace.' Actress Shirley Maclaine called the event a 'window of light' for the world. Whatever you thought of it, Glastonbury was a pleasant place to be. We sat at the top of Glastonbury Tor at the critical astrological moment, sunrise, with all our little children, waiting sleepily for golden light to emerge on the horizon. Warmed by the rising sun, we did feel moved and connected to everyone. Critics of the event called it 'the Moronic Convergence,' but we enjoyed being part of this peaceful, non-violent worldwide event.

Before we left Brighton, we decided to experiment with 'group visualization'. I'd always loved books and owned some on the theme of 'creating your own reality.' The 'New Age' hadn't yet become discredited as it has been now by the media – it was still fashionable to experiment and explore in many circles. We sat down together each night to affirm (say out loud) that we now had a beautiful house in the countryside. We'd agreed various details and stuck to this routine each evening. After we'd enjoyed the campsite in Glastonbury for a day or two, a couple of older campers decided they objected to our bus: we were asked to leave. Fed up, we drove down to the municipal car park, to park among rubbish bins swarming with summer wasps. There was a slight drizzle. A vivid rainbow appeared, arching from one full bin, across to another, cheering us up. At that moment another vehicle, a small van, drove in. Luci said, "This is it, our future..." We laughed about how right she'd been afterwards. Jim, ever friendly, rushed off to greet the newcomers. They turned out to be a couple who were looking for people to rent their house in Wales. It seemed our group visualization, conscious creation, had worked!

This couple, the G's offered us a change of location that has lasted over twenty years. We still live only miles from 'Panteg,' their home at the time. We arrived unaware how small and winding the roads would get, challenging in a double Decker bus! Trying to get into the G's driveway was a major operation: the first encounter with some of our neighbors was while blocking their route. After digging away some of the bank to widen the road, we got the bus into 'Panteg' driveway, where we stopped to wait for a month, as the couple prepared their live-in vehicle for a road trip to France.

Eventually the G's went and we were left to do our own thing. We grew vegetables, chopped wood, made candles, brought up our kids, had our 'feelings' and enjoyed socializing. There was a flow of people, experiences, trips and parenting that absorbed our time. Influences such as Atlantis and primal therapy had worked their way into our days, we were free and open about feelings – our own and other people's. There was an atmosphere of exploration and mutual sharing, young people having fun.

Of course, with my boyfriend and Jim around, there was also music. We did quite a lot with friends we'd met, going up to the nearby lake together, Luci and I taking the kids for trips out with them. One in particular, Paul, became someone we spent a lot of time with. No one noticed Luci was getting closer to him than the rest of us, not even his current girlfriend. One night Paul and Luci slept together. Jim's world was rocked to the core. Shortly afterwards Luci moved into the bus in the garden. Jim, having to watch Paul visit her, was devastated, the children were confused.

Shortly before a friend had taught us 'the Dynamic Meditation' as practised by Bhagwan Shree Rajneesh. It was a ritual that took an hour, involving breathing, catharsis (letting go and doing whatever you felt) chanting and meditating. We invited people to join us at 5.00am, before the kids woke up to do this everyday. When Luci left it was a lifeline, allowing Jim to cry, rage and explore all his intense emotions safely, within a structure. It was therapeutic for Jim to 'let it all out' and express his pain around others. We continued to do the dynamic meditation daily until October 1988. In this time both the couples that had moved into Panteg, had separated or were beginning this process.

CHANGES For the first time in our lives Luci and I began to experience changes in our relationship. The emotional 'closeness' we'd taken for granted all our lives began to crumble. Luci stayed living outside the house, I lived with Jim and the kids inside. She and Paul had a different way of looking at things and it was not sympathetic to the 'house people.' Suddenly we found ourselves divided, into 'us' and 'them,' a mini war. One day Jim got so fed up he called the police. Of course this just increased bad feeling between us. We didn't really know where anything was going, we could only use our therapy techniques to deal with the emotions stirred up. Wales is said to have that effect on people, the elemental landscape and ancient hills stirring up primal energies in the psyche! We definitely felt raw and stripped of defences, as if our old skins were falling away.

• • •

When the year was up I decided I'd had enough and travelled back to Brighton with Polly. My man had gone ahead for some civilization and culture! After the countryside Brighton seemed unsafe, dirty and noisy, with too many people too close together. I stayed a while but yearned for space and nature. I returned to Wales with Polly, to see how things were developing....

Jim had rented a room in a house up the road. A single man called S. lived there with his dog. For a while Luci was in the bus on her own. Then, moving into the same house as Jim she immediately became involved with S., a man not her type at all. Jim was not thrilled. It's interesting to look back and see how, no matter what dramas there were...we all kept coming back to each other. You might have thought we'd run a million miles away! Perhaps we would have, if there'd been no children!

Luci stayed with S. for five years and had a son, Llyr. At that time I began to feel I'd lost touch with her emotionally. She seemed distant, harder, less open. Sometimes the tensions between us became blazing arguments. Her relationship with S. confused me: she often said she didn't like him and didn't know why she was with him. Like a moth to a flame, I added to the crazy emotional hotpot by also moving into S.'s house. Eventually there were eleven people, three couples, Jim and four kids. This was the way things were then, relationships were formed and dissolved, in the spirit of the time. There was a large 'alternative' population drawn to our town, having in common this tendency to challenge social rules.

In the middle of this flux something significant fluttered between Jim and me. Living together in Panteg we'd developed a much deeper friendship. One cold night I'd 'borrowed' Jim's bedroom to sleep in, where I usually slept was icy-cold, Jim was out doing a gig, but it was cancelled. We ended up sharing a bed. To our surprise, an overwhelmingly sweet feeling opened up for both of us, like breathing honey through every part of our bodies, just from being near each other. It was not a sexual experience at the time. I was still (just about) with my boyfriend, so I told him. It was the way we were, communicating about everything. He wasn't pleased. Human nature being what it is, it blossomed into more. I had two 'boyfriends' for a while, a good experience for me!

Eventually my man had had enough. He told me to choose between them. It was obvious, our relationship on the rocks anyway, without hesitation I chose Jim, which plunged my man into jealousy. He roared, banged his head on the wall, verbally attacked and insulted Jim. We weren't surprised. After primal therapy, Atlantis and the dynamic meditation, we were used to intense behavior, saw 'letting it out' as healthy. Sometimes things went too far. We believed in honesty and being 'real' but with children sensitivity was required. In the climate of opening everything up we all went way out of balance. It was a reactionary time. The effect of all this on our children took years to emerge...

<u>FLUX AND ANOTHER BIRTH</u> After months of us all living together, Jim reclaimed his autonomy by moving into the woods in the bus. I would walk several miles to visit him, day or night. It was a pleasure walking through the dark woods, even at night.

Little did I know that that beneath the freedom from fear I felt at this time was a 'shadow side,' fears and vulnerabilities, packed away inside me, which would one day catch up. For now, we carried on with our 'crazy' ways, Polly, Kizzy and Minna were bundled together in an imposed sisterhood. Though they adored each other and had many benefits from their interactions, it was difficult for each of them. Polly had to adapt from centre of attention as an only child, to being one of a group. Kizzy and Minna had to adapt to her being around a lot more, to a new half brother, Llyr, *and* a new man in their mother's life. Until Jim moved out they had Daddy and step Daddy in the same house, Mummy and sister, who was now with Daddy... Polly had Daddy and Mummy, but Mummy had switched to Jim. Yet, Jim was Kizzy and Minna's Daddy. This conflict-producing mish-mash, broke down normal boundaries.

The positive side was plenty of contact, with none of the loneliness of nuclear family units. Everything was mutable and in flux, the adults so busy experimenting, it didn't occur to us the kids might feel differently about the ultimate value of all this. We didn't even think about the positive aspects of security and stability. We assumed as long as we were there, our kids would be fine. We gave them what we would have wanted, taking it for granted that it was right for them. There *are* things I would do very differently now, with the benefit of hindsight.

I was pregnant again. Pablo was born in April 1990, also at home. We wanted a water birth, but hiring a tub was expensive. So we bought a large children's swimming pool to put in an annex adjacent to my bedroom. The birth went well, apart from having to exclude the midwife, a kind, muddled, short-sighted ex sheep farmer who was getting too old for midwifery, forever fumbling, mumbling and dropping things. When we found another medical syringe under the Welsh dresser we knew we needed to take charge. We'd all done background reading on the subject of birth so were informed, having a passion for medical encyclopedias and books on health. We took matters into our own hands, asking the midwife to leave the room during the birth unless there was an emergency. Luckily there wasn't. Luci took charge and nature took its course. Polly, Kizzy and Minna joined Jim and me in the birthing pool. We had floating candles, the girls got into a party mood, giggling and eating green grapes. The warm water and happy atmosphere did wonders for my contractions. The atmosphere was relaxed, informal yet focused and finally Pablo's head and chest emerge; I'd been in labor about eight hours. Our baby hung suspended in the water, half in and half out of his mother. In the candlelight, the blue of the pool on his yellow hair made it look green as it waved in the water. We were all quiet, watching him. One more push and he was out.

We moved back into the bus in the woods with a contented and relaxed baby boy who seemed to love the trees with their fascinating rustling leaves. We had a peaceful and nurturing time, close to nature and all together. Five months later we were on the road again.

My ex boyfriend had a new partner who later bore him twins and a second son. Wherever Polly went there was a newly established family, where she felt like an outsider, working to belong, an echo of GabiLu's background. I worked hard to understand and to help her feel more central, valued and important.

Luci and S., also holidaying in Spain, met up with us to deliver Kizzy and Minna for 'our turn'. We parked the bus on the edge of a scrubby hillside. The kids played out on the hot dry earth while goats trekked up and down, bells jingling round their necks. The three girls were so creative, they never ran out of ideas for new games, amusing themselves dressing Pablo as a girl and taking photos of their efforts. One detail had been overlooked, we discovered later: there was no film in the camera!

• • •

Many foreign hippies had settled in the area. A young couple, one German and an Israeli, had a communal bath with their kids in a nearby hippy house. We were thinking of doing the same thing.

They went first. No one realized something was wrong with the gas-fired water heater. There was a dangerous build up of gas, the family began to slide into unconsciousness. Luckily one of the adults summoned enough strength to crawl to the door, let air in and save everyone's lives. The whole event took place just meters from the bus and had eerie overtones - the German/Jewish connection and the gas. It added to a dark feeling around Orgiva. I couldn't wait to leave the place.

We headed for the coastal village of Nerja for a change of mood and scenery, swimming in the sea and playing some tunes. It was the end of the season, the sun was weaker, more watery, and less hot. Everything felt tired, especially me, with Pablo only six months old and still breastfeeding. I needed to recover from my whole life: I could have lain on the beach resting forever! Having been on the move so long I didn't recognize the need to stop. Driving back to Britain slowly, the trip took a couple of months. On arrival in Wales we delivered the girls on Christmas Eve, my birthday.

In summer 1991 we set off on a tour around England with young Pablo and a new child in my belly. Yes, I was pregnant again!

<u>WALES AND SPAIN</u>   In Wales we lived a while parked next to tranquil Llanfair Lake, waking up to swim in undisturbed waters in the morning, often retreating to our bus when the crowds turned up. For the birth we rented a holiday cottage 'Felin Gogoyan'. After six months Pablo had become attached to the house, but it was time to leave. He stood firm and rigid in the doorway, making his one and a half year old protest, blocking the landlady from entering and us from exiting. She was amused

and patient, letting him be passionate about his tiny cause.

Saba was born in November 1991, again a home and water birth, only we had no time to get into the tub. Pablo had woken up in the night, sitting up and shouting 'Girl!' Soon afterwards Saba shot out like a rocket.... we managed to start filling the tub but she couldn't wait. There was no midwife, only Jim, my friend Irene and of course me, rocking, squatting, on all fours, waiting for the next contraction and out she came! I thought I was waiting to go into the water, but I was giving birth! Jim just managed to catch her. Luci turned up not long afterwards with the three girls, having missed the whole thing. Polly, by chance, was staying the night with her. Finally the midwife arrived. Our doctor turned up to administer stitches, while Jim bonded with his beautiful new daughter. The doctor pulled on her surgical gloves, ready to begin. Luci who'd just been on a midwifery course, had a quick look and asked, "does she really need stitches?" The doctor looked puzzled. Then slowly, sheepishly, to her credit, she removed her surgical gloves. "Not really," she admitted. The GabiLu birth team had triumphed once again!

Apart from situations like these, my relationship with Luci was strained. We were outwardly normal with each other but something had changed. We had become critical of each other, less at ease. We were also busier with our growing families and complex relationships with current men and exes. I found it a challenge having two infants under three. 'Baby Factory,' was developed for simultaneous nappy changing, Jim doing one child and me the other. As Jim was still a musician, he had time to be a hands-on father. We suffered none of the estrangement that many couples complain of, spending most of each day together, sharing experiences. The love we felt for each other was the centre of our life. We were almost equally involved in childcare, whether it was our two, or my three, or our five. Those were the permutations. Sometimes my ex took Polly. Luci and S. cared for Kizzy and Minna. Pablo and Saba we had all the time. We were one big extended family, all interconnected. Even so, there were growing tensions.

At last, in 1992, we found a house, 'Esgair Las'. The liberal-minded landlord had let the place to lesbian tenants before us, who had lived rent free, then later to a couple who paid rent by doing home improvements. Our landlord was a conservationist, easy-going and flexible and didn't mind the bus, allowing us to park it in the garden where it made a good venue for children's birthday parties. People either loved or hated that bus: one crazed woman in Kent had called it 'an abortion,' perhaps she meant 'abomination.' She was furious it was parked in a residential street with people living in it. Others would run out to meet us smiling and give us gifts. The Spanish were especially generous, making a fuss of us in our unusual home. In late summer of 1992 there was another trip, this time with Pablo and Saba to Northern Spain. The busking was excellent until disaster struck: Pablo fell on Jim's fiddle, smashing it. The sympathetic Spanish public helped us find a violin repairman: the tragedy was undone.

We made good money that summer; everyday our table in the bus was heavy with so many coins that we opened a Spanish deposit account. The bank was amused when we hauled in our bags of cash and impressed when they saw what the fiddle player could make!

The kids and I always went out busking with Jim. I hated staying at home cleaning the house. I'd read them stories and take care of them out there in public, even breastfeeding Saba, I wasn't shy. Sometimes the crowds took more interest in the woman and the cute blonde babies than in Jim. Once he stopped playing to join *them* watching *us*; the crowd loved that! Jim could be an incredible comedian, each show a one-off. I never knew when the urge to play up to the crowd would hit him. It all depended on their reactions and what was happening around him. Drunks and oddballs could be material for his spontaneous shows. He attracted huge crowds and a party atmosphere developed, people came to gush about how much they envied our lifestyle, not knowing how hard it could sometimes be. You had to have all kinds of strategies to cope with the lifestyle, endless energy and alertness, you couldn't switch off for a second.

By this time all three of GabiLu's parents, Pierre, Evelyn and Charles, were united by a common disrespect for our lifestyle. J. our stepmother, was the least judgmental, but she was living with a woman, so had made a non-mainstream lifestyle choice herself.

After a prosperous summer we drove the bus back to Esgair Las, to spend autumn in Cellan, with its wonderful trees and peace. But soon we were back in Spain to earn money for Christmas.

This time we took the car and caravan, judging the bus too much work. It was slowly sinking into the mud in our garden and would be an effort to get out of the drive. The caravan would be easier to travel in,... but we were wrong, it was much too small! It required military precision with four kids, (Polly stayed in Brighton with her father) two under five, and two adults. We couldn't get any space from each other. I made the girls sit without their feet hanging over their beds so they wouldn't kick the younger ones in the head.

This trip made me irritable and tense. There was too much washing up and so many clothes to wash; we had babies in nappies, making messes everywhere. It was noisy with all that chatter *and* it was snowing, the caravan walls were cold to touch, like living in a fridge. We only had ourselves to blame for our choice, but being a couple we blamed each other!

Back in the city of Vigo, during a busking act, we made a cardboard sign asking if anyone had a house to rent. In half an hour we had a first floor flat. Our hosts welcomed us warmly with small gifts, an embroidered handkerchief, toys and food. They were lovely, baby- sitting our kids and coming round often to check if we needed anything. We were accepted as the busking family, becoming minor celebrities in the town centre where Jim played. Sometimes Jim was offered a gig in a shop, bar or restaurant.

We stayed in Spain for Christmas and the New Year, but oddly it was melancholy. We were sad that Polly wasn't there and that we didn't really know anyone. The Spanish did celebrations with extravagance and flair, the streets exploded with people and vibrancy at midnight on New Years Eve. We joined in, aware that we had no family or real friends out there, which made us feel isolated and gave us a subtle attack of the blues.

We set off to Spain again, in the Spring, with all the girls. This time we went to a campsite in Lekeitio, a beautiful village on the northern coast. Polly was with us. During that trip 'The Brilliant Girls,' a busking act devised by Jim, was a hit. Everyone was charmed by the family and Polly's performance in particular was commented on. But some of the trip was spoiled by my health: I was suffering abscesses and intense toothaches. That was just the beginning of a severe health challenge that became serious for years.

We returned to Wales in October 1994, our travelling life ended. From then, until March 2003 we stayed at 'Esgair Las'. It's the longest I've ever settled in one place.

Illness

By this time Luci and S. had separated acrimoniously. She'd had a fling with his best friend, so their relationship ended abruptly, almost overnight. S. turned to Jim and me to help him make sense of this abandonment; we had seen it coming, but couldn't warn him, he wouldn't have believed it. Besides, my own relationship with Luci was still difficult. But like all members of my family, including my parents, I could be upset by and love someone at the same time. I had many emotions, which seemed to be springing forth in conjunction with my illness. The energy I was giving to parenting also took its toll. I gave it my all, but missed a sense of family of origin support in the background. The buried pain in my own life was knocking, but I tried to ignore it. I began a strict healing regime, consulting various medical professionals the world over, to try and make sense of my health problems. I began to understand what dying might feel like. It was dramatic. Everything was going wrong in my body. My legs were weak. I couldn't walk down the slightest slope. I had boils, ulcers and abscesses, as well as an almost permanent intense headache combined with a kind of buzzing sound. Sometimes I'd find it hard to form a word or sentence, my brain felt scrambled. I had such intense ear aches I lost some hearing permanently in my right ear; I still have to turn the other ear more toward someone to really hear them. I felt nauseous all the time, dizzy and 'wonky' if I moved my head too suddenly. I had terrible chest pain, yellow fingers and keratin growths on my feet. There was unbelievable bone pain, as if someone was drilling through my jaw with a red-hot drill.

Six of my teeth crumbled away, leaving unattractive gaps that embarrass me to this day. My energy felt so low as if my batteries had run out. I was used to having plenty of vitality.

One theory offered by my dentist was sensitivity to mercury that contributed to my health breakdown. There were also other factors. There are four files of papers in the attic filled with research I did on my problem. I decided to follow the mercury theory. My doctor had written 'mercury poisoning' on my file, considering I had fillings, the most likely source. So I consulted a Dr Levenson in London and had a test for body burden of mercury. The result indicated a significant level of mercury. A German laboratory confirmed this.

A routine was developed to support my liver and clean my blood of toxins. I have to keep to it, eat certain foods, mostly vegetables and organic vegetable juices to keep symptom free. I still have subtle problems with energy levels, but have come a long way since then. At the time I became ill, Luci and her new man were hostile and challenging about my 'problems.' Their conclusions about me didn't fit my feelings at all: communication broke down more and more, the relationship with my sister felt bleak. She seemed to me capable of being a real bitch, not that we don't all have our moments. I began to dislike her. But I never stopped loving her. All I wanted was to love and be loved by my family. It could all be so simple, but it's not. That's the strange thing. Life is full of conundrums that we should be able to solve but can't at times. Sometimes I hated Luci. It is said that hate is 'blocked love.' There seems to be truth in that.

Life in Esgair Las, involved parenting and 'counseling.' At least that's what people said I was doing. Some part of me seemed to collect people in need of help and support. Luci's new man said I was 'empathetic to a fault.' I found I had a flair for saying or doing just the right thing that could help someone with a difficulty in their lives. People urged me to get professional training and set up some kind of practice.

I didn't have time! I had too many children to care for and people who needed help! My health issues made me insecure about setting up anything away from home. It was necessary to be near the foods and equipment I needed. So the years at Esgair Las were devoted to my children, my own health and giving to others. I stayed still for the first time ever. It was a major learning experience. I got my most troubling symptoms under control. There was tendency to retch and vomit if I didn't stick strictly to this program. On my hands, under my rings, my skin was bleeding and rotting. What bothered me was my huge weight gain: I ballooned to about 16 stone. To his credit, Jim adapted to all of this, staying loving and affirming no matter how I mutated! Luci seemed disgusted by me. We grew further apart. I felt abandoned by my family, finding it hard to explain my life to anyone or reach out for help. My childhood had taught me to be independent. But one person I *had* been allowed to lean on, and her on me, was Luci. Now she'd had enough of 'us'... she certainly didn't want any part of my sordid problems!

Apart from all this, life was idyllic for the kids. They could roam free in the countryside and had plenty of friends to be with. We had time to give them attention. At first the three girls were often there and we were a family of seven. The girls created complex imaginative games; we had no television, computer or phone then, not even a washing machine. We had a joke of a cooker brought in from the bus. When we upgraded to a second hand dishwasher we had to wedge it shut each night with an axe. But no one cared, we had each other! There were great trees to climb, water holes to swim in, places to create dens or 'horse's stables' and 'pig pens' using junk that could be left out for days. There were no neighbors to offend or disturb.

Polly liked to initiate games of 'orphans' and 'poor little match girls in Victorian times.' She'd play 'woodchucks' with the little ones, leading Pablo and Saba over hill and dale in search of natural objects to collect, bossing them about happily. Or they would sit and draw or write poems and stories. Polly initiated long, elaborate projects that could take days. She loved organizing plays and dances and boss the others around. Saba was once cast as a doll, sitting silent and still with rouged cheeks the whole performance. At Esgair Las, we'd have meals outside on sunny days, or take the kids up to nearby Llanfair Lake to swim. Pablo and Saba had an incredible bond, Saba's nature the perfect complement to his. She has always been loving, patient and accommodating, both are affectionate and at ease with each other. They seem very wise and 'real' to me. One by one the girls have left home; each time we'd sob over their empty rooms. Now there are Pablo, Saba and often Llyr, Luci's son; he comes to stay, our bond goes way back and he entertains us with his surrealist sense of humor.

Polly too has stayed nearby, doing an acting degree, with a chance to use her variety of talents. We have a close relationship, sharing many aspects of our lives. Already her tutors have spotted her outstanding potential. I've no doubt she has what it takes to do whatever she sets her mind on. All three girls show great inventiveness and resourcefulness in their now independent lives.

With all our children, we'd a policy of allowing them to choose whether or not to go to school. We read, among others, John Holt's books 'How Children Learn,' and 'How Children Fail.' He argues that children learn naturally and don't need regulation, interference or control. He sees home not as an alternative to school, but as the best place to be educated no matter how good the school. His writings formed the basis of the 'un-schooling' movement. We felt it important that our children, unless they wanted it otherwise, be allowed authority over their own lives. This freedom of choice has been subtly undermined through ridicule by the media: homeschooling is presented as creating 'geeky' and socially maladapted children, a distortion that makes people more reluctant to differ from the mainstream. We had no T.V, computers, and read few newspapers at the time, we were immune to this conditioning.

We left our children free to choose. Kizzy did chose school, loving the structure and daily routine. Polly and Minna both preferred to have days off every week. The school was in those days, surprisingly relaxed about this, as they liked the girls who produced high quality work no matter their attendance. All the girls got good exam results. Kizzy received the £250 A level prize. Polly was so good at art she did her GCSE'S early and got an A,* the highest. Pablo and Saba both tried school intermittently. Pablo only really began properly at fourteen, then went everyday and passed his GCSE's with excellent results. Saba started at thirteen and showed the same flair.

In 1994 we began a business, offering a telecommunications service, which neither of us knew anything about. In August 1995 Jim bought his first business suit and in 1996 our first computer. Financial life became more complicated as our business grew, stress levels increased. But we learnt to overcome all kinds of challenges and making it through the first three years. After surviving the crucial first years we began to expand into electricity and gas. The business has become more interesting as we move into more 'green' and environmentally aware projects. Before that, one of the main companies we were doing business with was Enron. By late 2001 it was involved in a scandal that rocked the financial world. "Something is rotten in the state of Enron", stated the New York Times. The company had manipulated accounting rules, hiding the extent of their indebtedness. Enron was forced to file for bankruptcy in 2001. We lost a significant amount of money which had an affect on our business for some time. We carried on, hanging on in there, each year our strength increased as the business grew. Problems from the past were dealt with. Although we weren't prepared for some of the exasperating aspects of business slowly we understood more and more, some of it sobering; in the end we have the satisfaction of overcoming obstacles and becoming increasingly independent.

Meanwhile Evelyn, by now separated from Charles, had found a new man, Alan who, finally, gave something real to her life. It was inspiring to see, hear, how vitality began to return in her. There is nothing that helps a person blossom more than being loved. Alan challenges stereotypes of ageing, encouraging interaction with a wide variety of people and enthusiastically embracing new projects and adventures all over the world. Evelyn's concern nowadays is that they don't overdo it, as they tend to do more than the average twenty year old! Charles has also found love, with a woman about my age, whom I've not met.

<u>THE 12-STEP PROGRAM</u> The thing that was out of control in my life was still my relationship with Luci. Life wants movement and growth, the alternative is stagnation. For a couple of years my sister and others were causing concern. So much so that Jim and I signed up for a twelve-step program twice, not because *we* had a drug problem, but because others in the family had. We were taught (at the twelve-step program), that if we felt affected by an issue, it was *our* problem. There was much to learn: about family dynamics, dysfunctional relationships, addiction, boundaries, anger, self care, games, manipulation, enabling, people pleasing, co-dependency, forgiveness, caring, giving, self deception, denial; many things that helped us make some sense of subtle chaos and darkness settling over what had seemed to be something mutually beneficial and reciprocal between us and my sister's side of the family. We'd assumed we'd had a healthy dynamic between us, it was a lie. We had not. Some things I cannot detail here as there are issues of privacy were spiraling seriously out of control. I began to feel very strange, hurting about

my sister and her way of relating to members of her family. I couldn't reach her, she was like a stranger.

No matter how well someone can put on a front, our childhood continues to run on inside us all. We can deny, transcend, push away, overcome things, but always there's an effect. Our childhood issues were catching up and it was time to look, to face areas of low self-esteem and worthlessness.

Jim and I continued to reach out to the twelve-step family program for support. In matters of addiction, no matter how much a family member may wish it, no-one can force anyone to take part, it has to be a free choice. Our counselors advised taking the focus off others and putting it on ourselves, stressing self-care. The concept felt difficult to me, it was hard to admit I needed some even though I was feeling physically and emotionally exhausted. Problematically, as my own confusion increased I was getting better at offering support and care to others. I was good at this, using everything I learned in all the courses. Unfortunately, like any house built on unstable foundations, something had to give way. My strength was masking weakness, the two existing intertwined like snakes. My nurturing ability was a role, a compensation for my own lack and pain. I was giving what I'd not really had, but wished I'd had, attracting more and more people to care for, friends in addition to my children. Everyone seemed to need mothering or help, a world full of people in distress looking to me for support.

As the giving increased I was getting emptier and emptier. My background had taught me to just get on with it, losing touch more and more with what I needed. That twelve-step family program began to reveal truths about myself that I was reluctant to face.

It was complicated. I had become mystified and confused about my worth and identity doubting all my own perceptions as a way to try to end the feeling of nothing making sense. The twelve-step program helped me to validate my own perceptions, allowing me to reclaim my own truth. I learned to accept that I was powerless over others, there I had no control there. So began the harder job of coming to terms with myself and take control of my own life.

Demons

There are certain days in your life when you are required to face your demons, no matter how much you try to get out of it. Days when you run slap bang into something you don't want. You are thinking your day is about one thing, but really it's about something else. January 15th 2002, was my demon-facing day. I had a serious argument with my sister which had roots in the events which as I said, for privacy reasons cannot be detailed here. This argument changed our relationship permanently.

There'd been increased strain between us over Christmas. There was a coldness coming from Luci.

Her contempt for who I am that emerged during that argument can still activate painful shame in me. I was subjected to a tirade of venom and cruelty from which I tried to defend myself, but couldn't. I was so vulnerable at that time that my strength left me, I had no assertiveness left. Tired and sad, all I had left was pain and exhaustion. But Luci was fuelled by some purpose and mission to reject me. I seemed to disgust her. She became completely cold. I'd never seen her like it. We'd argued before, sometimes ferociously, but there was contact, never like this, this was new. There was no Mediterranean passion here, the kind of healthy 'air clearing' that makes everyone closer. I was floundering in a sea of toxic treacle. I was really drowning. I could find no handle on what was happening, no ground to hold me up. Wanting compassion from someone ice cold and full of hate for me my mind was working hard to find an explanation. What did she need? I couldn't find any softness in her. Jim was also bewildered. Luci announced I was 'banished' from her life. It was over. For two weeks it was hard to look anyone in the eye, I felt like the 'unclean,' worthless, contaminated, despised and grieving. It was like an amputation. Though we'd had years of estrangement, we were still entwined at the root, like two parasites, sustained by the blood of each other. I felt as if a heartless axe-man had chopped us apart, without concern for the bleeding and physical pain.

There was no one left, I was alone. Though my intellect knew it was all rubbish, that such behavior is its own call for help, Gabi had fallen. I had uncovered a vulnerable, hurt, worthless child in me, afraid, alone and in need. I sensed that behind Luci's bravado and show of disdain she might feel the same. There is an African saying that translates something like this 'I am because you are, you are because we are.' For me it was more like 'I'm not because you're not, you're not because we aren't!' Our culture of independence hides some truth, that we affect each other, we're interdependent and we need each other. There are invisible strands of connection that we rupture at our peril. That year Luci and her man experienced a similar 'blood bath.' It was almost a relief to know she was off attacking somebody else. For me trust was gone and has never really returned. Something was changed forever.

Wounds, Healing, and Moving On

Now it was my turn to be derailed. Throughout life, when I've felt bored, tense, frightened, stressed, lonely, unloved, confused, unsure, isolated, rejected, I've turned to words. Words are my friends. They can entertain, relax, comfort, inform, reassure, enlighten, connect and make me feel I belong. They have been a security, giving form to the formless, making sense of the chaotic, helping me feel safer when the world gets too much. Words can be hunters, capturing truths, tracking down what escapes. Our attic bulges with books, journals and magazines by the stack. Yet for all their power to define, express, clarify, bridge, convey passion, energy, aliveness, words are not life. They are not people. No matter how much I root around in words, digging deep to examine something, its people I long to trust, reach out to, be with and love.

Words had finally failed me. They would not reach the place my sister had opened up in me. It was a psychological wound hurting like a physical wound. Words couldn't help a place that raw. I felt knocked by another family rejection into hopelessness and despair. It was the same loss and grief I'd felt about Dad over the years.

I spent a couple of years on a creative writing course with the playwright Dic Edwards. Unendingly generous, with time and praise, he is supporting me writing a book, an agonizing process, I don't know why. My sister once said to me that writing is 'for lonely people.' It does make me feel alone, facing my own mind and myself. There's something weird about it, yet satisfying, when you manage to express something you didn't know you thought!

The children I've brought up, the partner I've talked to for nearly thirty years, these people love me unconditionally. With them I find relief from the fear and uncertainty inside: 'little Gabi' who sits in me, living on, despite the years passing. It's up to me now. I have to provide for myself love, patience, tenderness and time. I got a therapist and started to work with a new technique developed for trauma victims, EMDR. Evelyn is the only parent figure still to make contact and I'm grateful for that.

She really wants something new, after all the years of estrangement. Slowly we are getting to know each other and find out we are just flesh and blood. Pain, generational distress, patterns of abandonment, all the muck and mire of being human has led me, after all these years, to a simple truth: no matter how messed up we are, how much there is to learn, how wrong we can get it...we are all in this together. The teacher Louise Hay once said, "It's not 'them' and 'us.' It's all 'us.'

I've decided not to turn away from my sister, even if she turned away from me. I'll take care of myself around my sister, do things differently, look out for myself and do the best I can 'a day at a time,' as the twelve-steppers say. Luci will do what she does. Sometimes we connect, then I feel she has mellowed and changed. Other times I back off, knowing when things are not moving in the direction that is right for me. I can only hope one day we understand each other better, if we don't, so be it.

On July 3rd 2002 Polly gave birth to Leela, my first grandchild. It was another successful home and water birth. This time Luci wasn't there, but Polly's partner Jack, along with Pablo, Saba, Jim and I, were. The birth went well, Polly made lots of noise that must have been heard across the tiny village of Rhydowen. Born easily, caught by her Daddy Jack, (now a loved member of our family), in the water, Leela soon lay peacefully at her mother's breast, in the tub. Daughter of my daughter! Incredible.

Twelve-year Pablo said the birth was "the most amazing thing" he'd ever seen.

This baby girl helped my emotional life, drew me out of the desolation I felt, her tiny life an affirmation that life, even mine, goes on. All the kids help too of course, but Leela's newness accelerated this change. Her birth was a reminder that life springs back fresh and full of hope, her raw need pulled me out of self-absorbtion. I made a leap in myself to fully embrace everything again.

• • •

In 2004 Jim and I were on the way to a' twelve-step' meeting in Aberystwyth. We knew Luci had gone into labor, but we no longer spent time together. I sent her love and went off to the meeting. On the way, we received a text message from her. Things were not going well with her home birth; she might have to go into hospital. An ambulance was stationed outside, ready. She didn't ask me for help. I hadn't entered her house for two years, yet I knew I must go to her. Jim stopped the car in a lay by while I wrestled with my feelings. Should I go? Did she even want me there? Would she tell me to go away? Confused, I couldn't decide. That little voice we all have insisted, "go"! We turned the car round.

It was my first moment back in Luci's house since our row. Ignoring my memories of the past I put my focus on the child still inside my sister's body. Her partner didn't seem to know what to do, but as soon as I was in that house, I did. There was no doubt, only certainty. I knew she just needed to relax. The intensity of the situation made it easy to put our differences aside. I wanted and needed to give to her, touch her, reassure her, say the familiar things we'd said at all our shared births. GabiLu was resuscitated, just for now. I kept focusing on relaxation, touching and talking to her. I knew it would work and it did. Her contractions became normal. The ambulance man hovered to assess whether or not to take her to hospital, but all was well, her strength had come back, her power came through.

Baby Rocco entered the world. He looked at me with alert twinkling eyes and I was hooked. It was a special moment, as if all the denied love between Luci and me flowed from her tiny boy. Through this little baby there was warmth and connection... then it was time to let go. Jim and I left soon after he was born and that was that.

Luci did acknowledge my contribution to her birth and I felt our bond. But we quickly went back to our usual distance. This is the child of Luci's we've now seen the least of. Her other son, often comes to stay the night most weekends and feels like part of the family. Still, this new child has brought his parents closer. Luci and her partner have so much love to give to their tousled haired three year old, it warms my heart to see their devotion. A beautiful flower grows from all the muck.

As for Luci and Gabi? We'll always love each other but our connection from the past is now the real link. In the present being together isn't yet easy. I find myself longing for a softer, more affectionate, warmer sister. Time and communication may one day repair the damage.

• • •

In 2006 Polly's mother-in-law, died of lung cancer caused by asbestos. She died in almost exactly the same spot that Leela was born. They had a ritual when this grandmother was dying, of pouring tea from a matching rainbow teapot and cup. This ailing woman was always fascinated by the precise careful way Leela poured the tea, spilling not a drop. It gave her pleasure to share this intimacy her little granddaughter. Leela's childhood has been idyllic up to this point, secure and adored in her extended family. This death was the only bad thing so far. We prepared her for it.

By the time she threw a red rose on her grandmother's grave she knew roughly what to expect. After the funeral she was furiously angry with me though, my presence reminding her of her loss. For a while it was my fault I was her only remaining grandmother.

I've now learned to run a home and a business, how to have some routine and security. Jim and I grow vegetables on our allotment behind our house. I'm writing a book and continue healing my body and mind. We've never had such a normal life. Values have changed, youth movements have been absorbed into the culture and life has moved on. It all still feels like an adventure.

Throughout my lifetime I have had many different perspectives on the same situation, looking back each time through wiser eyes that allow wider vision. We 'share the same biology, regardless of ideology' as the songwriter Sting puts it. The human vulnerabilities, needs and drives that make us distinct, paradoxically unite us all. "All you need is love," said the Beatles and I think they've got something there. Love is the magic ingredient that provides resilience for all life's challenges. It comes naturally and thankfully it's free! The love of my life, partner Jim, has been the most constant I've ever known. He continually steps up for me, sharing everything and giving more. We've had the challenges most couples experience, but he is always willing to learn, grow and reach out to me. From this foundation extends the love I feel for my children, my children's children, my sister's children, my sister, my other sisters, my brothers, my Mum and my Dad.

The influence on Mum of *her* third partner, Alan, has helped bring out *her* softer side. She is more confident, less judgmental. I am grateful to her for attempting to create a connection with us, and to Alan for his tolerant personality. In the climate of twisted bitterness from the 'father figures' in our lives, Alan's acceptance of and interest in others is a breath of fresh air. Passion and intimacy matter, they are the perfume of life. Self esteem matters. That's the conclusion of my story so far, a story within millions of stories that ends with a feeling of life's incredible richness. It's all worth it, for the experience of being alive!

As for home, that place of belonging and unconditional love? I've discovered it's a feeling, it's where the heart is, it's anywhere where there's real love. Which is all anyone wants. To be continued when I've lived it...

• • •

Polly's turn now...number six of the seven women: an 'actor', in search of an 'author'. Polly is the busy one, all of twenty-five years old...trying to catch up on her missed chances at an acting school, so the 'author' will have to be me, Ingeborg Evelyn, her grandmother. I've seen so little of her, it's almost strange to admit I *am* such a thing... a grand-mother!

Nice she is so busy! How furious I was with her when I heard she was pregnant, seven years ago. Seeing history repeat itself.....

Up to then her life was uncharted and she could have had every opportunity. A granny's nagging is not appreciated!

Adorable little Leela, my first great-grand child appeared soon enough; another one of those water babies we've read about. She is much loved, and one hopes her gorgeous mother will still be able to fulfill all her dreams and talents.

I wait patiently to receive Polly's views and become more wary and conscious of my own position: the fulcrum of an old-fashioned scale: on one side my daughter, my daughter's daughter and my daughter's daughter's daughter.... on the other: my mother, my mother's mother and my mother's mother's mother; just look at us.... Here we are, all seven of us. We *appear* so neatly balanced.

EVELYN

Erika	M	Gabrielle
Cölestine	M	Polly
Josephine	M	Leela

Is this my last chance? How to weigh up the stamina of each of the seven maids with their mops, turning lives into idyllic contentment? And also how to 'weigh up' the lives on one side against the lives on the other... especially when two are still so young? What are the predominant qualities on the left hand side...what on the right... can one even begin to compare them, born in such different times? One thing is certain: those on the right are British with a Welsh, partly post-hippy flavor, and my goodness, what complicated lives so far! Did some 'rot' set in when I broke free, refusing to throw my life onto the altar of holy matrimony? Oh dear, evil Evelyn, living up to her name.... greedily wanting more, wanting something other than wife- and mother-hood. Then falling into the same old trap...*again*!

Life was so much easier on the '*old*' side of the diagram: find a man, become his wife, bring up the children, take up knitting or good works...and die. Will the Gabrielle-Polly-Leela team show a better way? *Is* there a better way? Meanwhile, I wait for Polly's contribution. She is up to her ears preparing homework for the next course at drama school... I fear the task of writing down thoughts about her life so far has no appeal.

First Polly and her family must have a holiday in France, to recover from that Welsh greyness.

Polly's Story

Now...at last. the perfect baby,

cooing at strangers as she is handed round during a
talk given by Jiddu Krishnamurti in Gabi's 'hippy'
days....that is how she emerges in my mind. She
was just as perfect when I first met her, chatting,
trusting and adorable, only three and content to
come to me, even leave her mother for a few hours
while we two held hands and wandered about.
"This is 'Glastonbury', 'Blueberry' and 'Sunshine'
she proclaimed, when I gave her three small Care-
bears, to break the ice...but there was none!

"Is this what breast-fed babies are like?" I asked
myself, as I noticed how she interacted with her
mother, the intensity of their eyes looking, it
seemed, right inside each other. I had never seen
such closeness before and felt a stab of jealousy
contemplating their intimacy.

In her earliest years she too became a victim,
finding herself pulled around as a 'visitor' between
two families: her father in Brighton with his new
dependants and her mother's new growing family.
Not only once did Polly experience splitting-
up parents, but even a second time there was the
continuing theme of blending and re-blending
families...when her father moved on. Such
'dysfunctional' patterns leave traces that may have
to be worked on.... in order to 'let them go...'
According to Gabi, who knows only too well about

such things: "Polly felt she wasn't central...this only emerged with time, but she also felt she had to look after her father, and she still does. She is upset by him, but loves him."

Crowding into Polly's being is the threatened loss of a young step-sister recently diagnosed with the rare disease of Pulmonary arterial Hypertension, apparently incurable. It stands to reason that happiness, under these circumstances, may, for a while, be hard to achieve.

Knowing which way to turn, when one is young and multi-talented, can become obstructed with all the twists of tempting choices. Polly has always shown a strong leaning to 'artiness', studying A-level Art, winning Eisteddfods In Wales and even trying her hand at 'making' beautiful objects...cards, jewelry. The first gift I ever had from any grandchild, were two handmade buttons, made of clay, painted with charming detail and stitched onto a card signed by Polly. She was probably about six or seven at the time and I've treasured them for almost two decades, not quite knowing what to sew them on.

The next time Polly came into my ken she was 13 years old; spending a few days with us she brought her cousin Minna with her. They travelled to London by train, I picked them up in Paddington. All three of us were undergoing a craze for painting... I showed them the Library on Stanmore Hill, where there happened to be my own first exhibition of pictures, paintings of children in mysteriously frightening situations... later we spent time painting together and also visiting the South Bank to see the sights, museums and Galleries.

Polly, from the very start, appeared to me on a different level of existence, with a detachment, apparently sympathetic, yet 'keeping- her distance' approach, perfectly poised and polite, accepting and mildly amused by everything that was going on. I was in awe of her perfection, not just physically, but of what felt like such a strong core. What would become of this creature, seemingly so self assured? Gabi's maternal assessment is that "Polly can be scary as she comes over with great authority, very sure of her opinions, though often it's a bluff and she is uncertain underneath". I suppose many people who seem authoritarian are like that!

It now appears she is extraordinarily talented as an actress, and that her acting school has high hopes for her. "There has been no-one like her for twenty-five years" is what the management says. Well, who was that talented creature and what became of her/ him? Our budding actress however, wishes she were at a more prestigious drama school.....

At this moment there appears to be a crisis. Polly, the goddess, has cracked: what has completely unhinged her is nothing other than a taste of holiday-life in the summer sunshine of France... the feeling of being fully alive and unstressed without dead-lines; of good food, lounging on the beach, playing with her little girl, and to hell with running a home, becoming an actress and looking out onto that grey Welsh sky every day. Anyone of her age on a grueling schedule such as hers would feel the same!

Speaking as someone who, at a similar age, had everything Polly has just now so enjoyed (sunshine, swimming, leisure,) I would just love to point out that opening up a career for oneself (as she will be in a position to do) is infinitely more rewarding in the long run...'something to die for' as the young say nowadays....that learning new skills is a real investment for the future, (huge, overwhelming amount of time stretching ahead into infinity....) which, seen from being only a quarter of a century old, can take place over decades and decades in a sunnier place than Wales, very soon after another two years have gone by. Two years is a blinking of an eyelid, when there is a quest for that elusive 'pot of gold. 'And she might say: "I don't care, I no longer want to live in dank, dark Wales, I will go abroad, take my chances....." Arguments would then centre on "what's it all about" but, alas, no-one can instill any sense in some-one else's brain... we all have to make choices, we don't like to be told. She may decide to change course altogether........ Our wondrous Polly sits on a volcano, and I watch, helplessly, from a distance.

"Life is long, Polly, get that career going...then move out into the world", is surely everyone's advice. A famous British film director might pick you out of the crowd, bring your talents to the world...do you really want to chuck it all up and instead cultivate an early crop of wrinkles in the hot sun, or produce more babies, who will speak other languages better than you?

Polly feels family is the most important thing in life. She wants to do something in the world AND be a good mother...and it's hard.

.......and so we must move to the seventh name on the scales.

Leela's Story

E-mails from Gabi are my daily fare, where would I be without them:

27th April 2008, "Here are Leela's own words... I'll keep going each time we meet. I managed to interview her, here is the result so far, word for word (she loves the idea of being 'in a book' and is v. co-operative)........

I was born on July the 3rd in 2002. My dad is Jack William and my mother is Polly. (Gabi must have started her off ...I don't see a six-year old doing that!)

I've lived in:

(1)   The Willows   (Wales))

(2)   Rhyd Fechan   "

(3)   Gabi's house   "

(4)   Mandy's house   (Brighton)

(5)   Temple Terrace   (Wales)

The one I like best is The Willows because it has bigger rooms than my last house. That one gave me illness, chickenpox, because I was breathing all the badness in... I got a really bad cough. What I liked about Rhyd Fechan was I had loads of kittens. They had to live under the stairs. Their bowl was bigger than the kittens! They had to have Whiskers pouches for food. Tabby was my friend. She used to come out and say hello to me. The sad thing was that Tabby had to leave. They all had to leave, Bawdry, Ginger and Tabby. There were more but I have forgotten their names-there were hundreds and hundreds.

Egg and Fizzy Water were their mum and dad. I also lived in Mandy's house in Brighton. Egg and Fizzy water went to her house and changed their names to Pumpkin and Pippin, so I still lived with them but not with the kittens.

Luckily now I've got a little kitten called Mish-Mish. I'll tell you what color she is. She is orange, black and white. She's beautiful and she's got a monkey face and she's really fluffy. She likes killing mice and she killed a blue-tit once and I felt sorry because I love blue tits. Guess what!

Mish Mish actually pulled a gut out of a dead slug and there was a dead mouse in there all mixed up together. And I've got a cat called Oscar.

He's tabby-colored and he's got a very pink nose. He likes killing mice too, because they are all very hungry.

What I remember about my grandmother is that she died and, well, I got very sad and we had to put her in a box and then Cameron (cousin) went to MacDonald's after the funeral and we went home. We had to throw flowers everywhere and then we came over to Gabi and Jim's house. I think Gabi can be my best grandmother now because Mimi used to be my best grandmother because she had grey hair which she put up in a bun. I want Gabi to dye her hair grey because she looks too much like a mother. She's all young and that's not right for grandmothers because Mimi had old and wrinkled skin.....

Gabi, and her grand-daughter Leela are silent, for a while. Then, on another day: "This is what Leela said, typed down word for word, no editing," by Gabi:

This is for 'the book', Gabi! It's about my violin. My violin has a special thing that has to go on the bottom of it, I can't remember what it's called...it's not the chin rest it's at the bottom of the chinrest, it's green, oh yes it's called the shoulder rest......and my violin has a special stick called a bow, and some soapy stuff called resin that you have to put on the bow, then you have to remember to put the resin back in the violin box.

My violin is called Lynn, and every time I play it I'm so into it that it hurts my arm and neck but I'm so into it that I can't actually let go of it, and anyway it won't let go because I'm going to play it at Glastonbury.

In violin you have to put lots of touch and care into it to be really good at it. Also to be really good you have to rub the bow on the strings and that's how you make the music...that's how I do it so good- I just concentrate for ages and ages and try and practise and practise.

There are four strings, G is for Gabi, D is for Daddy, A is for Abi and E is for egg.

My violin just glues me to it- it's really funny! It just won't let me go!

My violin has this red spot on it where you put your finger. The best thing about it is that it makes you strong and better at music...at first when you start your arms are all floppy and limp but it makes you get strong and tough. My violin is brown and the strings are made of horse fur, no, horse hair.... the hair that goes down the manes and tails....

I like the sound of the violin, that it makes, because it is musical and delicate and gentle music. I like music. It can be fiery but mine is sort of gentle like when you are at a pond with dancing swans. Playing it makes me space off into a different world....it's got a special arm that's glue-ing me to it! I just love it! When I'm older I'm going to play at Glastonbury.....

Then she had enough. Hope you enjoyed that, I did! (Gabi was the scribe)

The smallest person, the seventh daughter, and one day, mother no. seven, is in 'seventh heaven' when playing a violin. God forbid she has the gene, the one that drives you to spend half your life getting the tiniest detail to perfection, in order to pierce the hearts of others. Unless she has exceptional talent, please God, let this chalice pass! I am entitled to this view. (Evelyn is the scribe) According to the latest scientific research it takes 10.000 hours to develop a talent to the point of excellence.

(What good fortune Polly has such a patient mother, who baby-sits each day, while Polly does her course. Leela could not be in better hands.... and the spin-off is: I get all these delicious accounts straight across the ether. Leela has just come second in the 'creative writing' competition in her class, beaten by one 'Theo', her arch enemy. She is allowed to sit on a golden throne and wear a red cloak. They believe in that sort of thing in Wales, the home of Dylan Thomas. And Leela's Mum is doubly blessed: her husband does both, shopping and cooking. What more can a woman ask? To emigrate from 'potato-ey Wales'?

Both Gabi and Jim confess to feeling like 'church-wardens', trying to help Polly make the 'right 'decisions, not just for herself but also for all three generations...Gabi, Polly *and* Leela...while I confess to a mild attack of 'Schadenfreude', that they too may be experiencing the frustrations of parent-hood now, in their middle-years.

I must be careful not to make myself too unpopular with our prospective 'prima-donna'. How can she become one, I wonder, because her growing-up period was everything but straight-forward... such a sensitive small person, she must have suffered from witnessing her Dad running away, dumped off the hippy bus: she did promptly lose her voice from this shock and there was more:...being handed to a fire-man in Brighton, when the family was being rescued from the 4th floor of a Brighton house; well, it is all in Gabi's story, the shuttling to and fro between separated parents and observing the grown-ups trying out 'primal therapy' and other bizarre practices...what happened to her immature mind then? (Turn back to page 523 to unravel the muddle of her young life.) Polly, please continue this account in half a century from now! You will have to come to terms with many more ugly facts such as overpopulation, Aids, Global warming, melting icecaps, acid rain and terrorism, global financial meltdown...you may try to live according to different precepts with new, more *beautiful* theories, to allow our world to recover. Perhaps Leela will find these jottings one day, just as Josephine did in Neumarktl in 1894, when sorting out *her* mothers' belongings.....so, I wish you well, darling great-grand-daughter, I pray I live long enough to see you become a grown-up. When you too are a granny, better still, a great-granny, please study what *your* daughters have done, and what *their* daughters are up to. Write down all their lives to see if the patterns they make are similar to those in this book of ours. I have tried to imagine your life........

.....now, try to remember me, the 'Pomeranian Peasant', 'discrete', (a new word in my vocabulary), well advanced in years and *almost* British, except when getting through a British Christmas or even more painfully, when listening to German Lieder,.... then the tears stream, helplessly.

May you all stumble on happiness......it's there,... somewhere.

... what we call the beginning is often the end

And to make an end is to make a beginning

The end is where we start from.........

'Gerontion.'
T.S.Eliot

Lightning Source UK Ltd.
Milton Keynes UK
31 March 2010

152161UK00001B/2/P